ROAD TO THE ROBES

A Federal Judge Recollects Young Years & Early Times

by

Ruggero J. Aldisert

1663 LIBERTY DRIVE, SUITE 200
BLOOMINGTON, INDIANA 47403
(800) 839-8640
www.AuthorHouse.com

© 2005 Ruggero J. Aldisert. All Rights Reserved.

No part of this book may be reproduced, stored in a retrieval system, or transmitted by any means without the written permission of the author.

First published by AuthorHouse 03/01/05

ISBN: 1-4208-1692-6 (sc)
ISBN: 1-4208-1693-4 (dj)

Library of Congress Control Number: 2004099697

Printed in the United States of America
Bloomington, Indiana

This book is printed on acid-free paper.

BACK COVER PHOTO by James D. Macari.
FRONT AND BACK COVER DESIGN by Molly Gleason
Most of the photographs reproduced here are from the family collection. At one time, others had copyright protection in an era where the life of a copyright was 28 years. I am assured and represent that because these did not have their copyrights renewed, their work is now in the public domain.

Also by Ruggero J. Aldisert

Opinion Writing (West Group 1990)

The Judicial Process: Text, Materials and Cases (West Group 2d Ed. 1996)

Logic for Lawyers: A Guide to Clear Legal Thinking (NITA 3d Ed. 1997)

Winning on Appeal: Better Briefs and Oral Argument (NITA 2d Ed. 2003)

For Jack August and Luciana Aldisert in Portland, Oregon

and

Audrey Valentine and Lorenzo and Gianna Aldisert in Topanga, California,

so they may become familiar with young years and early times of their paternal grandfather,

and

the profound influence on him of his mother and father,

who are their great-grand parents,

John S. Aldisert and Elizabeth M. Aldisert

Acknowledgememts

The word, acknowledge, has two meanings. I invoke both of them here. To the extent that it means to recognize or confess, I represent that what I say in these pages is as authentic as my memory cells permit, except I admit to reconstructions of certain conversations which are my elaboration of a gist of what actually was said. The account of past generations of my father's family results from discussions with his relatives in Acquaformosa and Lungro in Southern Italy during four visits there in five year period from 1965 to 1969. This was the time when Agatha and I went searching in Italy to reunite with families whose members we knew only by name, and to locate the exact houses where our maternal and paternal grandparents were born. We found three of the four houses still standing.

To the extent that to acknowledge means to express gratitude or obligation for I do so freely in thanking friends who read various drafts of the manuscript and offered excellent suggestions. I am indebted to Jayme De Barros, Edward Carter, Erin Englebrecht, Patty Flournoy, Gary Gleason, Sue Bracco Gleason, Mimi Hillbrand, Michael T. Reagan and Judge Joseph F. Weis, Jr. I again thank Linda E. Schneider, Esq., of Pittsburgh, Pennsylvania, for research assistance (this being the fourth of my books in which she has done so). I thank Cynthia Miller, Director of the University of Pittsburgh Press, for publication advice, and I am especially indebted to Molly Gleason for her exquisite talent in designing the front and back covers.

A special word to members of my family who have been very supportive--daughter Lisa M. Aldisert of New York City, sons Robert L. Aldisert of Portland OR and Gregory J. Aldisert of Los Angeles, my two daughters-in-law, Jennifer Shea and Harley Jane (Kozak) Aldisert, who extended much love and support in this endeavor. My sister, Adrienne Aldisert Massucci, rummaged through her portion of the family photo collection to help me.

These friends and family have complimented me for a memory that goes back many generations, but they were kind enough not to quote Irving Cobb, "A good story teller is a person who has a good memory and hopes that other people haven't."

Although technically I retired in 1987, since that time I continue to be a very active "senior" federal judge, and in addition have written four serious books on the law, together with four supplemental editions. This has involved incredible time demands, valuable time that intrudes on the retirement time of Agatha and me. As in the case of the other books, she has soldiered on with me, and thanks to her patience and encouragement, our life has been extraordinarily happy and rewarding. For making all those good things happen, I can only profess my profound admiration and gratitude to over a half century of deepest love.

Foreword

The "Greatest Generation" is a flattering description, but not really the way those of us in Judge Aldisert's contemporary era feel about it. Yet, the events that molded that time – the Great Depression of the 1930's, the global conflict of the 1940's – did provide the testing ground for some persons of uncommon achievement. My friend and colleague, Rugi Aldisert, is in that category.

His life has spanned more than 80 years and included such careers as a Marine Corps officer, lawyer, judge, author of a number of books, law professor, lecturer, and leader of an influential ethnic society. Early in life, Judge Aldisert encountered bigotry – in some instances in its aggravated form. The white robes of the Ku Klux Klan that he confronted in his boyhood helped to shape his black-robe thinking on discrimination and equality.

The fascinating story of the legal defense he provided for a friend who was involved in a cloak and dagger operation in northern Italy during WWII reads like a novel of the espionage genre. In that case, fighting the full power of the federal government, Judge Aldisert became convinced of the truth of one of Justice Oliver Wendell Holmes' sayings that, in dealing with its citizens, government "must turn square corners."

I have known Rugi for more than 50 years. We shared years together at the bar, for a brief time on the bench of the Court of Common Pleas of

Allegheny County, Pennsylvania, and more than 30 years as colleagues on the United States Court of Appeals for the Third Circuit.

Rugi's exceptional energy in his work on the Court, legal educational endeavors, and writing widely cited books have left me in awe. Much of that work ethic came from his childhood, but much of the self-discipline and goal-setting were the result of his service in the Marine Corps during WWII. As was said of our late, beloved colleague on the Court of Appeals, James H. Hunter, III, if there had been no Marine Corps he would have invented it. That military service experience was also a defining element in his approach to his own work, as well as a criterion in evaluating that of the lawyers who appeared before him. Like Judge Learned Hand, Rugi does not suffer fools gladly, but is quick to praise those who, like him, perform with excellence.

Through his years of struggle, he was most fortunate to have the loving and uncompromising support of his wonderful wife Agatha. To her must go much of the credit for his accomplishments.

The reader will enjoy these reminiscences of the man underneath the black robe as I did, and will begin to understand the philosophy that is evident in his judicial writings.

Pittsburgh, Pennsylvania
April 2005

Joseph F. Weis, Jr.
Senior U.S. Circuit Judge,
United States Court of
Appeals for the Third
Circuit

Preface

There I was, just a few months back, sitting on the high bench with two other U.S. Circuit Judges of the United States Court of Appeals, as we were hearing the final moments of an argument by the U.S. Department of Justice. The case was very high profile and it involved the Department of the Interior and the U.S. Army Corps of Engineers. I had already made up my mind. I was going to rule against the United States Government, the most powerful country in the world. This would not be a novel experience because I am long in the tooth when it comes to making extremely difficult decisions on the federal appellate bench.

I am constantly aware of the profound responsibilities that go with the judicial commission I hold. After many years I am still in awe of what I have done and continue to do. I keep remembering that I started out as a kid born in Carnegie, Pennsylvania, a grimy industrial suburb of Pittsburgh that contained four steel mills and was surrounded by a half dozen coal mines. What is more, I was the son of an Italian immigrant who landed in Ellis Island in 1906 at the age of 16, alone and flat broke.

For some time now I have wanted to write about certain events in my long life that took place before a President known as LBJ nominated me to this judgeship. I have a story. I finally decided to tell it, and this is what this informal book is all about. It describes events of a rather humble background and experiences I had along the way to sitting on the highest federal court in the land to which a litigant had a right to appeal a case.

Above us is the U.S. Supreme Court, but you have no absolute right to go there, and that Court decides only 80 or so cases a year.

What's written here is not a full fledged Memoir, let alone an autobiography, but simply what I call it, *ROAD TO THE ROBES: A Federal Judge Recollects Young Years & Early Times*. I have not described much of my wonderful personal life with a fantastic wife of over 52 years and my three children and their families who mean so much to me. Rather it's a collection of snap shots taken against the back drop of important times in America–from the beginning of the Roaring Twenties to the turbulent and traumatic year of 1968.

What these pages describe is like a story a grandfather or a great-grandfather would tell to his Baby Boomers or the generations that followed, a story about the early days when the great waves of immigrants came to these shores from Southern, Central and Eastern European to work in the coal mines and steel mills in 12 hour shifts with a 24 hour shift every other Sunday. And how the children of these immigrants made up a large portion of those who came to be known as the Greatest Generation, who came of age during the Depression and left home for three or four years to fight in World War II in Africa, Europe and the far reaches of the Pacific; the men and women who then returned to help propel this country into the most powerful nation in the world.

Mine is a story full of life experiences from this era that formed me, a man who has been a state and federal judge for over half of his life, born when Woodrow Wilson was President which was a few years before a radio broadcast, when no dial telephones existed, and when you lifted the four inch hearing portion of the two-piece telephone, an operator answered and said "Number please." It's about my life which spans a generous slice of important American culture and history.

Come along with me as I informally travel back down my young and early road. Pretend that I'm your grandfather or great-grandfather reminiscing with you, for it is my hope that it will feel as familiar.

Santa Barbara, California
April 2005

Ruggero J. Aldisert
Senior U.S. Circuit Judge,
U.S. Court of Appeals
for the Third Circuit

Table of Contents

Acknowledgememts ix

Foreword xi

Preface xiii

Chapter One One Foot In America 1

Chapter Two Carnegie, Pennsylvania in the Twenties 15

Chapter Three The Ku Klux Klan 27

Chapter Four The Men of Carnegie's Mills and Mines 53

Chapter Five From Dolcedorme (Sweet slumber), Italy to Carnegie, Pennsylvania 65

Chapter Six Growing Up in the Italian Catholic Church 83

Chapter Seven Growing Up In School 89

Chapter Eight Growing up Playing 101

Chapter Nine Growing Up Italian 119

Chapter Ten Growing Up Eating 143

Chapter Eleven Growing Up in the Depression 151

Chapter Twelve Growing up in High School 161

Chapter Thirteen Growing up at Pitt 175

Chapter Fourteen The Marine Corps Influence 203

Chapter Fifteen The Birth of a Lawyer 231

Chapter Sixteen Hanging Out the Shingle 239

Chapter Seventeen The General Practice 255

Chapter Eighteen Criminal Court 281

Chapter Nineteen The Icardi Case: Part One 307

Chapter Twenty The Icardi Case: Part Two 331

Chapter Twenty-One The Road to the Common Pleas Court 357

Chapter Twenty-Two The Trial Judge Years 371

Chapter Twenty-Three The Long and Rocky Road to the Court of Appeals 397

Chapter One
One Foot In America

My mother was sobbing. "Please, God, help us. Please, God, don't let them hurt my babies!" she said. She was trembling and had her arms around my brother and me. We were in her bedroom, peaking underneath the blind that was drawn in a front window.

It was the summer of 1922, and this is the first thing that I remember in my life. My mother was terrified because I was only three years old, my brother Caesar was just a year older, my father was out of town and some visitors had "come a'calling." It was in the evening but still daylight when they came. Caesar and I had been playing in the front yard when we first saw them: They were marching around the corner where Shearer's Hill ends and Grandview Avenue turns toward our house.

They were the Ku Klux Klan.

Dressed in full regalia with white robes and white hoods, they marched in a single file, a small procession. After we saw them, we ran screaming to mother who had been on the porch. She immediately hustled us inside, locked the front door and rushed us upstairs. From her front bedroom window we watched them, ten or twelve of them, enter our yard in single file. Then silently they walked in a circle.

They said not a word. They simply walked in a circle in our tiny yard, around and around. They uttered no threats. They simply kept walking in that circle. Walking in that circle, dressed in long white robes that dragged along the ground, their heads covered with tall, pointed hoods with slits for the eyes, nose and mouth. No one spoke a word during their ritualistic exercise. In time they left. They left, as silently as they had come, probably to one of the houses nearby, to shed their robes and hoods, and return to their various homes as neighbors of the Aldisert family.

The Klan was sending my family a message. A message to get out. To get out of the neighborhood. To them we were not Americans, although my mother and we kids had been born in America and my father had been a naturalized citizen for almost 20 years.

To them we were Italians. We were foreigners, and as foreigners my parents had no right to buy a Grandview Avenue house in 1918 on Chestnut Hill, Carnegie, Pennsylvania. To them there were other places in Carnegie where we could live, Italian districts, where we could also buy a house. As foreigners, we had somehow despoiled the neighborhood, a neighborhood of homogenous Protestant English stock. We had no right to move into their neighborhood.

Grandview Avenue was clean and quiet with green lawns and trees and open space and it ran along the top of a hill that commanded a magnificent view of Chartiers Valley. It was for the good people, the nice people who had settled in this town. It was not for greenhorns, not for newcomers with strange-sounding names and the Papist religion.

I was born in November 1919 in that very room from which we watched the Klan and its ceremony, my parents' bedroom, on the second floor at our house at 412 Grandview Avenue, a little bungalow, perched high above the valley where the town of Carnegie, Pennsylvania lay. The year 1919 was a very inauspicious one, a day short of one year after the first Armistice Day. My arrival was sandwiched between days of the One-step and Ragtime and those of 22-Skiddoo; it heralded, with no causal relation, the advent of the Roaring Twenties.

It was a kind of dull year in which to be born. No one, I'm sure, remembers anything of major historical significance that happened in

1919. It was the first year after the World War; that's what they called it then, we hadn't assigned a Roman numeral to it yet. It was the year when the steel industry had its abortive steelworkers' strike that would influence Pittsburgh attitudes for a generation until the National Labor Relations Act went into effect. It was also the year when President Theodore Roosevelt died. History books don't help much for a point of public reference to my natal year; perforce, I have begun this account with something that happened three years later, the first thing I remember as a valid personal recollection.

A true recollection is an actual conjuring up from your own personal memory cells, not something visualized from what parents or relatives may have told you. Seeing my mother shake with fear and watching the men and women in white robes and hoods parading in our yard is a vivid recollection that has endured through the years. I will never forget it. Nor do I wish to.

We're not sure what permits our memory to recall vividly something that took place over 80 years ago and yet draw a blank on what we read in a book last week, but I have remembered that evening to this day.

It was the opening chapter of growing up with only one foot in America.

My mother was the third of 14 children born to Ottavio and Maria Antinone Magnacca of Steubenville, Ohio. Her father was born on November 6, 1866 in the village of Vastogirardi in the Italian province of Campobasso in what was then known as the Abruzzi, now called the Molise region. In the early 1880's, while in his teens, my maternal grandfather had emigrated and went to work for the Pennsylvania Railroad as it was pushing its rails west in Ohio.

Grandfather Ottavio's first paymaster believed that the name Magnacca name was too complicated, and instructed Ottavio that his name was no longer Magnacca, but Manack. Thus, my mother was baptized as Elizabeth Manack, and families of my grandfather's brothers also had to bear this strange name because of the whim of a paymaster at the railhead.

Although my grandfather had attended only five years of school in Italy, his fine handwriting, flare for figures and proficiency in English and Italian impressed the railroad construction bosses. Within a year he was lifted from the labor gang and assigned to office work in the rolling railhead.

Grandmother Maria was born in the same Italian village as grandfather Octavio but they did not meet until her father brought her to Steubenville when she was seventeen. Through the years the family has insisted, perhaps not too convincingly, that this was not an arranged marriage, yet within less than a year they were married on March 12, 1891. Like many women of her era, she had not attended school in Italy and never learned to read or write, but had an uncanny command of numbers.

Mother had been a very bright student in Steubenville's St. Peter's elementary school and the public high school. As a daughter of Italian immigrants at the turn of the century, she was a generation ahead of her time. Highly intelligent and extremely well-informed, she was a constant user of the Steubenville public library. A generation later, she would have gone to college. Instead of being encouraged by her mother, however, she was taunted and referred to as "book-in-the-hand," because of her love of reading, her chief taunter being her mother, who insisted that her daughter stop school after the eighth grade. Mother prevailed upon her father to intervene, who was successful until mother was about to enter the senior year in high school. My grandmother then laid down the law, "You've had enough of this foolish schooling. I've had enough. If you don't listen to me, get out of my house!" Mother went weeping to her father, who shrugged his shoulders and said, "Lisabetta, I've tried my best, but your mother is one stubborn woman." Grandmother believed that the role of women was to stay pregnant and live in the kitchen. In this respect, grandmother Maria was paradigmatic; she had 19 pregnancies and delivered 14 children, nine of who survived to adulthood. Her Italian was limited to an Abruzzese rural dialect, and even after living in America for over 50 years, she was incapable of uttering a simple declarative sentence in English without mixing it mostly with Italian.

My parents met in 1916 when a Carnegie friend of my father told him about a family in Steubenville that he had visited and had been invited to return. "John, they have three very talented, beautiful daughters and only one of them is married." Steubenville was only an hour and a half ride on the Pennsylvania Railroad from Carnegie, and he convinced my father to accompany him when he returned. A very successful merchant tailor, dad was 28 years old at the time and was immediately smitten by Elizabeth, one of the two eligible daughters. He asked her father's permission to call upon the following Sunday. My mother was 21, truly a striking beauty, an accomplished pianist and had perfect pitch when she sang. She and her older sister, Lena, knew the entire librettos of *la Traviata* and *La Boheme* by memory; they could play a duet at the piano while singing the various parts, my mother, a soprano, taking the feminine roles, Aunt Lena, a contralto, the male. Sunday afternoon at the Manack home was always a musical performance.

As the Sunday visits continued, John and Elizabeth fell in love, but as he was courting mother in 1916, he was not welcomed by my grandmother: "One daughter is already married to a tailor and I don't want two in the family!" She made it very unpleasant for Elizabeth and John who each Sunday took the train for the ride from Carnegie to Steubenville. In May of 1917 my mother and father made a decision considered very drastic in light of the Italian cultural mores of the day. They decided to elope. In retrospect, knowing my father and the personality of one who would leave his family in Italy and strike out on his own to come to America and rescue his sister, defying a potential mother-in-law who stood in his way to happiness was only another day at the office for him.

So, one fine day in May, as the song goes, my father surfaced in Steubenville, not by train but in his brand new 1917 Model T Ford. The couple went out for a "ride" that took them first across the Ohio River to New Cumberland on the West Virginia panhandle to spend the night with her brother, Ernie, who was in on the elopement conspiracy. Mother slept with Aunt Fern, to be sure. The elopers headed for Carnegie the next day. They had to take country roads, most of which were unpaved, and traveled from one country town to another. At one point, it was necessary to ford a shallow stream near Burgettstown, Pennsylvania; it was fordable except when it had rained. They went straight to the Pittsburgh office of dad's friend, Attorney John B. Fortunato, who was an ordained Presbyterian minister. They were married that day in his office.

But my mother did not consider herself married. No one was legally married, she said, until a priest performed the ceremony, so she slept with Aunt Silvia until Catholic Church nuptials could be arranged. Aunt

Clementina, always cheery and confident that she could solve any problem, said "*Ci penso io*," ("Don't worry about it, I"ll take care of it") and then proceeded to do just that. She arranged with the priest of her parish in Pittsburgh to perform the nuptials, Carnegie still not having a Roman Catholic parish that would admit Italians, and on May 24, 1917, mother and dad were married at St. Phillips Church in the Sheridan section of Pittsburgh. None of mother's family was present; only my father's two sisters and their husbands. The couple took off that night by train for a wedding trip to Atlantic City, New Jersey.

Mother was one of the early women's libbers, because after they returned from the wedding trip, mother received a message from her parents: "Come home. All is forgiven. We will welcome your new husband." Mother wrote back, "I'll come back to visit you, but first you must take the train and come to the house of my husband which is now my home and apologize to him for saying that he was not good enough for me to marry him. When you duly apologize, my husband and I will be pleased to visit you at any time." Her parents complied.

I was born in that house on a Carnegie hill in 1919--a native born American whose father and maternal grandparents had been Italian immigrants. Although I was born in America, the community regarded me as an Italian. And so did I.

Significantly, this was years before it became popular for women to go to hospitals to have their babies. Their mothers and sisters attended them when the time approached, and they maintained the vigil until the doctor arrived with his little black bag, and as Hollywood would tell us, they got the pot of water boiling. I am told that the doctor who delivered me was named McGrew, and mother and my aunts and *commare's* (godmothers) indicate that I came in as a heavyweight at 11 pounds. But they weighed me on the pasta scale in the kitchen. All Italian families had pasta scales in those days because pasta was always bought in bulk and not in neat boxes or plastic bags. The scales came in handy to weigh pasta and babies.

My parents bought the house on Grandview Avenue in 1918, and had made the transition from my father's business property in a small East Main Street Italian settlement to a semi-rural ambience in a neighborhood of solid English stock. It was quieter here. No trolleys clanged through the night on the principal line to and from Pittsburgh. On Grandview Avenue the air was fresh and clean. Our street was appropriately named because it overlooked the entire Chartiers valley from the south. We were high above the soot and smoke from the mills and the coal-burning railroad locomotives on the Pennsylvania Railroad's main East-West line that passed through the valley below. Each house had broad lawns and hedges and flower gardens and a stand of woodlands in the back. Grandview Avenue was ideal for the young couple, John and Elizabeth Aldisert, with two small children. But we were foreigners here.

My mother has described the Janus nature of our neighbors at that time. To us, they were very formal, but very polite, with no outward manifestations of hostility. Yet they were not the type who would run in to chat or borrow a cup of sugar. To our backs, they were something else. They deeply resented the intrusion of an Italian Catholic family into a homogenous sector of Protestant English stock.

My father had been a merchant tailor, a name given to those who crafted tailor-made suits for men, and he had been very successful in his trade. During the war, textile factories had been pressed into service to manufacture military uniforms. With the coming of the Armistice, these mills were converted to produce men's clothing. Geared up to mass produce uniforms, the mills were able to turn out ready-to-wear suits available at greatly reduced prices, much cheaper than tailor-made. As it has happened over the centuries, automation again affected a trade of skilled craftsmen. The advent of ready-to-wear men's suits wiped out my father's trade.

He later became a self taught forensic expert serving for 33 years as assistant chief deputy and chief deputy coroner of Allegheny County, supervising investigations into homicides and sudden deaths before police departments developed specialty squads. He presided at Coroner's inquests to determine cases of sudden deaths, and if a crime had been committed he functioned as a committing magistrate, the Coroner of Allegheny County not having relinquished powers conferred by *de Coronatoris*, one of the old British statutes received into Pennsylvania law upon becoming a Commonwealth. But before he embarked on this career, and immediately following the demise of his tailoring business, he worked as a traveling salesmen, a job that required him to be out-of-town for two or three day stretches.

In the years that followed I would often ask my father about the 1922 Ku Klux Klan visit to our house and he would say that there was no doubt in his mind that dressed in those robes and wearing those hoods had been our neighbors, and this was the reason that none of them spoke as they circled our yard. They did not dare to be recognized. Moreover, they chose a time when he was out-of-town, and he had asked some of his neighbors to keep an eye on his wife and children for a few days. They surely did.

I remember asking him what he would have done had he been home at the time. "I would have shot my revolver up in the air," he said, "and they would have crapped their pants and run."

The Klan demonstration in our yard was not repeated in the many years thereafter when we lived "on the hill," but we became accustomed to the huge crosses, some 20 feet tall, that the Klan burned on summer nights. The Klan burned crosses at two locations in Carnegie: on the high pasture at Forsythe Farm about a half mile to the south; and on Southern Grounds, a primitive ball field located only 100 yards to the east of our house.

Burning crosses on the hills sent messages throughout the valley. Mixed messages. For the foreigners, mainly Catholics, the message was "You're not welcome. You're not wanted." For others, the burning crosses were a symbol of inspiration: "Don't worry about these foreigners. The Klan is here and we're looking out for you."

As pre-schoolers, Caesar and I took these cross burnings in our stride. On the mornings after the crosses lit up the night, we would run over to Southern Grounds and play in the charred grass where the big crosses had fallen after flaring out. The charring took the form of a black cross in the grass, to be sure, but to our fertile imaginations this black form was not a cross, but the fuselage and wing of an airplane. We would jump into the blackened grass and play "airplane." We would pretend that we were aviators sitting in the pilots' seats and we pretended to zoom around like World War aces.

Our parents were less sanguine about these burnings.

But we did not move from our house on Grandview, and I suppose as I was growing up, we could say the Aldiserts and their neighbors maintained a peaceful co-belligerency. We played out a charade with the utmost hypocritical diplomacy – very formal and proper to each other's faces. It was a quintessential politeness. Behind our backs they called us "Those damned dirty dagoes." And behind their backs we shook our heads and felt sorry for the *'Mericani'* who didn't smile or laugh very much, were not very friendly, and what is worse, ate bacon and eggs for dinner. For dinner!

We went to school with their children, although in later years my brother, sister and I were the only kids on the hill who would go on to college. We did have one good neighborhood friend, Billy Hiles, who lived two doors away, who was our constant companion until about the third grade when he suddenly died of asthma. My brother and I were deeply saddened because he had been the only kid in the neighborhood with whom we played. Our childhood friends haled from another part of town. They, too, not unexpectedly, were the children of immigrants. The full turn in neighborhood relations came in the late Forties and Fifties when I finished law school and hung up my shingle as a lawyer in the home town. Most of the old neighborhood families became my clients, including some who had worn the Ku Klux Klan robes and hoods in the 1922 procession in our yard. I administered estates of the older generations, wrote wills for their children, handled their real estate transactions, got their divorces and at times got them out of jail. The kid from that family of foreigners, the kid with that strange-sounding first name, "Ruggero," became the person in whom they placed their confidence and to whom they turned for advice.

But almost thirty years had to pass before that came around. In the meantime, I acquired a wealth of experiences in Carnegie. It was there that I went through twelve years of public school. It was from there that I commuted by trolley and bus to obtain my both my undergraduate and law degrees at the University of Pittsburgh. And it was also from there that in 1942 I took the train to serve four years in the U.S. Marines.

My years in Carnegie from childhood to manhood were very important then, and as I look back today, my experiences in the 1920's and the 1930's did much to mold the person that I have become. Indeed, I like to think that some basic feelings that I hold strongly as a person and as a judge-- feelings about the absolute necessity for intercultural understanding--stem from my first memory, that summer evening when I was three years old. That summer evening when some neighbors "came a'calling."

Here I am, fat and smiling at age 2

I'm sitting in the chair, age 3 with my brother, who was 20 months older. The photo was taken the same year the Ku Klux Klan paid a visit to our house in their summer whites–robes and hoods. If you think Ruggero is a tough name to go by, my brother was named after his paternal and maternal grandfathers, respectively--Caesar Octavius. He would later become an obstetrician-gynecologist in Pittsburgh.

My father, John S. Aldisert, in 1917.

My mother, Elizabeth, when dad was courting her in 1916.

My father in his 1917 Ford Model "T" flivver. Mother and dad used this car to elope, and it was the family car a number of years.

Mother and dad on their wedding trip to Atlantic City, New Jersey in May, 1917

Chapter Two
Carnegie, Pennsylvania in the Twenties

Carnegie, Pennsylvania, my home town, was a mill town and railroad center with a number of coal mines and coal mine company towns near its outskirts. We were seven miles west of downtown Pittsburgh where the Monongahela and Allegheny rivers meet to form the Ohio, a place now called "The Point."

The Point is now the apex of Pittsburgh's business district, the Golden Triangle to form the Ohio, but in 1753 it was only a spot in the wilderness. That was the year when a young Lieut. Col. George Washington of the Virginia militia, on an exploratory expedition for the Ohio Land Company of Virginia, arrived at this spot and said that it was "extremely well situated for a fort, as it has the absolute command of both rivers." The British started building a fort, but before they could complete it, the French captured the rudimentary fortification and called it Fort Duquesne. In 1758 General John Forbes put it under new management with the name, Fort Pitt, in honor of the British Prime Minister, William Pitt.

I hesitate referring to Carnegie as a Pittsburgh suburb, because the modern connotation of "suburb" carries with it the notion of a bedroom community with no self-contained urban facilities except sprawling shopping malls, multiplex movie screens and fast food chains. During the Twenties and Thirties, Carnegie was a self-contained town that also served as a commercial center for surrounding farm towns and coal mining camps.

Growing up at that time and in that town as the son of an European immigrant father is an experience that cannot be duplicated today. For good or bad. Massive immigrant waves of economic, political and religious refugees from Europe have stopped. Only a trickle persists. Most of today's immigrants come from Mexico and Central America.

We no longer have satellite mill and mining towns and railroad centers adjacent to big cities like Carnegie was to Pittsburgh. Smokestack industries, as we once knew them, are virtually extinct. The automobile and airplane have practically replaced the passenger railroad train, the truck has diminished the use of the boxcar, and the coal-burning locomotive has given way to the diesel. Aluminum and plastic have replaced steel in everything from cans to automobiles, and imported steel from the Ruhr Valley and Korea has wiped out local industries. Instead of bituminous coal, natural gas or oil now heats our houses. Without immigrants and steel mills and coal mines and the railroad centers there can never be again towns like Carnegie, Pennsylvania that existed during my childhood.

To understand events of those years you must first understand the extent of how the monstrous industrial complex of Greater Pittsburgh became a magnet for hundreds of thousands of immigrants. The coal-coke-limestone-iron-ore-railroad-blast-furnace-open-hearth employment opportunities beckoned the men from worn out villages in Ireland, Southern Italy, Slovakia, Poland, the Ukraine, Russia, Hungary, Croatia, Serbia, and Lithuania. My father and my mother's parents heeded that call. Within two decades the immigrants and their children would become the huge majority of the people in Western Pennsylvania.

Within that small space of time, from about 1890 to 1910, everything in Western Pennsylvania--indeed, everything in the tri-state area, including the West Virginia panhandle and Eastern Ohio--revolved around the production of steel. Steel was king. Every business, every service industry, every phase of commercial life was ancillary to and an auxiliary of making steel. Coal was mined to make the coke that was mixed with iron ore hauled down from Lake Erie where it had been shipped by vessels from the Mesabi Range in Minnesota and together these were conjoined with limestone that came from the quarries. Where young George Washington told his men, "This is where we will build the fort," the industrial fathers of our land had taken a look at the three rivers and the outcropping of coal that lined their banks, and said, "This is where we will build the steel mills" – especially Andrew Carnegie, who, in 1848 at the age of 12, after only five years of education, had migrated to America from Scotland with his mother and father.

It was a natural. Coal, a key raw material, and natural gas, a key fuel in the manufacturing process, were abundant. Also at hand were the three huge rivers – the mighty Monongahela rising in the mountains of West Virginia and the sparkling green Allegheny from northern Pennsylvania, meeting at Pittsburgh to form the Ohio, the greatest tributary of the Mississippi. The rivers could be used to furnish bounteous supplies of water for the blast furnaces and Bessemer converters and the finishing mills. The rivers could also be used to carry away industrial waste, and transport massive barges of coal, coke, ore and limestone to the mill sites that had been erected on the river banks.

Earlier, the industrial fathers built mills in Pittsburgh to make iron products. Iron was made in small foundries, small when compared to gargantuan steel mills that would follow. These foundries supplied cannon and shot for Commodore Oliver Hazard Perry in the 1812 battle for Lake Erie, later for General Andrew Jackson in the Battle of New Orleans and for our army in the Mexican War in the 1840's. In 1852 the great Pittsburgh connection with the east coast took place when the railroad from Philadelphia was completed. It was this rail connection that made Pittsburgh a boom town, expanding greatly during the Civil War. The city produced iron, cannon, shot, other arms and ammunition, and shipping coal became a new industry.

At the war's end, Pittsburgh had become a formidable manufacturing center for the nation, but steel was yet to be its product. It was first a center for iron and glass making, providing 70 percent of our country's glass. The mills were not labor intensive. Iron and glass making were crafts, not mass production industries. Great railroad marshaling yards developed here as the railroads pushed their rails west.

This changed in 1873, when Andrew Carnegie began construction of the Edgar Thompson Works in Braddock with immense Bessemer furnaces to convert iron to steel. Carnegie founded the Nation's steel industry, and Pittsburgh became its capital.

Prior to the development of new smelting processes, Pittsburgh's industry required only a small cadre of skilled or semi-skilled labor to produce a limited amount of iron and glass products. With the advent of the open hearth and Bessemer Converters and the development of the blast furnace, massive quantities of unskilled labor were required and were required immediately. Monumental changes in steel manufacturing methods transformed the former iron foundries into only one part of a huge mass production industry, a new industry that required hundreds of thousands of unskilled laborers.

Making steel was highly labor intensive, and it was not necessary for this labor to be trained or proficient. No skills, only broad backs were required to mine coal, make coke, shovel slag and iron ore, tend furnaces, manhandle giant containers filled with molten pig iron, load slabs and blooms on railroad cars, lay railroad rails and maintain road beds. For all this, the steel mills required thousands of unskilled laborers. The word went out to farm villages of Europe from the immigrants already here. The mills, mines and railroads needed workers now. No skills required. On its part, the fledgling steel industry dispatched labor contractors to "the old country" to recruit a work force. Pittsburgh had become known as "the Steel City" and all the satellite towns around it, including my home town, were dependent upon this industry. Pittsburgh and its satellite towns became populated by immigrants from southern, central and eastern Europe who had heeded the call of "Help Wanted." All of this affected the environment into which I was born.

My childhood experiences could not be shared by my daughter and two sons, who grew up in the posh, upper-middle class, manicured neighborhood of Virginia Manor, Mt. Lebanon, Pennsylvania. They were children of a successful Pittsburgh lawyer who drove a Cadillac and who belonged to a country club. They did not grow up feeling that they were hyphenated-Americans, somehow inferior to kids from old line families – the 100 percent, large, economy-sized "Americans," the nativists who called us hunky and dago and wop and to whom we referred as "the *'Mericani.'*"

Carnegie lies about six miles from downtown Pittsburgh, nestled south of the Ohio and west of the Monongahela. In the 1920's it boasted

CARNEGIE, PENNSYLVANIA IN THE TWENTIES

a single major commercial thoroughfare, appropriately called Main Street, over which two trolley routes rumbled. Main Street, divided by a bridge over Chartiers Creek into East and West Main, served as our business district; it stretched for about a mile from the trolley barn on the east to Superior Mill on the west. A full complement of retail shops--food, variety and clothing stores--supported the community, as well as a coterie of professionals--physicians, dentists, chiropodists, engineers and lawyers.

We had a population of some 12,000, and for the most part, were a community of new immigrant families who had begun the influx at the turn of the century. These "strangers" constituted most of the people in Carnegie, but were abysmally ignored politically, and totally unrepresented in its social, educational or economic structure.

Before these immigrants came--and I suppose I can say before "we" came, my father having come from Italy--Carnegie had been a quiet semi-rural community set in the Chartiers Valley, through which flowed a creek of the same name. To the north were the hills known as Rosslyn Heights and Rosslyn Farms. To the south were Chestnut Street Hill and Johnny Bull Hill and beyond them, the higher ground of Forsythe Farm.

Carnegie had been settled primarily by English and Scottish-Irish stock. They were Protestants, mainly Presbyterians, but also a substantial number of Methodists, Lutherans and Baptists. They had created a quiet, homogeneous, small-town community. But it was a community that was to change suddenly into an industrial and commercial center, and was to change rapidly into a polyglot community.

The image of the Italians in the Twenties was not comparable to that enjoyed today. It was not a vision of sleek design, high fashion clothes, gourmet cuisine, fancy cars and endowed inheritors of a magnificent tradition in art, music and literature. Instead, the image was the common laborer who spoke broken English. The Hollywood type cast was the buffoonery of Henry Armetta, not the glamour of Sophia Loren. Italians were considered boorish, loud and ignorant, fit only to wield picks and shovels. The foods they ate were strange, purchased in peculiar Italian grocery stores where dried codfish, salami, sausages and cheese hung from the ceilings, barrels of olives guarded the doors and pasta, bought by the pound, stacked at the counter in open boxes. Over 50 years had to pass before the food the Italian-American ate in a ghetto life became the

American gourmet food of the Eighties when humble pizza replaced the hot dog as the most popular snack.

In those days it was far from chic to be known as an Italian. We were foreign in speech, food and religion. We did not fit the mold of the Carnegie nativists, and we were not welcome.

The original settlers of Carnegie lived in two communities, then named Mansfield Borough and Chartiers Township, but in the 1890's, some community leaders whose names disappear in the mists of history came up with a splendid idea. They petitioned the famous industrialist-philanthropist Andrew Carnegie who was spreading his largess by donating libraries to various communities in Western Pennsylvania. They asked him to erect a palatial library and auditorium in a park in the center of the two communities. In return, the grateful recipients would combine Mansfield and Chartiers into one town and christen the new municipality, Carnegie. The man who developed the great mills in Homestead and the Edgar Thompson Works in Rankin-Braddock, who founded the Carnegie Illinois Steel Corp, which was to be nucleus of the U.S. Steel Corporation, the man who made millions in grubby little mill towns, accepted the idea. A mill town was named after him and a new borough was christened on February 20, 1894.

At the same time, three new mills to make specialty steel were built. One was located in West Carnegie by the Superior Steel Company and two in East Carnegie by the Columbia Steel and Shafting Co. and the Union Electric Co. A fourth steel plant was McClintock Marshall Co., a fabricating plant specializing in steel girders and construction beams. Industrialists opened a number of new coal mines, small ones within the town limits, larger ones in the outskirts.

The Pennsylvania Railroad sounded a call for laborers, skilled and unskilled, to come to Carnegie, as it had done in Pittsburgh two decades earlier. So did Jay Gould, with his dream to compete with the PRR to St. Louis. Immigrants succumbed to the help-wanted calls and converged on Carnegie to work in the mills and railroads and mining camps. The call was heard by newer immigrants from eastern and southern Europe. They came mainly from Poland, the Ukraine, Russia and Italy, with a smattering from the Middle East.

CARNEGIE, PENNSYLVANIA IN THE TWENTIES

Before them had come the Catholic Irish in the nineteenth century's middle decades; a little later, the Germans. But the Carnegie area needed more strong backs. The quiet semi-rural town erupted into an industrial and commercial center that required a huge work force. At the turn of the century, Carnegie had burgeoned into a moderate-sized trading center. What was once an ethnically homogeneous, Protestant community became a Babel of foreigners who spoke with grating accents and erected strange religious structures of the Roman, Byzantine and Orthodox Catholic faiths. The newcomers raised high towers on their churches on which they installed huge bells that clanged every Sunday morning and disturbed the peace of those who remembered Carnegie as it was in the old days. The good old days. The quiet times.

And a great paradox came about. Old line families who owned the stores and controlled the community services became very prosperous. They left modest frame houses and moved to grand houses of brick or stone on Washington Avenue and Lincoln Avenue, and the upper reaches of which became known as Johnny Bull Hill. They expanded banking facilities. Carnegie supported three commercial banks, busy enough to require evening hours on Friday and Saturday; twelve savings and loan institutions for thrifty immigrants who believed that the prime tenet for staying in the new America was, in the short run, to save money to send for wives, families and relatives in the old country; in the long run, to save enough for a down payment on a house.

The old line families owned dry goods shops, specialty shops of men's and women's wear, shoe stores, a mini-department store known as Autenreith's, automobile service stations and automobile agencies. They managed two separate Five and Ten Cent stores--a Woolworth and a Murphy. They owned real estate agencies, operated a meat packing plant, grocery stores and butcher shops. They were the physicians and lawyers and dentists. They operated five motion picture houses in the hey-day of silent movies--the Carnegie, Grand, Liberty, Dixie and Lyric theaters. They became very prosperous indeed.

But Carnegie's population of 12,000, in and of itself, did not support the economic expansion. What had ignited and then fueled the economy was that the town gradually became the business and service hub of a dozen smaller farming communities and mining camps that lay to the south, west and north.

Located on the main East-West line of the Pennsylvania Railroad, the PRR, as known familiarly, Carnegie was a major railroad junction, boasting fourteen sets of parallel tracks as well as freight marshaling yards. The main lines of the PRR ran to the west through Rennerdale, Oakdale, McDonald and Burgettstown, through the West Virginia panhandle to Ohio and then terminated in St. Louis or Chicago. A subordinate PRR line ran to the south through Kirwan Heights and Bridgeville and on to "Little" Washington, Pennsylvania. Freight trains would pick up and return hopper cars for coal at a number of mines scattered from Carnegie to Washington. From farm towns and mining camps, many families took advantage of inexpensive and frequent train service to shop in our stores and avail themselves of physicians, dentists and other professionals, all of whom maintained evening hours on Fridays and Saturdays. Carnegie, itself a satellite of Pittsburgh, became in its own right a center of smaller satellites. A railroad train passed through every seven minutes.

We were also a major stop on commuter trains to Pittsburgh. From 7:00 a.m. until 9:30 a.m. one could hop a train to Pittsburgh every half hour with intermediate stops at Rossyln, Crafton-Ingram and Corliss stations. Regular return service from Pittsburgh's Union Station and Fourth Avenue began at 3:30 p.m. and extended until 6:30. Less frequent service was available at other times; the last train left Pittsburgh at 11:30 p.m. and was familiarly known as "the bummer."

Rail commuter service was curtailed sharply after World War II, and by the early Fifties was discontinued completely when "progress" came to Carnegie; when fast, convenient and inexpensive rail commuter service was replaced by long lines of automobiles, clogged bumper to bumper during the morning and evening rush hours, all struggling to find limited parking space in downtown Pittsburgh.

Before such changes, trolley service had been abundant and available 24 hours a day. For eight and a third cents (three car checks for a quarter) one could take the "Carnegie 27" from Carnegie for the 35-minute trip to downtown Pittsburgh. We also had our own local line, "Heidelberg 28," that carried you for five cents from the Pittsburgh city limits in East Carnegie, up East and West Main Street and over the Glendale Bridge through Scott Township and thence along the right-of-way to the adjacent borough of Heidelberg. This local trolley line made it possible for housewives to come in from the outskirts, do their shopping and return home with only ten cents expended for transportation.

In the early Twenties we also had another local trolley route; one that turned off East Main Street and went north on Chestnut and east on Arch street to swing under the railroad arches at Rossyln Station, and then north again up the hill to Rosslyn Farms, an elegant residential community perched on the hill that overlooked Chartiers Valley from the north. Here lived some of Carnegie's business or professional men but, for the most part, Rossyln Farms residents were corporation officials and business or professional men who worked in Pittsburgh. They had developed a country club and sponsored polo matches on summer Sunday afternoons. The increase of automobiles by the middle of the Twenties forced the Rosslyn Farms trolley route to discontinue. But the Rosslyn Farms elite continued to shop and use the services of Carnegie.

If the people from Rosslyn Farms constituted the most affluent of Carnegie business patrons and possessed the highest social graces, the men and women who lived in the outlying coal company towns and came to Carnegie for Saturday shopping represented the nether position. These coal miners--virtually all new Americans--were considered the dregs of Carnegie society with their shabby clothes and foreign tongues.

Perhaps more than anything else, the changing face of Carnegie was seen in the blackened faces of the coal miners walking to their homes. The faces were a daily reminder that the immigrants had come and had inundated the community.

What was the effect of these massive waves of new Americans on the old line residents of Carnegie? First, it transformed a sleepy little town into the bustling new business and service center. Old line shopkeepers expanded their stores, hired more employees and began to enjoy a comfortable life. To bankers Carnegie resembled a western boom town. Waiting rooms of physicians and dentists were constantly filled and patients spilled out to the sidewalks. New doctors and dentists came to town.

Shopkeepers, who before had merely scratched out a living, suddenly became comfortable. They no longer were mere tenants. They were able to purchase their Main Street storefront buildings as well as homes of their own. They became first time freeholders, or upgraded from frame houses to brick or stone, or they retained architects to build elaborate new houses especially designed for individual family needs. Carpenters, painters, plumbers, electricians and masons found themselves with more work than they could handle. They rode the crest of total prosperity. Wage earners employed by the hour or on salary no longer worried about part-time work. Mills and mines ran 24 hours a day in two or three shifts. Prosperity and physical comfort had come to the old line residents of Carnegie.

But a contradiction came about. Financial stability and physical comforts did not bring total happiness. A substantial percentage of old line residents became uncomfortable, disturbed and discontented. To be sure, prosperity came to them when their sleepy little town became a bustling commercial and industrial center, but with their new prosperity had come a social and neighborhood disaster. Thousands of foreigners had poured into their tight, homogenized community. Waves of new immigrants inundated the town. Children of foreigners sat next to their children in the expanding school system. Strange people with strange faces who wore strange clothes and had strange smells and talked in strange languages walked in and out of their stores on Main Street.

What was worse, these upstarts even dared to rent houses on the same streets of the Carnegie natives. When this happened, there went the block! There went the neighborhood! Old line families moved to higher grounds.

The newcomers brought strange religious practices. They had processions in the streets, with priests adorned in ostentatious vestments accompanied by chanting choirs and altar boys swinging incense burners. They followed ancient rituals in Latin. The Christian total monopoly was no more. A moderately sized Jewish community had sprung up and its members erected a wooden synagogue on Broadway near East Main. They opened butcher shops, grocery stores, fruit markets and a jewelry store. The Raskin family founded a lumber yard and Joseph Stern and Marcus Sherman each established a scrap metal yard. The Bales family opened Carnegie's largest restaurant. Harry Sutton, an optician, came to town and was followed by Harry A. Klee, a physician.

In the first two decades of the century a revolution, an economic and cultural and social revolution, had taken place. Prosperity had come to the Chartiers Valley with an expanded railroad center, four steel mills and even

CARNEGIE, PENNSYLVANIA IN THE TWENTIES

a brewery. It had become a retail commercial center that serviced outlying farm towns and the people from the nearby mining camps. It was bad enough to be white collar supervisors in the mines and mills and deal with these foreigners from a superior employment position, but the old line residents who themselves were blue collar workers suffered the most. In the mills and mines, they had to work side by side with these foreigners. They had to hear a constant stream of foreign languages, "hunky talk," or listen to crude, broken English. They complained that these newcomers showed no deference to natives of this country. They complained that they had to work side by side with "greenhorns" who had just gotten off the boat. They complained that they had to work alongside hunkies and dagoes, and this was most demeaning. Added to this mix was the reality that most native-born blue collar workers had very little formal education themselves and lacked even the rudiments of basic intercultural understanding. Although new immigrants had brought prosperity to the town and made many families financially affluent, if not wealthy, by becoming their new customers, patients and clients, many old-line Carnegieites disliked them intensely. The old-liners simply did not like foreigners in their midst. The nubile beast, xenophobia, nibbled at their breasts. The dislike was so prevalent that it consumed the members of respectable organizations like the Masonic Order and the Knights Templars, whose membership was open to Protestants only. It consumed many otherwise respectable people who regularly attended worship services at the Protestant churches--at Dr. James Mc Masters Mc Quilken's United Presbyterian or Dr. John Wishart's, First Presbyterian Church, both on Washington Avenue, and Rev. Taylor's First Baptist at Robert Avenue, the Methodist on Lydia Street, the Primitive Methodist on Anthony Street and the Lutheran on Washington Avenue.

And in 1923 it fueled the passions of the Klansmen of Realm of the Invisible Empire, Knights of the Ku Klux Klan, Inc.

Chapter Three
The Ku Klux Klan

The back of the Western Pennsylvania Ku Klux Klan was broken on Saturday, August 25, 1923 when I was four years old. Their decline as a dominating political and social force started dramatically one solitary day. It was not a sudden death, but on this one day the Klan suffered wounds so serious that it would never recover completely.

The demise of the KKK came about as an aftermath in one of the most frightening and violent experiences in Western Pennsylvania history, an event that has been neither widely chronicled nor broadcast. Ignoring this as an historical event—after the one day coverage in the Sunday papers—perhaps may have been justified at first, because Western Pennsylvania's social fabric in the Twenties was too fragile to broadcast the accounts too broadly or to repeat them as historical data. Reminders of hatred and oppression are counterproductive in developing a healthy community of diverse religious and ethnic groupings.

I recount it now to reveal the sociological climate when I was born and while I was growing up. I recount it to disclose the sheer numerical and political strength of the Ku Klux Klan in Western Pennsylvania in the early Twenties. I recount it also to emphasize that the Klan activity in the North was directed primarily against foreign immigrants, primarily Catholics, rather than the blacks. Today, over 80 years after the 1923 Carnegie events, the Klan is still active in various parts of our country, but is now a self-styled white supremacist organization. It originated that way in the South in Post-Civil war days and has now reverted to its original mission. But in the early Twenties in Pennsylvania it was not white supremacy that the Klan was principally espoused; it was not purely anti-African-American. Its main emphasis was anti-Catholic and xenophobia. It was a movement of Protestant extremists designed to terrorize the newly-arrived Catholic immigrants in America's industrial centers and coal-mining communities.

To understand what happened on that August Saturday in 1923, it is first necessary to recognize the purpose of the Klan in the Pennsylvania of the Twenties. Their members were native born Americans. They had witnessed the sudden influx of immigrants to their cities and the establishment of coal mining communities. Their members had experienced problems in the workplace because of the colossal infusion of foreigners. In Greater Pittsburgh, for example, the great steel strike of 1919 was predominantly undertaken by unskilled immigrants, while the native labor force remained at work. In Cambria County (Johnstown), the steel workers were united to go on strike, but imported African-Americans were recruited to break the strike. Attacks on unionism regularly portrayed "radicals" as exponents of foreign ideologies, as often as foreigners themselves. Professor Jenkins of Penn State University has written:

> The principles advocated by the KKK combined general nativist slogans (support for the Christian religion, white supremacy, pure Americanism, states' rights, pure womanhood) with explicitly anti-radical social views. They claimed, for example, to stand for closer relationship between capital and American (not immigrant) labor; to combat "unwarranted strikes by foreign labor agitators"; to prevent fires and the destruction of pr operty by lawless elements"; and to favor strict limitations on further foreign immigration. There was much appealing here for native-born workers."[1]

---

[1] Jenkins, The Ku Klux Klan in Pennsylvania, 1920-1930, reprinted in 69 Western Pennsylvania Historical Magazine 121, 122 (Apri

The Klan received its mortal wound that night. In the day, 30,000 members of the Klan[2] had gathered on the cow pasture on the hill of Forsythe Farm, Scott Township--within sight of our home. The Invisible Empire, Knights of the Ku Klux Klan, had gathered to celebrate what they called, with their penchant for "K's," "Karnegie Day," a mass rally, during which they planned to initiate 1,000 new members. They had assembled from the rural areas of Western Pennsylvania, Ohio, West Virginia, Kentucky and Maryland. They had driven to Carnegie in thousands of automobiles and chartered special trolley cars and railroad trains.

The Pittsburgh Sun reported that some 4,000 automobiles passed through the sentries guarding the entrance on Forsythe Farm. Others reached Carnegie by a 14-car chartered railroad train bringing with them their national leader, Dr. Hiram W. Evans, KKK Grand Wizard, from Atlanta. They debarked from the train in civilian clothes, carrying satchels and bundles but wearing white ribbons pinned to suits and dresses. Others arrived from Pittsburgh in specially chartered trolleys, also debarking with the identifying white ribbons. Shuttle service was provided from the train station and trolley stops to Forsythe Farm.

Two blocks parallel to our house, they streamed up our hill; they streamed up Chestnut Street by the thousands. Armed, hooded Klansmen directed traffic to the farm and stopped and searched those who sought entrance. Because the Klan is a secret organization, there was no admittance without the proper password.[3]

The gentle rise of the farm pasture formed a natural amphitheater for the conduct of the Klan ritual. Thousands gathered in full regalia under a blazing summer sun, but an assemblage of 30,000 was too spectacular to notice the oppressive heat. The thrill of witnessing a mass initiation of 1,000 new members was too exciting. Huge American flags formed a red and blue backdrop to the sea of white robes. Red, white and blue bunting was everywhere, especially on the ritual's centerpiece, a crudely constructed altar around which the neophytes were assembled.

---

[2] This is the figure used by the Pittsburgh Post Gazette on March 25, 1939 in an account written 16 years later in a series entitled, Great Stories of the Past." On August 27, 1923, the Pittsburgh Sun put the number at 20,000.

[3] The formal title is "Klansmen of the Realm of the Invisible Empire, Knights of the Ku Klux Klan, Inc."

The initiates were mostly young men, and many were from adjacent Washington County and nearby Lawrence (New Castle) County. Among the emotionally-charged initiates was Thomas R. Abbott, 27 years old, from nearby Atlasburg, Pennsylvania. For years he had served as a merchant seaman and had returned from his travels, settled down on a farm in the rolling hills of Washington County with a wife and two sons. The Klansmen bore strong Anglo or Saxon names like Abbott; names like McConnell, Wyand, Keck, Matthews, Burns, Malone, Hartsell, Bailey, Bartholomew, Ford, Fabian, Reithmiller, Bohn, List, Davis, Crawford, Cable, Wolf, Fitzroy, Earnest, Miller, and Williams.

Scheduled to preside at the mass initiation was Dr. Evans, the Grand Wizard himself. A mix-up in transportation arrangements caused his chartered train from Atlanta to arrive at the Carnegie station at 8:30 p.m., long after the ceremonies had been completed. In his stead was Sam D. Rich, Grand Keagle of all Pennsylvania Klans west of Harrisburg. Formerly of Kentucky, Rich had arrived in Pittsburgh three years before and had operated the Klan out of a downtown office fronting as an advertising agency. The membership fee was $10.00, of which the Grand Keagle was entitled to keep forty per cent. Not insignificantly, he stood to pocket $4,000 from the day's initiation.[4]

Exposed on the altar for the ceremony was an open bible on which were positioned two crossed swords, a paradigmatic blasphemy. A cross, 50-feet high, built of wood and oiled clothes, had been ignited at the beginning of the ceremonies.

The Malta Band of Wilkinsburg, Pennsylvania and a fife and drum corps paraded around the field where a circle was formed around the burning cross. Here the candidates for admission were "naturalized."

All this I know from the history of that day as recorded in the comprehensive coverage in Pittsburgh newspapers that reported the dramatic events that brought a close to "Karnegie Day 1923."

But there are some facts that I know from memory, recollections that now reach back 80 years. I remember that it was the day of my father's

---

[4] Professor Jenkins estimated that there were 125,000 klansmen in Pennsylvania by the end of 1924 "and possibly 250,000 within the next two years." Jenkins, n. 1, supra at 127-128.

birthday, his 35th, and mother was baking a cake and we were going to have a family birthday party that evening; birthdays were important events in the Aldisert family. I remember a steady drone of motors racing up Chestnut Street. Automobile engines were much noisier than now, mufflers having not reached the present state-of-the-art. But I especially remember what the eyes of a four-year-old saw on the Forsythe Farms cow pasture from his vantage point in his front yard.

I ran into the house, shouting that "millions" of people were on the hill and that they were all dressed in white. From early in the morning, my father had been painting some rooms inside the house. In response to my shouts, he and mother and my brother rushed out to the front yard. They then saw what I had seen. I had seen thousands of people dressed in white assembling the hillside of the Forsythe Farms pasture, the pasture where so many KKK crosses had burned before. They also heard what I could hear on the outside--the sounds of automobiles streaming up Chestnut Street.

It was one of the few times that I saw worry on my father's face, if not actual fear. I remember him saying: "I'm changing my clothes and we're all going 'down street' to Aunt Silvia's." Within minutes we piled into his Model T flivver and headed for Main Street, dashing down Ridge Avenue and Anthony Street, parallel to Chestnut.

My next recollection, and this memory persists, was the scene at the corner of Washington Avenue and East Main, at the drugstore of Winfield S. Smith, a short block from my aunt's house. We saw robed, hooded and rifle brandishing Klansmen directing traffic. The Klan appeared to have taken control of the town. Carnegie had truly become Karnegie.

The sidewalks were filled with curious, but very concerned, people. Many had left Southern, Central and Eastern European countries to avoid violence. In the past they had feared European oppression and tyranny, they now feared the Klan.

My father made a sudden U-turn and we returned to our house on the hill, the family Model T chugging along. And there we remained throughout the rest of the day and evening. My father stayed with us. My only other personal recollection of that day was the frequent screech of sirens from the valley below. I later learned that the Carnegie police apprehended all the self-styled Klan traffic directors and hauled them away to the hoosegow throughout the day. Those arrested bore names like Fitzroy, Wolf, Crawford, Flazit, Cable, Miller and Williams. Many had been wearing army uniforms under their robes.

In later years I asked my parents what we did upon our return home. At first, mother and dad simply smiled and said, "Son, don't you worry about that. It's all over now." When I grew older, my father filled in details. He had been appointed a deputy coroner that year, had a badge and was licensed to carry a firearm. He said that upon returning home, he had first called the chief of police, who told him, "John, don't worry. Those people will not bother you. But stay inside your home."

My father also called his boss, Coroner William J. McGregor, who gave him the same advice. And stay inside we did. But he recalled: "First I got out a box of shotgun shells and a box of .32 caliber ammunition. And we sat in the living room with the door closed with my shotgun and revolver at the ready."

I piece together the dramatic events that brought an end to "Karnegie Day" from oral history, from the reports of my father over the years, and a tale oft-told of the stuff of which legends are made. The danger of oft-told tales is that they become embellished in the repetition. Although I remembered much of the account, before I left Pittsburgh in 1987 to live in California, I went to the files of the Carnegie Library of Pittsburgh to read microfilmed accounts of the three daily newspapers at that time–the Pittsburgh Gazette Times, the Pittsburgh Sun and the Pittsburgh Press. I was truly amazed when I learned that the account rendered me as a child and repeated through the years was accurate. Absolutely accurate, except for one minor matter to which I shall allude later.

It is an account of how a decision of the Grand Wizard was to push the self-destruct button of the Klan in Western Pennsylvania. The truly awful consequences of what happened that evening seemed to shock the Klan's membership into a sense of sanity. It paved the way to the elimination of overt intolerance and hatred in the Carnegie area. It paved the way, but the process was gradual and took many years to accomplish. Many, many years.

The Karnegie Day aftermath served as a signal that the time had come to patch up differences and divisions, to respect one another's differences, and to live as neighbors. As Americans.

We go back to Forsythe Farms. The ritual was concluded. The sun was set. Dusk had settled. Power lines were stretched from the road and lights came on. Electric "KKK" signs and crosses were activated. Hand-held, kerosene-fed red lanterns swung through the pasture as Klansmen milled about. The initiation ritual had concluded, but the thousands were waiting. They were waiting for a message from Carnegie. It finally came.

At ten o'clock a messenger from Carnegie was escorted through the ranks of Klansmen in the field. He carried a message, roughly written on an envelope, announcing that everything was in readiness for the marchers.

The time had come for the army of 30,000 heavily armed, hooded and robed Klansmen to march on a community of 12,000.

It was a night march with red fire and blazing torches to light the way. It was a disciplined parade in military style with orderly uniformed ranks of hooded, masked and white-robed marchers, a march in which many would carry firearms, of all types – many rifles but many more handguns. It would be an organized march of uniformed men, and some women, equivalent to an Army corps, almost three infantry divisions in number. A KKK army corps was to descend upon our tiny community of men, women and children.

It was to descend at night from the hill. All was in readiness except for the precise time the march was to begin. The word had come. Forty-five minutes later, they began the march.

This was not to be a small Ike Clanton gang set to terrorize Tombstone in the western frontier in the 1880's. This was to be an invasion in the civilized, effete East in the 1920's.

> A newswriter would later describe the purpose of the march:
> This was to be more than a mere ceremonial of the dread masked and hooded order. It was to be a demonstration of

the power of the great secret society to the communities of the district.

The Klan moved out. In the lead was a white automobile filled with women of the Klan auxiliary. Erected on the car was a white cross and a huge American flag, both illuminated by special lights. A large platoon bearing a mass of American flags marched behind the lead car, followed by regiments of marchers. The Grand Wizard was in the front ranks behind the flag bearers. The Klan marched on.

Meanwhile in Carnegie word spread of the coming invasion. The word was spread that a KKK parade was to enter Carnegie from Glendale at the Third Street bridge. Hundreds began to converge at the Glendale-Carnegie line.

The Klan marched on. Over the Forsythe Road bridge and left on Wabash Avenue parallel to the P. & W. Va. railroad tracks and down Lincoln Avenue past the school. This was Johnny Bull Hill. This was more than friendly territory, it was hospitable.

The Klan marched on. Up tree-lined Washington Avenue, past the wide lawns that fronted opulent homes, where the establishment of Carnegie lived. This, too, was territory that welcomed them. The Klan marched on. Into Scott township again, past the Bell coal mine, up the grade to Carothers Avenue, the beginning of Glendale, through which ran the trolley shuttle "Heidelberg 28." The trolley was not running this Saturday night.

The Klan marched on. Through Glendale, settled mainly by newly arrived Polish immigrants, immigrants that had recently fled Cossacks. The Polish were not secure enough yet in the new land to oppose the sea of white that had invaded their street. The Klan marched on. Down Carothers Avenue to the Glendale Bridge, to the border of Carnegie borough, to the border where a reception party awaited.

And the march came to a halt.

Carnegie motorcycle policemen barred the way. Beside them in the front rank stood the burgess (mayor) of Carnegie, a young lawyer named John F. Conley. By his side was police chief Chris Keisling (whom I would later know very well and respect during my career as lawyer and state judge).

"You have no parade permit to enter Carnegie. Turn back," Conley said.

"Our lawyers say we don't need a permit!" came the reply.

Conley and Keisling huddled while the Klansmen chafed at the Glendale side of the bridge. It was an eerie sight. It was almost midnight. On the Klan side of the bridge were the glare of torches and red fire carried by the marchers. On the other side behind a thin line of police, a mob of Carnegie citizens began to form. An angry mob, mainly Catholics. Until Karnegie Day, they had been in fear of the Klan with their burning crosses and terror tactics. But their fear, and what is more, their patience, had begun to dissipate at the audacious news that a mass midnight parade through their town was planned by the KKK. Their fear had been displaced by indignation when they learned that the Klan had decided to humiliate them by entering the town on Third Street where the two major Catholic churches stood side by side--St. Joseph's and St. Luke's.

Patience was thrown to the summer night. These people, the new Americans, heretofore the very passive objects of disdain and terror by the cross-burning Klansmen, had suddenly become an angry mob. An undisciplined, unorganized, enraged and wrathful mob. A mob that jammed the streets and sidewalks near the bridge. A mob that was of one mind, "Let the bastards come. We're ready for them!"

Thus came to pass the great blunder of the Grand Wizard and the Grand Keagles. As leaders of an army of terror, they had neglected to reconnoiter a potential battlefield. They had purposely decided to enter Carnegie on the street where the Catholic churches stood. The entry here was a symbol of disdain, a demonstration of raw arrogant power. If it was only a parade that they wanted, they could have marched down Chestnut Street to Main Street and then marched the town and probably have encountered little opposition. This would have been the direct route from Forsythe Farms. From Forsythe Farm it would have been less than a mile to reach Main Street. But no, the Catholics had to be taught a lesson.

The Grand Keagles had not reckoned with the multi-storied flats that ringed the east side of Third Street at the Glendale entrance to Carnegie, the tenements erected across the street from the two churches, the apartments occupied mainly by first and second generation Irish families with a sprinkling of Italians and Poles. This was Irishtown.

The Grand Keagles had not known that adjacent to Main Street on a railroad siding were two open gondola cars filled with coal. Those lumps of coal and an assortment of bricks and cobblestones were handy for throwing, and generously qualified as "Irish confetti." The Keagles had not realized that sheer numbers of Klansmen did not intimidate; that instead, the Klan demonstration had produced the opposite effect. It had infuriated the heretofore passive Irish, German, Polish and Italian Catholics, who had seen the thousands of automobiles converge on their town, had seen the special trains and chartered trolleys discharge hordes of Klansmen, had seen the hooded and robed KKK take over traffic control, had received news by bits and pieces all day of the massive gathering on Forsythe Farms. They had heard rumors of the midnight parade, and to them, the sacrilege of entering the town on the street of Catholic churches.

There was heated, intense opposition to the Klan that night, but it was not organized. On the streets was merely a swarm of agitated people. Some packed Third Street on the Carnegie side of the bridge to stop by sheer numbers the onward march of the Klan. Others took to rooftops, armed with paving blocks, lumps of coal and bricks. Some carried clubs and stones. Others waved pistols.

At the bridge there was a stand-off. On one side was the leading phalanx of thousands of Klansmen. On the other side were Burgess Conley and Chief Keisling and a handful of police. Angry shouts filled the air from both sides. Suddenly, passing through the throngs on Third Street, with siren wailing, came an automobile filled with deputy sheriffs. Help for the Carnegie police had finally arrived.

The detail was commanded by Deputy Sheriff Jack Dillon, who emerged from the car, walked to the bridge, and what newspaper accounts described as "in stentorian tones," invoked a law that has been a part of British and American law since Alfred, the Great--the familiar "Riot Act." It is designed to dispel mobs, because under a Pennsylvania statute then in existence, the county could be held financially responsible for riot-induced damages unless the Sheriff "read them the riot act."

If any persons shall be unlawfully, riotously and tumultuously assembled together, to the number of twelve or more, so as to endanger the public peace, it shall be the duty of the Sheriff to go among the rioters, or as near to them as he can safely go, and then and there with a loud voice make proclamation in the name of the Commonwealth requiring and commanding all persons immediately to disperse themselves and peaceably to depart to their habitations, or to their lawful businesses.

Invoking the Pennsylvania Riot Act, Deputy Dillon shouted:
As a deputy of the sheriff of Allegheny County I advise you men to turn back. To march means trouble. We are here to see that peace and order is preserved in the Commonwealth of Pennsylvania.

Deputy Dillon represented the law, and his voice was loud and clear, but his words were ineffective. His audience was composed of Klansmen from small towns, mostly rural, of Pennsylvania, Ohio, West Virginia, Maryland and Kentucky. The audience came from towns where the KKK was the law, not mayors or burgesses, not chiefs of police, not sheriffs.

A single voice from among the Klansmen called, "Let's go!" With this signal the Klan started to cross the bridge. Their march was strong and orderly. The white car, containing women of the Klan auxiliary, displaying the large white cross and the lighted American flag moved forward. The car proceeded about ten feet. And the battle began.

The marchers were pelted with clubs and lumps of coal and bricks and stones. The white cross was torn down from the car and smashed. The large illuminated flag was dashed to the ground. The mob pushed the lead car to the side of the road.

The Klan marched on. First, the platoon of flag bearers, followed by the robed and hooded military ranks. Marchers ran up from the rear to come to the aid of their leaders.

The Klansmen attempted to wedge a path through the crowd, but the fury of the attack hurled the marchers back, yards at a time, forcing them to retreat over the Glendale Bridge, across Chartiers Creek, the boundary line between Glendale and Carnegie.

Shots were fired in the air as the fighting intensified along the line. Women and children rushed to safety. Scores of Klansmen and civilians engaged in bitter fist fights. Rough and tumble skirmishes took place before the last of the marchers were forced back across the bridge.

Once out of the borough, the Klansmen had an opportunity to form and prepare for a new advance. Ten minutes after they had been driven back, they swept back across the bridge in a powerful rush that broke the ranks of the protagonists.

Singing, "Onward Christian Soldiers," the Klansmen began to move slowly down Third Street, past the churches, moving gradually toward Main Street, their progress met by fierce opposition at every point. Fights broke the ranks. Shots were fired.

This was not Wabash or Lincoln or Washington Avenues, the friendly territory where the parade began with the highest spirits on Johnny Bull Hill with contagious enthusiasm in the ranks and a rousing welcome from the residents they passed, that is, to say, those residents who were not in the white-robed march themselves. This was Third Street, Carnegie. Irishtown.

Each moment saw the crowd on Third Street increasing, but by sheer weight of numbers the thousands of Klansmen were able to advance slowly. A hail of missiles continued. More shots were fired. Bystanders continued to run for shelter. Women and children screamed and headed for open doors. The street became packed with rioters. The fight intensified.

Cries of "Get a rope," "Lynch them," "Kill them" filled the air. Fist fighting, stone and brick and stick throwing, firing guns in the air. All ingredients of a full blown riot.

As shots were fired a Klansman dropped to the street. Blood splashed the front of his white robe and hood. Half a dozen men, who may have been members of the mob or may have been Klansmen who had stripped off their robes, carried the fallen Klansman to the nearby office of Dr. F. B. Jones, Jr. The doctor did his best, but the unknown Klansman died a short time later.

No marks of identity except widespread tattooing could be discovered when his body finally arrived at the morgue in Pittsburgh. He had a rose tattooed on the left shoulder, a Japanese woman on his right, a cross and a branch of a tree with the inscription, "In memory of my Father" on his right forearm, "Mutt" on the right leg, "Jeff" on the left, a picture of a woman below the right knee, and a pig and a chicken on the left foot.

No identification and no money – not a penny – was on his person. Later, at the morgue in the middle of the night, he was identified as young Thomas Abbott of Atlasburg, Pennsylvania, a small mining and farming town about 10 miles away. A few hours earlier the young dead man had taken a lifetime oath of service to the Klan. He left a widow, Emma Abbott and two sons, Thomas, aged three, and Frank, six-months.

The Klan marched on. But not for long. At the most they progressed only three or four blocks into Carnegie from the Glendale Bridge. Some made it to Main Street, by cutting through alleys, and they turned around to await instructions from their leaders. But the shooting and the brick hurling continued. Four wounded Klansmen were taken to Roach's meat market. Two of them had been shot, others injured by flying bricks.

Almost as fast as it had started, the riot ended. The front ranks of the Klansmen began to remove their robes and hoods. Rioters and spectators sought shelter in nearby houses and buildings. Ambulances began carrying away the seriously injured. The morgue ambulance that later would carry Abbott's body to the morgue in Pittsburgh was to be filled with injured who needed hospitalization. Others were carried to nearby doctors' offices or to their homes.

The deputy sheriffs made a second plea. They ordered the marchers to return to their meeting place. They implored the marchers to leave in order to prevent further disorder and rioting.

This time the Klan leaders listened. They ordered a return march. One half hour after the confrontation at the bridge began, the Klan turned back.

But it was not to be an orderly retreat. It was not a repetition of the disciplined light-hearted, glory march on Carnegie. It was a flight in disarray to the sanctuary of Forsythe Farms. In their retreat, hundreds discarded hoods and gowns. Hundreds of hand guns were tossed aside. One souvenir hunter collected 200 of them. Others claimed 20 to 50.

The Klan ran away. Thirty thousand of them. They ran back to Forsythe Farm, rushed through the motions of a concluding ritual, and quickly and sheepishly slunk away in the night. For the first time, these members of the Invisible Empire learned something about fear. They suddenly were in fear for their lives. As they returned to their homes, they did not hold heads up high. They did not boast that they were Klan members. None wore white ribbons pinned to proud breasts. They discarded hoods and gowns by the thousands, so much they feared being apprehended by an irate citizenry, or by uniformed police, county detectives and deputy sheriffs. But most of all they feared being shot or manhandled by angry citizens. Even the black robes of the Grand Keagles were found on the outskirts of Carnegie and as far away as the town of Oakdale, a mile away. Such was the extent the leadership degenerated. The terrorists had become terrified.

The breaking dawn found the streets deserted. Piles of bricks, lumps of coal and other missiles remained on Third Street where the rioting occurred. The two gondola cars on the siding near Main Street no longer were filled with coal. On the Forsythe hillside where the hooded marchers had gathered and held their ceremony a scattered few remained, gathering up their personal belongings. Long strings of electric lights were still lit. The hillside was filled with paper and debris. Great piles of empty soft drink cases stood about several empty tents. The band stands were still covered with bunting and the flaming crosses of electric lights were still standing.

The effect in Carnegie was immediate. The Klan was broken. What is more, their members were ridiculed. They could no longer terrorize if they were laughed at as comics dressed in white sheets.

The saga of August 25, 1923 was a story oft-repeated in the years that followed. I remembered it well, both as child and adult.

The oral history turned out to be fairly accurate when later matched against newspaper accounts, except in one detail. It was not until I checked official records that I learned that the slain Klansman Abbott was simply a young man who had joined the Klan that day. Fable had it that Abbott had been the Pennsylvania Grand Keagle himself, and that it was the death of the leader that smashed the KKK. But this was not the case.

The man accused of firing the shot that killed Abbott was 60-year old Patrick McDermott, a popular Carnegie undertaker. He was taken into custody in the early hours of Sunday, during the night of the riot. One witness swore that he had seen McDermott fire the shot. A few days later, on Wednesday, a Coroner's jury failed to believe the lone witness; McDermott was released for lack of evidence.

But the Klan would not let the matter die. Grand Keagle Rich issued a formal statement complaining that the constitutional rights of the 30,000-strong army had been violated by the citizens of Carnegie:

> When conditions come to such a stage in this enlightened age that peaceable Americans banding themselves in a patriotic organization are prevented from exercising the same rights as Catholics, Jews and Negroes, and which are guaranteed by that constitution formed by our forefathers, it is high time that action be taken. Catholics, Jewish, Italian and Negro people have paraded the byways of this Pittsburgh community and not once has a participant been harmed in the least by a Protestant spectator.[5]

On the day before the Coroner's inquest, 1,000 hooded Klansmen followed Abbott's body for twenty miles from his home in Atlasburg to a grave in a little country cemetery in the hills between McDonald and Sturgeon in Washington County.

At the insistence of her late husband's friends, early the next year the young widow Abbott swore out an information against McDermott charging him with the murder of her husband. On February 19, 1924, a grand jury indicted McDermott on the charge. In 1939, Reporter Ray Sprigle of the Pittsburgh Post Gazette, writing a series on the "Great Stories of the Past," would describe the court proceedings that followed:

> On November 16, 1924, McDermott went on trial for his life. Four witnesses, including the one who testified the year before at the coroner's inquest, swore that they

---

[5] As reported in the Pittsburgh Post, August 27, 1923, page 2, cols. 3-4.

saw McDermott fire the shot that killed Abbott. But four witnesses testified that McDermott was with them throughout the progress of the riot and that at no time did he have a gun. Other witnesses testified that at a preliminary hearing before a justice of the peace, one of the witnesses who identified McDermott as the killer asked to have McDermott pointed out to him so that he'd "know him later."

Judge E. H. Baird of Elk County was brought in to preside at the trial. Three witnesses – Harry Albright of Carnegie, B. L. Bickerton of Clairton, and B.F. Ellings of Wilkinsburg, a member of the degree team that participated in the initiation ceremonies – testified that they saw McDermott firing into the parade and saw Abbott fall. Defense counsel, John S. Robb, ripped into their testimony. As reported by the Pittsburgh Sun on November 19, 1924:

> The major part of his rancor was directed against Harry Albright of Carnegie, who had testified that he knew McDermott for 15 years and as McDermott stood firing at the Klansman Albright said to him: "You are a coward to shoot into a crowd like that." Attorney Robb characterized Albright as a braggart and blowhard who would not have the courage to make the remark he had declared he had made to McDermott under any circumstances much less when McDermott had a revolver in his hand. Mr. Robb said he couldn't understand how a man like Albright would have the courage even to testify as he had unless it was squirted into him by the Ku Klux Klan.
>
> Robb characterized the testimony of Bickerton, another Commonwealth witness, as unworthy of belief and that he was unable to point out McDermott at the coroner's inquest and that the coroner believed so little of his testimony given at the inquest that he waved him from the stand in disgust.
>
> As to B.F. Ellings, the third Commonwealth witness who said McDermott had committed the murder, Mr. Robb said he was a man without a spark of honesty or religion.

He said Ellings was the "little whipper snapper" who came to him in the office of Alderman Anderson and asked to have Patrick McDermott pointed out to him. Mr. Robb declared that Ellings had never seen the defendant until the hearing in the alderman's office.

In speaking of the Klan, Attorney Robb declared it was a society that had no place in America.

In 47 minutes the jury returned with a verdict of not guilty.

But the importance of Abbott's death was not his position in the Klan or his station in life; rather, his death served to quell the riot and to bring peace and order. It prevented what could have been a permanently divided community. The fatal injuries Abbott received affected more than one man. They led to the death of the Klan in Carnegie. The Klan would exist in other parts of Western Pennsylvania, in other parts of Allegheny County, but in my home town it was mortally wounded.

On one day the Klan was transformed from a power that had terrorized the new immigrant families in Carnegie – constituting the vast majority of the population – to a group of crazies dressed up in white sheets who were laughed at. You can not succeed as a terrorist if the objects of your terror laugh at you.

The Carnegie Klan riot also caused a real beginning. It was the beginning of intercultural and interreligious understanding in the town where I was born. It was the beginning of an attitude by the white Anglo Saxon establishment that the strange newcomers were here to stay as neighbors and that Carnegie natives might as well accept this fact and live in peace; it also was the beginning of an attitude by the "foreigners" that the "Americans" weren't so bad after all.

In 1939 Sprigle would write in the Pittsburgh Post-Gazette:
But young Klansman Thomas Abbott did not die in vain. The utter uselessness and the cruelty of his death and the events that led to it seemed to shock both the Klan elements and the groups that opposed them back to a sense of sanity. Intolerance and hatred died out many

years ago in the Carnegie district. The old divisions and differences are gone.

Sprigle was writing from a perspective of 16 years later. But what was begun in August 1923 took years, indeed many decades, to accomplish. For example, 35 years later I was to be the endorsed candidate of the Democratic Party for a seat on the Common Pleas Court of Allegheny County. Although the party was strong, and reputed to be one of the last of the great urban political machines, its leader, Pennsylvania Governor David L. Lawrence, called me in:

> Rugi, with a name like Aldisert, no one will know whether you are Catholic or Protestant, English or German or old line American. All the Italians in the county already know you. But if you go on the ballot as "Ruggero J. Aldisert" all the Ku Kluckers in the North Hills will cut you. They're good Democrats, but they just don't like Italians or Poles or Jews. It's up to you, but I would use just my initials, "R.J. Aldisert." They'll think you're one of them.

I filed under my initials only and in 1961 won the election as "R. J. Aldisert." But seven years later, when I was named to the U.S. Court of Appeals, President Johnson nominated "Ruggero J. Aldisert."

The Carnegie Klan riot, or rather the retelling of it over and over again through the years, the recounting of it so often that it became sort of a folk legend, inculcated personal permanent impressions in me. And we need to be reminded of this, because for good or bad, as I grew up in Carnegie, most of the community regarded me as "an Italian kid with that funny name, 'Ruggero'".

But the broader, permanent, indelible impression that the Klan riot made on me was that all forms of discrimination are bad. I didn't have to wait to study the Equal Protection Clause in law school many years later to understand this, or wait for the Civil Rights Acts of 1964 to recognize that it was wrong to practice "discrimination or segregation on the ground of race, color, religion, or national origin." I learned my lesson that August night in 1923 when I was four years old.

And through the years at the dinner table mother and dad taught us that people would call us names because we were of Italian heritage. We had to expect that and prepare for it. But most of all we were taught that if we wished to be free of taunts and jeers ourselves, because it hurt us and made feel bad, we had to respect others. We should not call others names, or discriminate by word or deed against anyone by reason of his or her religion, race or national origin.

"If you don't like being called 'dago', 'wop' or 'hunky', don't let me hear you call a negro "a nigger", or a Jew "a kike", or the people on the other hill "a bunch of Kluckers," my dad said. He said it over and over again.

I didn't need a Supreme Court in the Sixties to teach me something I learned in the early Twenties.

In our town, as I have said, that August night in 1923 was the time of the beginning.

Two years later, in September 1925, I entered first grade at Washington School on Lydia Street.

Sunday editions, August 26, 1923 of The Pittsburgh Press and The Pittsburgh Gazette Times describe the Ku Klux Klan march and subsequent riot.

KLANSMEN ATTACKED DURING CELEBRATION; ONE MAN IS KILLED

Continued from First Page.

As the sun rose above the horizon yesterday morning, the charred cross on the initiation hill looked down upon trampled ground and Carnegie streets strewn with coal, bricks, railroad ballast, cudgels and other weapons used in the disorder a few hours before. Only a few patrolmen and detectives were on West Main street, where the rioting occurred.

It is estimated that 20,000 members and candidates of the Ku Klux Klan attended the initiation, widely heralded, throughout Western Pennsylvania, on the hill above Carnegie Saturday night. Imperial Wizard Evans, head of the Klan in the United States, and many high officials of the Pennsylvania domain of the order, attended the ceremonies.

Parade Decided On.

In preparation for the big meeting, which was held on a 50-acre field, a 50-foot cross was erected, fireworks were put up, bomb pits were sunk, a band stand and speakers' stand were erected. More than 4,000 automobiles bearing klansmen or candidates were said to have passed into the field for the services. Red fire and oil lamps were burned for light.

It is understood that before the initiation began, a parade through Carnegie, a permit for which is reported to have been refused several weeks ago, was abandoned, but following the admittance of the big class of novices, a consultation of Klan officials is reported to have been held and the klansmen formed in line for the parade.

Led by an automobile draped in American flags and with an electrical "K. K. K." on the front, the line of robed men moved down the hill toward Glendale and Carnegie. The procession was stopped many times by the huge crowds of spectators which filled the roads.

Crowd Halts Procession.

As the marchers came to the Glendale Bridge, the division between Glendale and Carnegie, the procession was stopped by a block of automobiles and a threatening crowd. As the klansmen in the leading automobile, in which there was said to be four women, began to argue with the opposing forces, the crowd in Carnegie is said to have become larger, until it blocked West Main street for almost a square.

1-- Klansmen forming circle around initiates before initiation ceremonies were begun. 2–Head of parade that moved around field, led by the Malta Ban of Wilkinsburg. 3–Group of Klansmen form guard on outer circle where candidates took oath before a blazing cross. 4–Burning cross, 50 feet high, that was fired before ceremonies began. 5– Members of Wilkinsburg Klan degree team.

DEATH IN A WHITE ROBE

THIRTY thousand men and women, robed in white, massed on the gently sloping hillsides of a natural amphitheater on the old Forsythe Farm in Scott township, Allegheny county, under the blazing midsummer sun that afternoon of August 25, 1923.

Breathlessly they watched as more than a thousand similarly white-robed figures grouped about a rude altar in the center of that vast throng. On the altar was an open Bible. Across the opened Book were crossed swords. As one man, the thousand lifted their right arms and slowly repeated the solemn oath that bound them forever to the dread Invisible Empire of the Knights of the Ku Klux Klan.

Through the long summer afternoon, the ceremonies continued endlessly, while the thousands sweltered uncomplainingly beneath their robes and hoods.

At dusk, from a dozen nearby hill tops, crosses burst into flames, climax of the drama of the most solemn ceremonial of the Klan.

Since dawn that vast army had gathered — from Pennsylvania, from Ohio, from West Virginia, from Maryland and Kentucky. Hundreds of them had driven all night long to reach that isolated farm in Scott township. This was to be more than a mere ceremonial of the dread masked and hooded order. It was to be a demonstration of the power of this great secret society to the communities of the district.

Before sunrise of this August morning, white-robed Klansmen had taken positions at every crossroad and street intersection for miles surrounding the Forsythe farm, which had been acquired by the Klan.

As the thousands of automobiles, each bearing a white Klan flag, began to converge on the Klan ceremonial grounds, the robed sentinels directed the drivers to the proper roads. In Carnegie some of the self-appointed traffic men were soon stripped about their robes. Borough policemen who came on duty later placed the armed traffic men under arrest and led them to the borough lockup. That ended their participation in the Klan's record ceremonial.

Starting the Parade to Tragedy

With nightfall, the thousands on the farm massed in parade formation. A white automobile, bearing a great American flag illuminated by electric lights, headed the procession. Slowly the great procession moved toward the highway, down through Glendale and toward Carnegie.

But while the hordes of the Klan were massing in orderly parade formation, other uncounted thousands were massing in Carnegie. Word spread like wildfire that the Klan, denied a parade permit, was determined to defy the borough authorities and traverse the streets in Klan regalia.

By the time the Klan parade reached the bridge at the head of Third street, which marks the boundary between Scott township and Carnegie, thousands were massed along Third street and other thousands literally filled the side streets, alleyways and yards for blocks on either side of the street.

In 1939 Reporter Ray Sprigle of the Pittsburgh Post Gazette wrote a series of articles entitled "Great Stories of the Past." On March 23, 1939 he wrote "Death in White Robes."

TRIBUTE PAID SLAIN KLANSMAN AT MEETING IN HOTEL HERE

Silent tribute to the sacrifice made by the dead klansman was paid by Ku Klux Klan delegates at the meeting in the Fort Pitt Hotel during yesterday afternoon's session and arrangements perfected to care for the members of the dead man's family.

A statement was issued by Sam D. Rich, king kleagle of the Ku Klux Klan of Pennsylvania, following the close of the afternoon session.

The statement:

The tenets of the United States Constitution have been struck a foul blow by the action Saturday night of a mob of Carnegie residents in attacking parading Klansmen, during which Klansman Thomas R. Abbott of Burgettstown was murdered. When conditions come to such a stage in this enlightened age that peaceable Americans banding themselves into a patriotic organization are prevented from exercising the same rights as Catholics, Jews and Negroes, and which are guaranteed by that Constitution formed by our forefathers, it is high time action is taken. Catholics, Jewish, Italian and Negro people have paraded the byways of this Pittsburgh community and not once has a participant been harmed in the least by a Protestant spectator. The regretable and certainly ruthless of the un-American element of Carnegie citizenry Saturday night is just cause for a greater concentration on the part of 100 per cent American citizens with the view of preventing its recurrence. And we, as Klansmen, pledge ourselves to this just cause.

The Klan is here for every good purpose. Furthermore, it is here to stay. It is to be hoped those who desire our dissolution will refrain from committing murder in any attempt to destroy us.

It was reported last night that committees of klansmen from the Western Pennsylvania district had spent the day in Carnegie making investigations into the riot Saturday night. According to a report, all efforts are being made to learn the identity of the slayers of Abbott.

The statement of the Ku Klux Klan King Keagle Sam D. Rich in singling out certain groups—"Catholics, Jewish, Italian and Negro people," the very people who in 1923 were the object of the Klan's terror.

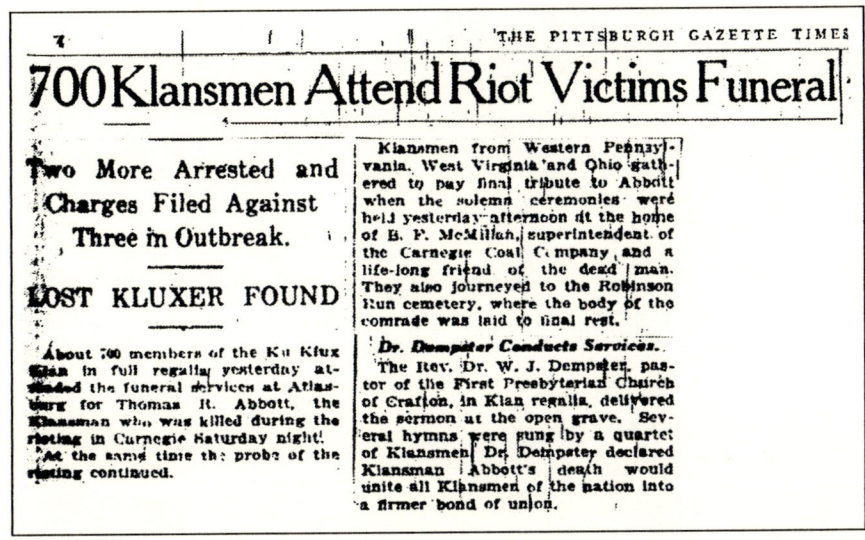

Indicating the power wielded by the Ku Klux Klan in Western Pennsylvania in 1923 is seen in this news report of the Klan gathering at the home of the Superintendent of the Carnegie Coal Company and in the sermon of a leading churchman stating that the death of the Klansman "would unite all Klansmen of the nation in a firmer bond of union."

Chapter Four
The Men of Carnegie's Mills and Mines

America has now probably forgotten the towns owned by the coal mining companies in Pennsylvania, West Virginia, Ohio and Kentucky. Our American literature does not devote very much to this phenomenon. Also called camps or patches, these towns began to diminish when the United Mine Workers Union brought strength and dignity to the miners in the early Thirties. Until the companies relinquished total control of miners' lives, the company towns served as America's resurrection of feudalism.

Coal was needed to make coke. And coke was needed to convert iron to steel. The mining companies sunk shafts in locations where it was most economically productive to extract the coal. More often than not, mine entrances were located in fields and woodlands, sometimes far from the nearest settlement. To attract a work force of substantially unskilled labor, it was necessary for the mine owners to build entire towns where they had sunk their shafts to retrieve the coal from the world famous Pittsburgh Seam that underlay the hills of Western Pennsylvania. These towns were built from scratch. Dirt streets were laid out and austere houses, duplexes and triplexes, were constructed of cheap lumber. Ramshackle settlements, similar to the hastily constructed mining towns of the frontier west, became known as company towns.

Several lay on the outskirts of Carnegie: Moon Run and Imperial in Robinson Township, Kirwan Heights in Scott Township, Castle Shannon, Library and Sygan in Bridgeville. Next to iron ore, coal was the most important ingredient in the manufacture of steel, a process that entailed a gigantic cooking concoction. Coal in its natural form was not used in the mills; rather it was first subject to a heating process in beehive ovens, lined with silica brick, to produce coke. Making coke removes volatile by-products from coal, such as ammonia, coal tar and gaseous compounds. Coke is to bituminous coal what charcoal is to wood.

The first step to make steel is to make iron, and this takes place in a huge blast furnace, which is a chimney-like structure about 100 feet high, made of steel and lined with brick. It is narrow at the top, increasing in diameter downward. The furnace is charged, or filled, at the top; filled with ore, coke and limestone that is carried to the top by hoists. Preheated compressed air is fed at the bottom through pipes and is passed onward through the charge. This causes the coke to oxidize eventually to carbon monoxide which reduces the iron ore and, in time, when the mix is thoroughly cooked, it appears as molten, or pig iron. This concoction is then transferred to huge ladles, great steel chambers two stories high, and transported by massive, moveable cranes.

The next step is to convert iron into steel at another furnace known as the Bessemer converter with a capacity as high as 30 tons. The converter is egg-shaped, often set on pivots so that it can be tilted to receive the molten iron, turned upright during the "blow" and tilted again to pour the molten steel product. In intense gas heat and hot air, sometimes reaching 3,000 degrees, the mixture cooks for eight to ten hours. Pouring out the steel is called "tapping," where the molten metal rushes out to the mammoth ladles heralding the birth of steel.

Andrew Carnegie erected Pittsburgh's first Bessemer at the Edgar Thompson Mill in Braddock. In August 1875 it made its first blow. Cold air shoots through the bottom of the furnace and through the molten iron. The heat increases tremendously, burning out impurities in the iron and forming steel. The process was simple, but the effect was extraordinary. In 1893, McClure's Magazine described the results:

Out of each pot roared alternately a ferocious geyser of saffron and sapphire flame, streaked with deeper yellow. From it a light streamed – a light that flung violet shadows everywhere and made the gray outside rain a beautiful blue. A fountain of sparks arose, gorgeous as ten thousand rockets, and fell with a beautiful curve, like the petals of some enormous flower.
Overhead the beams were glowing orange in a base of purple. The men were yellow where the light struck them, violet in shadow . . . . The pot began to burn with a whiter flame. Its fluttering, humming soar silenced all else . . . .

A shout was heard, and a tall crane swung a gigantic ladle under the converting vessel, which then mysteriously up-ended, exploding like a cannon a prodigious discharge of star-like pieces of white-hot slag. . . . Down came the vessel, until out of it streamed the smooth flow of terribly beautiful molten metal. As it ran nearly empty and the ladle swung away, the dropping slag fell to the ground exploding, leaping viciously, and the scene became gorgeous beyond belief, with orange and red and green flame.

Newer methods rendered the Bessemer converter obsolete by the Thirties; the last Bessemer in North America went out of commission in the 1960s.

The molten mass is then teemed, or poured, into ingot molds, where a cooling process solidifies it into 20 or 30-foot ingots. Ingots are heated again to become malleable and then transported to the primary mills, the slabbing or blooming mills, where they are rolled into slabs, or semi-finished shapes known as blooms. In Carnegie, the Superior Mill and Union Electric are what are known as blooming or rolling mills. After they receive the ingots in the size requested, gigantic machines roll the ingots into blooms, the way a housewife uses a rolling pin to roll dough into a pie crust. Although we lived a mile away from Superior Mills, when the wind shifted, we could hear the dim sounds of the rolling machines that transformed the steel ingots into rails for the railroads..

An enormous amount of unskilled labor was needed to dig the coal and to feed the ovens to make coke. A blast furnace would use about 2,100 tons of coke to run seven days. Each cokeoven would produce about two tons of coke a day. They operated only six days a week. Coke plants had to produce 350 tons a day to feed a single blast furnace. Mines had to produce coal 24 hours a day not only to feed coke ovens, but to run railroad locomotives, to fuel power plants, to meet other industrial needs and to heat the houses of Western Pennsylvania. The emerging steel industry of Western Pennsylvania, required coal miners by the thousands.

The steel industry required more than coal miners to sustain the new demands of mass production. Railroads required a substantial amount of unskilled labor, and railroads transported the coal to the coke ovens and the coke from the ovens to the blast furnaces. Men were also needed to work the rivers and to man the equipment that unloaded barges of iron ore and limestone at the mill sites.

It was in the steel mills, however, where the greatest demands for unskilled labor existed. Strong backs by the hundreds of thousands were needed to shovel the ore, coke and limestone into the hoists that fed the blast furnaces, load steel scrap into the charging machines at the Bessemer converters and to manhandle flaming iron ingots. Men were needed to remove impurities in the mix as steel cooks for eight to ten hours at temperatures exceeding 3,000 degrees. They were needed to tend the ladles and cranes. They had to manhandle the raw materials as well as the finished products.

At times the men shoveled for six and one-half hours non-stop in the blast furnaces, six and one-half hours of shoveling raw materials or raking out burned contents of hot furnaces or carrying bricks and cinder out of the hot bottoms.

But first you had to dig the coal. Twelve hour shifts slashed miles of passageways beneath the rolling hills in the blackness of the Pittsburgh Coal Seam. The men spent long shifts in the dark without a ray of sunshine, digging and blasting and shoveling to cut new shafts and horizontal "rooms." After the coal was removed from a "room" the miners had to move the coal forward to form a solid coal wall. The shot firers came in to bore holes in that wall and then inserted sticks of dynamite into the holes. When this was accomplished, the miners then scurried to the nearest "heading" (an alcove in the passageway) or to safety around the corner in the cross passageway.

Then came the cry "fire in the hole!" and the explosion followed. Chips and dust scattered through the room and also permeated the nearby subterranean passages. Unfortunately, it also penetrated the lungs of the miners. Inhalation of coal dust created a new medical phenomenon for its effects, "the Pittsburgh lung." We now call it black lung disease, pneumoconiosis.

While the coal dust was still settling, in came the loaders, swinging shovels to load the mine cars. This was devastating, back-breaking work. The men were paid by the tonnage they mined, not for the hours they worked. To pay for the privilege of working, the miner had to purchase the pick and shovel he used, as well as dynamite, black powder and the short fuses he carried in his pocket. The mine operators would later invest in the mechanical loader that operated on rails similar to the donkey-drawn mine cars. This equipment was able to fill as many wagons in an hour as it took a man to fill in three days, loading by hand.

We knew these men. They were the fathers of some of my friends at school. We would see them on the streets coming home from a shift after six p.m. They were totally blackened-- their clothing, faces, hands and shoes. They shuffled home, still wearing their work clothes and caps. They appeared as Halloween caricatures, with only the whites of their eyes recognizable and a red slash for a mouth. They always carried a lunch pail, the huge bucket, a three tier aluminum pail, with the lowest compartment holding two or three quarts for drinking water, tea or coffee, a compartment for bread, meat or cheese and another for a fruit or piece of home-made cake or pie.

The mining companies had yet to furnish bathhouses or locker rooms; not until the mines became unionized were such trappings of civilization installed. The miners shuffled the streets of Carnegie, blackened and sooted, until the early Thirties. Most of all, I remembered their stooped shuffle, too exhausted to walk briskly, too exhausted to talk, bent over moving at a slow and steady pace, looking straight ahead.

Then there were the railroad laborers, called the "Gandy Dancers." Massive quantities of labor were required to add new trackage and sidings, and to extend the freight and marshaling yards. In the golden years of expansion, the railroads carried in raw materials and hauled out finished products. They needed railroad labor to supply round the clock maintenance on the rights-of-way – to inspect and repair the stone ballast on which the wooden ties lay and to repair and replace the ties when needed. Railroad crews were required to be at hand 24 hours a day to rush to scenes of derailments and wrecks. The main line of the Pennsylvania Railroad had to be kept open at all costs.

In Thomas Bell's Out of This Furnace, a major character, Kracha, worked in a railroad gang in Pennsylvania around the turn of the century, before he headed west to work in a steel mill in Braddock. His work on the railroad gang is vividly described:

> He lined and surfaced track, renewed ties, replaced rails, cleaned ditches and culverts, repaired fences, put up cattle guards. During August, before seedtime, he became a farmer again, swinging a scythe on the weeds. He learned the names and uses of tools, to recognize cocked joints and broomed rails, to spot a tie that was pumping ballast, to use a Jim Crow, the U-shaped rail bender, to swing a twelve-pound sledge. He fought brush fires in dry weather and floodwaters in wet. Storms made silt of ballast, threatened trestles, uprooted trees and telegraph poles; in winter the ballast froze, the switches froze, spikes snapped like glass, snow chocked the flangeways and drifted in white hills across the tracks. His wages were ten cents an hour, and when bad times came and the company cut wages, nine. It was an excellent month when he made as much as twenty-five dollars.[6]

After the vintage work force was once in place here, labor contractors no longer had to go to Europe. A network of relatives and friends went into action. Immigration historians are well aware that immigration was not a random occurrence. The pioneer immigrants encouraged relatives, friends and neighbors from the same European village to leave. They

---

[6] Thomas Bell, Out of This Furnace 20-21 (U. of Pitts. Press 1990).

called it a chain migration. Letters to the old country from the new arrivals convinced thousands. From tired, worn-out villages in the old country, many thousands crossed the Atlantic to New York and took the trail to Pittsburgh.

Great numbers from the same village made the voyage and settled in the same town in America. They came to escape the poverty and despair of what was always described as "the old country." Whether recruited by the contractor in Europe or induced by the newly-arrived in America, the immigrants poured in. The mines and mills had no difficulty putting them to work. Because the companies had strong political ties with the federal government, many of the men coming to the mines and mills were able to enter without passports. At Ellis Island they were listed as "WOP" (without papers), and thus was born the derisive name still being applied to Americans of Italian origin. On they came to the mines and mills and railroads, eagerly seeking the riches of America, though many avoiding the large cities where pools of unskilled labor had existed from earlier immigrations.

In the mining camps near Carnegie, the companies laid out the company towns along a common model. They hastily erected wooden frame duplexes or triplexes and arrayed them along primitive streets. Usually one water pump served every two rows of houses. Outdoor privies drained into open runs converting them into open sewers. Infant diseases and typhoid rivaled mine accidents in mortality statistics.

The companies furnished large single houses for the superintendent and chief foremen. Completing the settlement were a church building, a one-room school house and the center of all community life--the company store.

Nothing symbolizes the oppressive nature of a company town better than the company store system that prevailed in all mining camps. The company's edict: "You had to buy at the company store." Although wage earners and consumers in a capitalistic democracy, the miners and their families were not free to shop where they pleased. They were required to buy food and clothing at the store at exorbitant prices. Little cash ever passed hands. Purchases at the store and rent for the house were deducted from their pay. They did their cooking on the kitchen coal stoves which served as the sole heating during the brutal Western Pennsylvania winters.

They bought the coal for their stoves, of course, at the company store at company store prices. And it was there that they had to buy their picks and shovels, miner's caps, and lunch pails. If their jobs involved blasting, it was there that they bought dynamite, black powder and blasting caps. A study by Lawrence Lynch published in the *Political Science Quarterly* found prices in the company store excessive; black powder, for example, was sold to employees at a 62 percent mark-up. Until the miners became more sophisticated, they often saw little cash on pay day, the company store having gobbled up the entire pay. Until prohibited by law, too often these deductions exceeded earnings, leaving the miner with a redline or "snake" to show for his toil. Until the unions gained some semblance of strength to stop the practice, the company had "snitches" who spied on miners, reporting to the superintendent names of those not buying goods at the company store.

Legislation in 1891 prohibited mine operators and manufacturers from operating company stores. The law was blatantly evaded, however, by incorporating separate store companies typically linked to the parent company by interlocking directorates. For example, Jones and Laughlin Steel Corporation operated the Pittsburgh Mercantile Company at its steel mills and captive coal mines.

The mine superintendent was the absolute dictator of work at the mine and absolute dictator of life in the company town. The foremen and straw bosses, tough and ruthless, who carried out his orders at the mine, were Anglo-Americans. The miners were mostly a polyglot group of uneducated peasant stock from southern, central and eastern Europe who had been herded together at Ellis Island and transported directly to the camps. They worked seven days a week in two twelve hour shifts, with one 24 hour shift every other Sunday.

At first, the immigrants lacked the ability to travel to Carnegie to purchase necessaries at regular retail rates. They were political and economic serfs, constantly in debt to the company. Undaunted, though, they persevered and in time were able to control their meager finances, and in turn, their lives. The advent of the Ford Model T brought transportation out of the boondocks. Several families would combine resources to purchase one car, and this provided a release from total confinement. They were able to shop in Carnegie stores. The miners were also able to take in boarders in the company town. The family head and his boarders worked different shifts so that when one miner rolled out of bed to start work, in crawled another. This "hot bed system" was also prevalent in steel workers' homes in Carnegie.

No elected officials governed the company town. It was America in name only. The mine superintendent's word was law. He maintained law and order and by edict proclaimed how the men would work at the mine and how they and their families would live in the company town. By mining company edict, expressly to prevent the entry of union organizers on mine property, those who lived in the company houses in the company towns, could not have visitors from the "outside." Only the company doctor could visit you in case of illness, and also, the undertaker. Joanna Bastolla De Lacio tells of her childhood in a company town:

> An interurban trolley line ran near our camp and went by the cemetery a few miles down the road. Most families could not pay for a full dress funeral. I remember funerals where the mourners put the casket on the street car and accompanied it to the cemetery where the priests and all the mourners got off, carrying the casket in a procession. A procession from the car stop to the grave. I remember a little dead baby being carried in a box on the street car on the way to the cemetery.

The mine superintendent enforced his brand of law and order through the infamous Pennsylvania Coal and Iron Police who rode big black horses up and down the muddy company streets with huge truncheons fastened to their saddles like cavalry sabers. These were private police, employed by the company, but endowed with all the power of a local, county or state police officer.

I remember these men dressed in black on black horses prancing through the streets of Carnegie in the Twenties. They were brought in at the slightest attempt to organize the Bell mine at the end of Washington Avenue. They wore black boots and black helmets styled after the London bobbies. With awesome six-shooters at their hips and truncheons swinging from their saddles, they were the Darth Vaders of the early Twentieth Century.

To the immigrants from Eastern Europe, they were the American counterparts of the Czar's cossacks, and this was the name by which they came to be known. These private police forces had been authorized by the Pennsylvania legislature as early as 1866 and approved by our state court system. Until the Franklin D. Roosevelt political revolution of 1932, the steel and coal industries and the Pennsylvania Railroad controlled the governor's office, the state legislature and the court system. The PRR was one of the largest stakeholders in the state's mining industry.

The Coal and Iron Police reached their zenith in the decade of the Twenties and it was precisely because of their abuses in those ten years that their downfall was pre-ordained. On February 10, 1929, John Barkowski, a miner at the mining camp at Imperial near Carnegie, was beaten to death by three coal and iron policemen. The "Barkowski case" became a cause celebrè throughout Pennsylvania. Michael A. Musmanno, a fiery young legislator from McKees Rocks, a town near Carnegie, introduced legislation to outlaw the company police. The campaign to eliminate them started in 1929. It was not until the 1934 election of George H. Earle III, the first Pennsylvania Democratic Governor in the twentieth century, before we would see a repeal of legislative enactments that had authorized coal and iron or industrial police.

This did not end the tyranny. Mining companies controlled the boroughs and townships where the mines were located and then were able to deputize local police forces to do their bidding. The steel and coal industrial complex also controlled Allegheny County politics, including the Sheriff's office.

Like the superintendents, foremen and straw bosses, these private policemen were all drawn from the old stock homogeneous population of the greater Carnegie area. They were Anglo-Americans. They were huge, strong men, but most of all, they spoke English. Knowing English conferred power and security in the mines. Mastery of the language secured terrible authority in Scottish-Irish mine foremen, motor bosses, tipple foremen, firebosses and weighmen. The new immigrants were the loaders, pickmen and laborers and they were paid by tonnage. They were at the special mercy of the weighmen whose calculations determined the amount of pay. It was not until the growth of the United Mine Workers in the early Thirties that the union was able to install the office of check weighmen who monitored every calculation of the company's man.

THE MEN OF CARNEGIE'S MILLS AND MINES

Early in the Twenties some miners began to leave the company towns and settle in Carnegie proper. Children had come along and it was necessary for them to go to adequate schools, and the mining towns offered only primitive one-room schools. Many of my elementary school classmates were newly-arrived refugees from the company towns.

Many men left the mines and found jobs in the Carnegie mills and railroads. No longer did they have to pay unconscionable rent for company houses or inflated prices for food and clothing at the company store. They learned about self-government and something about freedom of speech and assembly. They learned that they had precious rights of new Americans long denied to them by the mine superintendents. They also became acquainted with the various nationality churches that had sprung up in Carnegie – German, Polish, Ukrainian, Russian and Italian.

I have never forgotten the miners, the mill workers and the railroad labor gangs--the men of Carnegie and their counterparts of Western Pennsylvania. The phrase "back breaking" does not adequately describe what was demanded from their bodies in 12-hour work days, let alone the 24- hour shift every other Sunday. Serious injuries were a daily occurrence and industrial deaths were merely statistics. When a worker was killed, the company usually sent $300 or $400 to the widow and the mine or mill superintendent called out, "Get me another man!" The harshness endured by this immigrant generation, in eking out a bare existence in their early days in Western Pennsylvania, has no counterpart in the American labor experience, even when compared to work performed in the cotton fields in the early Nineteenth Century or by migrant agricultural workers in the Twentieth. Remembering the conditions under which they worked and lived of necessity has affected me as a citizen, as a lawyer and, admittedly, as a judge.

Chapter Five
From Dolcedorme (Sweet slumber), Italy to Carnegie, Pennsylvania

My father came to Carnegie in May 1905 at the age of 16. He came here as a result of a confluence of circumstances. He was a product of the sordid history of Southern Italy in the Nineteenth century, a history of government rule by despotic absentee rulers, that perpetuated a rigid landowner-share cropper-serf society, replete with inflexible class distinctions. My father would become a victim of this ignoble tradition.

Those who ruled Italy were akin to absentee landlords, caring not a whit for those who lived in the isolated mountain villages of the south. The ruling hierarchy perceived government to operate only as a cash cow for the financial benefit of themselves by means of all-inclusive, universal taxation. Their subjects in the southern provinces were impounded in worn out hill towns, isolated from each other because they lacked an adequate road system even for horses and carriages, confined to a wretched agricultural economy based on growing olives where the only soil was hardscrabble and where you could earn a comfortable living only if you owned huge tracts of land.

For the most part, the rulers were members of the Spanish-operated House of Bourbon based in Naples and were content only to maintain the status quo to preserve social conditions and social regulations that still bore trappings of a semi-feudal society. Harsh class distinctions, if not caste distinctions, in this social structure profoundly affected my father's entrance into this world and his childhood.

He was the fourth generation descendant in a family of wealth and social status, a family whose lands at one time extended for 25 kilometers on a side, once encompassing an area that surrounded more than one village, holdings so vast that a man on horseback could not traverse the perimeter in a single day.

Presiding over this domain was Raffaele Capparelli, born in the 1790's who passed on his holdings to his children, in part to Gennaro, my father's grandfather, who was born in 1826 and died in 1868. Gennaro had three daughters and four sons, among whom was my father's sire, Cesare, who was born in 1850 and who would live until 1930.

With passing generations Raffaele's original tract had been divided among his various descendants. By the time it passed to Cesare's generation, their share was much smaller than that of their grandfather's but was still formidable. They were the richest folks in town.

The town was Acquaformosa, a small village located in the northern section of the province of Cosenza (comparable to a state in America), which was the most northern province of the three in of the Calabria *regione* (an administrative region consisting of several provinces, e.g., Sicily, Tuscany, Lombardy). If you have a penchant to refer to the Italian peninsula as a boot, Calabria is the toe that points to Sicily.

Acquaformosa is 68 kilometers north of Cosenza, the provincial capital city, and 34 kilometers north of Castrovillari, the nearest market town that contained a district post office and telegraph station. The town sits relatively high in altitude, on the southern foothills of the Dolcedorme, the mountain massif that forms the southern terminus of the Apennines and runs south from Basilicata into Calabria.

When the air is clear and the light is right, you can stand facing south at a high point, as I have done, and looking to your left, you can see the Ionian Sea, 50 kilometers to the east across the plains where the ancient Greek settlement at Sibari was located. This was at one time a part of Magna Graeca, and the name Sibarite stems from the 60,000 or so ancient ribald

FROM DOLCEDORME (SWEET SLUMBER), ITALY TO CARNEGIE, PENNSYLVANIA

people who had partied in this area for a century or so. Looking to your right, you can see the Tyrranean Sea, 45 kilometers to the west. To reach the sea, you follow a winding road with hairpin turns that cuts through lowering foothills past the town of Sansosti to Belvedere Marittimo on the Tyrranean Sea. You get the train to Naples at Belvedere.

Acquaformosa is notable not only because you can see clear across Italy at the two seas that wash its coasts, but it is also famous as the site of an abbey opened in 1195 by the Prince of Altomonte, probably to give assistance to the Crusaders going to or returning from the battles in the Holy Land. It is also well-known because for 500 years its inhabitants have been of Albanian origin, not Italian. The language that they speak, even as I write, is Albanian, not Italian. Their church is the *rito bizantino*, not the Latin rite, although since 1919 it has been affiliated with the Vatican.

The Albanians had crossed the Adriatic and climbed the Dolcedorme range to reach highlands similar to those they left in the homeland. They were religious refugees; Christians who fled the Moslems who had invaded their homeland. Under the leadership of their national hero, Giorgio Castrioto, they had struggled mightily to repel the invaders. Their leader fell in battle in 1468 and the exodus across the narrow Adriatic to Italy began, coincidentally in the historic year of 1492. Today Castrioto is still venerated in the dozen or so Italo-Albanian villages of Calabria, Puglia and Sicily. He is generally known as "Skanderbeg," a bastardization of Iskander, or Alexander, and "bey" meaning "captain." An heroic statute of Skanderbeg forms the center piece in Rome's fashionable Piazza Albanese.

Legend has it that Albanians came to Acquaformosa around 1476 or 1478, but we know from the official records of the Prince of Altomonte that they were there at least by 1501.

The Caparelli's were Albanese. The men were taller and slimmer than the native Calabrese; their eyes generally blue or green, their skin fair. Many of the women were blue-eyed blonds. The Capparelli's were important people, and the man who sired my father was called "Don Cesare," a title of respect reflecting Spanish custom of the ages. You qualified for the title if your family had lots of money and were from the land-owning stock.

My father never became a Capparelli. He could not take the name because when my father was born in August 1888, Don Cesare could not bring himself around to marrying my father's mother, Filomena. The don was a 38-year old bachelor, my grandmother, barely 16. She was a servant girl, a maid in the household of Don Gennaro, the father of Don Cesare. Dons did not marry out of their class, and Filomena was not only a house servant, but moreover, she was an orphan with no clue to her parentage, other than that she, too, was Italo-Albanian, was born in the village of Sansosti, was cared for at birth by nuns, and when old enough to do household chores, was parceled out by the nuns to the wealthy Capparelli family as a servant.

Thus my biological paternal grandparents lived in the same house, as master and servant girl, at the time of my father's birth, and for the years that followed. It was acceptable for Cesare to bed down the servant girl and impregnate her numerous times, but, heaven's no, he could not marry her. He could not marry her because the *tradizione* would not permit it.

It was not a tradition that was Italian, because Italy did not become a unified nation until 1874, only 14 years before my father was born. Rather it was an unyielding ethic or mores or culture of the provinces of Southern Italy inbred by centuries of Spanish tradition. A member of the landed class married only a member of that class. He or she could never--absolutely never--marry beneath it, a genre or classification determined only by a Dun and Bradstreet rating, and very little else.

Spanish traditions permeated through southern Italy during the Nineteenth Century. It was a society dominated by royal decrees from Naples, implemented by hateful overseers and government agents whose sole interest was to see that a maximum amount of taxes were collected from all – from the wealthy landowners to the lowest peasant. The arbiters of social customs, the men and women who fashioned and executed social mores were the local dons and donnas. Social mores that visited no social stigma upon dons who impregnated servant girls. That's what they were there for – to clean, to cook and to bed down.

The history of this woe-begotten region of Italy is sordid. It was a land of tired old towns, generally isolated and perched on hill tops. The anopheles mosquito had wiped out the Adriatic, Ionian and Tyrranean coasts of Italy with the deadly malaria pestilence. Over the centuries entire centers of Greek civilizations in the south had been wiped out by malaria. By 500 B.C. Calabria had a degree of prosperity in its Magna Graeca

FROM DOLCEDORME (SWEET SLUMBER), ITALY TO CARNEGIE, PENNSYLVANIA

which has never been approached since: Sibaris (now Sibari), Kroton (now Crotone), and Rhegion (now Reggio Calabria) were Greek cities of considerable repute. Other important centers of ancient Greece were found at Vibo Valentia (Hipponium), Locri and Monesterace Marina.

Those who worked the soil were strong, they were men of the earth who tended a land dissipated by centuries of use. They tamed the slopes that were too steep for extensive farming, but here you could plant trees. It was an overworked soil that could yield olives from trees 1,000 years old and yield some almonds; a soil that could grow grapes, figs, lemons and chestnuts only if constantly nurtured with care; land that was worked into narrow terraces to produce tomatoes, eggplant, zucchini, peppers, melons and cherries to feed the family. Their ancestors had been tending this soil for countless generations.

In the village the men would leave town at 3:30 a.m. astride the family donkey, which took them outside the walls to the *campagna,* to the family-owned tract of land. They lived in the towns built in centuries past atop hills for protection against the Saracens and then the brigands, but each day the men ventured forth beyond the town walls to the family lands which were often far distant. They returned at nightfall, walking or riding home on their donkeys, after the labors of the day. A fifteen-hour day was the rule. Their sons were ordered to the fields as soon as they were strong enough so that their earnings could be added to the family purse. Incredibly, under the rule of the Bourbons, school attendance was compulsory for only the first three grades--from ages six to nine--but the law was not enforced. The father usually made this decision by following an old proverb of the Mezzogiorno:

"When hair grows between the legs, it is time to work."

At the end of the Nineteenth Century the great emigration began. They left their homes not because their land denied them, but because they had become too many for the land. They tilled their own soil as their fathers and grandfathers and generations before had. But with each generation there came a difference. The first ancestor-land owner surveyed vast domains with overseers and hired hands, the next generation had less to supervise and more to work by hand. The farm that could support one family with five sons fairly comfortably in 1860 could give only moderate subsistence to each family of the five sons when the father divided it up twenty years later. Dividing up that same original tract by the next generation at the turn of the century made the difference between comfortable and marginal living.

If you imagine a family living well from a land tract as expansive as an 18-hole golf course, you can visualize how drastic the family income deteriorated when the family was left with a plot of land for olive and figs trees as small as half of one rock strewn fairway; but nevertheless requiring 12-hour days for maintenance. These were the fortunate ones, the *contadini*, who worked their own land, as humble and desolate as it was.

Others were not so fortunate, having never owned land, or whose grandfathers had lost theirs to huge landowners, the *latifondi*. Such unfortunates were mere day laborers, the *giornalieri*, the most humiliating status of all. In between were the share croppers, whose land was "leased" to them as *affitturai* under the system of *mezzadria* under a fixed ratio, commonly 50 to 60 per cent of the expected yield, an expected yield to be determined by the owner, to be paid at the end of the year.

As a young father rode his donkey in the bleak pre-dawn blackness to go to the land, he could not help think of what would be in store for the two sons at home and the child on the way. He could not help ruminate, in slow and steady contemplation, of the true appeal of siren songs that were coming from America thousands of miles away.

In itself the call was tempting, but even more tantalizing was the effect on the male population in the villages. At the end of the first decade of the Twentieth Century, family life was shattering in Southern Italy. Two-thirds of the teen-age and adult male population were in the United States or Argentina, with some as far afield as Australia and New Zealand. In 1906, the exodus in Basilicata exceeded the birthrate.

Many men left their women behind, entire generations of them. To survive, the women of the villages had to become tillers of the soil. From the village wells, where first they gathered for the gossip of the early morning, they retraced their steps home with water jugs, or perhaps a bundle of kindling wood, delicately balanced on their heads. They then went into the fields. They became the women of the *campagna*, the workers of the fields, the *campagnole*. This was man's work, to be sure, but the men had gone, and the work had to be done, for to live one had to eat, and to eat, one had to grow and harvest the meager crops. So they coped. They slaved. They labored. But most of all they waited for the day their men would return or send for them to come to America.

The picture in Sicily was different, but only slightly. At an early time during the Graeco-Roman era, this small island had been a mountain paradise, but the Romans came and stripped the wooded hills of great trees to make timber to build the Roman fleet, to construct sea-going vessels of commerce and war, huge triremes where slaves manned the oars until the Mediterranean breezes filled the sails.

No reforestation replaced these trees. The original rich top soil, with no trees to hold it in place, washed down the mountainsides over the centuries. By the time of the great emigration from Sicily, the erosion process had denuded the land. Ninety percent of it consisted of hills and mountain ranges whose thin arid soil had been squandered and depleted over the centuries. Where the land mass did not take the form of cliffs along the sea, narrow strips of sea-level coastline became the fortunate receptacles of good earth, the rich top soil which had washed down from the hills. It was here along the coastline's fertile strips where generations of magnificent Sicilian farmers established a thriving industry of growing fruits, especially citrus, and vegetables.

In the weary mountain towns the Sicilian tillers of the soil experienced the same *la miseria* as did their counterparts on the mainland. For the most part, they learned to terrace the land and to tend their olive trees and plant their artichokes, but the earth was always thin and barren and they learned to grow what they could, where they could.

Clearly, the more fortunate owned fertile gentle plains on the south east area--from Agrigento to Caltanisetta and over to Catania---where olives, oranges, grapefruit, grapes, figs and lemons grew in abundance. All Sicilians are born with green thumbs, but the coast dwellers became masters in agriculture, and they would later carry these talents with them to America. And they too migrated because the land that supported one family in generations past could not support the families of their offspring. The acreage stayed the same but the mouths it had to feed had increased geometrically.

This was not the vast, boundless plains of the American Midwest, our famed farm belt, where pioneer farmers first plowed virgin land in the Nineteenth Century. This Sicily was a constricted island mountain that had been subjected to cultivation for over 2500 years. The Greeks started their colonization about 800 B.C. Pythagoras, Archimedes and Plato all lived here during the period of Magna Graeca.

Two rival houses ruled simultaneously in Southern Italy from the Thirteenth through the Fifteenth Centuries, one was French at Naples-- the House of Anjou---the other Spanish at Palermo, founded on claims as descendants of the Hohenstaufen.

None of these rulers were natives of Italy. In 1442 Alfonso V, "the Magnanimous," subdued the French at Naples and this meant that the entire region was to be ruled by Spanish monarchs until 1501.

This was succeeded by Spanish viceroy rule for two centuries with an intermittent Austrian rule from 1713 until 1734. Naples and Sicily accepted Charles, son of Philip V of Spain and Isabella Farnese, as king. Charles founded the Neapolitan House of Bourbon which was known as the Kingdom of the Two Sicilies.

Thus, the Spanish-dominated house of Bourbon ruled Calabria and southern Italy for over a century. The house ruled until 1874 when the kingdom became a part of the newly united Italy under the House of Savoy. It must be understood that until the unification of Italy, absentee Spanish and French rulers set the social structure for almost three centuries.

There was no tradition of self government; no benevolent monarch on the scene; no royal effort to improve the wretched social and economic conditions that prevailed throughout Calabria. The inhabitants lived off the land, their life style directly proportionate to the amount of acreage that they owned.

Calabria was *in* Italy, but not *of* Italy. Until after World War II, it was separated from the rest of the peninsula by mountains, by the absence of roads, by malaria, and until the latter half of the Nineteenth Century, by brigands. As recent as 1912, Baedeker warned his readers not to travel there unless they were provided with introductions to the local dons. No hotels existed anywhere except in the larger towns, and even these were generally squalid.

FROM DOLCEDORME (SWEET SLUMBER), ITALY TO CARNEGIE, PENNSYLVANIA

This then was the sociological and political background that greeted my father when he made his entrance into this world in Acquaformosa in 1888.

Acquaformosa was perched on the southern foothills of the Dolcedorme, the south end of the Apennines that run up the peninsula's spine to meet the Alps. Mount Pollino, named after Apollo, lies slightly to its north; it was once called Mount Apollino. But it was the Dolcedorme, snow dusted in the winter, but majestic and imposing the year round, with stands of forest and springtime wild flowers, that gave some color and respite to *la miseria* in Acquaformosa. It was to the Dolcedorme that families trekked in the summer, and it was here that the men hunted game in season.

All the towns of Southern Italy are hill towns, perched high to avoid the ravages of the anopheles mosquito on the coasts. They are examples of clustered living at its worst, with houses pasted together on narrow streets, compressed to form a fortress to withstand raids of Saracens or brigands. Acquaformosa was no exception.

In the confines of this wretched hill town, though living in its most palatial house, Filomena was permitted to keep her baby – my father, Giovanni. Don Cesare, as a member of the landed gentry, the *latifondi*, kept very busy supervising his vast holdings, for the most part an integrated olive oil industry. He owned tens of thousands of olive trees that required painstaking year-round care. He also owned the presses where the olives were crushed to squeeze out the oil, and the barrels and the cartage to haul casks of oil away to Castrovillari. He had vast holdings in fig trees and raised a modest amount of cattle, but essentially the bulk of the family wealth came from the olive trees.

When it came to business, Don Cesare was a very busy man. He was also very busy at night in his bedroom. Other children soon came from his union with Filomena: Silvia in 1890 and Clementina in 1897. Again, tradition stepped in: We can't have a flock of illegitimate children running around the house of Don Gennaro and his bachelor son, Don Cesare. What will people think? The nice people. People like us. So Silvia was farmed out to a childless couple in Policastrello, a few kilometers down the road from Acquaformosa, and Giovanni remained in the servant's quarters of the *palazzo Capparelli*.

My father would start school in 1894, and was simply known as "Giovanni--*padre ignoto*" (John--father, unknown), and survived the taunts. The school kids could go just so far in jeering him, however, because when their parents learned of this, they would pull their children aside and say, "Watch yourself. Don't you know who his father is?" In time, Filomena told Giovanni that he had a younger sister, Silvia, who lived in the town down the road and she confided in him the name of the foster family.

The brother started to visit the sister, getting on his horse and trotting down the mountainside to see her. They became very close as children: "Giovanni, you are the only real family I have," Silvia told him. Filomena encouraged this relationship. Don Cesare probably did not know about it, and he went on his way, making lots of money and lots of babies.

My father attended school for five years. Under the Bourbon tradition, five grades were sufficient to educate the handful of provincials who were motivated enough to attend. My father excelled in school from the very beginning. It was in the classroom where he learned the Italian language for the first time, for it was only in school where this language was spoken. In the home and on the streets of Acquaformosa, then as now, the language was and is Albanian. Five centuries of tradition are hard to break. Italian became a second language for my father, and all his life he would speak classical Italian, and not a dialect. He spoke the language with the precise academic inflection that he learned in school. He developed a beautiful classic penmanship and became proficient in arithmetic. Dad lived in America for 64 years and became a great master of the English language, but when it came to numbers, he always counted in Italian because that was the language in which he learned to count. Consciously wiping out memories of an unfortunate childhood, upon coming to America, he totally erased from his mind the Albanian language. He never spoke a word of it again. In mastering English, he lost almost all recollection of the language he spoke during his first 16 years.

It was in school that he also he made a decision that would profoundly affect him for the rest of his life as well as those who descended from him. In studying literature--the new Italian government permitting some study of Albanian traditions--my father was introduced to the work of an Italo-Albanian poet named "Aldisert." He liked the poetry, but more importantly, he was taken by the poet's name. "I was struck by the beauty of his poetry and the force of his name. A strong name. A powerful name.

FROM DOLCE DORME (SWEET SLUMBER), ITALY TO CARNEGIE, PENNSYLVANIA

I adopted it as my own and it sustained me through difficult times as a child," he would reminisce in later years. While in school he announced that hence forward Aldisert would be his family name, and he used it to offset the taunts of kids who called names. When at the age of 16, my father applied for an Italian passport to make his journey to America, he listed his name as "Giovanni Sansosti Aldisert."

In 1899, at the age of 12, he completed school and was apprenticed to the village tailor and it was in these formative years that he learned the *sarto* trade. He learned also that another daughter had been born to Filomena and had been christened, Clementina. This child, too, was immediately shipped out to another family. My father and his sister, Silvia, talked about this, my father insisting, "Don't worry, I'll find her."

And find Aunt Clementina he did, but before this took place, Silvia broke the news to him that her foster family was leaving for America. The brother and sister had a tearful farewell and she accompanied her foster family across the sea to Pennsylvania. Hearing that laboring jobs were available in Carnegie, it was in this town that my aunt's foster family, the brand new immigrants, finally settled.

Shortly after their arrival, however, they found themselves strapped for money. Railroad laborers, the "gandy dancers," were not paid munificent wages. So they did what many other immigrants in steel towns and mining camps did in Western Pennsylvania: They opened a "hot bed" boarding house for male immigrants. With more boarders than beds, and with the men working different 12-hour shifts in the mines, mills and railroads, one group of boarders could crawl into bed as soon as the other shift left. Working hours generally were from six to six.

Aunt Silvia was put to work in the boarding house--washing the filthy work clothes of the boarders, assisting in the cooking, packing lunches and scrubbing floors. She wrote to her brother and complained: "This is not the kind of life for a 13-year old girl." He agreed. He mounted his horse, a spirited white one he called Ghedeppi, and trotted the 20 miles to the market town of Castrovillari to obtain a passport. It was only after he obtained this document (which I have in my possession now) that he informed his mother of his intentions, and after an unpleasant confrontation with Don Cesare, he left the town and land of his birth.

But before doing so, he had another important visit to make. From the time when Clementina was four, she had realized that she had a brother. My father had appeared at her foster home one day and announced that he wanted to see his sister.

"You have no sister here," came the response from the lady of the house.

"Yes, I do and her name is Clementina."

He made periodic visits to her, the teen-aged boy and the child sister becoming very attached. She was only seven when the brother came to her house to tell her that he was going to America to see their sister.

"Come back, Giovanni. Don't forget me," she sobbed, and the brother and sister parted.

Dad took the train to Naples, boarded the *Prinz Adalbert* of the Compagnia Amburghese Americana steamship line on May 8, 1905, and was assigned steerage number 37/21. The total fare was 170 lire, about $34, and his health inspection card shows that "Aldisert, Giovanni of Acquaformosa, Cosenza" was daily inspected by the ship's surgeon until it docked at Ellis Island on May 24. He was passed by the Immigration Bureau on that day and he immediately took a train to Pittsburgh and from there to Carnegie.

His arrival sparked confrontation at the boarding house. "I have come for my sister," he announced and a heated discussion ensued with her foster parents.

"Silvia cannot leave," they insisted. "We are responsible for her. We are responsible to Don Cesare."

My father avowed that they should not talk about that, because nothing in the family arrangement was that Silvia was to come to America as a servant girl. "My sister shall not live the life of my mother," he said.

Aunt Silvia chimed in, "Yes, I want to go. I want to go with my brother. I'm leaving and nothing will stop me."

Nothing did.

FROM DOLCEDORME (SWEET SLUMBER), ITALY TO CARNEGIE, PENNSYLVANIA

The 16-year old brother and 14-year old sister found a place to live nearby and took up housekeeping. They vowed to stay together and remain in America.

If there ever were candidates for "Profiles in Courage," these two would win hands down. I have often thought of them at this stage of their lives, but especially a few years back when there was a public service announcement on television directed to the parents of teen-age children:

"It's 11 o'clock. Do you know where your children are?"

Yes, I know about two teenagers and where they were. They were not my kids. In fact they were my father and his sister. Where were they? They were thousands of miles from the nearest friend or family. Across huge seas from their native land. They were in the New World, but they do not know its language or its customs. But they were determined to succeed. My oh my, how they did succeed!

My father decided to practice the tailoring trade he had learned in Italy, and the two of them cast their lot in the land of promise.

He would later say that his decision to remain in America was not accidental, that he had decided early on to leave Italy and that the letter from his sister was only a triggering event that gave him the opportunity to justify a hurried departure. He had reasoned that prospects in Italy had been bleak. He had come from a family of large landowners. He was the illegitimate son of the greatest landowner in town but he did not ride on a handsome horse to survey the vast holdings of his father. He did not dress in the finery of a dandy and nod as sharecroppers and farm laborers bowed in obeisance as a son of Don Cesare while making his rounds. He was accorded none of this treatment. Instead he lived in servants' quarters of his father's manse and lived the humble life of a tailor's apprentice in a tired, worn-out isolated town on the Dolcedorme.

But in Carnegie, Pennsylvania, a new life beckoned. It was the time of economic miracles in that town. They were building new steel mills there, expanding the railroads and sinking new shafts in the mines as the mills and railroads called out for more coal. Coal. More coal. Prosperity had come to Carnegie and with it, a more comfortable class of business and professional men. It was time for them to dress the part that their new status demanded. My father, the new young tailor from Italy, helped them fill that need.

His specialty was designing and making tailor-made suits for men. Talented in design and extraordinarily skillful with the needle, he soon developed a well-paying clientele of Carnegie's leading business and professional men. He did not do alterations or general tailoring. He made only men's suits, elegant suits at that, and they were not inexpensive. Within two years my father had done so well that he was able to open his own shop and engage two apprentices of his own. He set up shop in the town's most prestigious address, the street floor of the Masonic Building at the corner of East Main and Broadway. His shop window bore the legend:

>JOHN S. ALDISERT
>MERCHANT TAILOR

It was the spring of 1907 and he was 18 years old.

It was in this year that he decided to return to Italy for a quick visit. The purpose: to tell personally his mother, whom he adored, that he and Silvia had decided to remain in America, permanently. It was the measure of the man that he had to tell his mother this face-to-face and not by means of a letter which would have to be read to her because she could not read or write.

He returned to Acquaformosa and explained all this to his mother, Filomena. Although disappointed that her first born son and daughter would be thousands of miles away, Filomena had the satisfaction of knowing that they would be together and that the brother would be ever watchful over his sister.

My father remained with his mother for only a week. The mission accomplished, he hurried to Naples and returned to Carnegie.

He would never see his mother and father again.

It would be almost 50 years before he ever returned to Italy. The umbilical cord with the homeland had been severed. Giovanni Sansosti Aldisert, the Italian, would become John S. Aldisert, the American.

FROM DOLCEDORME (SWEET SLUMBER), ITALY TO CARNEGIE, PENNSYLVANIA

My father was tall and thin, had fair skin and blue-green eyes, and his sister Silvia was a slim, blue-eyed blond, all in sharp contrast with the traditional brown-eyed, short, and dark features of typical Southern Italians, even those living in towns just a few kilometers from Italo-Albanian settlements. Life went well for the brother and sister. Within five years after he arrived penniless and searching for a sister, my father was able to purchase real estate on Carnegie's Main Street and to lease the storefront of his property to his good friend, Mario Castellani, a barber. At the age of 21, my father had become a landowner and a landlord.

Within a short time, Mario and Aunt Silvia would be wed and two years later, in 1913, at the age of 23, Aunt Silvia returned to Italy, this time with her one-year old son, Alexander. After meeting her husband's family in Rome, she returned to her family in the south. Clementina, a small child when Silvia had left in 1903, had now a become a vivacious, 16-year old beauty in the hill town of Lungro, the Albanian settlement adjacent to Acquaformosa. Upon reunion the two sisters became inseparable, giggling and talking and laughing incessantly. In addition to piercing questions about life in America, Clementina insisted on knowing everything that was to be known about her brother, John (and here I use the English name by which my father was known in the United States, rather than the Italian, Giovanni) and having her sister report and repeat as much as possible about the older brother whom she admired so much.

The sisters conjured up a secret plan. They took a horse and carriage to the telegraph station in Castrovillari and cabled their brother asking if Clementina could come to live with them in Carnegie. Within three days a postal messenger on horseback brought back my father's cabled response. It was one-word: "*vieni,*" the Italian imperative, "You come!" The sisters then presented their family with a *fait accompli*--their brother wanted to have the sister, Clementina, come to America and join the household. The two sisters and baby Alexander left the *paese* after a tearful farewell, boarded ship at Naples, and sailed to New York.

Silvia and Clementina, too, would never see their mother and father again.

But in Carnegie in 1913 the sisters and brother were not thinking about future years of separation. Rather, they were gleeful that the three of them were now together, the trio becoming attached to one another much more than siblings in an orthodox family setting. The three of them constituted the entire family: John, at 25, was the head, with Silvia, 23, and Clementina, 16. They were in a strange land, an ocean away from their nearest relatives, but they had each other. This would explain the strong ties that were to emerge among their families in the years that were to follow.

The years would pass, and changes were taking place in the old country. More children had been born to Don Cesare and Filomena -- a total of eight. The World War had come and gone and we were entering the decade of the Twenties. Don Cesare was now in his seventies; Filomena had turned 50. They were living together as man and wife in another family home in Lungro. The old caste system was disappearing. New social standards were emerging, even in the *paese*. The aging don finally decided to do the right thing for Filomena and his children. Cesare and Filomena were married in a quiet ceremony. A letter was dispatched to the three children in America, giving them to option to be legitimatized as members of the Capparelli family. The brother and two sisters refused.

We are a new family out here, they wrote back. We are not Capparelli's. Our name is Aldisert. That is the name on our passports. That is our name on our citizenship papers. That was our name we all used on our marriage licenses, brother and sisters alike. That is the name under which we started life anew here. That is the name under which we have succeeded in the new world. That is the name we will keep. Thanks, but no thanks.

This, then, was how John Aldisert came to Carnegie. The John Aldisert who was out of town on that summer day in 1922 when his neighbors paid a visit to his wife and little boys. When they paid a visit dressed in their summer whites.

FROM DOLCE DORME (SWEET SLUMBER), ITALY TO CARNEGIE, PENNSYLVANIA

Aunt Silvia with her children, Alexander and Irma in 1916. Ten years earlier, at the age of 13, she had written to her big brother, John, that her foster parents were using her as a scullery maid in Carnegie, Pennsylvania. Then 16 years old, her brother came to America to rescue his sister. They decided to stay. Aunt Silvia, a blue-eyed blonde, married Mario Castellani. Alexander would become a dentist in Framingham, Massachusetts.

Dad and his sister Clementina in 1914, shortly after she came to America at the age of 16. Later she would marry Pietro Ponzo, a professional musician who taught guitar and banjo and conducted his own string orchestra at radio station KDKA in Pittsburgh. They had four sons--Angelo, Robert, William and Ronald. The three older brothers served in World War II--in the Navy, Marines and Army, respectively. After the war the family lived in Newport News, Virginia. Angelo resumed his career in civil engineering; Robert and William practiced law together for years. The youngest brother, Ronald, became a very successful building contractor.

Chapter Six
Growing Up in the Italian Catholic Church

Today we are still cursed with some discrimination based on race, religion and ancestral origin. But in the Twenties religious and ancestral origin discrimination in Carnegie, as well as in many of the small towns of Western Pennsylvania, ran rampant and was multi-layered. Those discriminated against by one class were just as quick to discriminate against another class they deemed inferior to them. The antipathy of many old-line Protestant families toward the waves of new Catholic immigrants was of textbook quality, but an appalling discrimination took place within the Catholic Church itself. This led to the American urban phenomenon of the so-called nationality churches.

The Irish Catholics were the first victims of social and economic bigotry, intolerance and prejudice throughout America. The classic example was in Boston where employment signs proclaimed: "Help Wanted. No Irish Need Apply." The same was true in Carnegie. The nativists shared the antipathy toward the Irish, even the old-line Carnegie Scottish-Irish families who were descended from the relatively same ancestral stock. The animosity here was not based on ancestry. It was grounded on religion. Catholics were simply not welcome in "our" town.

But intolerance did not stop at the church door. The catholic clergy in the America did not practice what they preached at Sunday mass. In Carnegie, as was the case in many urban communities throughout the United States, the Catholic clergy in the territorial diocesan parishes opened their doors to the Irish only. This was not accidental. Precipitated by the potato famine in Ireland in the middle of the nineteenth century, the first waves of Catholic immigrants were Irish. With them they brought their religion. And their priests.

By official title it was the Roman Catholic hierarchy established in America; in practice it was the Irish Catholic Church. All the bishops were Irish, as were the monsignors and parish priests. After a few decades another wave of Catholics, the Germans, came to America. But the Catholic hierarchy was extremely insular, tremendously insecure in a Protestant America and very suspicious of strangers. Although the German newcomers were members of the same Holy Mother Church, they were not welcome. This was typical throughout the Eastern seaboard and further inland. The Roman Catholic Diocese of Pittsburgh was no exception.

The Carnegie parish priests could have recruited German-speaking priests to say the mass, but the Irish-American priests had another idea. They told the new immigrants: "Go build your own church!" And that is precisely what the Germans did. They built one next door, across the side street. They erected St. Joseph's Church on Third Street next to St. Luke's, the diocesan territorial parish.

Then came the Poles. They received the same message from the priests at St. Luke's: "You may be Catholics, but this parish is for the Irish only. Go build your own church." And build they did. They built three nationality parishes: St. Ignatius in Glendale, The Iron Church in West Carnegie and St. Mary's on Jane Street. Russians and Ukrainians--some Roman Catholic, some Byzantine and some Russian Orthodox--also arrived in large numbers and they built magnificent onion-domed structures on Jane Street, three in a row, all with magnificent bells that could be heard throughout the valley.

The Italians were the last to come. By this time other nationality parishes were already in place. Like the Germans and the Poles before them, they applied at St. Luke's and they received the same message. There

GROWING UP IN THE ITALIAN CATHOLIC CHURCH

was no room at the Roman Catholic inn for the Italians. Father Brennan, pastor at St. Luke's, publicly said that he did not like Italians and he did not want them in his parish even though the largest Italian colony in Carnegie was less than a quarter mile from his church. He was very outspoken about this. The Italian immigrants were all Catholics, but they were not welcome at the diocesan church.

Into the breach there stepped an enlightened churchman who was decades ahead of his time. He was Dr. James McMasters McQuilken, minister of the posh United Presbyterian Church. He welcomed the new Italian community into his church, brought Italian-speaking ministers to conduct services, established English language and citizenship classes. Dr. McQuilken helped his new flock with naturalization processes and vigorously sponsored evening classes to teach English to the newcomers. For the first two decades of the Twentieth century in Carnegie, however, the Italians were Catholics without a Catholic church.

This changed in 1923. An Italian missionary priest, Father Ercole Dominicis, a magnificent orator, had passed through the town, delivered a number of sermons and was enthusiastically received. Although he was touring Italian communities throughout Eastern United States, he was invited back to Carnegie again and again. Finally, a handful of community leaders, including my parents, were able to persuade him to settle in Carnegie and establish a nationality parish.

Administratively, this new parish, like the German and Polish nationality parishes in Carnegie, came under the Apostolic Delegate in Washington, D.C., and not under the Bishop of the Catholic Diocese of Pittsburgh. The diocesan bishop supervised only the liturgy and sacraments of baptism, confirmation, marriage, the last rites and burial. The diocese would extend not a penny to construct a new church.

Our families passed a hat and made a down payment on a livery stable on Mary Avenue, around the corner from other nationality churches on Jane Street. The stable was consecrated as the Church of the Holy Souls of Purgatory and served as the church until a brick structure complete with a traditional Italian bell tower was constructed next door. As I was growing up, the old livery stable served as the "Church hall" for wedding receptions, parties and meetings.

Mother served as our first church organist. At first she played at all Sunday masses, as well as weddings and funerals. In time, mother was able to recruit an assistant from the congregation by offering lessons on how to play the organ. Peculiarly enough, from time to time she was enlisted by Father Brennan, the nemesis of all things Italian, and later Father McCrory, to substitute for the organist at St. Luke's, especially for weddings, funerals and special masses. We often would chide mother: "You're the only Italian Father Brennan likes. He doesn't even like the Pope!"

With the opening of the Italian Catholic church, Holy Souls of Purgatory, Dr. McQuilken called his adopted Presbyterian flock together. "You now have your own church," he said. "You are free to go and practice the faith of your fathers and mothers, but you are also free and very welcome to stay with us." Most of them left the United Presbyterian Church and returned to the faith of their fathers and mothers. But they did not forget Dr. McQuilken. When he was encountered on the street, his Italian friends would remove their hats and greet "Father" McQuilken. The salutation was never "Doctor," "Minister," "Pastor" or "Reverend." It was always "Father," and this practice continued through the years.

As a family very instrumental in founding the church, it was imperative that all of us attend mass every Sunday. Here, we had to wear our finest clothes, be immaculately scrubbed, and even my intractable hair had to be neatly combed for at least a few minutes. After mass, we would stand alongside our parents on the sidewalk as they greeted friends and we were fussed over in the finest Italian tradition, a tradition that insists that children always be the objects of extravagant compliments: "*Che bellezzi. Sembre la madre, ma anche il padre!*" And always the subjects of crushing embraces and many wet kisses. And mind you, this took place every Sunday morning after 11:00 mass.

This was the high mass and we had to attend this one because mother was the organist. Women's lib had not yet reached the Catholic Church. Only men could sing in the choir at the high mass, an all male choir with a female director--my mother.

Our first stop after church was at the Italian bakery to get hot bread. Upon arrival home we had to change our clothes, change into something like school clothes because you were not allowed to wear play clothes on Sunday. We read the comics spread out on the living room floor as we awaited dinner. Afterwards we took turns listening to the ear phones of our crystal radio set and in later years the battery-operated set with its scratchy speaker horn.

Later in the afternoon, if weather permitted, my father took us for an automobile ride or we visited friends. When my parents visited another family, we children always accompanied them, a custom that my wife and I were to follow with our own children. It was a highly educational process because at a very early age we began to absorb serious adult talk on current events and private activities and public affairs.

These nationality churches of the newcomers--Polish, Russian, Ukrainian and Italian--operated as bastions of tradition and security. Served by bi-lingual clergy, they functioned as crucial institutions assuaging the hazards of immigrant life by providing guidance and mutual support. It was not until the late 1950's that a priest of Italian heritage from a nationality parish was assigned as the pastor of a territorial parish in the Pittsburgh diocese. Customs persist long in the Church.

In the Carnegie of the Twenties, there were no public departments of social service, no private social workers, no municipal, county, state or federal agencies to tend to the needs of minorities or new Americans. Labor unions were slow in gaining strength and furnishing leadership. It was the priest to whom the immigrants turned to for advice and counsel. Priests were the only persons of common ancestry who had the equivalent of a high school education, let alone a college degree. So important in the early decades of immigrant life these towering figures have been practically ignored by chroniclers of this era.

Also in the Carnegie of the Twenties, indeed, in the entire United States of the Twenties, no federal, state or local laws existed to forbid discrimination. The immigrants were minorities, but no government agencies protected them. No social agencies assisted them with complex problems of being strangers in a strange land. No powerful political lobbies advanced their cause as we see today in the powerhouses espousing the causes of popular minority groupings based on gender, religion, race and ancestral origin.

But without any government assistance, the immigrants of the Twenties survived. They prospered. They became an important reason how the United States transformed itself into the world power it would become at the end of the Twenties and Thirties.

They could not scream about discrimination, although they and their wives and children were subjected to it every day. They were the victims of economic, social and political discrimination in all forms, active and passive, direct and indirect. Yet they persevered. They said to themselves words that would become universally popular two generations later, "We shall overcome some day." And they did.

They were able to do so, in part, because the nationality parish priests emphasized to them that all men and women were children of God and were loved equally by the Almighty. The parishioners were told to walk the streets of Carnegie with heads held high. From the pulpits they were told, "You are now American citizens and no one can ever take that away from you."

Chapter Seven
Growing Up In School

At first Washington School had been the only elementary school in Carnegie, located on Lydia Street, a short block off East Main near Washington Avenue. It was a three story structure in the grand tradition of post-Civil War construction, built in the form of a cube, a building as long and as wide as it was high, erected in the center of a mammoth lot that allowed playground areas on all four sides. A second school was constructed at the west end of town to serve as a combination elementary-junior high school. It was initially known as the First Ward School, and because President Harding's funeral cortege passed through on the main line of the railroad nearby and the children were excused from class to watch it pass, someone got the idea to rename it Harding School.

With the influx of so many immigrants immediately prior to World War I, however, it became necessary to build a third school, which was erected in the second ward near Washington School on Lincoln Avenue and appropriately named Lincoln. Thus our town boasted three elementary schools, two named after great Presidents, and one after William Gamaliel Harding.

The school board's decision to build the third school solved two problems: It avoided overcrowding in existing schools and insulated the children of the WASP community from contacts with those newcomers with strange-sounding names. To do this the board worked out a masterpiece of gerrymandering. It drew snake-like boundary lines that placed most children of the foreign-born in Harding and Washington elementary schools, while children of old-line Protestant families were placed behind a *cordon sanitaire*: They would attend the new Lincoln school.

This did not mean that all children of the establishment families fit into the new school zone. By the accident of residence, some would be required to attend Harding and Washington. It was inauspicious for some of these families to live on what we may now call desegregated streets where the old-line families lived side by side with the newcomers.

But it did mean that children enrolled in the first six years at Lincoln would be the untouchables. They would be virtually free from ethnic contamination. School lines were drawn so that families on Johnny Bull Hill – on Wabash, Lincoln and Washington Avenues (the friendly territory through which the Klan began its ill-fated August 1923 march) could send their children to Lincoln.

It was under these circumstances that my brother Caesar had enrolled in Washington's first grade in 1923 one week after the Klan riot. I followed in 1925.

Our schoolmates were a fascinating mix of new Americans. Some 90 percent of us at Washington were Italians, Poles, Russians, Ukrainians, Jews, blacks, some Syrians (they did not call themselves Lebanese in those days) one Chinese family, and a smattering of Irish who lived too far away to attend St. Luke's parochial school. We were drawn from lower Chestnut, Ridge, Grandview, Forest, Anthony, Gormley, Plum, Academy, Boquet, Arch (known as "The Bogs"), East Main, Broadway, Walnut and Jane Streets and various crossways and alleys.

Carnegie had no nursery schools or kindergartens, so we entered first grade running at full speed. It was an old-fashioned structure with the traditional school room format: large rooms with one wall of windows and the other three with black boards made of slate, with narrow ledges below the boards to hold the white chalk and dusty felt erasers, and desks and seats bolted to the floor in rigid formation. No cozy group sessions here, the teacher's desk was in the center front with an American flag prominently displayed for the morning flag salute.

GROWING UP IN SCHOOL 91

Washington School boasted a cadre of dedicated teachers, all of whom were talented, competent and understanding. The teachers maintained discipline, but were models of grace and dignity. I think I know something about elementary school teachers. Having been a long-time trustee of the University of Pittsburgh, I have served on many boards of visitors in the university community, but one of the most interesting was service on the university's trail-blazing Learning and Research Center for grades K through six.

I know something about the potential that can be achieved at the preschool age, particularly under modern concepts of computer experience. I know the importance of having adept, proficient and dedicated teachers on the elementary school level. And I don't think I indulge in hyperbole in extolling the quality of primary school education received in those formative times. Looking back from the perspective of over 40 years as a judge, I am grateful for the education received, to be sure, but also for concepts of intercultural understanding I obtained from the Washington school teachers and later from those in Carnegie junior and senior high schools. The school board did a job of gerrymandering children of foreign born parents, but it did not shirk its responsibility in assigning top flight teachers to us.

None of the Washington school teachers was married and they were all women. In those days the woman had to choose between teaching or getting married. They were all devoted to their professions--Miss Westby, the principal, and Misses Richardson, Knepper, Chilton, Miller, Smith, Brown, DeLoche, McLain, Brown and Hoover. I am still able to remember them and their names after all these years because by deed and example they deserved to be remembered.

It was not until eighth grade that I had a male teacher and then, only two. One taught wood shop, the formal title was Manual Training; the other, civics.

Discipline problems rampant in modern schools were virtually unknown then, and this was probably because of the all-pervasive attitude toward education held by the first generation of immigrant parents. Those parents were denied for the most part education opportunities in the old country, and seemed united to ensure that their children would have schooling in the new land.

Parents drilled in our heads that teachers were to be respected. They were to be obeyed. If you had a disagreement with your teacher, you would find no solace at home. If you complained, there was an irrebuttable presumption that you, and not the teacher, were wrong.

Then, too, for the teachers, there was abundant compensation, a compensation other than financial. Perhaps, we call it psychic satisfaction today. A teacher was accorded universal respect by the community. When she walked down the street she was the object of great deference and admiration. With Shenstone, the community believed that "Deference is the most complicated, the most indirect, and the most elegant of all compliments."

The school system was the main force that eventually destroyed the jagged ethnic and religious tensions in the community prevalent in the postwar years of the Twenties. We learned more than that which was taught by rote drills, text books and home work. Attitudes were instilled. We learned that beneath a variegated surface there was unity in our diversity. We learned that your neighbor was entitled to respect and friendship regardless of ancestral origin, color or religion. Sure, we got this from the friendships drawn from our daily association with other kids, and this was very important. But the benefactions of those elementary school teachers can never be minimized.

These teachers taught us basics of intercultural understanding. In turn, children taught parents and aunts and uncles and grandparents, although I admit that my brother and I had very little to teach our parents. My parents were very special people and we learned by daily life at home that which was echoed in the classroom.

The janitor at our school was James Thornhill, an African-American. All the kids called him "Jim" and he liked us. We liked to watch him pull the ropes that rang the first bell, the big school bell that sounded throughout the valley and signalled that classes would begin in fifteen minutes; ten minutes later the "last bell" was rung and you only had five minutes to be inside and in your seats. But if we referred to him as "Jim" in the presence of our teachers, we were immediately lectured: "His name is Mr. Thornhill and you will refer to him as "Mister!"

The same admonition was forthcoming if we referred to the huge, affable black policeman at the Main Street crossing as "Joe." "He is Mr. Lewis to you, and don't you forget it," we were told. I suppose that if such corrections were forthcoming from teachers today, they would be prohibited by some of our kids and their parents as illegal infringements of the First Amendment right of free expression.

In the fall, the Jewish kids were absent from school on Rosh Hashanah and Yom Kippur. Our teachers carefully told us why they were absent and explained the nature of their religious holidays. Similarly, when members of the Orthodox faith celebrated Christmas and Easter later than we because of their observance of the Julian calendar, we were told why. Children were encouraged to bring to class objects of interest from their homes. We learned about Polish Easter bread, matzos, gorgeous Ukrainian Easter eggs, and, yes, Chinese fireworks.

Each school day began with a Bible reading from the Old Testament, and no one seemed offended. I was particularly attracted to the majestic language of the King James version, especially the Twenty-third Psalm. I thought it much more lyrical than our own Catholic Douay version. But neither my parents nor my priest objected. Our priest was Father Ercole Dominicis, a very sophisticated man from Rome. A scholar, composer and extremely erudite, he was over-qualified for a little parish in a small mill town. To be sure, we had a slight problem with the Lord's Prayer. The Protestant prayer ended with "For Thine is the Kingdom and the Power and the Glory forever and ever, Amen." As Catholics were told to abstain from reciting this last line because it was not part of our liturgy and we abstained from doing so. Fifty years later, the Vatican II Council added this passage to our version of the prayer. In retrospect, the editing during elementary school years was for naught.

We had the pledge of allegiance. We had the works--the Lord's Prayer, the Old Testament Bible reading and the flag salute.

My days at Washington were a very happy time, for I really liked school and did not look upon it as a drudgery. I found it exciting, I suppose because I did well from the very first and always made the honor roll. From our parents we were given the word: "It was not a question of making the honor roll, but what place on the roll did you stand."

For the first three grades we were evaluated in reading, numbers and penmanship: Very Good, Good, Fair, and Poor. I came out with a host of Very Goods each time except for penmanship. We studied the Palmer method, of "push-pulls" and "ovals" and I never mastered it and my handwriting today is still atrocious. This is not an inherited predilection. My mother wrote in the classical feminine Palmer method style, and my father wrote with a model masculine symmetry. I suppose my trouble is that I never got the hang of the push-pulls and the ovals with stiff hands and arm movement only in Room One from Miss Richardson.

We were not exposed to individual attention from the teachers. The rooms were big and the classes large. We did not have cozy little reading groups, and not much personal tutoring. It was drill, drill, drill. Reading 'n writing 'n 'rithmetic. First it was memorizing the alphabet, letter by letter. "For the 't' sound you put your tongue at the top of your mouth near your teeth. Try it. Say 't.' Very good. All together now, say 't.' That's very good."

"These are the numbers – 1 to 10. Let's try them together. 'One.' That was very good." And so it went in first and second grades. It was exercises on the desk with pencil and paper. It was exercises on the black board – yes, black, not green – with chalk and eraser. It was reading from the primer, sometimes quietly to yourself with lips moving, sometimes silent, sometimes whispering. It was reading aloud when called upon, or collectively as part of a vigorous class chorus. It was drawing pictures with crayons, wax ones. The birds were never so ferocious, and flowers so menacing as they appeared in my struggles with art.

By the third grade we were introduced to spelling with a vengeance. One hour at a time. Spelling bees were begun in earnest and they persisted through the eighth grade. We're too sophisticated today to concentrate on spelling in elementary grades. I think that's why I read briefs from high-powered lawyers with mistakes that would have raised the ire of Miss Miller in third grade or Miss Smith a year later.

We soon moved into geography and we first had to memorize the names and locations of all the states, all 48 of them, and their capitals, and then off to Europe and Africa and Asia, with insistence not only on location and capitals but much emphasis on their raw materials and manufactured goods. One of the tragedies of modern American education has been the decline in teaching geography. Small wonder that a study released in 1989-1990 revealed that Americans know less geography than our counterparts in the Western World. As a trustee of the University of Pittsburgh I fought a losing battle to preserve one of our premier departments--geography. We had to close it because public school systems and undergraduate curriculums no longer required faculty for teaching geography.

By fourth grade we were given history books, and by the sixth grade we had been introduced to all the Presidents. History was not taught by political or social or economic trends. Rather, the study of history was a chronological experience. We started with Columbus in 1492, quickly moved to Captain John Smith at Jamestown, had a full visit with the Pilgrims in 1620, and then leaped into the French and Indian war after short pauses with Dutch, English, and French explorers.

The wars we studied were all one-sided and America was always on the side of the angels through skirmishes with the Indians, the Revolution, the War of 1812 and not the War between the States, but the Civil War. We were a Pennsylvania school, the site of Gettysburg, and we believed in the Union, now and forever, a Union that did not tolerate states' rights.

We just glanced at the Spanish American war (we didn't know about William Randolph Hearst and really fixed those Spaniards trying to take our Cuba and our Philippines) and we learned that although the Kaiser could run rough shod over the Belgians, French and British, once he sank our *Lusitania*, we had to show him a thing or two and in the process give a lesson to our Allies on how real men fought wars and were not sissies. We learned that the only praiseworthy Presidents after Lincoln were Theodore Roosevelt and Woodrow Wilson.

But most of all was the emphasis on "Language," as it was called in elementary school, and "English" in later years. We learned "the parts of speech." Oh, how we learned them! Again it was drill, drill, drill. We had to parse the sentences that we read and those that we wrote. We didn't have to wait for a course in foreign languages to learn the difference between the nominative and objective, subjects and predicates, transitive and intransitive verbs and indirect and direct objects. We were given a sentence and had to go to the blackboard to diagram it: straight horizontal line for subject and predicate, forty-five degree angles to show articles and adjectives that modified nouns which were on horizontal lines; prepositions, on angle lines and also adverbs to modify adjectives or verbs; noun objects of the prepositions always parallel to the subject-predicate line. Yes, we learned "language;" we learned the basics–basics that my children never received with the modern emphasis in linguistics that characterized their elementary school education.

The years were happy ones for me at Washington School. The teachers kept us busy both in and out of school. We had lots of what we called "night work." Mother was the proctor at home. She insisted on knowing what was assigned every day and patiently sat with my brother and me at the dinner table until our work was finished. It was much more homework than my own children were to have 30 years later in Mt. Lebanon, a much larger and much more prestigious school system.

Mother was a very determined person when it came to school and school work. She was one of the few parents who ever visited our classes, the teachers often telling us to invite our parents. Our school was the precinct's polling place, and on election day--primary or general–mother showed up in class, usually with one or two of her friends, and because she had visited often, she knew the teachers and made a big production of introducing other mothers. She had started this with my brother and got to know the teachers then, so when I came along two years later and had the same teachers, it was always old home week for mother.

She was very patient, sitting with us at the dining table when we did the "night work." I sat at one end of the table, Caesar at the other end, mother in the middle. She checked all of our assignments and written work, and pointed out any errors. When this occurred, we had to correct the papers. If the corrections could not be made neatly, we had to write the paper over again. She was always very pleasant, but at the same time, very strict, constantly preaching, "Learn good study habits. Don't take short cuts." Even when we reached fifth and sixth grades and had to prepare for tests, she would go over the assignments page by page and give us an oral quiz.

The radio had come into our lives and there were programs we wanted to hear, but mother, the sergeant major, was adamant: No radio until both boys had finished home work to her satisfaction.

The Carnegie school experience put a premium on perfect attendance and lack of tardiness. If you were perfect for a school year you received an attractive certificate that contained a gold seal; if you repeated perfect attendance, you received a seal. My brother set a school system record of having a perfect attendance for seven of his first eight years. He had three certificates, with accompanying seals, prominently displayed in our house. I came in a poor second, with only one certificate with four seals.

Part of this was due to mother's insistence that we had to attend school; the other can be attributed to the way she practiced her own brand of medicine. If you had a cold, the usual affliction, she had one prescription--a jolt of whiskey. If you had a cough or sore throat, she would add honey to the whiskey and wrap our throats with flannel cloths liberally greased with Vick's salve. For many long winter days in school my brother and I had whiskey breaths and a Vicks salve body odor.

We had a distinct advantage of attending school in a small school system--your classmates became friends for life. A sizeable number of us went straight through twelve years together. Indeed, five or six of us were in the same home room through elementary, junior high and high school, one of whom, Evelyn Green, continued on with me for four more years at the University of Pittsburgh. We are still good friends and, now in our eighties, keep in touch by telephone or by mail.

We have valuable encounters in life, but one of the most special to me was the opportunity of going through school together, starting as toddlers, growing older and discovering gender mysteries as adolescence came upon us, electrified by the teenage experience and finally becoming adults. In 1987, our high school class had its 50th reunion with a splendid turnout, at which time we reiterated that we not only were members of the same senior class, but that most of us had gone through 12 years of school together. Many of us at this 50th class reunion had met as six-year olds, and we convened and reminisced for two days on the eve of our 70th birthdays. It doesn't get much better than that.

Washington School had its tough kids, but I cannot say that I was hassled much by bullies. The reasons for this were that most of the tough kids were my friends. I do remember one problem that I had for a short time with a kid named Charles Bradshaw who started to pick on me and call me dago and wop. He was bigger than I, and although I tried to avoid him, he started to make my life very uncomfortable. I had some good friends who were bigger, and tougher than he, and like me and unlike Bradshaw, were children of immigrants.

I collected them in the school yard one day, and reported that this "American" kid was picking on me, threatening me, calling me names and, in a burst of exaggeration, calling, them, my friends, names, saying that we were all a bunch of hunkies. They ganged up on him that afternoon for a little "attitude adjustment." I had no trouble with him thereafter.

When I was in the fifth grade the Boy Scouts organized a troop from the meanest neighborhood in town--Arch street, known as "the Bogs." It was more a sociological experiment than anything else and it proved to be very successful. The kids from "the Bogs," Arch Street, a rowdy neighborhood, could not call other scouts sissies if they themselves belonged to a Boy Scout troop. I felt honored when these kids invited me to join the troop even though I was not from their neighborhood. I stayed with them for about two years until the troop disbanded.

We did the usual merit badge projects and hiked every other Saturday morning to a rustic camp on Campbell's Run Road a few miles out in the country. We shared this camp with the town's established scout troop whose scoutmaster was John Passavant. He had trained our scoutmaster and he conducted the outdoors lessons at Saturday morning camp for both troops. As a young scout I admired this fine community leader who found the time to say a few words to each of us from the new troop.

Twenty years later he and I were members of the Carnegie Kiwanis Club and I later became his lawyer. The tenderfoot scout and the kind scoutmaster of an early era became the lawyer and the client. Such are the precious experiences of growing up in a small town in the Twenties and hanging out your shingle in the same town in the late Forties.

I was in the fifth grade when Washington School instituted safety patrols in which certain students were chosen to serve as guards at school crossings. I was chosen as captain by Miss Westby, the principal, and given the right to name my lieutenant. I selected my close pal, Andy Lezchak, the biggest kid in school who had recruited me into the scout troop. We became leaders of a patrol of six or seven fairly big guys who stood watch at street crossings and stomped through the school yard like gauleiters at morning and afternoon recess periods. I asked Miss Westby for an explanation of our school yard duties at recess times. She replied, "Ruggero, with your group keeping an eye on the children, it will not be necessary for teachers to go out in the yard." I got the message. We were to insure that big kids did not pick on the little ones, and I started to suspect that some members of the patrol had been offenders in the past, because after the patrol was organized everything became tranquil. We wore white Sam Brown belts and took our jobs seriously, and all was quiet on the Second Ward front.

If I encountered any trouble at all in grade school, it came from my name, Ruggero. As might be expected, it was not a case of every Tom, Dick and Ruggero. My name was difficult to spell and to pronounce. (Like most Italian names the emphasis is on the penultimate syllable and the "gg" is pronounced as the "g" in George.) The teachers had no difficulty with it, but, for reasons that still defy me, most kids called me "Rahjetta," until about fourth or fifth grade when my nickname "Rugi" took hold for good, and it's pronounced with the hard "g." Sure, some kids poked fun at the name, but not too much. You don't poke too much fun at another's "strange" name if you, yourself, answer to Popivchak, Matwiezceck, Krovchychyn, Zbalishen, Wosnyak, Bondarenko, Battaglia, Santavicca, Magliocca, Panebianco, Bevilacqua or George Washington Yee Linn.

All judges today are confronted with the doctrine of equal protection of the laws. Every state or federal judge every day, at trial or on appeal, must be prepared to face this issue. Ingrained in our consciousness, the ringing doctrine starts with the stirring premise of the Declaration of Independence "All men are created equal." By the majesty of the Fourteenth Amendment states may not deny any person "the equal protection of the laws."

I'm an expert on this venerable doctrine, and not necessarily because I have been a judge for a very long time. I really learned about equal protection at school and grasped it well at a very early age. It was not in political science classes as an undergraduate at the university nor in the law school curriculum, although I studied the courses there. My education in this field started long before that. It began in September 1925 when I enrolled as a first grader in Washington Elementary School.

Chapter Eight
Growing up Playing

The life of a child is play. It's a mixed world of reality and imagination. I enjoyed both facets of this world, and as I look back, my life of play covered not only fact and fancy, but two discrete locations: "on the hill" where I lived and "down street" at Aunt Silvia's house.

At home it was play in the countryside. Although only five blocks up steep grades from Main Street, our house was perched on top of a hill. From the left side and rear we had a stunning view of the valley below. We had a front yard with two umbrella trees and hedges on either side of a concrete walk that led to the street. Our house faced an open field, four or five acres of pasture and trees, and across the street only one house stood between us and the ball field, known as Southern Grounds, about 100 yards to the east. The Sweetall family lived there and had a cow who grazed in that little pasture across the street from us. The Sweetall's kept her in a tiny barn, the size of a one-car garage. She was most docile, and I loved to touch her, always because she made me believe that we were living in the country, and not in a city.

A small level terrace served as our back yard and, although it was in grass, we did not keep it trimmed as we did the front. It was here that mother would hang the laundry to dry on clotheslines that stretched from the house to the trees. The younger I was, the more formidable appeared the woods in our back yard that tumbled to Ridge Avenue, the street below. I spent many hours "exploring a dense forest," of the back of our house, which in later years I realized was only about 50 yards deep and 100 yards wide.

But the real woods were located in the back of the ball field at Southern Grounds and covered about a mile. Behind home plate--there was no backstop--certain narrow paths beckoned the young explorer. One led to the lower reaches of Whiskey Run near Noblestown Road in East Carnegie, a little stream of some historical significance, for its name dated back to Western Pennsylvania's Whiskey Rebellion during President George Washington's time when the farmers chose to dump their whiskey in this stream rather than pay what they considered an exorbitant tax on liquor.

Another trail was more exciting. It twisted downgrade with many turns through lovely stands of oak, birch, beech, maple, wild cherry and hawthorn trees. Intermittent shafts of sunlight poked through the branches so that the path through the woods was not a foreboding darkness. Near the valley floor, the trail brought you to a natural spring that spouted from a cluster of rocks on the hillside. This was a ritual, for the water was pure and icy cold and it was much fun to stop for a drink. It was a totally primitive setting. No cups or glasses were available, and the most popular way to drink was to cup your hands and catch the water as it flowed out, but often we used a more exotic method by pulling hollow green stalks from nearby plants and using the stalks as natural straws to sip the water as it emerged from the rocks.

But the spring in the woods was only a way station. The trail continued down grade until it arrived at the upper reaches of Whiskey Run under the high trestle of the P & W Va. railroad (which we persisted in calling the "Wabash" because the predecessor railroad was Jay Gould's ill-fated Wabash Railroad designed to compete with the Pennsylvania Railroad to the west). This was a magnificent railroad bridge that crossed the canyon between Carnegie and Rook Station where a railroad "roundhouse" was located. At times, we were able to sneak by the railroad police and catch a look into this wonder world where the railroad engines were brought in for repair and maintenance. Especially fascinating was a gigantic rotating circular platform that was able to swing the huge steam locomotives from one track to another, or to guide the black shiny monsters into a proper alcove within the roundhouse for repairs. Rook Station was the last stop before the railroad tracks swooped eastward through the tunnel in Pittsburgh's Mt. Washington, crossed the Monongahela river over a private bridge and arrived at Wabash terminal, the end of the line in downtown Pittsburgh at the corner of Liberty Avenue and Stanwix Street.

The trestle between Carnegie and Rook still stands and is in use by the Norfolk and Western railroad for hauling freight, but there are no magic woods below it now, and sadly, no storybook sylvan spring. An elevated four lane interstate highway bridge now runs under it and cuts the perspective of height and the grace of its supporting trestles. Four lanes of drab concrete on filled land now paves over the exciting woodlands of my childhood.

When we played in the wooded trails, we didn't walk or stroll. My brother and I, or any of the kids with us, always acted out roles. You do this when you are only four or five years old. We played cowboys and Indians or pirates, and when I explored these paths alone, I still acted out roles I had seen in the silent movies.

The trestle was there to be climbed. To be climbed as high as your imagination, or more properly, your fears, permitted. Here, too, a great imagination came in handy. Climbing the railroad trestle was climbing the mast of the Jolly Roger. I could climb only so high before I became gripped in terror, and at times became the subject of taunts of other kids. It was not until later years when I discovered that I had acrophobia that I learned the source of my terror in climbing the pirates' mast. That explains also why I was always ill at ease when we walked the open ties on the railroad bridge. We had to look down to see where we were walking, but between the ties we could see way down, far to the deep valley below.

Playing in the woods and stopping at the spring and climbing the railroad trestle were always much fun, but another place to explore was a natural gully abutting Southern Grounds about 20 yards deep and extending 100 by 300 yards south of the grassy outfield. In the early Twenties this was sometimes used as a skeet range and I was entranced by the men and shotguns and the call of "pull" as clay pigeons were released to sail over the gulch. To a five year old, the sound of firing and the tart smell of cordite and the sight of blue smoke propelled from the gun barrels was much more graphic than the silent western movies we saw on Saturday afternoons.

At the south end of the same gully were ruins of a brickyard that went out of business at the end of the Civil War. (In retrospect the Civil War seems a very long time ago, but you must recall that I was born only a little over 50 years after Generals Grant and Lee signed the peace treaty at Appomattox). Remnants of kilns poked out of the ground and pieces of red bricks could be found in the weeds, accumulations of decades past. A favorite pastime was to search for hunks of brick and remnants of clay pigeons flung from the skeet range. Sometimes we discovered an intact clay pigeon and this was akin to finding treasure trove.

We also took what we called long hikes. We hiked up Grandview Avenue, past a rudimentary dirt tennis court at Gormley Avenue where the Grandview changed its name to Summit Street and then up to Chestnut Street to the road bridge that crossed over the Wabash railroad. Here was the boundary between Carnegie and Scott township and here, too, was another change of street names with Chestnut Street now becoming Forsythe Road. The road was named after the farmer who had extensive holdings on both sides of the country lane. We would turn left and climb the high Forsythe pasture where a herd of cows always grazed. This hillside bore the traces of fallen Klan crosses long after the burnings had taken place.

Our neighborhood was an idyllic place to spend a childhood, especially at a time when there were no kindergartens, let alone nursery schools. But it lacked one essential--there weren't many kids with whom to play. Our immediate neighbors were childless, but our good pal, Billy Hiles, lived two doors away and was about my brother's age. We spent hours in a barn behind the Hiles' house that had been converted into a garage where inside was a magnificent hulk of an aged four-door touring car that no longer had wheels and was propped up on blocks. I still recall the smell of the engine and old leather seats and the mildewed fabric top and the barrels of oil and grease. Garages were meant to smell that way in the early days of automobiling.

In the early Twenties my father had a Ford Model T open roadster. Starting it was a ritual that we always enjoyed watching. First he had to adjust the spark and the accelerator which were stalks on the steering column. Then he would proceed to the front of the car to start the engine with a crank. There was a trick to this. First, you had to pull the choke that projected as a ring right under the radiator. You could not grasp the crank too tightly with your hand because often when the engine started, the crank would violently kick back. If you held the crank too firmly this kick could break your arm. I was about four or five when my father sold his Model T and bought a second hand two-door Willys Overland. It made news on the hill because it was the first car in the neighborhood of the type then known as "closed cars," automobiles that had genuine glass windows that could be wound up and down. I remember breaking the news to Billy who jumped up and down, exclaiming, "Are you sure? Is it really a closed car?" On the day dad drove the car home for the first time we waited on the curb for almost two hours and when he arrived, Billy joined my brother and me in jumping up and down and screaming "Yea!" And we asked my father to please start the motor with the new fangled electric starter. No more hand cranks here.

Billy is responsible for my nickname "Rugi" or "Rugy" pronounced with a hard "g." Unfortunately, as a said before, Billy, our only playmate on the hill, suffered from asthma, and died when he was only eight or nine. The spelling of my nickname underwent changes. I first wrote it as "Rugy," but too many people read it as "Rudy." In later years I attempted to dispel this by writing it as "Rugi." One thing's for sure, you don't know anyone else in the world called "Rugi" or "Rugy." I'll give you odds on that.

Kids need more than environment or ambience to have a happy life. Kids need friends with whom to play. Brother Caesar and I found our friends, not on the hill, but on Main Street where my father's sister, Aunt Silvia Castellani, lived with her husband Uncle Mario and four children, Alex, Irma, Adele and Richard. We were especially close to my aunt and her family and we spent much time with them. She lived in my father's former property in a small enclave of immigrant families in the heart of Carnegie's business district. Uncle Mario had a barber shop and the family lived behind and above the shop. All neighbors lived the same way, with a business on Main Street and living quarters behind and above, a living pattern you still see today in most European communities.

This enclave loomed very large in my growing up. Starting from the west, it began with Jim Bassano's shoe repair shop behind which he and his wife and child lived with his wife's, the Bevilacqua's. Harry A. Klee, M.D., son of a Jewish immigrant, had his office next door and then followed a house first occupied by a tailor named Berlingeri, who later moved and his house was bought by Joe and Josephine Burrafato, a childless couple who operated a fruit market. Josephine was a member of the Farinella family who conducted a fruit market and soda parlor across the street. Next came the Yee Linn's who operated a hand laundry and lived immediately next to my aunt. We were friends with all their family–Lucy, Martha Washington, Margaret, George Washington, William and Herbert Hoover Yee Linn. Directly across was the Steinmetz bakery complex, operated by a German immigrant and his family. The complex contained a retail store, a bakery and family living quarters. It still flourishes today in the same location. Next door to the east of my aunt lived Tony and Rosa Muracca who rented their office front to Clyde Kocher, a real estate broker and insurance agent. Tony was a gandy dancer on the Pennsylvania railroad. When he returned from work he always bathed and shaved and emerged well-scrubbed and neat, boasting a perennial bronzed face from working outdoors six days a week 52 weeks a year. This most rugged of men was also the most gentle. He was always kind to us and nurtured a splendid flower and vegetable garden in his back yard.

Next to the Muracca's was a rental property whose changing tenants never conformed with the stability of the enclave's community. Next to it lived the Leo Paolino family. Leo was a tailor, born in the same *paese* as my father. Our families were very close. There was an exchange of best man at the Aldisert and Paolino weddings and there were various godfather and godmother exchanges when children were baptized. As a result, the titles *compare* and *commare* flowed in every conversation. My mother was *"Commar'Lizabetta,"* my father was *"Compare John,"* but the most popular name was attached to Mrs. Paolino, to whom all in the neighborhood referred to in the one word, *"Comm'Annie."*

Next to the Paolino's lived *Comm'Annie's* mother and father and their family, the Peluso's. The father, Eugenio, operated a shoe repair shop. I always liked his strong name, and he had a son whose name had a similar lilt – Egidio, who early in life was dubbed "Jad," and the name still sticks. The enclave ended with the Peluso's, whose house abutted the large commercial building housing the Carnegie Union Printing Company, which printed the Carnegie Union, one of Carnegie's two weekly newspapers. The plant extended from Main Street to Brown Way as did its neighbor, the Glenn P. Knouse butcher shop.

It was in this enclave of that I spent much childhood playtime. Families have shorthand expressions to indicate geographical locations. Thus, my Castellani cousins always referred to our house as "up the hill"; we referred to them as "down street." As a young kid I lived "down street" as much as I did "up the hill."

"Down street" we did not have the open fields and deep woods and trails to explore and country roads along which to hike. We had something more valuable: We had kids our age with whom to play, and we had their families who didn't think something was wrong with us because we were foreigners.

The core of our friends were from the enclave. There lived my cousin, Rich Castellani, Nino and Eddie Paolino, Georgie and Billy Yee Linn, Pete Bevilacqua, Carl, Alois and Raymond Steinmetz. Living in the alley called Brown Way were Petey and Eddie Liwoscz; and later, my school friend, Oliver Brooks, an African-American, would join us. This was the nucleus, but we were often joined by others, especially various Russian or Ukrainian kids from nearby Jane Street. We played in the back yards, usually, in Aunt Silvia's, for although she had a small flower garden, she had a relatively large open area under a huge beech tree where we played games or just sat around and talked. We talked about everything; like most kids, we never ran out of something to say. We did not use the popular expression, "marbles," but we had shooters and commies and aggies, and spent hours in various contests.

My aunt had a well in her back yard. In retrospect, it was remarkable because their house was only about four blocks from the polluted Chartiers creek and located on Main Street with its street car line, yet there was this well that was known simply as "the pump." It produced chlorine-free, pure cold water, and the Castellani's made it available to the entire neighborhood--white and black, Italian, Irish, Russian, Ukrainian, Russian, Polish, German. Aunt Silvia's back porch abutted the pump and this became the cross roads of neighborhood activity.

When we weren't in the back yard, we were out in Brown Way, sometimes playing a form of "it" or "I spy," but more often we played baseball; not a hard, white leather, red-stitched Spalding baseball, for we saved that for when the gang came "up the hill" to play at Southern

Grounds, but rubber balls, sometimes solid ones made of sponge rubber, or hollow ones that were cheaper but with a lesser life span. We usually bought them for a nickel or a dime at an establishment at the corner of East Main and Broadway formally called Carnegie News, but everyone called it "the paper store." The proprietor was a laconic, old line Carnegieite with a Hollywood-sounding name, Case Foster. He always wore a hat in the store and we made bets that he was totally bald, but we never found out, because, in his entire lifetime, we never saw him without a hat.

When we played ball, we usually picked up sides. A captain was chosen for each team who alternatively named his players. Because I am fairly uncoordinated in sports, I was usually the last to be chosen. Nobody really wanted me on his side, but I survived. As I look back, the alley was not a bad baseball field for kids our age. Each family had a high wooden fence along the alley separating its yard from the alley. Across the alley was an even higher fence that ran across the back yards of two Ukrainian churches and a Russian Church. The parishioners lived mainly on Jane Street and seemed to get along splendidly during the week, and quarrelled only in their choice of what church to attend on Sunday. They had a common recreation hall, the Uke's hall, in which Saturday night dances were often held. It was known as the "boom-boom."

With relatively high fences on both sides of the alley, and with very little or no vehicular traffic, it was possible to get a good game going without the ball going out of bounds, but you had to learn to play the bounce off the fence. At times, of course, the heavy hitters poked balls over fences and it took some scampering to retrieve them. The most popular game could be played with less than full teams. It was called "rounders." The game would be initiated by someone yelling "hose for rounders!" This qualified him to be the batter. Others would chime in "catcher," "pitcher," "first base" and so on. As the person at bat was put out, he had to take the post of "last in the field" as others moved up through the infield through pitcher and catcher. When a player caught the ball on the fly, however, he was automatically "in hose," or at bat.

We could not afford store-bought bats, for lives of baseball bats were very short when thrown on a brick street, so we used old broom sticks. On one occasion my brother's bat broke as he hit the ball and a piece of it went flying through the window of Cy Heney's house where lived a childless African American couple. Cy was a popular barber and his wife was always kind to us kids, considering the noise we always made. At the sound of smashing glass, Mrs. Heney came out on her porch with hands on her hips and said "Okay, who's going to pay for it?" My father did.

But there were other games and things we did together. We would walk the half block to the high school, then up the steps to Library Avenue to play in the green park that surrounded Andrew Carnegie's gift to the town. Or we would forage for scrap iron or newspapers to sell to Markus and Julius Sherman for pennies and nickels at the Broadway scrap yard at the end of the alley.

When my father was busy, my mother and we kids sometimes would spend the evenings "down street," and we would play a game called "scrip the den" on the sidewalk across from the Carnegie fire house next to Cheesebrough's restaurant at the corner where Walnut intersects with East Main. The person who was "it" had to find and tag the other players to return them to the den, but if an untagged player could race to the den without being tagged, then all the captives in the den were eligible to run out again. This was a very noisy and lively game, but we had to be careful to quit before ten. Carnegie had a ten o'clock curfew, and that meant kids 16 years of age or under had to be off the streets when a siren blew at this time unless accompanied by adults. Our nemesis was a Carnegie cop whom we called "Redbeard" although his correct name was Red Baird. He patrolled the streets in an open police car and we believed that his only job was to grab us kids. Twenty five years later I was to serve in the Kiwanis club with Red who still served as an active policeman.

The closeness of our family with Aunt Silvia made it almost a single extended Aldisert-Castellani family. Adele and Richard were our age, but as kids we got to know the friends of our older cousins, Alex, eight years older than I and Irma, five. When you are six or seven years old, it was something very special to get to know "big people," albeit they were only teenagers, who actually talked to us and treated us as friends.

Alex belonged to a sandlot baseball team, the Wilson A.C., a member of a Greater Pittsburgh twilight league. Their home field was Southern Grounds, virtually next door to our house, and it was in our cellar where the team kept its bases (sacks of lime) and the machine for marking the base lines. We went to all their home games and most away games because my father would fill up the Overland with players and we kids would sit on their laps.

I still remember these wonderful guys-- Mike Carrick, catcher; Bob Peel, first base; Foggy Freshwater, second; Leo La Sota, shortstop; cousin Al played third. Other players who switched from infield to outfield as demanded were Dave Fitzmaurice (who later would become International President of the Electrical Workers of America), Woodie and Bill Wilson, Wetch Kapeluck and Huncie. The pitchers were John Gilbert, Bill Klem and sometimes Woodie Wilson. I served as official scorer for several seasons and my father occasionally served as umpire.

Hey, this was really living. They were real life baseball players. They were "big people." They were old--14 and 15 years old--and when they would pass you on the street they would say "Hi, Rugi. Hi yah doin'?"

Small town life in the extended Aldisert-Castellani family was a constant joy. But play in the winter time was for Grandview Avenue and not "down street." The snows came often in those days and Caesar and I were ready for it, ready with our Flexible Flyer sleds. Upper Grandview was a slight grade which we called "Shearer's hill" because they were the only family on the block. We would go to the top and ride down and swing right on the corner and come to a stop not far from our house. We would then drag our sleds with a clothes line rope where Grandview dipped down to Southern Grounds and met Forest Avenue, an unpaved street on the boundary between Carnegie and Scott Township.

At first we were only permitted to sled down to where Forest met the top of Ridge Avenue, but as we grew older, our parents let us go all the way down Ridge. "Watch out for the cars!" was the admonition, but at that time there were only four or five cars a day that used the hill. A symbiotic relationship existed between the automobiles and the sledders, because you could not get a fast sledding surface on the street until the cars had traversed the hills and packed down the snow.

There was night sledding, too, but only on special days when the borough authorities roped off Chestnut Street and permitted a mile run from the very top. The mile run was for more for teenagers or young adults who would start at the top of the Forsythe cow pasture, turn right on Forsythe Road, which changed its name to Chestnut Street when the road entered Carnegie, and then shoot straight downhill all the way to Lydia Street, a block from East Main. On this final block the borough had spread ashes so that the sleds could stop before reaching the main thoroughfare.

The dazzling performers on these nights were those older people who had built large bob sleds with steel runners. They roared down Chestnut hill clanging bells and chains which they used at the end of the ride to sprag the sleigh to a stop, a spectacular stop in a blast of ashes that splashed high in the air just a few yards from where the street cars ran on East Main.

When we were not sledding, we played in the snow. We wore rubber galoshes with metal fasteners, wool Lumberjacks, tassel caps, scarfs and gloves, and built snowmen in the yard, or rolled the snow into compact two-foot widths that we used as building blocks to build forts. Once the forts were built we proceeded to have serious snowball battles. The forts took seemingly hours to plan or build, and the battles lasted only minutes.

When it snowed, the rural setting of Grandview Avenue became a true winter wonderland. Tree branches were heavily weighted, pristine white, and the air sparkled cold and dry. To look down upon the valley below was to behold a setting of a real-life Christmas card: thick white coatings on roofs and yards, streets piled with snow and divulging tracks where an occasional car traveled, wisps of smoke rising from the chimneys. The beauty of a heavy snowfall is a cherished memory of a Carnegie winter.

Inside, the winter scene was not picture perfect. Bituminous coal in the furnace produced soot in massive quantities, fouling the air, layering dust on the furniture, floor and dinner table, blackening wallpaper, dirtying the carpets and coating the dishes. We ordered coal by the ton that was dumped either at curbside or on the front lawn. From there my brother and I carried it to the coal chute on the side of the house by a wheelbarrow. To make the trip it was necessary to lay planks across the grass. The wheelbarrow was emptied with a crash into the cellar below producing a rush of coal dust, into the cellar where mother did the family wash and in the wintertime hung the laundry out to dry indoors.

You shoveled coal into the hungry furnace and at bed time you banked it high so that by morning a few hot coals would remain. Otherwise it was necessary to build the fire from scratch with newspapers and kindling wood. Were this not dirty enough, periodically you had to remove the ashes and truck them out of the cellar and dump them over the hillside. To enjoy wonderland of winter you had a price to pay.

We played in the house with erector sets and tinker toys from Christmastide, or sprawled on the living room floor reading books. My brother and I went through the entire series of Tom Swift: Tom and his electric locomotive, his machine gun, his submarine and his what-have-you. Our parents encouraged us to read and we were regular patrons at the library. At night on week ends or when school work was completed, the family played cards. We played 500, a rudimentary form of bridge, and Parcheesi, "A Game of India," where you rolled dice and advanced your marker along designed pathways. The object was to arrive "Home," or to land on a space where your opponent's marker lay, forcing him or her to start over again.

Then came the radio! KDKA in Pittsburgh was the world's first commercial broadcasting station and went on the air in 1924 announcing the Coolidge election returns. My father purchased a crystal set operated by two batteries in the form of cylinders about eight inches high and three inches wide. No speaker here, just one set of earphones. In time we received a larger radio with a speaker, no longer did we have to rely on earphones, and to get the proper reception--it was always better at night--dad had to string a long aerial from our roof to a tall tree in the back woods.

I was six years old when my sister was born. At first we called her Betty Marie, and although she was too young to play with, in the winter time, we could wrap her up and take her for sled rides. Later, when she started school, my mother insisted that we call her by her baptismal name "Adrienne." And so it was until my sister turned 70. "I'd like to be called 'Betty Marie' again," she announced. Go figure.

The Twenties were also the era when the movies came into their own. At first there were the silent movies, very popular at Carnegie's five picture shows--the Lyric and the Grand on West Main and the Liberty, Carnegie and Dixie on East Main. As kids we could go to the Lyric on Saturday afternoons to see Westerns for a nickel, other shows cost a dime. Most of the theaters had lady piano players who perched up front and played dramatic pieces throughout the show. I never did learn how the pianists chose their music or how they could read it in the dark. The silent movies were always exciting, the actors being masters of pantomime, with terse dialogue flashed as sub-titles to augment the histrionics. Outdoor night scenes always appeared in a bluish green tint.

We could not go to the movies on school nights, so our parents dropped us off, or went to the show with us on Friday nights or Saturday afternoons. The houses were dark on Sundays; Pennsylvania Blue Laws prohibited them for many years.

Our family went "down street" every Saturday evening, but this was not a time for play. Saturdays were a big event in Carnegie, the stores being open until nine. Every Saturday morning the borough street department men washed down Main Street with fire hoses. This was the day that many stores displayed wares on the sidewalks, including the A&P and P.H. Butler and all the produce stores and independent grocers. Outside their shops, butchers arrayed crates of live chickens and turkeys, sometimes carcasses of pigs and sides of calves and steers. In proper season we would see dressed rabbits, deer and pheasants.

But Saturday evening was something special. First you had to take your weekly bath, get dressed up and go to Aunt Silvia's on Main Street. From about seven until a little after nine we witnessed a tradition of small towns the world over, the stroll or promenade along the town's main street. In Italian towns this is known as the *passegiata*, a parade of townsfolk, dressed in finery. In some places the promenade took place every evening, but in Carnegie, it was a Saturday night spectacle only. It was about a half mile walk, from Chestnut Street on East Main to the Railroad Station on West Main. The street was brightly lit by street lights and store fronts. It was a night to walk with friends or to visit with those you met along the way. My father often walked with his friends, John Castelli, the jeweler, and Leo Paolino, the tailor, discussing, in English and Italian, the news of the day and exchanging notes on the families and the church. After our own early stroll was over, we kids had to sit in front of the barber shop where mother, Aunt Silvia, Rosa Muracca and *Comm'Annie* usually sat in chairs brought out from the barber shop, constantly admonishing us not to dirty our "good" clothes. The older Castellani and Paolino children would greet friends, and thus at an early age we became acquainted with various generations of the town.

"Growing Up Playing" was fun, although, as I look back on it, it was highly structured. You could play on the week days and only during the day on Saturday. Sundays were out of bounds, for you went to church in the morning, had the mammoth Sunday dinner in the middle of the afternoon, and spent the rest of the day with the "big people." The "big people" helped you grow up in a hurry.

I'm certain that playing with your gang of friends as kids was not always a barrel of laughs and I probably underwent my share of emotional trauma because I was uncoordinated in sports. Being the last to be chosen in any pick-up ball team no doubt produced some anguish at the time, an unpleasant experience now probably totally repressed because I learned later that how far you can hit a baseball ball is not society's sole way of measuring success. Nevertheless each child covets, if not the constant wish to be liked and accepted by peers, at least an intense yearning not to be the subject of derision. At times childhood friends can be cruel, because the art of diplomacy comes later in life, but being part of a gang – I use this term in a non-pejorative sense merely to describe my playmates – was, in retrospect, a great experience. It augmented lessons learned at home that you could not have it your own way all the time, and that many decisions in society, even a community composed of kids alone, are reached by group consensus rather than your personal preference. The "mama's boys" who go through childhood without the give and take of buddies at play are destined for major disappointments in later years.

I could not catch or hit the ball or run as fast as my friends, but I could flick the aggies or shooters or commies with accuracy and dexterity when playing marbles, especially "knuckle down board tight," whatever that meant. But this did not diminish my zeal to be with the gang. What got me accepted I suppose was that what I lacked in proficiency I made up for with enthusiasm.

Playing with my friends was an enriching experience. We can say that all of us are created equal, but some are born better ball players than others. I have not met a constitutional law scholar to explain that one to me.

Mother and dad with their two boys in the early Twenties in a visit to mother's home in Steubenville, Ohio. The back yard is not very impressive, but my maternal grandfather Octavius operated a very successful liquor store in the front of the property on Sixth Street directly across from the Pennsylvania Railroad station. After he purchased the property, grandfather installed one of the first modern bathrooms in the city.

The back porch of Aunt Silvia's house in the late Twenties. From the left is cousin, Richard, my age, Aunt Silvia, Uncle Mario and mother. Can you believe that these horrible dresses were considered fashionable in the Jazz Age? At the Castellani pump on the right, the gathering place for the entire neighborhood, is Peter Bevilacqua, a boyhood friend, who would later became an outstanding end on the Carnegie High School football team.

My brother and I (age six) posing with mother in our dress up clothes.

Chapter Nine
Growing Up Italian

When I was born in 1919 the average Italian immigrant in Carnegie had been in the United States for about ten years. The typical immigrant (and I will refer to the immigrant in the masculine gender, for in most cases, the man had been the first to arrive) possessed the same attributes as those settling elsewhere in the United States:

- For the most part, he came from a very old hill town in southern Italy, or Sicily. Although some migrated from northern or central Italy, generally, the great migration was from that distressed part of Italy now known as the *mezzogiorno* (southern Italy and Sicily).

- He came from the Abruzzi, Campania (the greater Naples area), Basilicata, Calabria, Sicily, and to a lesser extent, Puglia. He did not migrate from any large city. Certainly, he did not come from Rome, Florence or Venice. He was not an aficionado of Galileo, Michelangelo, Da Vinci or Rafael, but had at least a passing acquaintance with Verdi and Puccini.

- He was part of the great exodus that started in the mid part of the first decade of the century. For example 778,000 emigrants left Italy in 1906.

- When he left Italy, he had no firm intention of abandoning his home town and family; he intended to make his money in the new world and then return in a year or so.

- He had been an unskilled tiller of the soil, strong and sturdy, accustomed to long hours of back-breaking labor in the fields, tending olive and fig trees and grape vines, and gathering and transporting wood and charcoal.

- He had little or no formal education, was often illiterate. To have attended five years of school was regarded as being highly educated in the paese. In southern Italy, outside of the city of Naples, schools in the villages were limited to five grades. Only the first three grades were compulsory.

- He came to the Greater Pittsburgh area because of the exhortation of a labor contractor representing mills, mines and railroads, or through the importuning of a friend or relative who had preceded him.

It is important to distinguish Italian immigrants who packed the tenements of Manhattan and Brooklyn, South Philadelphia and Boston's North End from those who made their way to Western Pennsylvania. Little Italy's in the seaboard cities had special urban problems not present in other parts of the country, problems implicating sociological, behavioral and political anxieties and apprehensions not found elsewhere in this country.

Most American literature on the life of the Italian immigrant, including excellent scholarly works by Italian-Americans, has confined itself, for the most part, to the New York City experience. Unfortunately, this has skewed the image of the immigrants who did not settle there or in Boston or Philadelphia. By the force of sheer numbers, these eastern urban immigrants established Little Italy's in large crowded sections of the cities. Especially in New York, because of their isolation, they maintained the *via vecchia,* the old ways of the *Mezzogiorno* (Southern Italy and Sicily) through the first and second generations. They lived much more segregated lives than those who pushed west after clearing Ellis Island.

Those in Pittsburgh were not familiar with the traditional *festa's* of New York or the particular saints whose lives they celebrated. In the Mulberry district they honored St. Rocco, who although born in France and canonized in northern Italy, was revered by the New York Italians for his cures of the maimed and diseased. The saint with the largest constituency was St. Gennaro, the patron saint of Naples. In each of these celebrations, statues were paraded through the streets. They rushed to show their faith by pinning dollar bills or large denominations to the floats. In Pittsburgh we laughed at so-called sophisticated New York *paesani.*

In the Lower East Side, the Sicilians honored Santo Gandolfo, patron saint of a small town in Agrigento. Each year the New York Italians sponsored a huge celebration in honor of the Madonna of Mt. Carmel, where the dollar-bill festooned statue of Our Lady was followed by hordes of penitents marching barefoot on pavements burning with the heat of July in appreciation for previous favors bestowed in answer to various supplications.

There were comparatively few intermarriages in the Eastern Seaboard Little Italy's. Very little economic or political progress emancipated from these self-constructed ghettos. City administrations isolated these communities, and generally, the police permitted the creation of criminal organizations. This was organized extortion by a group known as the *mano nero*, the black hand, that extorted a tribute from all Italian businesses – the grocery store, the barber shop, the produce store, the tailor, the small contractor. The city administrations proceeded on the theory that "so long as these guys give us a piece of the action and keep things quiet, we won't interfere." Because Southern Italians had been antipathetic to police authority for generations, very few complaints were ever lodged, thus giving unfettered rise to the New York organized crime families. This was a New York phenomenon; current fiction improperly suggests was nation-wide in its organization and operation.

It is important to separate reality from the caricatures produced by our fiction, or displayed in the movies, television or depicted in the media.

As is the case in most ethnic, religious or racial segments of our society, the stereotype often displaces actuality. This being especially true in the case of the Italian-American, because novelists and playwrights, even those of Italian origin, have been content to strive for excitement with much dramatic license than to concentrate on verisimilitude. The great artistic works of Francis Ford Coppolo, Martin Scorcese and Mario Puzo on organized crime in the New York-Boston-Philadelphia axis places an undue emphasis on only a small segment of Italian-American customs and mores.

I have a vivid recollection of the Western Pennsylvania Italian immigrant at the time I was growing up. As I grew older and became active in Italian-American fraternal activities in Western Pennsylvania and later in urban communities throughout the United States, I became intimately knowledgeable with conditions of these men and women.

The man was not typified by the unfortunate Hollywood version of the Italian-American male--the loud and crude dictator in his home who made a serf of his wife and cowering vassals of his children. To be sure, some were this way, but they were the exception.

To comprehend how these pioneer men and women conducted themselves in America, as I clearly and fondly remember them, requires that you understand how they lived in the old country. Describing the Calabrian in 1915, Norman Douglas, in *Old Calabria*, depicts the life of those who left the worn out hill towns of the Italian south:

> You must watch the peasants coming home at night from their field work if you wish to see the true [southern Italian] type--whiskered, short and wiry, and of dark complexion. There is that indescribable mark of *race* in these countrymen; they are different in features and character from the [northern] Italians; it is an ascetic, a Spanish type. [He] is strangely scornful of luxury and even comfort; a creature of few but well chosen words, straightforward, indifferent to pain and suffering, and dwelling by preference, when religiously minded, on the harsher aspects of his faith. A note of unworldliness is discoverable in his outlook upon life. Dealing with such men, one feels that they are well disposed not from

impulse, but from some sense of preordained obligation. Greek and other strains have infused versatility and a more smiling exterior; but the groundwork of the whole remain that of *homo ibericus* of austere gentlemanliness.[7]

That is how I remember the men in the early years of my childhood---men of few words always deliberately spoken, straightforward in relationships, deciding things not by impulse but from a sense of cautious obligation to their families. They had one objective in life: to have their families evade and escape the all-consuming memories of a life they left behind in Italy. They had to protect them, all of them, from *la miseria*, the desperate poverty that plagued the south of Italy. Their goals in the new world were twofold--to provide a living for their families and good marriages for their children.

What Douglas called "austere gentlemanliness" I would describe as a rustic courtliness. After decades passed and I had become a lawyer, many of these men and women had become clients. More important, I enjoyed a long time association with them in a national fraternal organization of Americans of Italian origin -- fourteen years as national president of the Order Italian Sons and Daughters of America (ISDA). Although the national headquarters were in Pittsburgh with a large membership in Western Pennsylvania and Cleveland, during my presidency we established lodges on Brooklyn, Long Island, Buffalo, Miami and the Greater Los Angeles area. From personal experience I can attest that such courtliness persisted in these original immigrants after many years in this country.

And so the tillers of an impoverished land in Italy's southern provinces and Sicily came to Western Pennsylvania and settled in our town. They were masters of the *zappa*, the combination pick-hoe used to cultivate the barren land back home. For the most part they were illiterate, but these *zappatori* had the muscle and the hardiness to wield the American-style pick and shovel in all phases of construction work. They would become the Americans who did the digging, hammering, chopping, sawing, and lifting; they hauled rocks, dressed stone and chiseled chunks of marble. They would shovel coke and iron ore for 12 hours in the steel mills, or disappear for 12 hours at a stretch in dank coal mine shafts, or as "gandy

---

[7] Norman Douglas, Old Calabria 112 (1956)

dancers" on the railroads–lifting rails, replacing ties and shoveling ballast 12 months of the year.

The coastal Sicilians came with additional skills. In the homeland, they not only grew their produce, *la frutta e verdura*, but they had mastered mercantile skills as well. Not only could most of these farmer-merchants read and write, but they worked wonders with arithmetic, possessing a native sense of business acumen developed over the centuries on an island that had depended upon trade and commerce for its very existence. Sicilians are Italians, but more so; they are also the product of the centuries of occupations--Greek, Arabic, Spanish, Norman, German, Scandinavian and French. You see this even in the food they ate. You must not confuse the garlic and tomato sauces of Naples with the Sicilian cuisine that their immigrants carried with them to America, a cuisine reflecting historic Arab influences on the island -- raisins, pine nuts, almonds and super sweet desserts spiced with cinnamon, sesame, almond and pumpkin.

When the fruit growers arrived in the States, they carried traditions with them and soon opened corner fruit stands. All the produce markets in Carnegie were owned by Sicilians.

That is how I remember many Italian immigrants in Carnegie in the Twenties when I was growing up. In their "free" time they worked in their gardens and grew tomatoes, beans, lettuce and peppers. Compared to the hardscrabble back home, the lush Pennsylvania soil produced miracles.

But still another class of immigrants came. Although many of them originated in the devitalized hill towns, they were not the unskilled *zappatori* or *campagnoli*; they had learned a trade in the *paese*. They were the *artigani*, tradesmen who generally finished five years of education in the primitive schools, and at the age of nine or ten were parceled out after school hours to work for a tailor, barber, stonemason or carpenter. They swept floors, ran errands, and observed the "master" at work, sometimes assisting in basic tasks. By the age of twelve they were able to start a full-time, and generally unpaid, apprenticeship. They carried these skills to America. In Carnegie, the Italians soon replaced all the other barbers, with the exception of Cy Heney who was an African-American. All tailors in Carnegie were Italian, and my father was to be one of them. Sixteen years old and penniless when he arrived, within two years he had his own shop and had apprentices of his own.

The women would soon come. The men had sent for them, because although the labor on the job or mill or mine was arduous, the men soon recognized that the Carnegie life style was far more comfortable than that experienced in the *paese;* and that an exquisite hope for the future lay here and not in the old country. Through the informal network, the word had come to the hill towns that America offered the magnificent opportunity for entire families to start a new life.

An old saying in the *Mezzogiorno* became the practice in America as well:

"The father is the head of the family, and the mother, the center."

Once transplanted, the women were not the sorrowful, black clad figures as they often appeared in the old country. They were better dressed, better looking and as intelligent as the men. If the average immigrant was a day laborer, his wife was of the managerial class. The father turned over his earnings to her for complete management, keeping only a small allowance for his daily needs. It was she who organized the home, who gave birth to and looked after the children, cooked and cleaned and did the marketing. She washed the clothes on Monday and ironed on Tuesday. She saw to it that the children got to school on time, had their bath on Saturday night and appeared at Sunday mass in starched shirts and dresses. The man brought home the cash, tended to his garden in spring and summer, bought the grapes at harvest time, made his wine in October and his sausage in November and December. In the house, the wife did everything else.

If friends and relatives were coming for Sunday dinner or a holiday or a Christening, it was she who planned and prepared the meal. She knew when the bread or cake was to come out of the oven, when the soup was to be placed on the table, when the water had come to a boil at the proper time for the pasta, when the roast was to come out from the oven with the potatoes, when the salad had to be carried to the table, when the homemade cake was to be served with a flourish and coffee tendered piping hot. She knew the final ritual: to bring out the fruit, freshly washed, and the cheese that accompanied it.

She attended no culinary school to learn all this. Her teachers had been her mother and grandmothers. She was the mistress of the kitchen, and a whole lot more. She was the willing participant in the somewhat apocryphal scenario that the man was the absolute master of the house. He may have been on the lowest rung of the social scale in the community, the most servile day laborer with the most demeaning, degrading, ignoble occupation in the work force, but once he crossed the threshold of his house he became *un uomo di rispetto,* a man of magnificent respect. And his wife made this possible.

She made it possible by following centuries of tradition that if the man was the breadwinner and supported his family and treated them moderately well, he had to be accorded total respect and obedience. This did not make him an absolute despot within the confines of his home, for here the innate sophistication of the rustic woman from *la campagna* came into play. The kitchen was the exclusive and unconditional domain of the woman; if not a principality it was at least a protectorate, vigorously administered by its monarch. The man was the boss of the whole house, but the woman reigned supreme in the kitchen. And because the kitchen was the center of all family life--it was here where the children were kept as infants and where they felt comfortable during their childhood, and it was at the kitchen table where the mother and father had their coffee and talked about the day's happenings after the children had gone to bed--the allocation of the ultimate authority to the man was more evanescent than real. Yes, the man was master of the house except for the kitchen, but all life in the house was centered in the kitchen.

It was the mother who bestowed upon the father the figure of respect in the eyes of the children. They were made to understand from the earliest age that the father could do no wrong. Tradition dictated that the mother would not tolerate any criticism of the father by the children. In practice, if the mother concurred with the child's complaint, it was the mother who communicated the "suggestion" to the father with consummate diplomacy yet firmness, in the guise that it was coming only from her.

It must be said with great truth and force that the wife waited on the Italian husband hand and foot, but this devotion was even more embellished when it came to treatment of her children, especially her sons. The girl child was singled out for training. By the age of ten she had to learn the rudiments of cooking and baking. At an even earlier age she was expected to do know how to clean the house, do laundry and wash and dry dishes.

While the girls were doing all this, the boys were pampered by the mother. To the mother it was demeaning for boys to do "women's" work; those were chores to be performed by their sisters. The son's role in life was to receive an education and to get a good job. The Italian mother was determined that, if at all possible, the sons had to be trained to earn more money at less arduous physical labor than their father. She was the straw boss who constantly emphasized the importance of education and insisted that boys complete high school if at all possible. Not formally educated herself, the immigrant mother measured everything in dollars and cents insofar as educating her sons was concerned. It was not for the purpose of broadening their horizons of knowledge in the abstract, or for cultural enhancement. It was solely for heightening employment opportunities.

To coddle the son and attend to his every whim was one thing, but unfortunately, the doting mother syndrome produced an extremely unfortunate parochial and provincial sociological effect when the son was old enough to look upon the opposite sex with interest. The mother had ground rules: the girl had to be of Italian descent, being a Catholic was not enough. The girl had to be Italian because only an Italian girl, trained in the tradition, knew how to cook for her son, how to wash and iron his clothes and make his bed, how to keep a proper house and how to extend to her son at all times the proper respect. A matter of intense feeling, it was an ingrained fervently, passionately, profoundly held belief that was not subject to rational discourse. The future happiness of her son was at stake, and if entreaties to her son were of no avail, there was recourse to novenas at church, prayers to St. Anthony, and supplications to Our Lady of Nice Italian Girls.

We saw in place a double standard. When it came to the daughter's association with a man, an Italian man was preferred, but if the non-Italian demonstrated that he loved and respected the daughter, his ancestral heritage was no absolute barrier. But with the daughters, the sociological problem was more with the father than the mother: Nice Italian girls did not go out with boys; the American custom of "dating" was not for Italian girls. Girls who did date were "loose." The daughter had to meet a nice boy at church and, if the father knew the family well, then the families could arrange social events where the young folks could meet in the presence of the parents or aunts and uncles as chaperones. Here, the father was adhering to the ways of the *campanilismo*, the traditions of the *paese*. In Carnegie it took some years for fathers to be dislodged of these medieval notions, but when the barriers came toppling down, it was as much through the intervention of the mothers who recognized the frustrations and unhappiness of the daughters, as it was for the yearnings of the daughters to be free of the "old ways."

The barriers came down more easily in a small town like Carnegie than in the Eastern Seaboard where the Italian colonies were much larger. In Carnegie the daughter could effectively ask, "Who is there in this town for me to show some interest? Give me three names that you feel are good enough for me." And here the father was stumped because in his mind no one was good enough for his daughter. He simply did not know, or did not want to be committed as to who was good enough for his daughter. Slowly, the mother would rock on her chair and, referring to the daughter would quietly say *"da` ragione alla figlia"*--the daughter is right; she speaks with good reasoning.

But with her sons it was always a different matter: They could not possibly be happy, they could not be extended the slavish attention conferred upon them by doting mothers unless they married an Italian girl. Just like their mother.

The Aldisert household was not a typical immigrant family for discrete reasons:
- First, my father had migrated when he was 16; his childhood had been in the *paese*, but he reached his maturity in the United States. His work in the Coroner's Office and his avocation (politics) brought him into daily communication with lawyers, physicians, the police, judges and the public-at-large. He was indeed an Italian-American, but in most ways, he was much more American than Italian.
- Second, although of immigrant parents, my mother was born in the United States, had attended eight years of school under the direction of Irish Catholic nuns and three years in the public high school in

Steubenville, Ohio and had been an excellent student. She was an accomplished pianist and organist. She loved to sing, had perfect pitch, and, with her sister, Lena, knew the complete scores and librettos of *La Traviata* and *La Boheme* as well as the great classical and popular standards.

- Our house was not bi-lingual, as my father deliberately choose to perfect his English. At home he spoke Italian only when conversing with friends or by phone or when he talked with his two sisters.

- My father read five newspapers daily, the three Pittsburgh dailies and Italian language papers, *Il Progresso*, out of New York and *Il Popolo* from Philadelphia. He also subscribed to the *Saturday Evening Post* and *Collier's* magazines.

- My father did not suffer fools gladly, was impatient with superstitions, intolerant of prejudices and customs of the *paese* that ran counter to a modern American lifestyle. In retrospect, he was a pioneer in women's liberation. Yet he had a passionate belief that the cultural inheritances of Italy--law, art, music, food, literature, science, engineering from the Roman times through the Renaissance era--should be incorporated into the American way of life. He had an all-pervasive, abiding pride in his Italian ancestry.

- He was a true *paterfamilias* and demanded to know what the children did each day, or more important, what we thought about things. The forum was the dinner table. The family ate together and this was a command performance. No kitchen snacks here or taking a plate to our room or outside. The evening and Sunday dinner served as a family forum. My father led the discussion of current events, and even from the third grade on, we had to jump in with dialogues of history and geography, for dad and mother would invariably inquire, "Now, what did you learn in school today?"

Thus, the great paradox: Although labeled Italians by our neighbors and friends, the Aldisert family carried little sociological or behavioral baggage characteristic of many Italian immigrant families. There was a solid reason for this. My father was born Italian, but became a self-educated American from the day he landed at Ellis Island at the age of 16. My mother was born in Ohio of Italian parents, but was a voracious reader, starting in her childhood. And they, especially dad, adopted what Gunnar Myrdal described as the American Creed in 1944 in *The American Dilemma*. Although emphasizing the racial, religious, ethnic, regional and economic diversity in this country, he argued that Americans had "something in common: a social *ethos*, a political creed." He said this was "the essential dignity of the individual human being, of the fundamental equality of all men, and of certain inalienable rights to freedom, justice, and a fair opportunity."

When dad talked at the dinner table, he constantly made the point that although we were Roman Catholics, the men and women who settled this country in the 17th century and the men who framed the Declaration of Independence and drafted the Constitution were Protestants and these men emphasized that "All Men are Created Equal" and equality of opportunity. "You don't find these principles anywhere in Europe except in England, certainly not in Italy," dad would often say, and the prescient comment, "When you come down to it, these are Protestant values that make possible government protection of Catholics and Jews and others who are not Protestants."

My parents ridiculed superstitions of the *paese* that were transported to these shores. Endemic among many immigrants was the *malocchio*, "the evil eye," a belief that illness or bad luck could be traced to somebody's having cast the evil eye upon you. Thus, if one would extend a complimentary statement to another, like commenting how attractive a baby or a child was, the speaker had to immediately punctuate his or her remarks with a *"grazie di Dio*, a "God bless" and "Thanks be to God." Absent the invocation of the deity to attest to the truthfulness of the statement, the utterance, although complimentary, was not only suspect, but judged to be a casting of the evil eye. There was a defense to *malocchio* that could be employed to fend off the spell. One could openly or covertly extend the proper hand signal---extending the hand with index and little finger projecting and the three other fingers clasped. This was a time-tested technique to deflect wicked and mischievous consequences.

Then, too, there were the practitioners who could treat adverse physical symptoms, especially headaches, obviously caused by the evil eye and not by physiological reasons. The practitioner was usually female and she was possessed with power to restore the patient to good health or, at a minimum, to predict the course of the unwellness. A cold table knife or spoon across the forehead was an accepted practice, although the results never made the pages of the New England Journal of Medicine. To predict the length of the indisposition, the practitioner dropped olive oil in water in a soup dish. If the oil formed a circle in the water, the prognosis was a temporary indisposition; if the oil took the form of scattered spots, it forecast long-term consequences. The "skill" was passed down from mother to daughter, and also transportable, from Southern Italy to the United States.

Other superstitions added to the home-grown American varieties of bad luck superstitions: placing a loaf of bread upside down, whether on a table or in storage; continuing to walk or ride when a black cat crossed one's path--to avoid the hex a woman had either to change direction or halt until another person or carriage went forward. Seeing a female hunchback was bad luck and could be avoided only by touching iron, a key in your pocket would do, or if you were of the male sex, by touching your genitals, but seeing a male hunchback was always good luck. It was bad luck to spill salt and this could be vitiated by taking a pinch and throwing it over your left shoulder. You never poured anything except palm down in the direction of your thumb; to do otherwise was an indication that you were a traitor to someone present.

The Southern Italian infatuation with the Madonna was also carried across the sea. In the old country you could not depend upon the individual saints to help you. There was historical proof of this. When the various city states waged war with each other, each warring faction had its own patron saint. Because invariably one side always lost, the reasoning went that you just couldn't depend on those male or female saints. It was necessary to turn to a universal wonder worker, who could be all things to all people. So they appealed to the Virgin Mary. She was venerated, however, not as the

Mother of God, but as a demi-god endowed with vast powers in her own right. And thus came to pass a Madonna with at least 300 personalities.

She could not be one person to all people, so she became the object of specialized venerations, like the Madonna of the Big Hill, or the Madonna of Rainy Weather or the Madonna of the Good Olive Harvest. She became the an accessible wonder-worker attached to a particular district or phenomenon. An inhabitant of Lungro would stand a poor chance of his prayers getting answered by the Madonna of Vastogirardi. If a man had a headache, it was no use applying to the Madonna of the Hens, who dealt with diseases of women. You would find yourself in a pretty fix if you expected financial assistance from the Madonna of the Mountain when everyone knew that she was a weather specialist. In that case you had to pray to the Madonna of the Payroll or Our Lady of the California Lottery.

The Madonna played a dominant role in all things good or bad. When things did not work out right, like when you didn't hit on the numbers, the fault was never yours, it was always that of the ever present demi-god, and you vented your frustration with the popular Italian curse, "*porca Madonna*" ("the Mother of God is a pig!"). Many people did not want to learn anything about their saints or Madonnas or deities or to argue about them. They only wished to love and have good luck and be loved and protected in return, reserving to themselves the right to punish their deities when their deities deserved it. Hence the popular *porca* curse. Countless cases are on record where pictures or statues of Our Lady had been thrown into a ditch for not doing what they were told, or for not keeping their share of the bargain. During the Vesuvius eruption of 1906 a goodly number were subjected to this punishment, as well as after the Reggio Calabria and Messina earthquake because Our Lady and other saints failed to protect their worshipers from the calamity. After all, so many candles were lit, so many festivals were held, yet so little protection was forthcoming from Our Lady. "She" had breached the contract..

Our family never got too involved in the Madonna cult. We had one rather modest statue at home, perched on top of a book case in the living room, but this was St. Elizabeth of Hungary that my father had picked up somewhere in honor of his wife. The story went that St. Elizabeth had been the wife of the king of Hungary and she wanted to help the poor, but the mean old king would not let her. One day she slipped out of the castle with loaves of bread hidden under her robe. She was caught by the king. "What are you hiding there?" he demanded, and when the queen demurred he opened the outer garment and lo and behold the loaves had been transformed into a bouquet of flowers. Our St. Elizabeth statute showed her holding the flowers.

Mother was the religious leader in our house, but in time of need, she did not rely on lesser authorities like saints. She went straight to The Boss. An intercession could be forthcoming only if God was willing. "*Se Dio vuole.*" Only God, not His angels and His saints.

The Italian language was also used as euphemisms in certain Italian families to discuss some subjects where English would have been taboo. When we were very little, my grandmother referred to us as *piscialetti* (those who wet the bed); or *caccasotto* (one who has a diaper full.)

But it bears repetition that the home of John and Elizabeth Aldisert was not the home of the typical immigrant. As emphasized before, my mother was born here, and my father came here as a young teen-ager, and immediately established his own tailoring trade. He soon became more American than Italian. One of his customers was a Carnegie lawyer, James H. Duff, who was the town's Republican leader and who would later become Pennsylvania's Attorney General, and still later, its governor. Mr. Duff introduced my father to the political process and John S. Aldisert soon became recognized as a political leader of the Italians in Carnegie.

My father received much joy in recounting an incident in which Mr. Duff admonished him for taking a highly visible role in a particular election campaign. "John," Mr. Duff said, "I want you to maintain a lower profile, because I know that you are not old enough to vote." To which my father replied, "That's alright, Mr. Duff, don't worry. I'm not even a citizen yet!" James Duff would later become my father's political sponsor in 1923 when dad was appointed as a Deputy Coroner of Allegheny County, thus initiating his professional career that spanned 33 years.

America entered the Twenties with the Volstead Act and the Eighteenth Amendment on the books--the Prohibition era. Substantially condemned throughout the United States, Prohibition was especially anathema to the

Italian immigrants. Drinking wine was an inherent part of their daily life style. It was also part of the culture of France and Spain but the French and the Spaniards had not migrated to the United States in the millions. The Italians refused to obey laws that they deemed silly. With the advent of the bootlegging, it was not surprising the original group who manufactured and distributed illicit spirits were Americans of Italian descent because they had a ready market for their wares. Soon the bootleggers found an expanded market among other Americans and in time bootlegging was dominated by Italian immigrants in most metropolitan areas. Carnegie was no exception, except that the bootlegging was generally localized in small neighborhoods. I remember the moonshine stills set up in houses below us on the hill. When the prevailing winds blew from the east to the west, up the valley, we had no problems. On the occasions when a north wind came our way, however, problems arose. The change of the wind carried the zesty, astringent stench of sour mash. And we had to contend with this until the normal wind flow returned.

The several local bootleggers whom we would see in church on Sundays, operated retail outlets of Golden Wedding, a popular rye whiskey, and familiar labels of scotch, transported from Canada through Niagara Falls or Buffalo down the highway bordering Lake Erie through the northwest corner of Pennsylvania, and then via Route 19 to Pittsburgh.

Other than bootlegging in the Twenties, in the decades that followed there was not much Italian American organized crime in the Western Pennsylvania area. To be sure, there were the area "books" (groups that ran the numbers lottery based on the last three digits of the total stock sale on the New York Stock Exchange that paid $7.20 to a penny) that operated throughout Pittsburgh neighborhoods and Allegheny County towns. The numbers game, being neighborhood based, was not dominated by any particular ethnic group. It was a kind of Equal Opportunity Employment illegal business, winked at by the authorities and according to the ethnic neighborhood operated by Italians, African-Americans, Slavs, Irish and "100% Americans."

Among Americans of Italian descent, bootleggers constituted the organized crime that flourished in the Twenties and early Thirties. The illegal operations in Western Pennsylvania did no compare with the stereotypical "crime families" of Boston, New York, New Jersey and Philadelphia. We were spared the wide spread corruption of the East

Coast Mafia or Cosa Nostra with its widespread domination of extortion, loan sharking, domination in building supply industries, construction work, trucking companies, prostitution and infiltration into the labor movement.

And thereby hangs a tale. During the height of the depression several representatives of New York crime families came to Pittsburgh and met with the top bootleggers. They sought "permission" to operate in Pittsburgh and Western Pennsylvania. The leading bootleggers turned them down flat. "We have a good thing going on. The general public tolerates our breaking the law because they consume our wine, beer and whiskey. This is a city of hardworking steelworkers with families and children and we do not want your rackets here."

The emissaries returned to New York, but returned time and time again to try to persuade the bootleggers, to no avail. The New Yorkers then made threats, said that they would be back, and expected a yes answer at that time. Several of these New York emissaries returned on the appointed day planning to make an offer that could not be refused. While enjoying their expressos in a Wylie Avenue coffee shop prior to the time of the expected meeting, some other "customers" walked in, and opened up with Thompson sub-machine guns.

The New York crime family got the message. They never came back.

Following the bootlegging era, organized crime in Greater Pittsburgh took the form of the "numbers." The police and district attorneys took a very pragmatic view of numbers operations. No politician could be elected or stay in office if he or she called for the outright ban on numbers. The brute fact was that a majority of the voters played the lottery; it was known as "the poor man's stock market." The compromise with law and order afficionados was that no numbers operator was permitted to function in too large an area. He was not permitted to grow too big or to conduct the business city-wide or over a large county area. Numbers were illegal, but so long as it functioned in a small neighborhood area, no serious attempts were made to break it up. Writing numbers flourished until state lotteries took hold, and like bootlegging, it, too, lost their illegal business when the nature of their activity became legitimate.

Nor did organized crime make any headway into organized labor. Had they even attempted to muscle in, the union members would have bashed in their heads and sent them packing back to New York City. It must be remembered that Pittsburgh was always a bastion of organized labor, first in the craft unions of the AFL, and later as the birthplace of the industrial unionism in the United States, the Committee of Industrial Organizations, later the Congress of Industrial Organizations, the CIO. Prior to the CIO, all unions were organized by particular crafts in a company. Industrial unions placed all workers of an industry in one unions, regardless of the task. The labor movement in Western Pennsylvania was hard driving and scrapping and militant and although it struggled bitterly with management, the union officers were basically honest. With one or two exceptions, extortion and labor racketeering, mainstays of the organized crime in the East, did not get off the ground in Greater Pittsburgh.

The reputation of the average American of Italian descent has been cursed by the Mafia. The Mafia's dramatic deeds which are popularized in books, movies, radio, and television--have cast a long shadow. Criminal deeds from Al Capone in Chicago to the New York, New Jersey and Philadelphia families spawned the image that crime is dominated by one ethnic group, and therefore if you are of this ancestry, you lack law-abiding tendencies. Logicians call this the fallacy of hasty generalization. This image has been the cause of widespread discrimination against Americans of Italian origin even though, statistically, the exact opposite is true. A recent estimate is that there are about 20,000,000 Americans who can trace their ancestry to one person of Italian descent, and it is generously estimated that, at its peak, the Mafia had about 4,000 members in various "families" throughout the United States. The sins of one out of 5,000 are being visited upon an entire sector of American society.

The Italian immigrant did not bring with him any concept of community group activity. No social, fraternal, civic or charitable organizations existed in the tiny towns in which they lived in the old country. When the Italian immigrants arrived here, they brought no experience in collective or cooperative endeavors. They not only lacked organizational skills, and the understanding of compromise inherent in group cooperation, but originally they had no desire to organize as a social or political force.

In the new world, their primitive efforts to organize group activities took the form of neighborhood club houses where they could meet in the evening with their *connazionali*, to play cards---*briscoli* and *tre sette* were the most popular games---to play the game of *bocce* (lawn bowls) in neat courts illuminated for night play. Their clubhouse was their cantina where they drank their wine.

They had both a distrust for and lack of familiarity with insurance companies, so they organized many of these neighborhood clubs along the lines of *mutuo sicorso*, mutual help, where for a few cents a week each member contributed to a mortuary benefit fund that would pay $500 as a death benefit, this sum representing the cost of a funeral and burial plot. The clubs were very parochial or provincial--sometimes membership was limited to those from the same home town, but more often than not, from the same province or region. These clubs continued until well into the middle of the Twentieth century.

With the breakdown of Italian districts in urban areas and the movement to suburbia and the aging, if not disappearance of the immigrant generation, these clubs disappeared, or were assimilated into the two major fraternal organizations–the Italian Sons and Daughters of America and the Sons of Italy.

The immigration generation, as once I knew it so well, is now gone. Yet their magnificent contributions are legion. Recorded elsewhere are accounts of rising from ditch digger to general contractor, from corner store to huge mercantile establishment. But their greatest accomplishment was to instill in their children the absolute necessity to become American and pursue the American dream. To become assimilated into the mainstream as much as possible, to learn the English language, to venerate the work ethic and give 100 percent at your job, to obtain the best education possible, to marry well, to own a house, to feed and nourish your children. To become an American in the fullest sense, yet at the same time be a guardian of a rich cultural heritage of a lineage that can be traced back to the time of the Romans.

My father, John S. Aldisert, Chief Deputy Coroner, Allegheny County (Pittsburgh) Pennsylvania pictured at his desk in the 1940's.

The family in 1933. My sister Adrienne was 8 years old. Along with her brothers, she, too, graduated from the University of Pittsburgh, served for a time as Assistant Dean of Women and then as a secretary in various corporate executive offices. She married Dr. Elmo F. Massucci, a neurologist with the Veteran's Administration in Washington, D.C., and adjunct instructor at the Georgetown University Medical School. They made their home in Chevy Chase, Maryland.

Mother and dad in 1940.

In 1954 at the age of 34 I was elected national president of the Order Italian Sons and Daughters of America (ISDA), and served in that capacity for 14 years. A major problem facing Americans of Italian origin was the implication that most, if not all, Americans of Italian descent were law breakers because of the publicity given Al Capone and the New York Mafia families. My organization led campaigns demanding that the federal government use maximum efforts to destroy organized crime. Cy Hungerford, famed *Pittsburgh Post Gazette* cartoonist, assisted our campaign with the above editorial cartoon entitled "Taking a Bad Rap." Although the ISDA national office was in Pittsburgh, during we expanded grearly, maintaining or initiating new lodges in Ohio, Western New York,

Florida, West Virginia, Southern California, Brooklyn, Long Island, Windsor, Canada, as well as Pennsylvania. We published a weekly full-sized four-page newspaper, *Unione*, originally bi-lingual and later solely in English, distributed to all members. We established a cultural heritage foundation and a fraternal benefits life insurance society that in 2004 had assets of over $20 million.

Chapter Ten
Growing Up Eating

Italian food in the United States is now commonplace and treated as a gourmet delight. This has not always been so. In the Twenties only Italians in America, or guests in their houses, ate Italian food. The corner grocery stores did not carry lines of pasta, olive oil, garlic, exotic cheeses, olives, sausage, salami, basil, squid, anchovies, canned Italian tomatoes, rosemary or tomato paste. No commercial pizza, no pizzerias existed. Commercial pizza did not appear on the American scene until after World War II. Unless you visited an Italian grocery, you could buy only two brands of Italian food--canned Heinz spaghetti or the Franco-American brand. The canned spaghetti was overcooked and mushy; the antonym of *al dente,* and the tomato sauce had a strong ketchup flavor. Ketchup!

But every community with a sizeable Italian population had at least one Italian grocery. Carnegie had a fair number--Basilio Morelli in East Carnegie, Jack Silvestri and Enzo Capoferri on Arch Street, Saracena's on East Main at Washington, and Joe Roman and Isaia Battistelli on West Main. The tell-tale symbol, as olfactory as visual, was the ever present *baccalá*, the dried cod fish, that seemed to hang everywhere or displayed open in wooden boxes. *Baccalá* was very popular because it was very cheap and refrigeration of seafood had not yet been perfected. Most Italians were Catholics and the Friday no-meat edict of the American bishops was meticulously observed.

Magnificent cheeses competed for attention. Massive rounds of *parmigiana, romano,* and *pecorino,* dominated the back counter, always in the open because they were in demand daily as the mainstay for pasta and did not require refrigeration. The ever popular *provolone* took the form of many shapes--royal torpedoes hanging from the ceiling, accompanied by their attendants, some as twine wrapped balls and cylinders. The mighty *provolone* was king, the mainstay for sandwiches, especially with hot and fatty *capacola.*

Mozzarella, not the yellow hard kind now found in supermarkets or used for pizza, but the soft white ball wrapped in waxed paper and stored in liquid, but always in the refrigerated case. Sometimes you could find the very good stuff made with buffalo milk. Always the pungent *gorganzola,* elder statesman of the cheese family, older brother of roquefort, more aged, more runny, more powerful.

The Italian store was an extravaganza of sights and smells. Pasta came in twenty pound wooden boxes and you bought it loose in long 24 inch strands. The grocer had to break spaghetti or spaghettini or linguini or perciatelli in half to have it weighed on the scale and put in a paper bag. Other wooden boxes contained, ziti (we called them sewer pipes), penne and mostacciolli. Rigatoni was another matter, it had to lifted out of the box with a scoop. Barrels of olives stood guard-- all kinds, black ones dried and cured in olive oil and hot pepper, and green ones of all sizes

Perched on top of the counter was a large open and aromatic can of *alici,* anchovies, which too, were sold by the ounce or sometimes appeared in small oval-shaped tins with an opening key that never seemed to work. On the display in the refrigerated counter were the various salamis–Genoa, or smaller versions, *soprassata,* hard and fatty made from a pig's head and always *capacola. Prosciuto* was available for those who could afford it; it had to be cut very thin from the side of the specially cured ham from Parma, Italy. Here, too, protected from the heady aromas of other cheeses was the delicate *ricotta,* sold in bulk, as still is the custom in Italy today.

We bought Italian bread and rolls from Benvenuto's, the local Italian baker, on Railroad Street near Harding School, or from Cirrone's, the larger bakery in Bridgeville, a few miles up the road. We couldn't handle store-bought white bread. "It has no crust! It's good for toast only!" went the lament. Bertolli olive oil came in rectangular gallon cans; getting a smaller size can made no sense because we used it every day for cooking and salads. We always had wine vinegar, for it was the only kind for salads, and if the store did not have it, we used the dregs of home-made wine. We stocked up with cans of *tonno*, tuna fish, Italian-packed in virgin olive oil, that we dumped from the can directly on to the plate and mixed with white onion slices. We didn't buy gnocchi or ravioli or pizza, for these were *fatta in casa* (homemade) and not sold in stores. And to make the proper sauce for pasta you had to buy canned tomatoes packed in Italy. Canned tomatoes sold by the A & P could not produce the necessary flavor.

Italians in Carnegie always ate well, even during the depression. Often the objects of derision, and subject to various forms of discrimination and slights, we ate like kings compared to the general Carnegie population. "We" knew it, but "they" didn't. A senseless rhyme that was often thrown our way comes to mind, even after 80 years:

Hunky, dago,
sheeney, wop.
I eat chicken
You eat slop.

It wasn't until I started to visit Italy, and especially its south, from which most of the Italian-Americans originated, that I learned that there is a difference between Italian cooking and Italian-American cooking. Italian-American cooking is much more elaborate than in the old country. For the most part Italians came to this country from sad hill towns of the Abruzzi, Campania, Puglia, Basilicata, Calabria and Sicilia. Economic refugees, they were forced to migrate because, as previously explained, the proliferation of families made it impossible for the limited family hectares to support grand-children and great grandchildren and great-great grandchildren of the original property owners. Living in poverty in the hill towns, they had their daily pasta, but seldom did the sauce contain meat. Meat was too scarce. It was served only on holidays or in the form of home-made sausage and salami and *soprassata*, prepared from occasional slaughter of a limited number of family pigs. The universal popularity of spaghetti and meat balls is more an American phenomenon than Italian. Italian immigrants were thrilled to purchase beef, veal, and pork because, unlike in the old country, these were always available and inexpensive enough to prepare lavish meat dishes, heavy sauces and to treat themselves to meat dishes in a style of splendor unknown in the *paese* thousands of miles away.

So here we ate well. We hadn't heard of cholesterol and triglycerides and low sodium in the Twenties. Our mothers were told that lots of milk and eggs and bacon and fatty red meat were good for kids and they did us proud.

My mother's people were Abruzzese, a region that was west, not south, of Rome where the inhabitants were expert cooks and accustomed to eat better than their neighbors to the South. Their mountainous region was filled with deer and wild boar, and upper verdant pastureland furnished an abundance of fine natural ingredients for the great regional dishes. It was to be expected that the Aldisert kitchen would follow the Abruzzese traditions--home made *tagliarini, gnocchi* and a special thin pasta cut in two inch squares popular in my maternal grandparents' home town of Vastogirardi and known as *tacca'nelli*. To make this mother created a thin pasta sheet on a large wooden square, rolled with an ancient broom handle lovingly known as the pasta stick (and sometimes used as a cudgel in disciplining her sons). A special light tomato sauce only was used for this delicacy flavored with chicken, including chicken feet.

Sunday dinner at home was more than a meal; it was a ritual. It started at around 2 p.m. with pasta, heaps of it, store bought spaghettini, ziti, fusilli, rigatoni, perciatelli, linguini, or home-made taglialini, ravioli, or gnocchi. My brother and I always had seconds. And the pasta was just the beginning. Next came roast – beef, pork, veal, lamb, or chicken--with accompanying roast potatoes. Another course then appeared, consisting of the meat used in the tomato sauce, the *ragu,* which was served with a green vegetable, usually peas or green beans. A green salad – lettuce or dandelion or endive – always with oil and wine vinegar dressing, came as a change of pace, and dessert was a must--usually home-made cake or pie or cookies, and always fruit and sometimes cheese. My father and mother always had wine. As we kids grew older we had wine as well, at first diluted with water, but later full strength. When Italian kids reached high school age, very few got excited about the "new" spectacle of surreptiously drinking wine and booze. Very few of us drank to excess, because to us drinking hard liquor was not a novel experience.

Italians were creatures of habit in Carnegie. Mother always washed clothes on Monday and this was a day-long operation, long before automatic washers appeared. It required manual soaking in one of the twin laundry tubs, rinsing in the other and then running the clothes through the ringer. No automatic drier in those days, the clothes were hung out to dry either outdoors or indoors, depending on the weather. This left little time to cook an elaborate meal, so we usually had our "American" meal on Monday--steak and mashed potatoes and salad. In later years, I was sometimes faced with the kidding on the square in a contrived Italian accent: "Rugi, you like-a da spaghett?" I would answer, "You're damn right. At our house, we eat your American steak and potatoes on wash day!"

Tuesday and Wednesday were optional days. On one of these days, summer or winter, our main course was soup, more often than not with a beef stock and tiny *ditalini*. The meat course consisted of boiled beef with a vegetable. Sometimes, we had what is now called "wedding soup." This was a massive operation. It was necessary first to make a chicken broth with most of the hen. Some of the chicken meat was reserved, to be put in the grinder to make tiny meat balls. At the appropriate time, the meat was removed from the soup and endive placed in the broth. In the meantime in another pot *acini di pepi* or *pastina* was put to boil and later put in with the endive. My mother prepared small squares of French toast to serve as croutons which she placed in the huge soup bowl at the last minute before she triumphantly paraded it into the dining room. It is known as "wedding soup" today, not so much as a celbratory gesture, but to make a special event because it took so much time to make it more often. With all the time required for preparing it at home, I report that Campbell's is now selling a commercial version "Italian Wedding Soup" that I consider first rate.

If not soup as a main course, we had a roast of some kind--veal, lamb, beef, always flavored with generous cloves of garlic wrapped in parsley, and much, much natural gravy. Thursday, we returned to pasta with meat sauce in healthy portions. The meat in the *ragu* varied. Sometimes it was simply large cubes of veal and pork, sometimes beef in combination with pork. At our house pork was considered the best flavor and we very seldom had a sauce prepared with beef alone. A special treat were meat balls, made with a combination of ground pork and beef, breadcrumbs, eggs and garlic. And sometimes there was a glorious *bracciola*, a single cut of round steak that was covered with hard boiled eggs, flavored bread crumbs and parsley and garlic and then rolled and tied with string. Although serving as the main flavor for the pasta *sugo*, this was served as a magnificent course in itself, a loaf regally sliced and garnished with peas.

Friday was a disaster. Because we were about 400 miles form the nearest seashore and lacked air delivery or refrigerated trucks, fresh fish was not available in Pittsburgh; seafood was flaccid and rancid, but Catholic discipline prevailed. When I was growing up even the day after Thanksgiving, we simply did not eat meat on Friday. It was a mortal sin, requiring I suppose the same penance as murder. As expert a cook as my mother was, she could not prepare broiled or fried fish that passed muster. An exception was *merluzzo in umido*, a cod fish baked in tomato and onion. It was a welcome relief when mother prepared *calamari*, or a pasta made with a tuna fish sauce, or *aglia e olio* (garlic and oil and red pepper).

Saturday dinner was the lightest meal of the week. We acknowledged the sparseness as a necessary prelude to the gargantuan Sunday dinner. We had hot dogs, or sandwiches--ham or "party lunch," a concoction of ground ham, pickles and mayonnaise. We ate in a hurry, for this was the night to take our weekly bath and dress up for the promenade "down street." Saturday night was always dress up time in Carnegie. Sometimes, we'd have pizza, and this was homemade by my mother. Mother made pizza on the day she baked bread. Her favorite was a topping of anchovies and green onion on the tomato and provolone base.

At least twice a year my father made sausage. All members of the family pitched in, including baby sister Betty Marie. Dad would trim a pork shoulder and cut it into cubes. He was insisted that fat gave sausage its real taste. He first ground the meat with a coarse cutter, mixed it with salt, fennel, and hot pepper and let it set for a while. In the meantime, while the seasoning taking place, some of us would rinse the salt-cured sheep's casing. That chore completed, the seasoning completed, the casing was placed on the grinder now fitted with a fine cutting blade. We took turns on the grinder's handle and the sausage emerged. Dad tied the sausage into links with white thread and then coiled the finished product on the table. The final step was to puncture the casings with a needle. This was done to allow the meat to dry. Because this was before the age of freezers, the sausage was hung high to dry, some in the kitchen, but most among the rafters in the cellar. This was the same way it had been done in Calabria and the Abruzzi for generations.

The total family participation in our home was not an isolated phenomenon. It was a family ritual in all Italian households. Sometimes we broiled the sausage as a Tuesday or Wednesday meat course, or a main ingredient in the *ragu* for pasta, or we'd fry it with eggs for the grandest, most tasteful, and most cholesterol-ridden breakfast one could ask for.

And so I ate my way through childhood. I ate with a profound dislike for what we called "American" food. The arch enemy was sliced store-bought bread; chewing gum bread, we called it in our house, and extended universal pity for those who went through life without regularly eating crusty Italian style or home-made bread. We described sandwiches made with store-bought bread "aspirins" because they would be gone in a gulp or two. A real sandwich had to be made with Italian bread, my favorite sandwich being fried green peppers and eggs.

We ate well, even in the depression, and with the exception of the many meat courses, what we ate were essentially meals prepared for the most humble of our forebears in the Italian hill towns.

As a child I would never have dreamed that the strange foods of peasant folk of Southern Italy would become the gourmet food of modern America. It would indeed have been an impossible dream to have thought that pizzas, the delicacy my mother always prepared with the left over dough from her bread-making, would in my lifetime surpass the hot dog as our Nation's favorite finger food. Even in my university days before the war, there was nary a pizzaria to be found. You could treat yourself to a slice of pizza only if the lady of the house was baking bread at home that day.

Chapter Eleven
Growing Up in the Depression

You knew that times were bad. You knew it even though you were only ten or eleven years old. You knew it in many ways. You saw groups of men clustered at street corners, idle men just standing there loafing, talking among themselves; men who ordinarily would have been at work. The air in our own smoky city basin was cleaner, for the mills no longer operated at full capacity, and less coal was burned to heat houses. It was quieter. Fewer trains rolled by, rumbles from the rolling mills were muted. Fewer automobiles rattled down the streets.

But most of all, you knew it because every time adults got into a conversation, their talk turned to the depression and how people were hurting. And you knew it when your schoolmates sadly reported that their fathers had been "laid off."

We can talk about recessions of the Seventies, steel mill layoffs of the Eighties, the world wide recession of the Nineties and the economic downturn caused by lack corporate accountability at the start of this century. But compared to the early Thirties even the worst of current times would be the best of times if measured by Great Depression standards.

We had no Social Security payments for the elderly or the disabled. Older employees in the mills and factories were simply cast off. No state unemployment compensation, sweetened by federal funds, took care of you after you were laid off. Primitive private, church and public relief plans helped a little, a very little. We did not have the generous federally funded and state administered welfare plans, regardless of how such programs may be criticized or called into doubt today. Entitlement is what they call it now. No financial aid to dependent children existed in those days. No Medicare. No Medicaid.

Many memories of the depression still persist. In our immediate neighborhood, my father was the only household head who still had a full time job. He was a career self-taught forensic specialist serving as the county's chief deputy coroner. An unmarried school teacher, Dorothy Hiles, lived two doors away and she, too, had full employment. But dad and Miss Hiles were the exceptions. A railroad engineer up the street was lucky to get one day's work out of ten. Maury Strong, (full name Samuel Marcellus Strong, Jr.) who lived next door, a white collar worker for the Pennsylvania Railroad, waited four years before he was called back. Four years of doing nothing. Four years of reading the daily newspaper (three cents), listening to the radio, getting dressed up every evening to walk "down street." Maury's father, Samuel, a 40-year veteran at Columbia Steel and Shafting, was laid off, never recalled, and never received a pension. Mr. Delmar, another neighbor, had been a well-paid union motion picture projectionist and lived in the large red brick house, the Sweethall house, the newest and most impressive one on the block. He, too, was laid off. Theaters had found ways for one projectionist to do the work of three. The Delmar's survived by selling bread baked by Mrs. Delmar with their oldest son, Bill, peddling and delivering it from door to door. We were regular customers. Bill never left our house without my mother giving him a sandwich or something on which to nibble. On one Thanksgiving Day he came to our door while we were eating dinner and we gave him a huge drumstick. As he left I ran to the front door and watched and still remember Bill chomping on the huge turkey leg as he continued his rounds, carrying the bread basket, but now with a spring in his step. His father never was recalled to work; a bank foreclosed on their house. The family moved away and was never heard of again.

Even when the depression hit rock bottom--from 1930 through mid-1936--before President Franklin D. Roosevelt created and activated his Public Works Administration and Works Progress Administration and

GROWING UP IN THE DEPRESSION 153

other pump-priming devices and agencies, even during what we called "the depths" of the depression, Italian families ate well. They ate better than their friends and neighbors. They were able to do this because they returned to the ways of the *paese* in the old country, making nutritious and appetizing meals with less expensive ingredients, with no meat or cheaper cuts. They were able to do this also because most Italian families had gardens in which they grew lettuce, endive, potatoes, cabbages, beans, peas, beets, carrots, and especially, tomatoes. Pasta was the mainstay and it was inexpensive.

Chic restaurants now feature what they herald as gourmet pasta sauces but many of these are dishes that we Italians ate during the depression. A quick sauce of *marinara*--tomatoes, parsley, and garlic; or a sauce plain tomatoes and basil or *'matricciana*, tomatoes, onion, bacon and a pinch of *pepe rossa*. The old standby and *pasta e fagioli*, pasta and beans with a ham bone thrown in for flavor and great *minestra's* with spinach or *escarole* (endive) and beans and carrots and potatoes. We could pick up big beef bones at the butcher's for pennies and with inexpensive pieces of beef chuck, have the makings of great beef soups, flavored with a little tomato and celery, into which you poured various shapes of pasta. Or we had homemade *gnocchi,* one of the most filling of all tasty Italian dishes, and one of the cheapest to prepare--boiled potatoes, flour and an egg. Yes, we Italians ate well.

Yet, you may ask, why didn't non-Italians eat this same Italian food as tasty and as inexpensive and as nutritious as it is? The answer is that Italian food was not a commonplace menu sixty years ago. Today, pizza is known by every child, but if you had asked a non-Italian in the Twenties and Thirties if they knew what pizza was, they would have shrugged their shoulders and said "I dunno."

Today all American children are taught to roll spaghetti with a fork almost as soon as they move from Gerber's baby foods. Yet I remember when kids my age, invited to dinner by us, embarked on maiden spaghetti voyages, struggling to get the hang of twirling, and often in despair giving up and resorting to cutting the strands in small pieces to eat with a spoon. I can still remember my father at the head of the table, smiling and encouraging them on: "Roll them, son, roll them." Nor were their parents more adept in handling spaghetti or other long strands of pasta. Rolling spaghetti with a fork was a trick known only by the Italians, they believed, for often we were described with some affection by our friends as "spaghetti rasslers."

Eating well at home was one of the few bright memories of the depression years. We had the apple sellers on Main Street, forlorn men trying to sell a shiny red apple for a nickel. On the sidewalk in front of the A&P and P.H. Butler stores were 24-pound bags of flour, white bags that bore the logo of the Red Cross. These were distributed to the destitute, and even as a young child, I shared the anguish of proud men shouldering the relief food but walking home, embarrassed, heads down and unsmiling.

Less than ten years after the Ku Klux Klan tried to terrorize Italians and other foreigners, a sociological paradox took place in Carnegie. Families were going hungry, and the Italian priest, Father Ercole Dominicis, and his parishioners determined to do something about it. Our church opened a noon-time soup kitchen to serve the entire town; to serve a hot meal to anyone who was hungry, regardless of age, race, creed or national origin. Parishioners donated ingredients from their gardens. Salvatore Viviano, the owner of the town's macaroni factory, donated his products from time to time. He kept his factory working throughout the depression by greatly reducing wages of his employees. The average wage there was six cents an hour, but the men and women were happy to bring home 60 cents after the ten hour day, or $3.60 at the close of the six-day work week. Struggling retail shop owners occasionally helped out the soup kitchen with cash donations.

The soup line flourished through the depression years, Monday through Saturday, not operating on Sunday because of Sunday masses. Family heads, mostly men, came to the kitchen every day to get their only hot meal of the day. Parishioners encouraged all children to stop by for lunch, school cafeterias being unknown in Carnegie. Men and women took turns at cooking vats of soup and cauldrons of pasta and vegetables, for although it was called a soup kitchen, other hearty dishes were served. The generosity of the Italian families during this critical time was an extremely important factor in bringing about inter-group understanding in the community. Notwithstanding early xenophobic feelings of a few years past, old line inhabitants simply could not continue to bite the hand that was feeding them. It was the only free meal in town and it was hot and nourishing.

Retail prices hit rock bottom during the depression years. A loaf of bread sold for 10 cents, a pound of boiled ham 25 cents, but most people purchased sliced bologna, a ground meat substance that had the texture and taste of a mild weiner, that sold for 15 cents a pound and was familiarly known as "jumbo." It is still a favorite in Pittsburgh. At a diner you could buy a lunch for 15 cents, two hamburgers and a bottle of soda pop. Houses were heated by bituminous (soft) coal; a ton of mine-run coal delivered at $2.50 a ton; if you preferred a better grade of coal it would cost a dollar more. A good quality men's wool suit with vest and two pairs of trousers could be purchased for $21. Daily newspapers were three cents, the Sunday edition was ten cents. Postcards could be mailed for a penny, a letter for two cents. Yet we had home mail delivery twice a day, including Saturdays.

Murphy's and McCrory's, the Five and Ten national chains, flourished. We could buy articles for five and ten cents. For just one nickel you could make a phone call or buy a Coke or an ice cream cone or an Eskimo Pie or a cup of coffee. You could buy a new Chevy coupe for $659 if you could afford it. A pity, too, because gasoline was eleven cents a gallon.

The movies and the radio provided recreation. We saw Westerns at the Lyric, Liberty, and Dixie theaters. Tim McCoy, Ken Maynard, Buck Jones, Richard Dix, William Boyd and the Lone Ranger, had taken over where Tom Mix and Tony left off (Oh, yes, Tony was Tom's horse). A newcomer named John Wayne was becoming popular. Depending upon the feature, admission to a Saturday matinee was either five or ten cents for kids. But for first run movies, you went to the Carnegie Theater where admission was 15 cents until six p.m. and 20 cents thereafter. No movies played on Sunday because the Pennsylvania Blue Laws were still in effect.

I grew up in the golden age of radio. Stand up comedians made us laugh--Jack Benny, Eddie Cantor, Fred Allen, Bob Hope, Lum 'n Abner, and Don Ameche's Chase and Sanborn Hour with Edgar Bergen and his Charlie McCarthy. There were Gracie Allen and George Burns and the Easy Aces. We listened to Walter Winchell with his "Good evening, Mr. and Mrs. America and all the ships at sea" and Jimmy Fidler's Hollywood Gossip. On Monday evening at nine was the *Lux Radio Theater* with Cecil B. DeMille, radio condensations of leading motion pictures. We had a choice of great radio drama in the evenings--*Gang Busters, Mr. District Attorney, One Man's Family, Mr. Keen, Tracer of Lost Persons, I Love a Mystery, Duffy's Tavern, Hollywood Hotel, The Green Hornet, Information Please, The March of Time*, and *Major Bowes' Amateur Hour*. We were terrified by *Light's Out* and the ever popular, "Who knows...what evil...lurks in the hearts of men? *The Shadow* knows!" In the afternoons our mothers listened to the original soap operas: *Romance of Helen Trent, Backstage Wife*, and *Our Gal Sunday*.

Special radio programs for kids started around five o'clock--*Superman, Tom Mix, Sergeant Preston of the Yukon, Captain Midnight*, and *Jack Armstrong, the All-American Boy*. And always at a quarter to six, *Little Orphan Annie* came on with her secret rings and Ovaltine mugs. One hour later was Floyd Gibbons with the national news and later, Lowell Thomas.

But no entertainment program ever had the following generated by *Amos 'n' Andy*, the comedy in which two Caucasian actors role played a number of African-American characters, including Amos and Andy, master of the malapropism ("I's regusted'), the operators of Harlem's Fresh Air Taxi Cab Company; together with Kingfish, head of the Mystic Knights of the Sea, his wife, Madam Queen, and Calhoun, the lawyer. The fifteen minute program aired at seven o'clock five nights a week and was so popular that motion picture houses would interrupt the movie at seven and pipe the program into the theater. Large signs appeared at theater marquees advertising this in order to offset the decline of attendance at this hour. Retail stores turned up their radios to benefit customers.

Later a rival network created *Myrt and Marge*, to run at the same time. This evening soap opera featured a savvy New York chorus girl who took an ingenue under her wing only to told later, as we already knew, that the young woman was her long lost daughter.

Sports events were well covered, and Carnegie stores would place radio speakers in vestibules so that customers could follow broadcasts of the World Series and evening prize fights. On New Year's Day at 5 p.m. we always tuned in the Rose Bowl game, the only football bowl game of the time.

For music we had the Lucky Strike Hit Parade and Horace Heidt and his Musical Knights and the Kraft Music Hall with Bing Crosby and Bob Burns. On Sunday afternoon, always a major symphony orchestra took to the airwaves. Except Sunday, every night national broadcasts of live big bands from famous dance halls and night clubs followed the 11 o'clock news. That's how we got to know the great orchestras of the swing era-- Tommy Dorsey (with a new singer named Frank Sinatra), Jimmy Dorsey, Kay Kyser, Sammy Kaye, Guy Lombardo, Artie Shaw, Lawrence Welk, Benny Goodman, Fred Waring, Vincent Lopez, Glen Miller, Ted Weems, Jan Garber, Paul Pendarvis, and the Spitalmy's--Maurice and Phil.

Radio programs took our minds off the hard times and in their hey day were more entertaining and more imaginative with more variety and higher quality than present day television.

We underwent basic political changes at this time. Until the Thirties, Pennsylvania and Pittsburgh and Carnegie were Republican strongholds. There had not been a Democratic President since Woodrow Wilson. But a strong phenomenon flashed across the country in 1928. The Democratic candidate was Al Smith, the popular governor of New York. He was the first national political figure to use the radio as a political medium and, as a Roman Catholic, he appealed to strong segments of traditional Republican voters. Governor Smith called it "raddio." Smith's candidacy cracked traditional Republican bastions, even though he was defeated by Herbert Hoover.

The year Hoover took office, Black Friday took place on the New York Stock Exchange. Unemployment skyrocketed, breadlines spread and shanty towns sprouted, and the person who bore the brunt of criticism was the President. Throughout the country voices railed against him and his party.

Carnegie was no exception. Seemingly everybody, including most of our family's closest friends, excoriated Hoover and the Republicans. This placed us in an awkward position, because my father was holding office as chief deputy coroner under a Republican Coroner, William J. Mc Gregor, M.D., and dad was very loyal to his employer. As a political appointee, he had to. At the age of 11 or 12 I found myself involved very much in political arguments in the schoolyard and at play. There was no question that I had to be loyal to my father's views. His job depended on a Republican office holder.

I still remember the election campaign of 1932. The economy had reached rock bottom. Unrest and violence ran rampant in the coal mines around town. I still remember vividly one day during a strike at the Bell Coal Mine on the upper reaches of Washington Avenue. The miners attempted a parade down Washington Avenue to show their strength. The Pennsylvania Coal and Iron Police, the uniformed private force with high black helmets like London Bobbies, were paid by the employers but endowed with the full powers of the state police. I saw the mounted Coal and Iron Police charging into the paraders on huge black horses. They made a rush attack into the line of marchers, swinging long wooden truncheons like Cossacks on a saber charge. Assisting them on foot, specially deputized men dressed in street clothes but wearing red arm bands for identification, waded into the fray with pick handles. I had seen violence in the movies and heard vicious blows struck on the radio, but this was the first time I had been eye and ear witness to the real thing. Over 70 years has passed, but I still remember the crack of a black truncheon smashing the skull of a coal miner. I have never forgotten that sound, nor the sight of blood erupting all over his face, a sad bloody face. It was frightening. And it also was a burning political issue in 1932--the right of workers to unionize.

It was a foregone conclusion that Roosevelt would clobber Hoover. The Democrats promised to repeal the Eighteenth Amendment, the Prohibition laws. During the campaign, I heard a person say, "Now, really, not everybody is going to vote for Roosevelt. The gangsters and the bootleggers will have to vote for Hoover to keep their rackets going!"

Nevertheless, our family remained loyal to the Republican party. We remained loyal until the next election for county coroner. A Democrat was elected and he chose to retain my father to run his office as chief deputy. Overnight our family became Democrats. With a huge sigh of relief, I went forth to proclaim that Roosevelt was the greatest President in our history.

It was during the Great Depression that I made the transition from sub teen to young adulthood. I grew up in a hurry because I saw first hand the misery of unemployment and all-pervasive deprivation of comforts. Wild teen age years? In junior high school? Wildness comes from idleness or luxury, and this was not to be had. Instead there seemed to have been a determination among the young to make do, to find entertainment without spending money, to find some happy hours amidst the bleakness, and this we discovered by visiting each other in our homes--four or five together---

to listen to radio programs and catch the lilt and swing of the big band era and sing songs and pretend to swoon. And especially, to giggle over those girls whom we had ignored for so many years, those girls who had started to fill out their sweaters.

The dating age had come on us when everyone was broke, so a "heavy date" took the form of meeting a girl just inside the New Carnegie Theater at 5:45 p.m., just fifteen minutes before the admission price changed from 15 cents to 20 and walking her home and meeting her mother at the late hour of 8 o'clock with the girl saying, "Mother, look who I ran into at the movie and he walked me home. Can we have some lemonade or hot chocolate?"

Oh, those wild sub-teen and teenage years in the Great Depression.

Chapter Twelve
Growing up in High School

If there was anything resembling a town square in Carnegie, it was the area surrounding what we called "the Fountain." Consisting of a round, ornate cast iron structure painted silver that rose about 20 feet, the Fountain was already a majestic relic of a past era when I entered high school. At its base were two huge drinking troughs for horses with water running over the sides to underground drains.

The Fountain and a high curb that extended on the two sides not occupied by the drinking troughs constituted a divider between two parallel streets: Broadway Extension Street and Beechwood Avenue. The two streets, along both of which traffic moved in both directions, were conjoined for about 100 yards near their intersection with East Main Street. The Fountain and curb kept cars from Broadway Extension from crossing over to Beechwood and vice versa. The Masonic Hall stood at the corner of Beechwood and East Main, while the Bell Drug Store occupied the corner of Broadway Extension and East Main. Moving away from East Main, Broadway Extension eventually intersected with Robert Street, where stood Carnegie High School. Beechwood, meanwhile, eventually split away from Broadway Extension and ran up the hill to the Andrew Carnegie Library park.

Carnegie had its traditions and jealously guarded them. Shortly after the classes entered Carnegie High School in the Gay Nineties–the first graduating class was in 1899–a tradition was born. And it still persisted almost 40 years later when I entered as a freshman, a ninth grader. On the first Friday after Labor Day, the boys in the freshman class would assemble at the library, then descend en masse down Beechwood Avenue to the Fountain where the sophomores awaited. This was a rite of passage. The mission of freshmen was to avoid being dunked in the horse troughs by sophomores; the sophomores' task was to insure that every freshman got dunked.

After only four days of high school, on Friday morning, September 8, 1933, the freshman home room teachers made an announcement: "All freshman boys are expected to meet in front of the Library at no later than 6:45 p.m. You are expected to leave at 7 p.m. to go to the Fountain for you know what." No school-wide public address systems in those days.

It was a community event. Hundreds of spectators–including many high school kids--cheered from the sidelines awaiting the coming melee. But certain ground rules prevailed. You could push or grab or carry and forcibly dunk the head into the water, but you could not punch, pull hair or kick. The dunking went off in 1933 as it had since 1895. We valiant freshmen, more a mob than an organized phalanx, collided with another mob, differing from us only in that they were one year older. After about 30 minutes of disorganized shoving and pushing, eventually all of us got dunked, but once the fracas reached a crescendo with gallons of water splashed through the air, everybody was soaking wet. It was impossible to distinguish the dunkers from the dunkees.

There were 248 of us when we entered high school; four years later only 115 received diplomas. Under today's standards, that's quite an attrition, but I make bold to suggest several reasons for it. First, some of our kids had come from three or four Catholic elementary schools, where the quality of education varied from mediocre to extremely poor. Many of the high school courses proved to be too difficult. Moreover, these were four years of the depth of the Great Depression, and many families left Carnegie to seek employment in other climes. Then, too, many girls were required to assist in household chores, and a high school education for them was not deemed necessary for them in many immigrant families. And I still remember a good friend telling me with tears rolling down her cheeks that she left school because she was too embarrassed to continue because her skirts and dresses were too threadbare or patched.

Ours was a small town's high school with a general enrollment of four grades, ninth through twelfth, that vacillated between 600 and 700. In interscholastic athletic competition we played schools of comparable size. This was 20 years before the school district consolidation fever came to Western Pennsylvania and the boroughs of Carnegie, Rosslyn Farms and Crafton were combined into one district they called Carlynton. After this took place, all the traditions of Carnegie and Crafton high schools, 50 years of strong rivalry, disappeared.

I'm glad I went to a small high school. I knew most of the kids in my first year class because we had attended junior high together in the seventh and eighth grades; the. only new kids were those who came from the Catholic grade schools.

It was an old fashioned curriculum strictly divided into academic and commercial. I always regretted I did not take typewriting, but this was not permitted because I was not registered in the commercial segment. It would have delivered me from the hunt and peck method that I still use. But the academic courses were splendidly well taught. I had four solid years of Latin with Miss Nesbit--Introductory Latin, Caesar's Commentaries, Cicero and Virgil. From this sturdy base I have been able to learn Italian, and catch the drift reading French or Spanish. Mathematics also was very strong–two years of algebra followed by plane and solid geometry. Added to this were substantial courses in English and history. My science was limited to two courses in biology. I steered clear from chemistry and physics because they were taught by only one teacher, H.H. "Hard Head" Lee, a dinosaur whose reputation preceded him.

The high school building was extremely attractive from the outside. Its front was not a boxy square or rectangle, but a convex shape, curved and rounded like the exterior of a sphere or circle replete with Romanesque arches. On the first floor the rounded front was an outside lobby where all gathered before and after school. The semi-circular design carried to the second floor in the form on one huge room containing 200 or 300 desks, known as "Study Hall." During school hours this is where you were compelled to go if you did not have a class at a particular hour. Study Hall was strictly monitored by one or two faculty members.

There was no assembly room to accommodate the entire student body, and as was the case in every other Carnegie school building, no cafeteria. Back in 1890 when they built the high school, the school board was not interested in frills. They built a gymnasium that also served for basketball practice, but it was a two story cage with no seats for an audience. Our teams played home games at the Harding elementary school gym.

Upon going through the front doors passing through the open lobby you faced a wide flight of stairs to the second floor, and all around you was wood. Wood steps, wood floors, wood walls in the corridors. To clean the floors, instead of soap and water they used sawdust and oil. It would take some difficulty to conjure up a more dangerous fire trap. Permeating the entire building always was the smell of oil, except in the main basement where there was one rest room for the 300 or 400 male students. No urinals here, but only a long wall of slate with a small gutter at its base, ostensibly flushed by a stream of water, but the minuscule amount of trickled water could not carry away the ever larger yellow reservoir that seemed always to overflow. The "boys room" was an historical landmark that memorialized 40 years of peeing on a wall.

So you had your choice of smelling oil or nitrates, but you had to be careful not to have holes in your shoes because the floors from the *ancien régime* were cracked, and it was commonplace for an errant sliver to catch the unwary.

I discovered when I later attended the University of Pittsburgh that in this sub-standard building I received a better college preparatory education than most of my college classmates.

What eased my introduction to high school social life was that my brother Caesar was a junior and my cousin, Adele, a sophomore, and I had known many of their friends over the years. As freshmen we had no organized class activities; it was a year of studying, watching the upperclassmen and learning customs and slang of the school.

Later in my first year I was invited to join Zeta Tau, a newly formed high school fraternity, organized by a handful of junior class members, including my brother. They chose four of five of us freshmen, and we met in an unused garage on the W. W. Hack property across the alley from the high school. We became a branch of the Carnegie Athletic Club, fielded teams in basketball, and softball and organized a glee club. On special occasions we wore uniforms: white duck trousers, white shirts with red shields emblazoned with "Z" and "T." The *Carnegie Union*, one of Carnegie's two weekly newspapers, covered our activities and once sent a photographer to photograph us in our white uniforms. The fraternity was active for two years, but when the organizing class graduated, especially Jim McDonald our president, the fraternity became inactive. But to a freshman, it was an opportunity of becoming friends of leading upperclassmen.

Toward the end of the first year, I approached Jim, a long time friend of brother Caesar's, and a frequent visitor in our home. I knew that an assistant manager of the football team was to be chosen from my class next year and that Jim was to be the senior student manager. I told him I was interested in the position. He smiled and said, "You got it."

I didn't believe him until shortly afterwards, Dick Schumacher, who was my algebra teacher and also the football coach, stopped me one day and said that he was pleased that I was joining his staff as one of two assistant student managers.

In the modern era of high schools, head coaches are able to hire several assistant coaches, coordinators, various trainers and office staff, but in my high school years Dick Schumacher did not have a single assistant. His staff consisted of three student assistants--a student manager and two assistant managers.

We managers doled out uniforms and practice jerseys that the players hung on nails (no lockers) in a large basement room. We made minor repairs on football shoes and had to be able to tighten or replace cleats during a game. At football practice, often we would lead daily calisthenics to free up the coach. And we were the trainers. No whirlpool baths, no multiple massage tables, only one table and one heat lamp. We were responsible for carrying the footballs in huge sacks to the practice field; at home games we had to make certain that the game ball was delivered to the officials and always carry a spare new football.

With a proper note from the coach, a player could be released from class or study hall during the last hour of the school day to undergo treatment for an ache or injury. Student managers had standing authority to leave class at any time to open the "locker room" and tend to the player's needs.

Dr. Harry A. Klee, a local general practitioner, was the school physician. Not satisfied with instructions I received from players on how to tape ankles, I asked Dr. Klee for advice. "Come down to my office and I'll show you how," he said, and later he did.

The coach was pleased with my new specialty, and from then on I became the de facto trainer. When there was a time out at games, the coach always trotted out to the players who assembled in a circle on the field. He asked me to go with him with my black bag of liniments, band aids, iodine, Mercurochrome, bandages and rolls of adhesive tape. I carried smelling salts in my pocket and frequently used it when a player's "bell was rung." Sometimes during these time-outs I ministered to ankle injuries by taping over their high top shoes.

Football players were the glory boys of high schools, and although I was not a player, I was considered a member of the team and became the beneficiary of adulation sent their way. In any event, on November 9, 1933, I was elected president of my class. We sponsored a number of social activities, and used our class colors (white and blue) and spring flowers to decorate the Harding Gym for the annual Sophomore Hop on May 31. It was not until April that most of us guys on the dance committee had to face the horrible dilemma—the dance was only a month away, none of us knew how to dance and we didn't want the girls to know. We went to each other's houses and played radio music, stumbled with each other in primitive attempts to learn, all with gallant assists from mothers, older sisters or cousins.

In my junior year I almost was expelled, at least that's what Principal R. Edward Knarr told me after I made a speech at our class organization meeting. The day before the meeting he had advised me that I was ineligible to run again for class president. "You've got to give somebody else a chance," he said. In discussing this with my parents, I told them I wanted to give a speech on democracy and the right of the students to choose their class officers. "If you feel strong about it, son, go to it," dad said. That night I wrote out my remarks, memorized them and rehearsed in front of my father.

Present at the election meeting was Principal Knarr and Miss Frances Moore, my home room teacher and class advisor. I presided at the opening of the meeting and announced that the purpose was to elect class officers, but before nominations were made, Mr. Knarr had an announcement to make. He made a brief statement that because I had been president last year, another person should have the right to serve. My closest friend, Chuck Byrne, was the only nomination. I then said that before Chuck should take over the meeting, I had something to say.

I looked directly at Mr. Knarr and then turned to the class and told them that although I accepted Mr. Knarr's ruling, I had a few comments about what I perceived to be a contradiction of what was being taught in our classrooms about freedoms and the right of Americans to choose their representatives in a democratic society. I then threw down the gauntlet. I said that the administration and faculty of Carnegie High School today had violated all the precepts they taught in class—they denied members of this junior class the right to have class officers of their own choice.

It took a little while to make my presentation, and when I concluded there was total silence. Knarr came over to me, said, "After this meeting, in my office." He walked out. The class elected the remaining officers. After the meeting adjourned, I was immediately surrounded. Many patted me on the back. More than one friend said, "Rugi, they're going to get you now. What in the hell are you going to do? They're going to kick your ass out of here. You said all that stuff right to his face." Knarr was a tough, autocratic principal and he made sure that the faculty and student body understood that his word was the law. My friends wished me good luck. My sole answer was that the principal wanted to see me immediately.

The door to the principal's office was open when I walked in. He walked over and closed it. "You know, Ruggero, when I came down here I first decided that I was going to expel you," he said, "but the more I think about, perhaps I will give you a stern warning instead. You must understand that a student cannot publicly criticize the faculty authority in this school." He then asked me point blank if I considered that I might be expelled by delivering those remarks. I told him that my father and I discussed that possibility. "Your father! Did he know about this?" he asked. I then explained that my father supported me 100 per cent, that we decided that if Mr. Knarr expelled me I was to take an appeal to Superintendent of Schools Norman L. Glasser who knew me quite well because his daughter was my good friend and classmate. Knarr grunted and told me to return to home room.

When I returned to my home room, Miss Moore winked at me.

But from that day forward, I owned Carnegie High School. The "word" fulminated through the school community, through the faculty and all four classes, freshmen to seniors, that Rugi Aldisert had publicly stood up to the principal. In the following days and weeks I was a like "The Man Who Shot Liberty Valance" and became known to every kid in school.

In my senior year I was again elected class president.

One of my first projects was to establish a high school newspaper. I prepared a detailed proposal, suggesting names for editors and writers, mimeograph operators and estimated costs. It was to be distributed free, the only expense would be paper and mimeograph ink. The project was summarily dismissed by H.H. "Hard Head" Lee, vice-principal in charge of student activities. He told me that it was impossible to create a new activity. When I started to discuss it, he interrupted. "Look, I've made the decision, and that's it."

I was not deterred. I came across a beat-up mimeograph machine that I bought for $5.00 and decided that my friends and I could publish an unofficial school paper. Because the two national photo magazines were LIFE and LOOK, and as a play on the letter "C" in Carnegie, we called our paper "SEE." Our motto was "What SEE doesn't see isn't worth seeing." We mimeographed and assembled the paper at my house. The lead story in the first edition was that we had asked the school to sponsor a student newspaper, but had been turned down by H.H. Lee. We prominently published a masthead with the names and titles of all who worked on it, many of them being student leaders. Our unofficial school paper was an immediate success. We obtained advertisements, sold SEE in front of the school, and all shared the net profits. It became very popular because we covered stories, wrote editorials and had some columnists, of which the gossip column was most popular. Buoyed by its popularity, the school eventually had a change of heart in the second semester and agreed to take over official sponsorship. Thereafter, we put out a slicker product every other week, but it pained me to lose one of my editors. A student at St. Luke's, he did not attend our school.

As editor, my credo was to get as many student names in different articles and columns. "They have to believe that they belong, not only the BMOC's." (Big Men on Campus) I was quick to recruit reporters and typists, men and women, from each class to provide continuation. But before the year ended, "Hard Head" had the last word. He instructed the student editors of the year book that there be no mention of SEE, the official student newspaper. Neverthless, SEE continued as the high school paper from 1937 until 1956 when Carnegie became part of the new Carlynton School district.

In the 1936 Holiday season, I went into the Christmas tree business. I had learned that you could purchase a bundle of three trees at the Pittsburgh Produce Yards for $3.00, and then sell each tree for $3.00. I gathered five close friends and proposed my plan. The owner of a retail store offered to let us use his sidewalks at the corner of East Main Street and Mary Street. He would not charge us rent but he would have free choice of any tree and wreaths. The project would be a partnership in which each of us would contribute cash for the original tree purchases, and each partner's interest would be based on the percentage of money contributed for the original capital. No salaries would be paid. We would use all sale proceeds to purchase additional trees on the theory that the more we sold, the more cash we'd have to buy more trees. Because we were still in the depression, cash was hard to come by. I put in $5.00, but each of my friends could pony up only a dollar each. It was agreed that I would own 50 per cent of the enterprise and each of others 10 per cent. A friend of my father's lent us a dilapidated pickup truck, and we were in business.

Our business was called YXTA (Your Christmas Tree Association) but from the very beginning most people thought this was a high school project. We made no attempt to dissuade anybody from this impression. My partners went door to door taking orders for trees. One of my guys approached his neighbor who was active in the local numbers book and he supplied us with order pads. Every time an order was taken and a deposit made, we would have a record and the purchaser could have a receipt. We had standard rates for different tree sizes and offered free delivery. As deposits came in, we had sufficient cash to purchase a large stock in various sizes. By the final week we had a huge inventory, started to make deliveries and handle brisk sales. Fellow students joined the sales force–no compensation, they simply wanted to be a part of the action. By Christmas Eve we had sold out the entire inventory.

It was time to divvy up the proceeds. Each of my partners received $50 for his $1.00 investment; for my $5.00 I netted $250. In 2004 dollars this amounted to $674 and $3370 respectively.

I had been able to contribute such a large share of the original capital because I was the only guy in the crowd who had a steady part time job. Knowing that I had been working weekends at the Heidelberg Pharmacy, located in a neighboring town, Ben Kahn, owner of Bell Drug Store located close by the high school at East Main and Broadway, offered me a job to work from six to ten on Tuesday and Friday nights and on Saturday from noon till closing. Bell Drug was the school hangout, located less than 100 yards from the high school; on a corner that became known as Times Square.

In the evening I was almost totally occupied at the fountain, great fun--making ice cream cones, drawing cokes, making ice cream sodas, building sundaes and banana splits. Cigarettes were 20 cents a pack; we also sold individual cigarettes for two cents. No law prevented sales to minors. I loved the job because I enjoyed kibitzing with the high school crowd. I worked there throughout my junior and senior years; in time I was on a first name basis with almost every kid in school.

Keeping in mind that this was 70 years ago, that's about three generations past, there were some embarrassing moments when working behind the drug and sundries counter. In those days all stock in a drug store was behind the counter. Some of the girls I knew from school would come to the counter and ask if Georgia (the regular, full time employee) or any other female clerk available. Explaining that I was the only clerk on duty, I would lean over quietly and say, "Don't be embarrassed, we have Kotex and Tampax already wrapped for you to take out. Which do you want?" This may mean nothing today, but at that time it was a very delicate subject, a source of much fluster or outright shame for a woman to ask for such a personal item from a male teen age friend.

Then, too, there were the guys and older men who quietly leaned over the counter and whispered, "rubbers" or "cundrums." Yes, that's what men called them, never "condoms." In *sotte voce* I gave them their change and handed the purchase to the customer as if shaking hands.

June of 1937 came, and high school was over. I had done well in my studies, always ranking among the first three or four of my class. In my junior year I had been elected to the original Carnegie High School chapter of the National Honor Society, and when it came to the graduation ceremonies at the Carnegie Library auditorium, I was named Salutatorian and delivered the Commencement speech (attacking President Roosevelt's court-packing scheme).

Most important, I received an honor scholarship to the University of Pittsburgh:

UNIVERSITY OF PITTSBURGH

Certificate of Award

Be it known by these presents

that an

HONOR SCHOLARSHIP

is awarded to

RUGGERO JOHN ALDISERT

In Recognition of Good Character and of Scholastic

Attainment and upon the Recommendation of the

Principal and faculty of the

CARNEGIE HIGH SCHOOL

The reverse side of the certificate stated the conditions: This honor scholarship award has a value of $150 a year ($75 for each semester) to be applied on tuition charged if the recipient registers for a full program of work of at least fifteen credits a semester in The College, School of Engineering, School of Mines, School of Business

Administration, or the School of Education at the University of Pittsburgh.

It is presumed that ordinarily this tuition allowance will be continued for four years provided that the recipient maintains at least a 1.5 quality point average (Between B and C grade) in his scholastic work, and provided that the dean of the school in which the student is registered approves the continuation of the scholarship at the end of each year.

Without this scholarship aid-reflecting 50 per cent of the full tuition of $300--I would have been unable to go to college.

What I learned in the classroom those four years of high school would stay with me forever—old fashioned, time-tested academic courses that exercised your mind and taught straight thinking, and teachers who gave us indomitable exposure to English and history. But what also helped me go in as a boy in September, 1933 and come out a young man in June, 1937 was my participation in school activities. Having participated in leadership roles, I was spared the tentativeness, the self-consciousness, the feeling of insecurity generally associated with teen age years.

In high school I was the big frog in the little pond. With not a little trepidation, I looked forward to entering the University of Pittsburgh.

As student manager of the Carnegie High School football team in 1936, I am pictured with my two assistants. On the left is Howard Wilson, Jr., who would became a career dentist in the U.S. Army Dental Corps and retired with the rank of Colonel. George Foster Doak would later become a Minute Clerk of the Court of Common Pleas when I served as a judge. He would later be promoted to Chief Minute Clerk.

My senior year in high school. I was going through my bow tie period at the time and the class year book described it as my "passion."

May 1937. My high school graduation photo.

Chapter Thirteen
Growing up at Pitt

It took a change of trolley cars to go from my home in Carnegie to the University of Pittsburgh in the Oakland district of the city. First, the old Carnegie 27 route from the home town to the corner of Penn and Stanwix in downtown Pittsburgh; from there you took any route going East on Forbes Avenue because they all passed the Cathedral of Learning, the University's main building, to their destination in East Liberty and other points east.

Street car tokens (we called them "checks" in Pittsburgh) were three for a quarter and I used four a day, one for each route. Pittsburgh transfers were not acceptable on the Carnegie route. "Commuters" is what they call Pitt students today who live at home; "street car students" is what they called us back then. And we made up about 90 percent of the undergraduate student body.

No dorms then, just an assortment of fraternity houses for men fraternities and women fraternities. Dean of Women Thyrsa Agnes Amos said, they could not be called "sororities" because that word stem means "sisterly" and it was important that women, too, belong to fraternities, defined as groups formally organized for a common purpose, interest and pleasure, instead of being merely an ensemble of sisters. A handful of students rented apartments in the Oakland area, living quarters that would give the term "flea bag" a bad name.

No Student Union Building existed with a choice of fast food restaurants and cafés, and comfortable lounges and palatial student activity offices as you will find now in the William Pitt Union, the impressive building that occupies a full block on Bigelow Boulevard between Forbes and Fifth Avenues. Today's student union was then the elegant Schenley Hotel.

Only two floors in the unfinished Cathedral of Learning were allocated for student activities. Located on the eighth floor were all student publications offices, the Dean of Men's office, the university public relations office (one occupant, Robert X. Graham) and a YMCA sandwich shop that sold packaged sandwiches (if you liked ham sandwiches usually grey in color) and soft drinks. For amenities, there were a few tables, but mainly an assortment of folding chairs. On this floor, one restroom was available for men, two stalls and two urinals. The women had to go to the twelfth floor ladies room. On that floor the Dean of Women's staff had attractive quarters. There, too, were tiny offices for women organizations and some university offices.

With the exception of the deans' offices, all corridors and rooms had primitive walls of salmon colored building blocks accented by grey mortar, once oozing but now dried. Your illumination, such as it was, came from naked light bulbs at the end of black wires that dangled from unfinished ceilings.

Throughout my undergraduate days, all my classrooms were in the first three floors of the Cathedral, or in its basement, and each had unfinished walls, ceilings and concrete floors. And the dangling light bulbs. There was one exception. If you were fortunate to have a class in one of the finished Nationality Rooms, you were treated to magnificent surroundings that had been elaborately decorated to reflect the ethnic culture of the particular room; also comfortable seats and desks and plenty of light from lovely windows.

The severe trauma that I expected when going from a high school of 600 to 700 students to the University of Pittsburgh with its 25,000 undergrad and graduate students never materialized. For registration for classes hundreds of students milled around tables in the three story Common Room, splendidly Gothic-arched, that was the centerpiece of the Cathedral. We were throughly confused, but somehow signed up for the required number of first year courses. I registered as a political science major with a minor in English and history. In the years that followed, I would later regret that I did not major in English. But I came away from registration with both agitation and apprehensiveness. So many people, and all of them strangers.

A University event that soon followed put me at ease. An optional program for men was a freshman orientation weekend at a YMCA camp called Kon-O-Kee near Zelienople, Butler County, Pennsylvania. The weekend outing was designed to encourage us to participate in university activities. Various student organizations had open booths where upperclassmen explained their programs. We lived in tents, at least one upper class man bunking with us.

That's how I met Jack Hoeveler, a sophomore, active in student government and on the business staff of the monthly humor magazine, The Pitt Panther. We would later become close friends and remained so during and after our University days. After the war, he remained in France with various State Department agencies, and upon retirement became an expatriate in Paris with a vacation home in Tunisia. As a child he had been educated in Switzerland until the stock market crashed and wiped out his family financially. He worked his way through Pitt by operating a two-man sausage business with another Pitt student, and was able to establish a regular clientele by preparing sausage to meet individual seasoning and flavoring preferences; making home deliveries.

Meeting Jack was important to me, because I had met a man whose family once had a butler and maids, yet was commuting like I was and was working his way through school. Although Pitt's tuition was only $300 a year, (that's $4,000 in 2004 dollars) and although I had a scholarship paying half, we all had expenses to meet, and most of us had to scrounge for part-time jobs in order to go to college. It was 1937, still the time of the Great Depression.

At the camp I met John Martinco, the campus editor of The Pitt News (comparable to city editor in a metropolitan paper). I had a long talk with him and he invited me to try out for a reporter's position. He told me to see him the following Monday for a test assignment. I also met Bill Stark, student president of the Men's Debating Association, who was very enthusiastic about the program and encouraged me to try out for the freshman debate team. In the evening there was a giant bonfire and informal groups were set up for bull sessions. Martinco had explained that The Pitt News appeared Monday, Wednesday and Friday, but that we wrote everyday. I passed the writing tests Martinco had given me on Monday and was given other assignments during the week, and on Friday received the good news that I had made the reporting staff.

During the same week I visited the debate office where Bill Stark had a desk. He introduced me to Roy Umble, the freshman coach. A meeting of the first year applicants took place later in the week, a schedule of tryouts was distributed, but most of all I was impressed by the brief remarks Stark delivered. He stressed that the debate program discussed serious national and international issues. "This isn't a Joe College rah, rah, rah group. This is for serious minds." He then went into a short talk on the Spanish Civil War.

He opened our eyes, and explained that after the fall of the Spanish monarchy of 1931, the Republic of Spain had been proclaimed, first had been dominated by middle class liberals and moderate socialists, but in 1936 the Popular Front, composed of liberals, socialists and communists had taken over the government. In July of 1936, General Francisco Franco led a Spanish army revolt in Morocco and then invaded his homeland, seeking to overthrow the government by force. The Civil War then broke out. Those supporting the government were called Loyalists, and the Franco followers, the Rebels.

Thus began the war of the surrogates. From the very first, and throughout the war, Germany and Italy aided General Franco with an abundance of planes, tanks and other materiel. By war's end Germany supplied some 1,000 aviators and technicians; had sent probably about 70,000 "volunteers." Unfortunately, the Loyalists became dependent on the Soviet Union for supplies. France and England had sought to bring about a cease fire, and shortly after they accomplished tentative agreement, but soon the diplomacy solution failed. The Soviets were generous in military aid. They did this for the sole purpose of achieving their own political goals. But this aid was no match for the assistance rendered Franco.

Stark concluded his remarks with an admonition: "You probably did not discuss the Spanish Civil War in high school, but you must learn to follow it now. By June of this year, the Loyalists were on the run. To many thinkers, this looks like a dress rehearsal for Hitler and Mussolini."

Coach Umble closed the meeting with the few remarks and emphasized that the Civil War in Spain would be one of the subjects we would research and discuss during the year. Within a few months I was selected as a member of the freshman debate team.

In that first year at Pitt, I probably spent less time in class or preparing lessons than I did with The Pitt News and the debate team. I was not a stranger to public speaking. My father had been the first national president of the Order Italian Sons and Daughters of America, and had been enrolling children of the original immigrant generation members. During my last year in high school and in the summer of 1937, he persuaded me to make a number of speeches at various meetings. "I want a young person who could speak well to other young people," he told me. Because this experience had made me comfortable when speaking before a group, I had no difficulty with the freshman team in its intercollegiate program.

In the summer of 1938, I was fortunate to land a nighttime copy boy job at the Pittsburgh Bureau of the International News Service. The regular staff left at 1 a.m., and that was my starting time; the only person on the "graveyard shift," from 1 to 8 a.m. I had to tend the teletype machine for incoming copy, read it, and, by pneumatic tubes, send it to either the news editor or the sports editor next door at the Pittsburgh Sun-Telegraph. Through the night I inserted carbon paper into six-page books of thin typing paper for use by the reporters in the morning.

Because INS and the Sun-Telegraph were properties of William Randolph Hearst, almost every night there was a directive from "the Chief" dictating exactly where various front page news stories should be displayed. I sent these directives directly to the managing editor.

Then, too, I had to transmit on the teletype network articles previously written by the Pittsburgh INS staff. These "overnights" had been punched out in teletype tape, but not sent out over the wire. This delay had something to do with different time zones or the value of the news stories or no deadline demands. Specific tapes had to be sent out at specific times, and I was given a timetable.

I took my lunch hour at 4 a.m., locked the door of the bureau and walked the quiet streets of downtown Pittsburgh in warm summer nights. My usual lunch was at an all-night White Tower diner or at at restaurant called The Brass Rail. The countermen learned to recognize me and as I entered, would start to prepare my usual order–two hamburgers at five cents each and a bottle of root beer for another nickel.

When I started our second year at Pitt in September 1938, the news concentrated on the occupation by Hitler of the Sudetenland area of Czechoslovakia. This was a German speaking ethnic group that never had been part of Germany, but for a century or more was a part of the multi-ethnic Hapsburg Austro-Hungarian empire. Upon dissolution of the empire after World War I, Sudentenland was included in the new nation of Czechoslovakia. We were all very much interested in Czechoslovakia because the constitution creating that country had been drawn up in Pittsburgh in 1918.

On September 29, 1938, Neville Chamberlain, Prime Minister of Great Britain, signed an agreement with Adolph Hitler in Munich. Chamberlain triumphantly returned to London, exclaiming, "Peace in our time."

We were not so sure.

It became apparent to some of us that a dark cloud of serious international problems would prevent our University experience from being four years of fun and games. In our first year it had been the Spanish Civil War; as we entered the second year, the Munich agreement greeted us.

I tried out for the varsity debating team under Professor Charles Lomas and became active. Three propositions would serve as debate team subjects for the year. The principal national subject was the Roosevelt plan of stimulating the economy by sponsoring government work projecting, known as "pump priming." A secondary subject was "Resolved: That all labor unions should be incorporated." But third subject was one very much in demand: "Resolved: That the United States should enter into an economic and military alliance." Hitler's invasion of the Sudentenland had become one of the debate subjects.

After a few months of tryouts, I was selected as a member of the varsity debate team. We took turns taking the affirmative and negative sides of the three questions, and made many appearances throughout Western Pennsylvania. In the beginning of the second semester I received the news that although only a sophomore I was selected to serve on the first team, the four debaters who would represent the University in major intercollegiate debates.

The team consisted of Edward Springer and Hyman Richman, who were seniors; Abe Wolowitz, a junior, and me. With Professor Lomas as our coach, we started our tour on April 11 in Washington, D.C. for a debate and then proceeded to Richmond, Virginia where Ed Springer and I were assigned the negative on the British Alliance question in a debate with Randolph Macon which was broadcast over a local radio station. Our tour took us to debates with Georgetown, the University of Tennessee, the University of North Carolina, the University of Georgia and Duke.

After Duke we moved to the Grand Eastern Tournament at Winthrop College, South Carolina. Titled the Strawberry Leaf Tournament, this was a great intercollegiate debate tournament that attracted representatives from 75 colleges. There we participated in five debates a day for three days. It was a great intellectual experience for me as, well as the first time I had traveled in the South; and especially memorable for socializing and debating teams from all-women colleges. With their fetching accents and controlled eye fluttering, I did not care how the judges evaluated our debating skills because I soon learned that southern charm was not a figment of fiction writers' imagination.

In addition to debating I was getting more important reporting assignments from Bob Adams, the new campus editor of The Pitt News, and was receiving by-lines. Shortly after I returned from the southern trip, the highlight of the University's debate program, Professor Lomas called me in and suggested, very diplomatically, that I should make a choice between the debate team and The News. "You can't do both and do a good job in either," he said.

Shortly thereafter, however, the choice became easier. John Martinco, then editor-in-chief, and Bob Adams offered me a newly created position of assistant campus editor indicating that this was a stepping stone to the important campus editor spot the following year, a position that I knew carried with it a modest financial stipend. This offer, with its accouterments, made the decision for me even though I had truly enjoyed the debate program.

In the 1939 summer I was able to get placed in the Allegheny County Parks Department which not only administered the park system, but also the annual Allegheny County Free Fair and Exposition. At that time the county had a substantial agricultural area, and an old fashioned county fair was held at South Park, the county's largest park. Although the U.S. Farm Bureau recruited the individual agricultural participants, the Fair Office solicited Pittsburgh's many corporations and retail businesses to take part as well, to sponsor elaborate booths to exhibit their industrial and commercial contributions to the community.

Director of the Fair was George E. Kelly, head of the county parks department, who also served as a partner of a major Pittsburgh advertising agency, whose principal client was the Allegheny County Democratic Committee. A brilliant writer and idea man, he created a summer staff to prepare for the fair by borrowing personnel from other county offices most of whom were former newspaper reporters. In addition he brought on board three temporary summer workers--a retired advertising layout specialist, a school principal and myself.

Although the permanent fair staff was responsible for assigning spaces to the exhibitors, our group's principal purpose was to promote public interest in the big event that took place the first few days of September and closed on Labor Day. In effect we served as a public relations agency. We wrote brochures and handouts to be distributed throughout the county, and produced a steady stream of news releases for the metropolitan daily newspapers, the radio stations and a host of local weekly papers. In addition, we prepared a rather elaborate multi-page program for distribution at the fair, that laid out backgrounds of exhibitors and the entertainers who would be appearing on the stage to entertain the crowds.

From day one they sat me at a typewriter and gave me my marching orders, "Start writing." At first, they edited my copy, telling me that I had to write "with punchier sentences," but I was a quick learner, and soon I mastered their professional style. They not only taught, but they practiced, the four W's of a news story's first paragraph: Tell the reader Who, What, When and Where. Today's "news" stories seem to ignore this credo. Instead, a "hook" or editorial slant, has replaced straight news reporting in so many newspapers, including the *New York Times* and the *Los Angeles Times* where editorializing is not limited to the editorial or op ed pages.

This crew of old timers, including Lee Curran, David T. Jones and Frank Butler, had no problem in taking two and three hours for lunch. "Hold down the fort, guys," they would tell me and Dr. Neal V. Musmanno, a Stowe Township school principal (Neal would later serve as Director of Education for the Commonwealth of Pennsylvania). As a result Neal and I had free rein for a number of writing projects. But these old timers taught me a lot, and my experience with them was superb training for the editor positions I would later assume on The Pitt News.

They regaled us with yarns of old days when they worked with all three Pittsburgh daily newspapers. They were fine writers with a keen eye for the pungent phrase. Especially gratifying was working with H. D. Mc Donald, in charge of layouts and graphic designs for all publications, from whom I received a crash course in the mysteries of various printing fonts—serifs and sans serifs—and what he called the necessity to surround text with proper white space. "You need to use air around print to catch the reader's eye," he said.

Working with these professionals that summer was equivalent to a course in advanced journalism. By Labor Day we all had become close friends. And the next summer, most of us returned to work together again on the 1940 fair.

After the fair closed, Hitler furnished another greeting as I entered my third year at the University – Nazi armies invaded Poland on September 1, 1939.

Because Great Britain had a collective security pact with Poland, the world held its breath to see what it would do. Neville Chamberlain sent Germany an ultimatum to cease and withdraw. It was ignored. We waited throughout the next day. Nothing happened. On September 3rd, he sent a second and final ultimatum early in the morning and requested an immediate reply. Receiving none, Chamberlain appeared on the radio at 11:15 a.m. and announced that, honoring its treaty with Poland, "We are at war."

I was now campus editor of The News, responsible for filling the front page and about two thirds or three quarters of page four, depending on how many ads the business staff had placed. I had learned so much in the summer working with the professional journalists that I was able to sit in the editor's chair with maximum confidence, to wield a thick editing pencil with ease, and to take reporters aside in small groups and furnish practical tips in news writing that I, myself, had not thoroughly acquired in my previous two years on the paper.

I was completely familiar with the entire University environment–its administration, its faculty and its student body, knowledge acquired after a year and a half of reporting and a few months as assistant campus editor. I knew which reporters could be counted on, as well as those who required cajoling and those I had to let go. I devoted substantial time to freshmen applicants, and soon was able to decide whom I wanted on my reporter staff.

I decided not to sign up for 8:30 a.m., first hour classes. I needed quiet time to plan the day because later The News office became too noisy. Crowded into one room was the entire staff--editorial and business, news and sports, editorial page editors and columnists, make-up, copy desk. Along one wall was a line of clackety manual Underwood typewriters. In these close quarters we soon understood what togetherness meant.

Most of the 1939-1940 school year was a period Winston Churchill would call "the Twilight War" with both sides on a static line, facing each other while building their armies. We went to classes and put out the newspaper, but when it came to informal conversations, we usually talked about the war in Europe.

My plate was full during my junior year. The student governing body was called the Student Faculty Association (SFA) and lively politics surrounded the student election process. The fraternities usually controlled with a slate, but in 1939 the non-fraternity people, called GDI (Gawd

Damned Independents), led by my friend Jack Hoeveler, persuaded me to run. I was elected, and took my responsibilities seriously.

It was in this third year, largely through my position as a member of SFA and my role of campus editor of The News, that I became well known throughout the campus. I was elected into membership of Gamma Circle of Omicron Delta Kappa, the men's scholarship/leadership society. Also at that time the University had a long tradition of choosing one man and one woman as "Senior Worthies," based on their contributions to the University community. It was a rather formal ceremony at an assembly that involved displaying a huge wooden spoon on stage. As the two worthies were chosen they were escorted to the stage and the spoon was ceremoniously "dipped" over their heads. Adele Yorio was chosen as the woman, and I was dipped as the man. As senior worthies we were given custody of the spoon and charged with sponsoring the junior worthies for the next year's ceremony.

At the year's end the faculty-student publications board selected me to be next year's editor-in-chief of The News.

On April 24, 1940 my picture appeared in the Pittsburgh Sun-Telegraph over a headline and story:

Stoops To Conquer

> Ruggero Aldisert, 20 of Carnegie, is an editor by day and a copy boy by night.
>
> Ruggero is the newly-elected editor-in-chief of The Pitt News, student tri-weekly at the University of Pittsburgh.
>
> He has been Campus Editor of the paper for the past year. As such, he championed Pitt students who charged they were denied equal parking rights with members of the neighboring Pittsburgh Athletic Association.
>
> On Saturday nights, he is a copy boy in the Sun Telegraph editorial rooms. As copy boy, he speeds stories from the editorial room to the composing room and the news service via pneumatic tubes.
>
> "Rugy" has printers ink in his blood.

> His father is John S. Aldisert, chief deputy coroner and former publisher of "L'Araldo" an Italian weekly. His father is also national president of the Italian Sons and Daughters of America.
>
> As a senior at Carnegie High School "Rugy" founded the Carnegie High School "See."
>
> Last summer he did publicity work for the Allegheny County Free Fair. Before coming to the Sun-Telegraph two months ago, he was a copy boy for International News Service in Pittsburgh.

I continued to work week-ends at the Sun-Tele the remainder of my third year at the University. But on May 10, the no-shooting "Twilight War" came to an end. As Winston Churchill reported,

> During the night of May 9/10, heralded by widespread attacks against airfields, communications, headquarters and magazines, all the German forces in the Bock and Rumstedt Army Groups sprung forward towards France across the frontiers of Belgium, Holland and Luxembourg. Complete tactical surprise was achieved in nearly every case. Out of the darkness came suddenly innumerable parties of well-armed ardent storm troops, often with light artillery, and long before daybreak a hundred and fifty miles of front were aflame. Holland and Belgium, assaulted without the slightest pretext of warning, cried aloud for help. The Dutch had trusted their water-line; all the sluices not seized or betrayed were opened and the Dutch frontier guards fired upon the invaders. The Belgians succeeded in destroying the bridges of the Meuse, but the Germans captured intact two across the Albert Canal.

Four German Armies, with 55 divisions, smashed to the West. Ten Panzer divisions led the assault.

I was scheduled to work at The Sun-Tele on the night of Saturday, May 11, 1940, as a copy boy. At that time there were no computers, no offset printing technology. A reporter would bang out a story on his typewriter.

(Yes, the gender is correct. At that time, most women were relegated to the Society page.) When he finished the story, he would shout "Copy" and a copy boy would hurry to his desk, pick up the story and rush it to a large horseshoe-shaped desk known as the Copy Desk. When a copy editor completed his work, he, too, would yell "Copy," and the copy boy would pick it up and then carry it to the pneumatic tubes station. Here we would insert the story in a tube which was rushed by compressed air to the composing room. There a linotype operator, sitting at a keyboard similar to a typewriter, would transfer the copy to individual lines of lead type. A pot of molten lead was attached to every linotype machine to produce the lead for each line of type

Those were my normal duties as a copy boy. But on the morning of Friday, May 10, I was at The Pitt News office when I received a telephone call from Alec Zehner, my boss, the city editor of the Pittsburgh Sun Telegraph. "Can you drop what you're doing and come to work today? All hell is breaking loose in Europe. Take a cab and we'll pay for it!"

I worked until after midnight and was on the job at seven the next morning. My main duties were to tear off stories from the International News Service teletype machine and carry them to a hastily organized "war" desk where sat both Zehner and the news editor. From time to time came the familiar yell "copy." This meant that I was to bring it to rewrite men who were combining different teletype dispatches into a coherent story on the war.

Those two days—Friday, May 10 and Saturday, May 11--served as my front row seat on the great opening battle of World War II. On Friday Prime Minister Neville Chamberlain was replaced by Winston Churchill, First Lord of the Admiralty. Hour by hour we received reports on how the blitzkrieg crushed everything in its way, how the defenses of the French, Belgian and Dutch crumbled and how the British Expeditionary Force (BEF) was in full retreat. I can still remember the pandemonium in the huge Sun-Telegraph news room. Whenever a story came through on the teletype, the machine rang a bell; if it was a bulletin, it rang three times; the most urgent category was "flash," calling for five bells. Bells were ringing all day. On Friday and Saturday, we put out a number of extra editions; each required a front page makeover and new screaming headlines.

But the Panzer divisions were too much for the defenders. By May 22, ten Panzer divisions completed an end run south of the defense line and then wheeled north, pushing the BEF and the French armies to the sea. Five days later the incredible Dunkirk evacuation back to England began.

On the day he became Prime Minister Churchill would describe the disaster that had begun on Friday, May 10:

> Now at last the slowly gathered, long pent-up fury of the storm broke upon us. Four or five millions of men met each other in the first shock of the most merciless of all the wars of which record has been kept. Within a week the front in France, behind which we have been accustomed to dwell through the hard years of the former war and the opening phase of this, was to be irretrievably broken. Within three weeks the long-famed French Army was to collapse in rout and ruin, and the British Army had to be hurled to the sea with all its equipment lost. Within six weeks we were to find ourselves alone, almost disarmed, with the triumphant Germany and Italy at our throats, with the whole of Europe Open to Hitler's power, and Japan glowering on the other side of the globe.

This, then was the backdrop of my junior year at the University of Pittsburgh.

When classes ended, I again worked in the Allegheny County Fair Office, but as a veteran. I was given more responsibilities in both writing and in administrative matters at the fair grounds during days of the fair. Specifically, I was in charge of the main stand (normally, the judges' stand for trotting horse races) from which I coordinated the program for the main stage, supervised guest high school bands and the many parades in which the exhibitors walked their livestock around the race track.

By Labor day, 1940, I was back on campus and during the first month of my senior year the highly controversial National Selective Training and Service Act was enacted. This was the fancy name for the draft. Reflecting the bitter differences on the war in Europe that racked our country, the draft act passed by only one vote in the U.S. House of Representatives. On campus the draft act commanded more than pure academic interest as we published our first issue of the year on September 18, 1940.

We are often reminded how America was fragmented during the Vietnam war and in the 2004 summer over the Iraq war. Perhaps it's a gap in several generations that the print and electronic media do not remind us of the violent division of opinions that ran rampant in 1939-1941 about our entering the European conflict. To be sure, most Americans hated Nazi Germany and were enthusiastically supportive of Great Britain, but at the same time were loathe to get involved into a shooting war. It took the horrors of one day, the attack on Pearl Harbor on December 7, 1941, to bring about enthusiastic American unity. And it took less than 24 hours for this to come to pass. But in the autumn of 1940 it was no surprise that the opposition was not limited to any particular age group. For the most part, University students, the great idealists of the populace were extremely vocal in opposing our entering the war. We had experienced the same opposition to entering the war in audiences we had faced two years before when a major intercollegiate debate topic had been whether the United States should enter a military alliance with Great Britain.

As I took over The Pitt News, I decided that as a newspaper we would not take a position in our editorials. Although I had the authority as editor-in-chief to do so, I did not believe that I or the senior editors as a group, had the right to convert personal views as the views as of an official student newspaper, that it was inappropriate to do this with a student body so deeply divided. At the same time, I encouraged columnists and letters to the editor that would express individual views. But here, too, I was careful in having a balanced presentation, in encouraging diverse views.

In that memorable autumn we were faced also with President Roosevelt's decision to seek a third term, thus breaking the precedent set by George Washington. Here, too, I had to separate my personal views from official newspaper policy, even though at the time I was vice-chairman of the Young Democrats of Pennsylvania and was in charge of organizing Roosevelt College Clubs from Harrisburg, Pennsylvania to the Ohio border. As we approached the November election, however, I pushed the envelope a little.

Franklin Delano Roosevelt, Jr., a recent graduate of the University of Virginia, had come to town on October 23, 1940, and I had presided at three

Young Democrats rallies (aided by the Democratic payroll) in Pittsburgh to hear him speak. Under my by-line and not an unsigned editorial, I wrote a breezy piece that concluded:

> [FDR, Jr.] had just concluded a Rooseveltian speech that kept 1,000 people following every twitch of his lips, when I leaned over and said, "Your father will be proud of his son tonight."
>
> He squeezed my arm and said, "Thanks, fella."
>
> I liked this guy. I think I'd like his dad, too.

We received an angry Letter to the Editor criticizing my last sentence. I gave the letter prominent display.

Continuing our coverage of the election, we ran an editorial on October 30, 1940:

Youth in Politics
And Modern Democracy

> We are pleased to note the activities on campus of the Roosevelt and Wilkie college clubs.
>
> Historians agree upon one point: That in stable times the nation is ruled by the older, most conservative elements; and that in dynamic times, in times of stress and change, it is the young men who are the guiding factor.
>
> These are times of strain. We believe that we under-twenty-one, we who cannot directly effect but who can be effected, must more than compensate for our inability to vote.
>
> Democracy, it has been proven, is not merely rule of the majority, it is the rule of experts and authorities. These, while their principles of government may coincide with those of the majority, are far more capable, in themselves, of administering those principles than are the masses as a whole.

> We must believe that. If we do not, we must return to the idea of the old town meeting, with some seventy million people standing in squares throughout the nation and signifying their approval of each legislative measure by raising a hand.

Since September I had been content to have pro and con views on the war discussed by our columnists, and always sought an even balance. As the months passed, however, it was becoming more difficult to ignore the war crisis in my editorials. An entire city in Holland, Rotterdam, was completely leveled by Stuka dive bombers. The fire bombing of London continued almost every night. The bravery of the British people was getting to me. Thus, one year before Pearl Harbor, on December 6, 1940, our lead editorial began:

> The United States is, of course, at war.

> Naturally, war is not fought by the solider alone. Someone has to make the gun, the ships, the airplanes, the tanks, the uniforms, the food. The United States at the present time is at work supplying war materials for her allies. Few Americans are fighting at the front. Now.

Others editorials followed. On December 11, 1940 one piece concluded:

> In the United States we have such things as an independent labor movement, free intellectual inquiry and a toleration of the divergent opinions and groups. Even more important than these is the promise of the democratic process which allows dissatisfied individuals to organize political pressure groups without fear of a Gestapo, provided only that these individuals have enough guts and intelligence to organize.

> In America moreover, we know garbage when we smell it. The Nazis have declared the highest end of man is to engage in the violent subjugation of so called inferior races. Garbage has become, for them, a digestible delicacy, the Aryan superman possesses super stomach as well.

> In the face of this racial nonsense we must affirm that our society is worth saving, worth fighting for; yes, and if need be, worth dying for.

A spate of letters to the editor followed. We printed every one, pro and con.

Entering the new year, on January 6, 1941, we said, inter alia:

Belated Analysis
FDR's Speech

> The President quite logically came out for complete non-isolation in his speech to the nation last Sunday. One writer has said that President Roosevelt's policy, if he has a policy, is one of educating the American people to collective security.

> On Sunday in his speech to the majority of the nation—industrial workers, the city clerks, the small business men, the farmers and the old people—he completed his educational program. He asked for an all-out collective security—a collective security of the British Empire and of the United States of America.

The months would pass, and nearing the end of my editorship on May 16, 1941, we said, in part:

Discussion:
Power After the War

> We all know by now that we are in this war up to our necks, as close up as we can go without getting them cut.

> And we are going to take the fatal step in a very few weeks. The President has said that convoys mean shooting and shooting means war. And by war he means real honest-to-God-war. Not the piddling around we have been doing up to now.

Honors Week followed in early May. Our successors as editors of student publications were announced. I was named as one of 12 in the Class of 1941 University Hall of Fame, and later received the George Wharton Pepper Award as the Outstanding Senior man:

**UNIVERSITY OF PITTSBURGH
SENIOR AWARD**
The University of Pittsburgh recognizes
RUGGERO JOHN ALDISERT
As the Senior Man of the
CLASS OF 1941
who best combines character, scholarship, leadership, activities and social bearing

Extending from the Cathedral of Learning east to the Heinz Chapel is the Senior Walk, honoring those who received this award. Carved in stone at its beginning is an inscription describing the qualifications. There follows a designated stone for each year on which is inscribed the name of that year's Senior Awardee. I have treasured this accolade as that historic year's representative as much as any honor or award I have ever received.

I stepped down as editor on May 19, 1941. We had published 91 issues and it was time for me to reminisce.

> Although it has been one swift year for us as Editor, this was also our fourth year on the News staff and at Pitt. And the Pitt we have known in this period is the Pitt which has come through us through the News office.
>
> We have learned to like this Pitt, it was somewhat different from that which we met four years ago. It is a more pleasant Pitt now, the more amicable student-administration relationships. Publications men and women are now working with a definitely organized student-faculty publications board, instead of working against a vague set up then known only to us freshman as "the administration."
>
> And as we are going to remember this Pitt which we like and which has been transmitted to us through this

News office, so we will never forget this paper and the "draggers"; the day and night shifts of the staff, the typists, the reporters, the proof readers, the copy editors.

They have worked anonymously without thought of personal gain or glory. Theirs has been a quiet, undemonstrative performance, unappreciated by many, yet skillful and noiseless in operation.

It is they who showed us that the real Pitt spirit is not found in synthetic football cheers and beery alumni songs and faked applause at annual banquets and flashy globs of yellows keys and rings.

Their spirit, or that thing which we call real spirit, is not self conscious, it is not dramatic, it is not prepared.

The student with real spirit does not fit his actions into a preconceived pattern, rather, it is his action which forms the pattern of the spirit which is Pitt's.

I left the campus with a spring in my step and planned to enter law school in the fall, subject, of course, to a call to the service.

But another tribute was yet to come. I was the subject of an editorial in the May 13, 1941 edition of the Pittsburgh Sun Telegraph:

Aldisert and Alger
Both Begin with "A"

As thousands of young men and women prepare for commencement exercises, no longer can it be said that today's college youth receive their sheepskins with no knowledge of the working world to come. A vivid example of this is Ruggero Aldisert, who has been named the outstanding senior in the graduating class of 1,812 at the University of Pittsburgh. Ruggero, without ever becoming a "grind," combined a job with his college course.
Several summers he helped with publicity for the Allegheny County Fair at South Park. During another period he was copy boy in the Sun Telegraph newsroom. Even with his

jobs, he managed to find time for school activities. Starting out as a reporter on the Pitt News, Ruggero became it's editor in his senior year, at the same time he was President of Omicron Delta Kappa fraternity.

He, like so many other graduates, is proof that the "will to succeed" is still a living thing and not an outmoded fable of Horatio Alger days.

I had decided to enter law school in the fall, but first I had to get a summer job and I needed to make some money and looked around for the best paying job. University honors aside, I was not above doing manual labor if the pay was attractive enough, so by the middle of June I signed on to work in the National Mining Company's coal mine at Sygan, near Bridgeville, about five miles south of Carnegie. I received employee number 886 and my the job description was assistant timberman. My pay $6.00 for the 8-hour, steady third shift from 11 p.m. to 7 a.m. This came to $.75 an hour, but was three times the amount I received the previous summer writing publicity for the Allegheny County Fair Office. Coal was not dug this shift, only repair crews worked the mine. Our job was to reinforce with timber the overheads of new coal "rooms" cut by miners in the day and evening. I became a member of the United Mine Workers of America union, and carried its card as well as that of The Pitt News local of the National Newspapers Guild.

My brother Caesar, who had completed his second year at Pitt's Medical School, had obtained summer work in a steel mill, and together we had bought a 1933 Plymouth sedan for $80. At the end of my shift, I dashed home where Caesar would be waiting at the curb, lunch box in hand. Without turning off the Plymouth's motor, I got out of the car and he jumped in and raced away to be at the mill by 8 o'clock. We called our car, "Plym baby."

In September I returned to the Cathedral of Learning on the Pitt campus. The School of Law with its classrooms, library of faculty offices occupied the 13th and 14th floors and this was a different environment from the unfinished floors where my undergraduate classes and activities had taken place. The class rooms and library had been completed. The floors were finished and furnished, everywhere there was elegance and comfort.

I enjoyed the intellectual challenge in studying courses in contracts, torts, criminal law, property, civil procedure and judicial administration. I enjoyed it every day until Sunday, December 7, 1941.

I cut class on Monday and enlisted in the U.S. Marine Corps.

Campus (city) Editor of The Pitt News 1939-1940. I was responsible for filling the entire first page (newspaper size, not tabloid) and, depending on the size of the ads, most of page 4. We published Monday, Wednesday and Friday of each week.

Editor-in-chief 1940-1941. I always wore a coat and tie, as did most of the students prominent in student activities. This was not exactly a dress code, but a tradition at the University of Pittsburgh. Because reporters on the newspaper regularly interviewed faculty and administration officers, they followed the tradition, as did members of the Men's Debating Association.

Cortland Bacall, business manager of The Pitt News, and I pictured boarding a Pennsylvania Central Airlines (PCA) on our way to Detroit to attend a national conference of college newspaper executives. The date is November 5, 1940, the day after the Roosevelt-Willkie election. In my hand is a copy of the Pittsburgh Press showing a picture of the President who successfully ran for the third term, breaking the tradition started by George Washington. It was my first trip on an airplane. PCA was a forerunner of Allegheny Airlines which later became USAirways.

The yearbook picture of the Senior Awardee of the class of 1941.

Frick Acres 1940 view of the Cathedral of Learning and the Heinz Chapel on the University of Pittsburgh campus. During this period almost all undergraduate classes and student activities, except sports, were located in the Cathedral. It is still the nerve center of the greatly expanded University campus. Photo courtesy Library and Archives Division, Historical Society of Western Pennsylvania, Pittsburgh, PA.

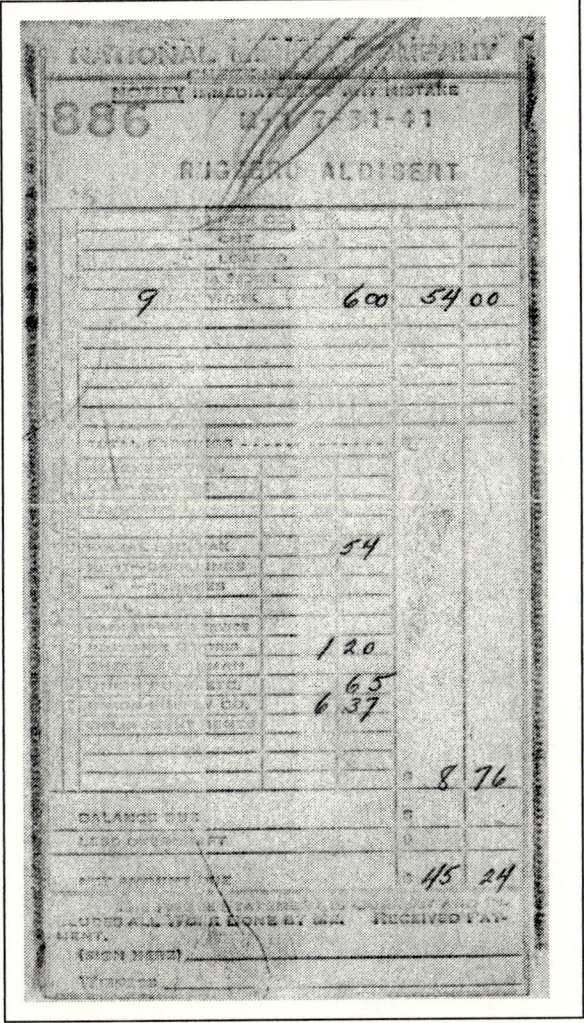

Summer 1941. My pay envelope for working nine days at $6.00 a day, pay period ending July 31, 1941. What does the honor graduate do after Commencement exercises in June 1941? He looks for a summer job that will pay the most until he enters law school in September. Working in a coal mine would paid twice as much as a white collar job-- 75 cents an hour (that's $9.66 in today's dollars). Through the intervention of Dr. Dante Pigossi, a family friend and company doctor the National Mining Company at Sygan, Pennsylvania, I got a job as assistant timberman. on the the steady third trick, or from 11 p.m. to 7 a.m., during which maintenance took place in the mine shafts. Digging coal took place only during the morning and evening shifts. Miners always work in pairs, using the "buddy" system. My buddy was Steve, a wonderful gnarled old veteran of the mines, an immigrant from Poland. He was the a timberman who fastened planks to the overhead of the mine shafts, to create wooden ceiling. This was designed to keep prevent coal loosened by the dynamiting of "rooms" or forward walls from falling on the miners. My job was to hand planks to him and hold them in place while he pounded. At first he called me "boy" and seldom talked except during our lunch break at 3 or 4 a.m. After a few weeks he got word somehow that I had graduated form college. Our relationship changed immediately. Thereafter, he proudly introduced me to fellow worker as his "friend" who, in his words, "was going to make me smart." It actually worked out the other way. I learned much from him as a person and still remember Steve with great affection.

Chapter Fourteen
The Marine Corps Influence

My years in the U. S. Marine Corps influenced me as much as any experience in life. I went in as a private at the beginning of World War II and ended up as a captain at war's end. During the war years I grew up in a hurry. My growth continued after the war for five more years in the Corps as a reserve officer attaining the rank of major. The nine years of military service taught me many things, but especially it was a crash course in responsibility and discipline.

No other organization teaches it better than the Marines.

They admonish Marine Corps officers not to become an "I.D"--an impotent dinosaur, "docile fossil with a fossil dossal." They drilled combat principles into our skulls daily in officers' school, principles that we practiced daily in the field, especially in the forward areas of the Pacific.

Marine Corps discipline is a credo, but basic precepts of responsible decision-making stood me well upon re-entering civilian life, finishing my final years in law school at the University of Pittsburgh, with a four year hiatus between my first and second years, then practicing my profession as lawyer and judge for almost 60 years. Many lawyers and too many judges, slog through their professional careers as I.D.'s, constantly at a loss on how to begin to make a decision.

They train a Marine officer to estimate a military problem and then follow a definite pattern. You begin with an estimate--your troops, the enemy, terrain, weather, ammunition supply, food supply, location of adjacent units. From the estimate you reach a decision, then you form a plan and issue an order to implement it. The formula is simple: estimate> decide> plan> order.

Making a decision is the military commander's most important mission. Napoleon and Frederick the Great are often quoted: "A good decision arrived at too early or too late is too bad. He who estimates best will win in the end." In the forward areas Marine officers are exposed to countless situations on which you must form an estimate. The rudiments of estimate-decision-plan-order, although fashioned in a military concept, serve as the *vade mecum* for all practitioners in the legal profession:

THE MISSION

Military: Your company is assigned as the advance guard. Your orders: advance to the front, drive off enemy patrols to permit main body to move forward, set up defensive position for main body to deploy.
Civilian:
Lawyer: Represent your client's interest in a business transaction or as an advocate in a courtroom.
Judge: As a trial judge, to determine credibility and find facts, if non-jury. To decide if the burden of proof has been met. To rule on evidentiary matters. To instruct the jury properly. As an appellate judge, to decide if the trial judge committed a reversible error, not an insignificant error, remembering always that a litigant is entitled to a fair trial, not a perfect one.

SURVEY OF OPPOSING STRENGTHS

Military: Don't attack where enemy is strong. Attack where he is weakest--weak in manpower, terrain, supporting arms. Hit the weakest point so that your reserves can follow the unit making the main effort. Mission of leaders--company commander, platoon leaders, squad leaders: look for weakness and shift the main effort there; know the terrain, disposition of troops, possibility of re-enforcement, time and space to maneuver, weather, status of supply and evacuation.

Civilian:

Lawyer: Know what facts and law favor your adversary and where he is weak. Know where you are strong and where you are weak. Act accordingly.

Judge: Know the law thoroughly to understand the strengths and weaknesses of the legal arguments before you.

ENEMY COURSES OF ACTION

Military: Conceptualize all courses of action the enemy is physically capable of making. Base fire: stationary or mobile? Can he outflank you? If so, in what direction?

Civilian:

Lawyer: Investigate your opponent's case thoroughly to anticipate possible defenses to your attack. Does the opponent have an alternative course of action to your attack?

Judge: Do not prejudge until testimony or final arguments are completed. Litigants may shift positions during trial or on appeal, or between written brief and oral argument.

YOUR COURSE OF ACTION

Military: Conceptualize what courses of action you are capable of making. Amount of fire power for direct assault. What are possibilities of performing a flanking action?

Civilian:

Lawyer: What is your "battle plan" whether negotiating or trying a case? What are alternative courses of action?

Judge: Same as previous section. Do not prejudge until testimony or final argument is completed. Litigants may shift positions during trial or on appeal, or between brief writing and oral argument.

DECISION, PLAN AND ORDER

Military: After your reconnaissance, survey opposing strengths, the enemy's courses of action, your courses of action, before you decide to attack. Your decision is what? where? when? why? and how?
Civilian:
Lawyer: Because you represent a client, the decision is made for you. You must formulate your plan and implement it by answering the same five questions presented to the military.
Judge: You, too, must answer the questions what? why? and how? Your decision is "what." Answer it as clearly as possible by explaining "why" you are doing it. Describe "how" you reached "what" by faithful adherence to logical order containing premises that are true and valid.

The Marines taught me the real meaning of responsibility. Two weeks after I arrived at my first overseas post in the Pacific as a brand new second lieutenant, the artillery battalion commander called me in: "We're short of officers here and I'm giving you a temporary assignment as commanding officer of an understaffed battery. You'll be the only officer, but there's a good sergeant," he said. I was still wet behind the ears and was named C.O. of a battery, the only commissioned officer.

We were on a tiny atoll, Johnston Island, 1328 miles south and west of Honolulu. It was one of the three outlying American bases in the middle of nowhere in the Pacific, the others being Midway and Wake, which had been fortified for one purpose–to keep the Japanese from invading the Hawaiian Islands. An atoll is essentially a reef, the high points of which constitute islands that ring a lagoon. These atolls contained a substantial number of jungle islands, each of which having an ocean side and a lagoon side.

But there were no jungles on this atoll. When I arrived on Johnston, the "big" island was a little over the size of a carrier–1000 yards long, 300 yards wide, elevation 14 feet. Not a smidgeon of vegetation, merely coral. A half mile to the east was Sand Island, about three acres in size, large enough to support an 90 mm. anti-aircraft battery on a tiny spit extending

THE MARINE CORPS INFLUENCE   207

from a glorified sand dune. On this tiny island also was a small Naval detachment that tended a diesel storage tank and a rudimentary dock to service submarines on their last stop for fuel on their way to Japanese convoy targets in the East.

The Japanese had been successful in capturing Wake Island as part of the overall Pearl Harbor operation. A few months before I arrived in the Pacific they had attempted a massive attack on Midway, and were unsuccessful. The Japanese now occupied Wake, and when I arrived at Johnston, the only other outpost standing between the Japanese and Hawaii was Midway.

We were only half of a Marine Corps Defense Battalion defending Johnston; the other half of our battalion had been sent to Wake Island, and our comrades were now prisoners of war. I arrived a little over a year after the Pearl Harbor attack, and a few months after the Marines had begun the first offense of the war in the Pacific by landing on Guadalcanal several thousands miles to the south.

To understand how primitive our defenses had been in the Pacific at the beginning of 1943, you must understand that there were only two aircraft carriers that were operational at the end of 1942. Out in the islands we were not told this. "You and Midway are our stationary aircraft carriers," we were told.

The armament on this tiny atoll consisted of two 90 mm. anti aircraft batteries of four guns each, a seacoast artillery battery of three 5 inch naval cannons, a four gun three-inch anti-aircraft battery manned by Seabee enlisted men, a searchlight battery and a battery of several sections of 40 mm. anti aircraft guns and .50 caliber machine guns.

The 90 mm. gun batteries had state of the art fire control equipment, that could direct the elevation and azimuth (the left and right movements) and the correct setting on the fuses to explode the projectiles, but we were denied an accurate component to be sent to the fire control instrument called the "director" to compute this data--the exact altitude of enemy planes. Army units on other installations had radars to calculate the height of the target exactly, but the Marines did not get this equipment until 1944–two years after Pearl Harbor. Instead, we had to resort to highly subjective guess work. We had to utilize a stereoscopic height-finder that was a 15 feet long metal cylinder about 20 inches in diameter with telescopes at each end. This instrument produced three dimensional viewing. We had to choose the man who had the best stereoscopic vision in the outfit, that is, the ability to use dials and estimate the proper depth of target as it appeared to him in his scope. The dialed impression was fed to fire control and was used to calculate the range of the target. The height-finder technique had been used by anti-aircraft batteries since the Twenties, but fortunately all naval vessels had radar control from the earliest days of Pacific combat.

The searchlight battery was designed to illuminate targets, but the training was somewhat limited. On Johnston Island blackout was 100 per cent with no exceptions, including uncovered cigarette smoking at night

No trees or any other vegetation existed on Johnston, just coral sand that glared bright white during the day for the 500 Marines and Seabees (Naval Construction Battalions). We all lived in dugouts in those early days. Seabees operated dredges by day to retrieve sand from the ocean bottom and pile it on the island to extend its length as fast as possible. The plan for the Seabees was to increase the island's size in order to have a landing strip that would be long enough to handle combat aircraft.

At first, two amphibian planes, Navy PBY's, top speed, 105 knots, constituted our sole aircraft protection. They flew dawn and twilight patrols taking off and landing in the lagoon between the reef and the shore. Seabees were soon able to create a coral runway of proper length for a dive bombing squadron to use, and soon a squadron of SBD's (Dauntless Dive Bombers) arrived, to become our major defense against an attack by sea. But the Seabees continued to dredge and extend the size of the island because the high command planned to use this forward atoll as a bomber's base.

After a few months I was replaced in my original assignment by an Annapolis graduate who had received specialized training in radar. Thereafter, I served variously as range officer and executive officer of Johnston's 90 mm battery; and my final assignment there was commanding officer of the 90 mm battery on Sand Island.

1943 was the critical year in the Pacific because in the year before, battles at Midway in June and Guadalcanal in August, collectively, represented the turning point of the Pacific war. At Guadalcanal, the Japanese threw everything they had against us—mounting massive naval encounters, landing many thousands of reinforcements to prevent us from keeping that island, with its airstrip, as a forward base. A few months later the Marines smashed into Tarawa in the Gilberts, south of the Japanese massive fortifications of the Marshall Islands.

In the three-day battle for Tarawa November 20-23, 1943, Marine casualties came to 3,301 killed, wounded and missing in action, most occurring on D-day. This was a high price to pay for a few hundred acres of coral. My commanding General of the Fifth Amphibious Corps, (VAC), Holland M. Smith, later would write:

> From the beginning the decision of the Joint Chiefs to seize Tarawa was a mistake and from their original mistake grew the terrible drama of errors, errors of omission rather than commission, resulting in these needless casualties... We should have left Tarawa " to wither on the vine."

The planners grossly erred in predicting the tides, and although this was the first landing against a heavily fortified island and the first to use amphibious tractors, they guessed wrong on the number of tractors needed—they required double the amount than they used, and most of them got hung up on the reefs. Most of the Marines killed on D-Day were caught in the amphibious tractors stranded on the reefs—truly sitting ducks—or were wiped out as they waded to shore.

On Johnston we received details of Tarawa from observers who passed through on their return to Pearl Harbor. The general consensus: "We lost a lot of good guys in this fucked up operation." This was solemn news, but because Tarawa and the Gilbert Islands, now forward air bases, changed the status of Johnston. We were no longer the forward American outpost in the Central Pacific. Accordingly, the Johnston Island Marine detachment was alerted to prepare for an amphibious landing for some future operation. For weeks scuttlebutt ran rampant at to where we were going, or how much of the island's detachment would remain where we were.

Our sailing orders soon came. Our battalion was ordered to furnish a reinforced 90 mm. battery, and officers were told that we were to participate in an operation in the Marshall Islands. When they formed the new unit, I was selected as its executive officer.

To be sure, there was the up side of the Gilberts' operation, but we did not know it as we prepared to stage for the Marshalls. From Tarawa we were able to send aircraft to neutralize the enemy as we proceeded into the Marshall Islands two months later. The blood lost in the Gilberts would make possible great bloodless victories in the Marshalls. But as we prepared to make a combat landing 1500 miles to the west and south, we thought only of Tarawa.

The C.O. of the newly formed 90 mm. battery was Capt. Gilbert Hole, who was the relatively new commander of the 90 mm. battery on Johnston Island (where I previously served as executive officer before he arrived) while I commanded the battery on Sand Island. Because we were on different islands, we did not know each other very well, but after we staged for the Marshalls and shared the same stateroom on the troop transport, our chemistry matched and we generally liked each other. Accompanying this troop transport was an LST (Landing Ship Tank) carrying our artillery, tractors, bulldozers, jeeps, fire control equipment and ammunition..

"Rugi, let's face it," Hole said to me. "At least half of these troops are from your battery. They know you better than me. The guys from my outfit know you as well. Two things more. I'm new to 90 mm. guns and this is my first command of a large number of troops. I'm the B. C. and you're the exec, and I intend that you, my executive officer, run this battery. O.K.?" After we landed, we shared the same tent and in time would consider ourselves as each other's best friend.

When we reached the Marshalls area, our task force was ordered to circle in wide arcs until further orders. We were now considered reserve corps artillery of the Fifth Amphibious Corps, (VAC) Fleet Marine Force, General Holland M. "Howling Mad" Smith commanding. We received word that the real fighting had taken place on Kwajalein Atoll, with the 7th Army Division landing on its south end , and the 4th Marine Division landing on Roi-Namur islands at the north end on the atoll. Kwajalein was secure in a matter of days. Learning the lessons from Tarawa, the plan was to by-pass other strongly defended atolls in the Marshalls.

The key to this strategy was Majuro Atoll, 220 miles west of Kwajalein, and in the center of strong highly-defended Japanese atolls—5 miles from Mille, 175 miles from Jaluit, 75 miles from Maleolap, and 150 miles from Wotje. Intelligence indicated that Majuro had little or no defenders. On January 31, 1944 a Fifth Amphibious Corps Reconnaissance Company made a quick landing and proved the intelligence to be correct. The early seizure of Majuro atoll was important because of its intended use as an advanced air and naval base. Its lagoon is about 21 miles long by five miles wide and extends generally east and west.

We soon got our orders--to land on Majuro to reinforce the 1st Marine AAA Battalion setting up on Uliga (Rosalie) Island. Our task force's mission: to repulse any enemy air approach from the northwest and to set up a perimeter defense for the battalion on the line where the jungle began. Immediately, runways were laid out for squadrons of F4F and F4U fighter bombers and twin engine bombers that soon began twice-daily bombing on the heavily defended Japanese installations only a few air miles away. General Smith's strategy proved absolutely correct, "Bomb the hell out of them and let them wither on the vine."

We set up our guns on Majuro—2,343 miles from Pearl Harbor and 2,448 miles from Tokyo. We took inventory of our reinforced artillery battery, jerry-rigged because VAC headquarters in Pearl Harbor sent us additional personnel who joined us the day we landed. We received a state–of–the–art fire control radar with a skilled crew, a .50 caliber machine gun section of trained gunners, an unexplained shipment of six .30 caliber Browning water-cooled machine guns and two squads of infantry.

A few weeks after we landed, a captain, who had been a Quantico instructor of mine, reached me. "I'm commanding a company of light tanks that were used in the landing," he said. "We're now shipping back to Pearl. For some reason I can't fit the last damned tank on the LST. The convoy is set to sail and I don't have the time to reload. It's a real SNAFU situation. I need a favor from you. The best solution would be for you to take this damn tank off my hands. I've prepared some papers saying that you made the request and I have acceded." One of his tankers drove the clanking tank to my battery area and parked it across the company street from my tent. When the battalion commander asked me about it one day, I said that it came in a package that VAC headquarters in Pearl had sent to us.

One of my interesting assignments in the combat area tour was company commander of a Provisional Reconnaissance Company (VAC) that left Majuro on two LCI's (Landing Craft Infantry). This remarkable vessel could sail open seas with a capacity of 100 men and yet ride right up to a beach without transferring the troops to Higgins boats or Amphtracks (amphibious tractors) for the landings. Our patrols were described in *THE MARSHALLS: Increasing the Tempo* (Official Marine Corps Publication 1954):

> During the month of April [1944], Marine and Army forces reconnoitered three other atolls, the last to be secured in the Marshalls before the end of the war.
>
> On 17 April a force of 199 Marines from the First Defense Battalion VAC [Fifth Amphibious Corps], embarked from Majuro on two LCI(L)'s with the mission of reconnoitering Erikub and Aur Atolls. Erikub lies a mere five miles from Wotje, and Aur only ten miles from Maloelap. Despite the proximity of the small atolls to the two formidable Japanese bases, no enemy was found on either. The Marines returned to Majuro only four days after departing it.

Our provisional company was a self-contained unit escorted by a DE (a destroyer escort, smaller than a destroyer), with two fighter planes furnishing temporary air cover during the landings. These by-passed atolls were strategically located and our mission was to reconnoiter them to discover whether any Japanese were hiding there.

After we returned and cleaned up, we were given a second assignment to explore a third atoll. This mission, too, was reported in *THE MARSHALLS:*

> Troops from this organization also conducted reconnaissance of Arno Atoll which had been reconnoitered shortly after the occupation of Majuro. No enemy was found on Arno.

We found no Japanese on the islands, but met many natives in primitive villages. As we would enter a village the entire populace would assemble to greet us. They knew we were coming; there are no secrets on small islands.

We would follow the same ritual in each village. As commanding officer I would make a little speech, translated by Johnny, our native translator, and I would conclude: "In the name of Franklin Delano Roosevelt, President of the United States, I do declare that this island is now under the protection of the United States. You are no longer under the power of the Emperor of Japan."

We possessed a large American flag on a line and pulley, and Johnny would scamper up a coconut tree to attach the pulley and line. At the conclusion of my remarks, the detail came to attention, and at my command "Present Arms" the riflemen brought their rifles to the proper position, and officers and sergeants executed the hand salute. A sergeant pulled the line and the American flag was hoisted to the top of the tree. This always impressed the natives. The chief would respond with brief words and present me with a gift, usually one or two chicken eggs, and often a woven mat or *buka*, which served as a bed, symbolizing a welcome to the village.

THE MARSHALLS carried an explanation by a civil affairs officer of the purpose of the ceremony that took place on the various patrols:

> After the proclamation explanation and the posting formality, the American flag was raised . . . one platoon at present arms, staff officers at hand salute, natives in a group in the center. A marine photographer made a picture record of each raising. The ceremony appealed to the natives, and was an aid in inculcating the idea that they were under American protection and no longer subject to Japanese rule.

We had no photographer, but as we would leave a village we would bring down the flag and retrieve it for use at the next village.

For the most part the natives had been baptized by Christian missionaries at the turn of the century and had equated morality with clothing. Thus, the women were dressed in long old-fashion Mother Hubbard dresses that extended from the neck to the ankle. This was hardly a costume to be worn in the tropics— we were on the equator–but the women wore them all the time even when they waded into the lagoon to perform daily ablutions. They suffered from extreme skin rashes as a result, and many were victims of yaws, a venereal disease.

But there was one rather large island described to us by the natives as "the bad lands." Johnny could not help us here, and we landed there with some trepidation. We soon encountered the natives. They wore few clothes and these covered only the waist; both men and women were generously tattooed. I soon decided that because they and their forbears had not succumbed to the missionaries, they were regarded as "bad people."

We impressed them with our ritual, especially after we hoisted the red, white and blue, but at one point they suddenly they became very disturbed– very nervous and very audible- gesticulating toward us. Johnny jumped into the breach and inquired what was wrong. He broke into a smile and explained to me. One of my corporals, Leslie Watson, had removed his helmet. He was very blond and the natives had never seem blond hair before. Johnny said, "They think he is a god."

"Good, tell them that he is a god, but a good one. He's an American god who has come to help them." I turned to Watson. "Keep your helmet off and don't smile. They think you're a god and I order you to act like one," I said.

The amphibious reconnaissances were generally uneventful, but as we headed back to Majuro on the last day of our patrol to Erikub and Aur, a Marine Corps fighter bomber zoomed close to us, waggled its wings and eventually made Morse Code contact with us. "You made the wrong ninety degree turn. You are now headed for Mille." This was the strongly defended Japanese atoll that our aircraft bombed every day. "Turn about 180 degrees."

I had previous troubles with the Navy captain of my landing craft, who also commanded the "flotilla" of two craft. He was only a lieutenant junior grade. On on approaching the first island of our patrol, had refused to take his craft ashore to land us. "Afraid of unknown reefs," he said. As a result, we had to shift to rubber boats, and by the time we hit the beach from a half mile out, we were exposed in broad daylight instead of protected by the dark at 3 a.m. as originally planned. Fortunately, no Japanese were present to repel us, but the Navy officer eliminated the critical element of surprise. From then on, as we proceeded from island to island, my relationship with this man was not exactly cordial.

When faced with this wrong turn debacle that could have wiped us out, he asked if I would please not include it in the official report of the patrol. I made no promises, but I didn't give him the satisfaction that I did not intend to do it. But the incident merited a footnote in *THE MARSHALLS*:

> One pilot subsequently recalled that as he was returning from a mission he spotted two LCI (L)'s which had reconnoitered Aur Atoll and were one the way back to Majuro. Somehow the two vessels made an incorrect turn and were inadvertently heading for Mille. The pilot flew low over the craft, sending them a message in Morse by means of a flashing light. He thus notified them of their error and in all probability saved the lives of the men on board.

I would spend 13 months in the Marshall Islands under field conditions, and that means not having the luxury of a flush toilet, washing my face and shaving in cold water in my steel helmet, eating Army Tropical rations B, based on a ten day diet cycle consisting of Spam for 20 of the 30 meals. And when I returned to civilization after being on Johnston and in the Marshalls for such a long time, I had the treats of all treats—I saw a Caucasian woman for the first time in 20 months! Up to that time the only women I had even seen were the Micronesian natives on the jungle atolls of Aur, Erikub and Arno atolls during the time I was commanding the Fifth Amphibious Corps Provisional Reconnaissance Company. There had been no women on Johnston, nor on the islands that we occupied on Majuro Atoll.

When I returned to the States I was a seasoned Marine Corps officer and was assigned for temporary duty at Marine Corps Headquarters, as the most junior officer in the Division of Plans and Policy, the unit that was studying options for the invasion of the Japanese homeland and Formosa (now Taiwan). My commanding officer was Col. David M. Shoup who was awarded the Medal of Honor at Tarawa. In later years he would become Commandant of the Marine Corps.

My Marine Corps training taught me preparation, discipline and responsibility that I have applied throughout my career as lawyer and judge. Trial judges require monumental self-discipline. If the court is scheduled to open at 9:30 a.m., the judge should be on the bench at that time. The litigants, lawyers and witnesses are there, and so is the jury. The judge may be the boss in the courtroom, but to command respect, the judge must earn it. This is self-discipline. If the judge is to hold others responsible for not obeying society's rules, the judge must obey these rules as well.

Self-discipline also means making a decision without undue delay, whether ruling from the trial bench or as an appellate judge deciding an appeal and writing an opinion. I fervently believe in the axiom: Justice delayed is justice denied. This also means doing justice without fear or favor, regardless of who appears before you as litigant or lawyer. Judges who do not do this lack personal discipline.

You can't be a good lawyer or a good judge unless you possess a profound sense of preparedness and responsibility. My nine years in the Marines, on active and reserve duty, gave me a post graduate education in these ideals. At home our parents had constantly drilled into us the importance of duty, obligation and accountability. I had some experience with responsibility in high school, and a massive dose of it at the University of Pittsburgh as editor-in-chief of its student newspaper, published three days a week. Years as a Marine officer inculcated in me, however, an understanding that you cannot perform properly in society unless you are willing to both make decisions and then justify them. This is the unstated notion that undergirds the entire concept of professional or judicial ethics.

An unspoken accusation of lack of responsibility lies at the heart of the pervasive criticisms of the legal profession. I could go through the litany-- lack of adequate preparation, failure to follow procedural rules, blundering, faltering and floundering in many aspects of the practice-- whether giving advice, writing an instrument, negotiating, appearing in a trial court or writing or orally arguing appeals. Part of this stems from taking short cuts; part, from shooting from the hip without adequate preparation, taking cases you are not competent to handle--in the vernacular, "biting off more than you can chew." It all goes back to one's sense of professional responsibility.

THE MARINE CORPS INFLUENCE 217

In the 14 years I practiced law as a sole practitioner, I needed extraordinary self-discipline in parceling my time. Lincoln's adage was ever important: "A lawyer's time and advice are his stock in trade." If you work for a law firm, utilizing every moment of your time to be productive does not matter much except for the managing partner's constant call for billable hours. When you're a sole practitioner, non-productive time has the effect of a lockout or general strike. The rent continues to run and the secretary and the telephone company have to be paid and the mortgage and the car payments have to be met.

When you served as a Marine Corps officer in a forward area during the war you had to be prepared always to make decisions; even not to decide was in itself a decision. To make decisions is to assume responsibility. Failure to reason properly in defending your decision is a sign of weakness. Your men will know it. Your superior officers will know it. And when you do this when you practice law, your clients will know it. Your adversary will know it. And judges will know it, too.

Private first class, summer 1942.

Brand new 2d Lieut., October 1942.

Johnston Island, November 1943. Pictured are four battery commanders of the 16th Defense Battalion, Fifth Amphibious Corps. From the left, 1st Lieut. David Logg, 40 mm battery; Captain Mike Mickelson, Godbold battery 90 mm; I am next, a 1st lieut, Lewis battery 90 mm on Sand Island; and Captain "Swede" Larsen, Seabee battery 3-inch. Our two 90 mm batteries were named after the commanders of the battalion's two other 90 mm batteries that were stationed on Wake Island. The undermanned Marine Corps detachment on Wake was captured by the Japanese shortly after Pearl Harbor in December 1941. Both Godbold and Lewis survived almost four years of internment.

Johnston Island, December 1943. As a Christmas card artillery officers posed in front of their newly erected Neissen hut. Previously, most of us had lived underground. The Navy had opened a laundry and we were showing off starched khakis. From the left, 2d Lieut. Gus Hardardt (of the New York Automat family), Marine Gunner Glenn C. O'Dare, 1st Lieut Robert C. Bain, who in later years served as a judge in Portsmouth, Virginia; Capt. Mickelson, yours truly and 2d Lieut. Howard Williams. Capt. Larsen had been rotated back to Hawaii for reassigment.

December 1943. A view of Lewis battery on Sand Island, one mile east of Johnston, which I commanded. These gun emplacements constituted most of the entire island. Because of the high water threshold we could not excavate the gun positions; instead we erected pyramids of sand to protect the artillerymen, their artillery pieces and ammunition. My battle station was at the top of the pyramid in the right foreground. The guns are located in the other pyramids. There was not a bit of vegetation on either island at Johnston Atoll.

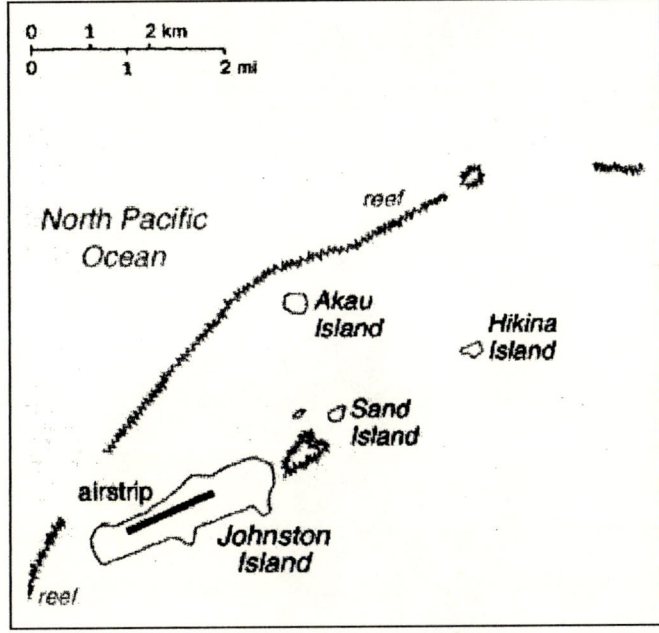

A current map of what is now called Johnston Atoll. Johnston is now over 3,500 yards long and over 800 yards wide. When I arrived there in early 1943 it was 1,000 yards by 300, and 14 feet high. Sand Island is still the same size. Akau and Hikina Islands are man-made and did not exist during World War II.

The sun was hot and blinding. I alternated days between wearing shorts and short-sleeved shirts and full khakis as pictured at my command post. which is on top of the pyramid. During the 11 months I was on Johnston, we never had a cloud in the sky or a drop of rain. When I arrived in early 1943 Johnston and Midway were our last outlying military bases in the Central Pacific after the fall of Wake Island in December, 1941.

THE MARINE CORPS INFLUENCE 225

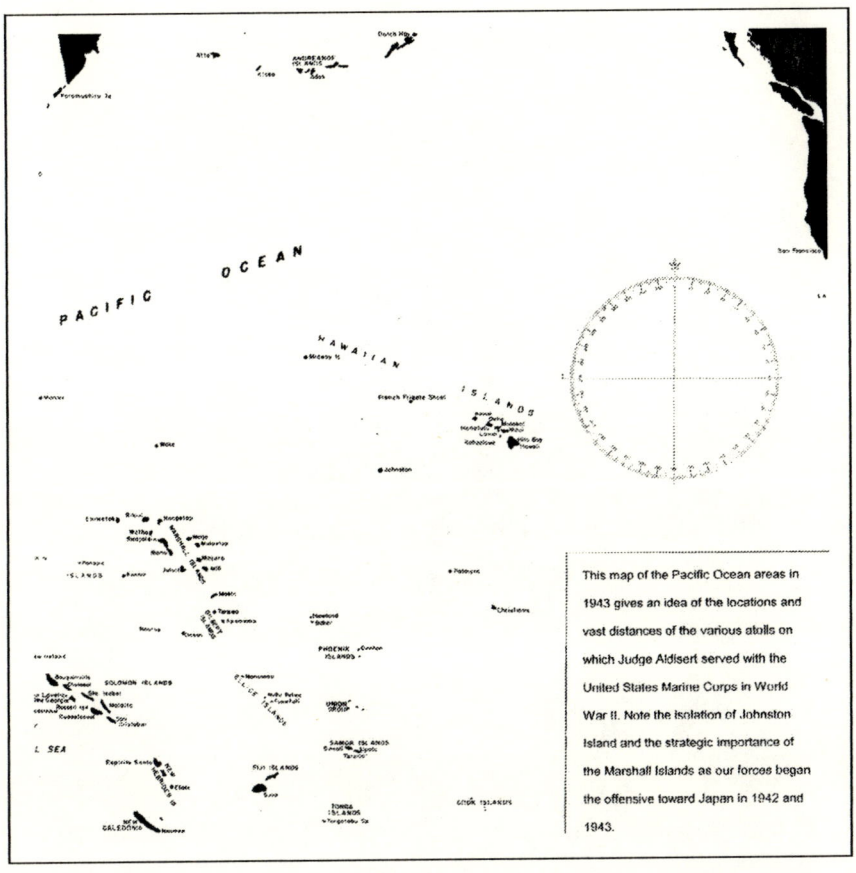

This map of the Pacific Ocean areas in 1943 gives an idea of the locations and vast distances of the various atolls on which Judge Aldisert served with the United States Marine Corps in World War II. Note the isolation of Johnston Island and the strategic importance of the Marshall Islands as our forces began the offensive toward Japan in 1942 and 1943.

Top, previous page: Driving my jeep through King Battery's company street on Majuro, Marshall Islands in March 1944. After the horrendous casualties on D-Day on Tarawa, the Pacific command decided to avoid strongly defended atolls in the Marshalls. Thus, they chose Majuro atoll where we landed with no resistance and built a large airstrip from which to bomb the nearby Japanese bases. At the same time the large Majuro lagoon served as an excellent forward harbor for the fleet.

Bottom, previous page: Majuro, Marshall Islands June 1944. The battalion commander of the 1st AAA Battalion, Fifth Amphibious Corps meets with his 90 mm battery commanders. I am in the center and had recently assumed command of Fox Battery after serving as executive officer of King Battery. This was shortly after D-Day in Normandy.

Above: Marshall Islands, 1944. This photograph taken on Eniwetok is typical of the practice of raising the American flag to notify natives that their islands were no longer under the control of the Emperor of Japan and that the inhabitants were now under the protection of Franklin D. Roosevelt, President of the United States. There is a little difference between what is pictured here and the patrols I led on Erikub, Aur and Arno Atolls. We had many more troops participating than the handful pictured here, and our villages were much larger with 100 or so native men, women and children. Additionally, we had no civil affairs officers who are pictured here in pith helmets.

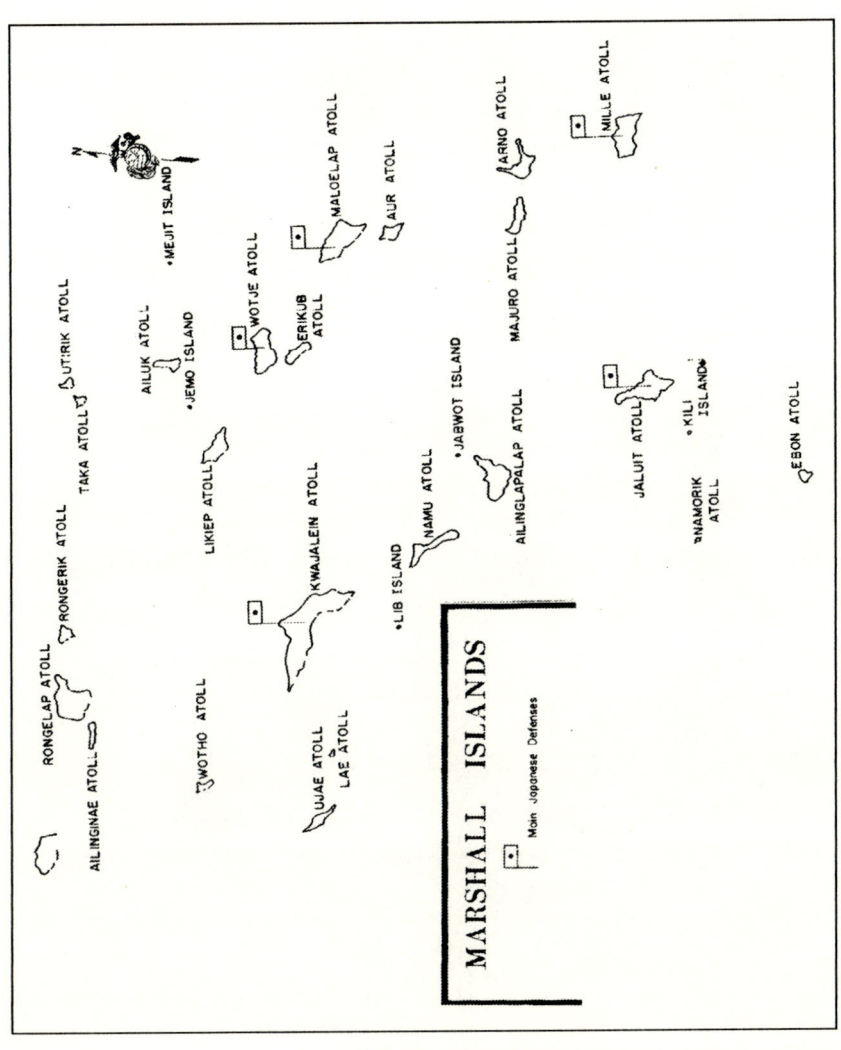

1945 Promoted to captain, back in the States on duty at U. S. Marine Corps Headquarters, Washington, D.C.

Chapter Fifteen
The Birth of a Lawyer

It was the afternoon of December 8, 1947. The place, Courtroom No. 1 of Criminal Court on the third floor of the old Richardson-designed courthouse in Pittsburgh. Presiding was Judge Samuel A. Weiss.

> If it please the court, my name is Ruggero J. Aldisert and I have entered my appearance for the defendant who is present and standing by my side. He is prepared to enter a plea of guilty to the indictment charging him with forgery.

I had become a lawyer and this was my first case after having been admitted to the bar only a few hours earlier that day in a ceremony before Judge Harry Montgomery in the Assignment Room of Common Pleas Court.

I was no stranger to the courthouse. For three months I had roamed its courtrooms while serving my Pennsylvania preceptorship, a system in which law school graduates had to clerk with a lawyer--without pay--for six months after taking the bar examination before they could be admitted to the bar. Before this, however, I had returned to law school in February, 1946 to pick up where I had left off four years before. I was admitted as second year student amidst a motley crew. Some had started law school in

September 1944 and were proceeding in a normal schedule, but a goodly number of us had put in a year or a year and a half before the war.

The law school at the University of Pittsburgh had an accelerated program with year-around classes for those of us who were in a hurry to get on with our lives. After taking the second semester in 1946, I continued that summer, the took a complete year beginning in September, 1946 and had to finish in the summer of 1947. The Pennsylvania bar examinations were scheduled for the second week in August, 1947, and my study group of five guys took our final law school exams on Monday and Tuesday and the Pennsylvania bar exams on Thursday and Friday of the same week.

The five of us attended classes or studied together seven days a week that summer, putting in 18-hour days, boning up on the bar exams; especially on subjects that we had taken in 1941 and early 1942. None of us expected to pass the bars, because we could not take a formal bar review course. In those days you had to go to Philadelphia to do that. Yet, when the results were announced, four of us had passed. The "togetherness" we experienced during that summer made us a true band of brothers and we remained very close friends thereafter.

World War II veterans had special favors in the required preceptorship time; mine had been cut in half. My preceptor, Premo J. Columbus, had been a former Assistant U. S. Attorney, and advised me to become a courthouse groupie and watch masters of the bar at work. His practice was limited to four or five large criminal cases a year in federal court and he was between cases during the time I was with him so he sent me up to the courthouse rather than to run errands for him:

> Watch what the good guys do. Defense counsel and prosecutors alike. See how they open to a jury and handle witnesses. Watch their body language. Observe how they romance a jury. They are more resourceful in criminal court, but also keep tab what is taking place on the civil side. If a good lawyer is on a case, follow him throughout the trial from the opening speech to the judge's charge. Get the feel of a courtroom so that when it's time for you to start you'll be comfortable.

I had got the feel and had become comfortable.

To be sure, my father led me by the hand through the courtroom corridors. By 1947 he had been in the Coroner's Office for 24 years as Chief Deputy Coroner, and knew all the judges, and equally important for a new lawyer-to-be, he knew all the court attachés--the court criers, bailiffs, tipstaves and minute clerks. He knew them all because he was always the first witness for the prosecution in homicide cases. He established the chain of custody of evidence—the firearm, the knife, the bottle of poison which the police turned over to him. He identified the person who performed the autopsy, and furnished the report of the coroner's inquest in which he served as the committing magistrate.

> As he brought me around the courthouse he would say: Shake hands with my son, Rugi. He'll be trying cases pretty soon in your courtroom. I'd appreciate it if you'd help him out and show him the ropes. Son, this is my friend (name). Listen to his advice and you won't go wrong.

Dad was a special friend of Jack, the Chief Crier in Criminal Court, whose job it was to recruit pro bono lawyers for defendants who could not afford counsel and whom the Legal Aid Society people could not represent because of overloads or conflicts of interest.

Long before the U.S. Supreme Court made it mandatory, every defendant in Allegheny County, Pennsylvania had to be represented by counsel, whether the offense was a felony or misdemeanor, and whether the plea was guilty or not guilty. Jack promised my father: "John, I'll keep him busy every day of the week, if he wants it."

I wanted it. And I was kept busy for the better part of my first 18 months of practice, and as a result, I became a very experienced trial lawyer.

Sure, I floundered at first, and made mistakes. Lots of them. I got outmaneuvered by experienced D.A.'s and got suckered by police witnesses who held back testimony on direct examination only to release damaging evidence against my client through my clumsy cross examination. At first sometimes hearsay evidence rolled past me when I was too inept to block its admission. But I learned by making mistakes, and when you learn this way you usually don't make the same mistake twice, and certainly not three times. I made too many objections and got slammed around by the judges. At first I was too intense and too emotional and some times got tongue tied when I should have been calm and urbane. To the jury I looked worried instead of putting on the lawyer's show of utmost confidence. But I learned. Oh, how I learned! The pedagogues say that one learns by two techniques: (1) reading and listening and (2) practical experience. I got the giant economy size dose of both.

When I walked into a courtroom, or perhaps it was strutting when I got the hang of it, every day during that early period of my life at the bar. I acquired trial experience that many lawyers never get today. Every morning, five days a week, I showed up in a criminal courtroom and soon I stopped getting my head bashed in. I stopped leaving my own blood on the courtroom floors. Soon I started to receive the top accolade--praise from the court attachés: "You're getting good, Rugi!"

After the Chief Crier would assign me a case, I'd enter my appearance, sign papers for a plea of not guilty and demand a jury trial. Sure, there was not much time to prepare, but what made the system work was that the assistant D.A. got the case even later than I did, moreover I had the advantage of sitting through the prosecution's case and learning the details at about the same time as the prosecutor. Thus, I jumped into the world of robbery, rape, burglary, breaking and entering, larceny, receiving stolen goods, aggravated and simple assault and battery, attempted murder, drunk driving, involuntary manslaughter, vehicular homicide, fornication and bastardy, forgery and embezzlement.

I mastered the elements and nuances of each crime and soon gleaned the strategies used by the prosecution to establish its cases. I learned the routine of police work and the courtroom mannerisms of individual prosecutors. I knew what to expect from the few who were good prosecuters and how to tap dance around those who were not. I learned sentencing proclivities of the various judges and assimilated their idiosyncrasies in the conduct of a trial. I grasped what annoyed them, and what pleased them, judge by judge.

I learned how to deal and plead. Because my main objective was to polish professional skills of a litigator by trying a case from opening speech to jury verdict, my clients got the best of both worlds--trying a case or pleading it. I was not courtroom shy, like most lawyers were then and still are today. I was not afraid to face a jury and gradually became very comfortable in relationships with them and the judges. The police and the D.A.'s no longer intimidated me. Nevertheless, if in the midst of a case, I determined that I could work out a good deal for my client, I did not hesitate to plea bargain.

During 1949, my second full year of practice, I defended in a number of murder cases. No moment in the practice of law is more disquieting, worrisome or fraught with apprehension than to sit at counsel table with your client and hear the prosecutor in his opening statement to the jury intone these sink-in-the-pit-of-the-stomach words: "Ladies and gentlemen of the jury, we are asking the death penalty in this case."

Compared to this, all other moments of courtroom drama--even detrimental surprises, unlucky and devastating, that come rushing in the midst of a trial and threaten large-scale financial stakes in a high profile civil case—all these are serendipitous encounters by comparison. You grow up in a hurry when you defend in a case where the state asks the death penalty, even if the only reasons they do it is to intimate you into making a plea bargain. Professionally speaking, I matured rapidly between 1948 and 1950.

When I practiced law, court-appointed counsel were, with one exception, pro bono performers; we did not get paid. We were compensated by the state only in murder cases. In the late forties we received $150 a case; it was later increased to $500 plus $100 for an investigator. I received a number of these appointments as a result of requests from jail inmates awaiting trial. This began after I was successful in acquitting a young night club entertainer charged with knifing a man in the back. We pleaded self defense and won. I began to receive notes from jail: "I hear you're a good stabbin' lawyer and I want you to handle my case."

It was in criminal court then that I earned my spurs as a trial lawyer. I earned them after months and months of daily pro bono work, and I started to get lucky. The word got around of my successes and I soon began to be retained by private, fee-paying defendants, but I still continued to be appointed pro bono by the judges during those early years.

Meanwhile, little by little, I developed a private practice, largely in my home town of Carnegie. I made myself available to my fellow townspeople behaving evening office hours in Cafrnegie. Leonard De Fonso, a good friend, allowed me to hang my shingle in his real estate office at 137 West Main street, a block away from Third street, the scene of the 1923 KKK riot, a short distance from Superior Mill. We were near the corner of Second Street, sandwiched between two bars. A third bar and flea bag hotel were on the other side of the side street. Across Main Street were the railroad tracks. This was not a posh location. It was not a sleek office complex like Century City, Los Angeles, but my clients were not corporate executives arriving in limousines.

On April, 17, 1948 I was the guest of honor at a gala banquet at the Hotel William Penn in Pittsburgh's largest ballroom. The parishioners of my Carnegie Church, Holy Souls, decided to pay public tribute to me as first member of my parish to become a lawyer. Over 1250 guests attended. In addition to my fellow parishioners---all of the immigrant generation and their children--hundreds of my father's friends were in attendance to honor him vicariously. They honored him in this manner because although he was a highly regarded leader in Pittsburgh fraternal and community circles, he had always resisted attempts to honor him with a testimonial dinner, even though he had served as national president of the Italian Sons and Daughters of America. His friends utilized his formidable community influence to see that his son was launched on his legal career with sufficient pomp and ceremony. Every trial judge in the county was on the dais that night. The main speaker was Pennsylvania's attorney general. No other lawyer has launched his career with such a public send-off.

The decision to fly solo had been a gamble. I had turned down two job opportunities. Judson A. Crane, the Pitt law schcol dean, had recommended me to a prominent practitioner who belonged to the right church and country club, who was an extremely able lawyer with a highly selective practice with fairly well-to-do clients. He was in need of an associate who would eventually take over his practice. I had interviewed with him and had been offered the position. I mulled over the offer for a few days and declined. It was tempting but I declined for the unspoken reason that although he was willing to take me on, I was not certain that his socialite clientele was ready to have an American of Italian origin serve as their lawyer. I did offer this explanation to the dean, explaining to him that in 1947 the doors of all major Pittsburgh law firms, except one, were closed to Americans of Italian descent, not only as partners, but as associates as well.

He told me that he was dumbstruck and would check out my statement. A few days later he called me into his office and said, "Rugi, I may know more law than you, but you know more about sociology."

A law firm headed by a very able, but very controversial, lawyer, offered me a position as an associate, but I felt that although he was a brilliant and I could learn much from him, he was too mean-spirited and too disputatious in the community for me to set sail with him.

So I began my practice as a sole practitioner on December 8, 1947, exactly six years and one day after Pearl Harbor. When I concluded my remarks as a court-appointed counsel in a plea of guilty to a charge of forgery, Judge Sammy Weiss thanked me for a job well done, but concluded, "Mr. Aldisert, don't take any checks as a fee from this man."

Fourteen years later I became a judicial colleague of Judge Weiss.

Chapter Sixteen
Hanging Out the Shingle

At first I had night office hours four evenings a week, starting at 7:30 p.m., but gradually reduced this to three nights, and finally, two. After I got married in 1952, after five years of practice, I closed my night office. But in those first years I had become a general practitioner serving my home town neighbors, ministering to the legal needs of those who had known me or my family from childhood. Also strangers came to me because I had made myself available for them. Because I offered night office hours in the town where they lived, they could consult me without taking a day off work to make the trip to downtown Pittsburgh.

Law is now much more complicated than it was in the Forties and Fifties. We have been inundated by a host of federal and state statutes, regulations by every government layer from the municipal wage tax agency to the federal Environmental Protection Agency.

Sixty years ago the average person consulted a lawyer because of a personal or business relationship between one person and another, as an individual or in corporate form. Under ordinary circumstances to render proper advice, the lawyer did not need a squad of research associates. The lawyer had to apply only certain fundamental concepts of the law, usually covered by law school courses, or at least readily retrievable in the books with a minimum of research.

It is another world today, light years away in complexity, and this makes it most difficult, if not impossible, for a one-person office to handle a general practice as I did from 1947 through 1961. Today in the cities there are still many sole practitioners, but for the most part, they tend to specialize in one field of the law, and depend upon referrals from other lawyers. In the small towns, especially in rural America, there are still many sole practitioners with the type of practice I had almost 60 years ago. But it isn't easy.

In that era, in a quieter hour, in a "kinder and gentler Nation," most requests for legal advice could be handled by a quick reference to a few concepts of the common law and a small number of statutes. Most problems could easily be evaluated, if not solved completely, at an original consultation. Often two parties to the sale and purchase of a small mom and pop retail operation would present themselves at your office, furnish you with the details, and within a few days they could return to memorialize a written sales agreement and bill of sale, which you had prepared. It was a transaction where only two sets of individuals were involved, a person-to-person transaction. It was a business transaction between two private parties. Today it is not that simple.

A comparable transaction may require consideration of the Uniform Commercial Code, precepts of common law contract law, federal, state, county and municipal taxation; environmental health, zoning and occupancy requirements; state and federal laws dealing with labor organizations, unemployment compensation and employment discrimination. If food and beverages are involved, an additional half dozen government agencies get into the act. Billable hours mount up and the paper work and correspondence tend to resemble a gigantic corporate merger, yet it's still only a transfer of a mom and pop operation.

Moreover, present today is a specter that was virtually non-existent when I practiced law--the threat of a future malpractice action against you by your client. Today, too much wheel spinning goes on, too many expensive procedures are resorted to, too much preventative law is being practiced by lawyers under the rubric, C.Y.A.--"Cover your ass!"

Back then we were in the post war era, suffering the economic and societal trauma of four years of war. When the G.I.'s came back, they faced a number of situations which required legal advice. Many got married, or were married during the war, and they were ready to purchase a house or lot by taking advantage of the 100 per cent financing of the G.I. Bill. Many G.I.'s called upon me to represent them during all phases of the transaction, from signing the agreement of sale, preparing the deed, searching the title and attending the closing.

At this time, the real estate title companies had not yet gobbled up the real estate title business. A lawyer could obtain a decent fee by tracing the title of real estate to determine if proper title had passed through the years, that all proper parties had signed the conveyances or wills in the chain and insure that the land was free of court judgments, mortgage, tax liens and other encumbrances. I soon became expert at title searching, doing the work after court hours or on Saturday mornings. I also had the advantage of working, for the most part, in the relatively small geographical area of Carnegie. Once I had traced the past ownership of a common tract in a given title search, it became an integral part of my master title abstract file. In future searches it was no longer necessary for me to trace each title back to William Penn and colonial Pennsylvania.

When only a few months into my practice, a real estate developer laid out a plan of 25 lots on land that had been in his family for generations. I was called upon to examine the title for the purchaser of the third lot sold out of the plan. I discovered a defect in the seller's title that had not been discovered by lawyers who had examined the first two purchasers out of the plan. I notified the seller, who came to my office in an extremely agitated condition, and I carefully explained the difficulty. He asked if I could remove the defect and fortunately, without too much effort, I was able to do it. I closed the transaction for my client, but the seller remained afterwards. He thanked me for clearing his title and asked for my bill. I told him that there would be no charge. "I am dumb-founded," he explained. "You have saved my ass and you're not charging me. I have never heard that from a lawyer before."

Thereafter, in a procedure that probably violated the tie-in prohibitions of anti-trust laws, he insisted that every purchaser of the 22 remaining lots retain me as their lawyer, and that if they had already retained another lawyer there was a surcharge of $35.00 payable to me on the sale of every lot, this amount being the then current fee for attending a real estate closing of a modest-price lot. During the next few years he sold all the remaining lots and I became his lawyer and remained so throughout my practice.

With fees coming in from real estate transactions, I was off and running. I gradually built a general family practice in Carnegie. A social trauma of the era involved problems resulting from war-time marriages. School friends and their families came to me to obtain divorces. For the most part, these were uncontested matters with no children involved and no property distributions. Very little work was involved and the going rate was about $50.00 in court costs and a $150.00 attorney fee. Measured against today's fee structures, this sounds very minimal, but if the 1949 fee and costs are expanded by the Consumer Price Index factor, this amounted to $1560.17 in our inflated dollars, but I doubt that you can represent a party in a no fault divorce with no property problems today for less that $5000.

As early as my first year of practice, clients retained me to represent them in administering decedents' estates. Often this involved simply registering a will to record the chain of title of real estate. Where personal property was involved--this means any property other than land-- I had to take out letters of administration, prepare and file an inventory, advertise that claims had to be filed against the estate within six months, pay all debts on the basis of statutory priorities, oversee assessments of state inheritance taxes, prepare an accounting of the administration for examination by the probate court, known in Pennsylvania as the Orphan's Court, and appear at a hearing with the executor or administrator with a written proposed distribution. I did much of this throughout my practice, and for the most part, the estates and the corresponding fees, were modest, but in a general practice, because the law of averages comes into play, some of the estates were quite substantial. Early on, I established a set procedure for estate administration, which I taught my various secretaries, making most of these cases somewhat routine.

In every client consultation on any matters, no matter what was involved, I asked if the client had a will. In most cases, he or she did not. Whenever appropriate, I drafted a will, and usually did not charge for these services. But every will carried my name and address on the blue back that covers most legal papers, and many wills contained the expression:

> I direct that the executor retain my lawyer, Ruggero J. Aldisert, as attorney in the administration of my estate.

HANGING OUT THE SHINGLE 243

In that first year, the Carnegie practice grew. I represented parties in neighborhood squabbles before the local justice of the peace--we called them "squires" in those days. They presided over criminal cases of simple or aggravated assault and battery, petty larceny, malicious mischief, public drunkenness, disorderly conduct, surety of the peace. I attempted to settle these matters before the squires instead of having them reach the grand jury stage in Pittsburgh. I often represented the prosecutor and here, too, I tried to convince both my clients and the defendants that a civil settlement was much to be preferred than a prosecution of a misdemeanor.

And so it was criminal court by day and Carnegie practice by night, but in January 1948, I also had opened my Pittsburgh office.

I moved into Suite 600 of the Jones Law Building directly across the street from the City-County Building that served as the courthouse for civil cases. My father arranged with Earl T. "Pete" Adair that I could use his office from 9 a.m. until 4 p.m., because during that time he was in Criminal Courtroom No. 1 as a senior assistant D.A. handling pleas. He had no private practice in the law but was a well known dog show judge, doing extensive traveling on weekends. His advice to me as a new lawyer:

> Always take a train. An airplane can always fall down; if you have to fly, take a two engine plane because in case of an emergency they can land on a pasture.

All attorneys in the suite had other jobs, so throughout the day I virtually had the office to myself with a very bright secretary, Dorothy Zinkhan, who served all of us. I would keep her busier than all the other lawyers combined, for although each maintained an office in the suite, their outside activities kept them out of the building most of the day. Generally they checked in the morning to read the mail and came back at lunchtime to receive telephone messages.

My suite-mates were astounded when I installed extensive book shelves and proceeded to establish a law library. None of the lawyers had a law book to his name. During my preceptorship I had seen a lot of shoddy practicing, and visiting various offices, I often commented on the absence of a library in many offices. To which the universal response seemed to follow these lines: "Yah gotta lot to learn, kid. You don't need books in this game. All yah need is street smarts."

I remembered some of them when I became a judge, and when they appeared before me in the most simple case, I occasionally would shake them up by suggesting that they write a brief on a point and hand it up the following morning. They would squirm, because they hadn't written a single brief in their entire practice of law. For suggested jury instructions, they would hand up canned points for charge with old citations, usually pilfered from some other office. Nevertheless, they were very financially successful lawyers. When I asked for the briefs, often they would squirm, and ask to speak to me at sidebar:

> "Christ, Rugi, whatayah tryin' tah do to me. You know the Goddam law, inside and out, better'n I can find. You doan need any help from me. C'mon now. Gimme a break".

I would sit back and smile, and say: "O.K.", and they would go back to counsel table in their expensive suits, gold jewelry flashing, and their clients beaming.

From my first days at the bar I ran into too much of this as I watched lawyers perform and I decided early on that I would not take shortcuts. West Publishing Company was eager to stake a new lawyer to a complete library, with no down payment, easy monthly installments and no interest charged. So I infused Suite 600 with the first library it had ever seen: Purdon's Pennsylvania Statutes, Vale's Pennsylvania Digest, the U.S. Code Annotated, Goodrich Amram on Pennsylvania Practice, Corpus Juris Secundum, and the Atlantic Reporter version of Pennsylvania appellate cases. I made an original investment of $1156.00 for this library in January, 1948, and $300 more a year later.

It was the Marine Corps training all over again. Prepare. Prepare. Prepare. Do it right. Don't take shortcuts. That's how I started in the beginning of 1948 and that's how I practiced law for 14 years.

My expenses were modest that first year. From January through July my monthly share of the rent at 600 Jones Law Building was $46.44, the secretary $37.50. But by mid-year I recognized that I had outgrown my time-share arrangements. It was necessary that I have a private office of my own and in August I moved to the ninth floor of the same building to share Suite 933 with two other lawyers. It was a pretentious suite with a mammoth reception room. I paid one half of the secretary's salary, $90.00

a month, and my share of the rent. But my practice was growing and I could afford it. Here, too, not a law book was to be seen, so I trundled up my entire library with its book shelves and installed it anew in the reception room. I remained in these quarters for about two years and I can't remember either of my two suite mates ever cracking a law book.

At first my clientele consisted of blue collar worker families and their modest problems. My charges were modest and I attempted to adhere to the minimum fee bill of the Allegheny County Bar Association: $10 for drafting a will, deed or mortgage; $25 for attending a squire's hearing; and $50 for brief court hearing before a judge. My records show that I generally received $25 to $50 as a retainer for a criminal case or divorce, that I charged $50 to draw a partnership agreement, $20 to $25 for a contract, $35 to $50 to represent a landlord in eviction proceedings, $65 in a landlord-tenant dispute, $40 to process a mechanic's lien claim, $50 for a change of name petition, $75 to appear at a Coroner's inquest, and $100 to appear before an examiner of the Pennsylvania Liquor Control Board.

The biggest fee I received during my first year was from representing some siblings against their brother in a family squabble over a very valuable stock certificate. The oldest brother, who had possession of the certificate, had taken a hard nosed attitude and refused to distribute dividends with his younger siblings. He kept a meticulous and honest accounting, was not spending the money, but simply refused to make any distribution to his brother and sisters. It was they who came to me for advice and at first I attempted to solve it amicably. I telephoned him and was bluntly told, "Mind your own business. This is a family matter." He was holding the certificates as executor of his father's estate, even though the estate had been closed years before. A few days later I filed a petition for a preliminary injunction and we were before a judge immediately. After a brief hearing at which the defendant appeared without counsel and defended his action by saying "I'm doing what father would want me to do," I obtained an order requiring an immediate distribution of past dividends, a surrender of the certificate and the issuance of separate certificates for each brother and sister.

The court handed down its order within a week. The court designated me to obtain new certificates at a stock brokerage in the names of each sibling and to prepare a schedule of dividend distribution. The brothers and sisters paid me $1050.00, and were pleased to do so, because the matter was accomplished so quickly. Based on the Consumer Price Index comparison, that fee was equivalent to $8000.00 in today's dollars.

And so went the first year's experience, handling a general practice much as the family doctor in those days conducted a practice of treating burns, cuts and bruises, usual childhood diseases, chest colds, sore throats, flu, heart conditions, removing tonsils and delivering babies.
Even in that first year I moved beyond general family practice and began to create various business organizations for clients and to develop an expertise as a business lawyer. Representing business clients would bring me much satisfaction and success in the years to come. In that first year, the businesses were small, but the experience would stand me in good stead when I started to represent million dollar enterprises.

I had no prior personal business experience, but I had an equivalent--I served as an officer in the U.S. Marines. I knew how to handle personnel and recognized the importance of creating and maintaining a loyal work force through incentives. I knew that it was important first to recognize a specific problem, make an inventory of all possible solutions and then make a recommendation. Before attempting to solve an isolated business problem, I wanted first to learn the whole picture. After you are given a specific objective, in the military, before proceeding you need an intelligence report, then a reconnaissance before making a plan to commit the forces under your command. I believe that a good lawyer had to do the same, whether he was preparing for trial and giving advice to a business institution. And that's how I started to handle my early business clients in 1948.

About six months into the practice, three men whom I knew from Carnegie came to my night office for a limited purpose--to draw a partnership agreement. In 15 minutes I had basic information as to the equal financial shares to be contributed and the agreement that all profits and expenses were to be shared equally. They then asked how much I would charge to draw the agreement and I gave a small figure that met with their approval. As they got up to leave, I said, "Look, I'm closing up for the night. I want to know more about your business and I won't charge you for it, so let's go to Bales restaurant, have a cup of coffee and talk." We talked for two hours and I became more than a scrivener retained to draw up an instrument. I became their business adviser, lawyer for their families and received many referrals from them.

Their business venture turned out to be a great success story. They were three mill workers, friends from the work place who pooled their savings accumulated during the war as servicemen to launch a new business. "We don't want to work in the mill all our lives," they said. I pointed out some of the problems they would face and some of the pitfalls of launching a new business. I prepared not only a partnership agreement but a schedule of working hours. Each would continue to work in the mill on different shifts so that at least one owner would be on the premises at all times. I persuaded them to find a new location, because their original choice had inadequate parking, prepared a lease for one year only with the option to renew annually for a five year period and the right of first refusal in the event of a sale. I gave them rudimentary advice on how to keep books, insisted that they obtain adequate liability and workmen's compensation insurance coverage. Within a year they were doing so well that each of them married and I had to revise the partnership agreement and recommend that they subscribe to an accounting service. Each of them quit the mill and devoted full time to a very successful retail business which I later placed under a corporate umbrella. They had started out with a small coffee shop that later expanded into a bar. They then bought a restaurant and operated it separately, and still later purchased an adjacent hardware store. They often attributed the success of their venture to the advice I gave them in the beginning and through the years. My success here stemmed from my decision to learn as much as I could about their business plans. In discussions I raised more questions than I answered and forced them to think about dimensions of their enterprise that had never occurred to them.

I followed this pattern through the years, in even more elaborate detail and concept, especially business clients who could afford to pay me for the time I put into studying their operations. At the same time I broadened my own horizons on business operations.

At about the same time, another mill worker and his son came in to see me. They lived in the adjacent town of Heidelberg, a small hamlet near some old worked-out coal mines, a town where there had been talk of building a race track. They wanted to get in on the ground floor in operating a taxi company. "We don't have much money to pay a lawyer or to buy many cabs and we intend to start out with just one cab." I took a $50 retainer, "Just to look into to it." I had only a faint idea how these things worked so the next day I telephoned Art Diskin, a law school friend who was a staff attorney for the Pennsylvania Public Utilities Commission. He introduced me to the esoteric world of certificates of public convenience and public utility law. He agreed to send me the appropriate application forms and instructions how to fill them out, together with copies of the governing regulations. When the batch of papers arrived I spent an entire week-end poring over them--a minimum of 12 or 14 hours all for a $50 retainer. But I was ready to advise my clients. I had become an instant public utilities "expert."

Because I then knew what to expect, I called my clients in and explained what was going to be necessary, gave an estimate of my fee and we went ahead. Six months into the practice of law I went through the entire procedure of obtaining the "certificate of public convenience" that would enable them to operate a taxi company, including participating in a contested hearing before an Public Utilities examiner because the huge Yellow Cab Company of Pittsburgh had protested. I had to follow the same procedure for one taxicab as required for a company with a huge fleet. It took much of my time and my clients were pleased. And so was I.

A number of years later a friend who specialized in insuring large trailer trucks introduced me to one of his clients who operated a flotilla of tractor trailers that delivered finished steel rolls from Pittsburgh mills to auto companies in Michigan. We had a drink, and the talk came around to certificated rights of the Interstate Commerce Commission and the Pennsylvania Public Utility Commission. When I started to use words like "certificated rights," my insurance friend said, "I didn't know you were a public utilities expert!" I flicked the ash from my cigar and told them that I had organized a taxi company over the opposition of Yellow Cab Company. I did not go into many details, but a week later I got a call from the big rig operator, who became a good client and stayed with me until I became a judge.

But most of my early business clients were older men, very experienced in commercial affairs, and I acquired much from their wisdom. A good lawyer always learns from his clients. I remember with affection two gentlemen from Carnegie who asked me to represent them in the sale of the saloon next door to my night office. When they first called me, they wanted me to "draw up papers," reported that they were in total agreement in the deal except for one point and that perhaps I could help them. I had known them both over the years as friends of the family. Isaia, the seller, also operated a very successful Italian grocery store and Gus, the purchaser, had previously sold a bar in another part of town. After a short fling at retirement, he decided to return to the business. I welcomed them when they arrived at my Carnegie office at the appointed time. Unfortunately, the one point that had not been agreed upon was the sales price.

Each was a prototypical old world Italian, very dignified and very formal, and each was a very successful and shrewd businessman. Each spoke a very fractured English, however, so I suggested that because the problem was the amount of money, perhaps it would be easier if they spoke Italian to one another. *"Signori, parlate italiana, per piacere."*

This was a mistake. Both insisted that they would be more comfortable in speaking English, and so I blithely said something like, "Let the bidding begin." And so they began. They understood each other perfectly, but I had a helluva time following some of their talk. They spoke their own patois: "one" was "un", then in succession, "du", "tree", "fo", "fie", "sei", "sebben", "ott", "ny" and "ten." Neither used the world "thousand"; it came out, in singular or plural form, as "tous." Finally, after much gesticulating, dramatic voice inflections, facial grimaces and deliberate pauses to relight dreadful Italian tobies, which were suffocating me in the small office, they came to about "tree tous" apart and were at impasse. Neither would budge. Finally, one turned to me, "Avvocat, whatch u tink?" I said nothing, but smiled and shrugged my shoulders. The other asked the same question. I continued to smile and raised my hands palms up and shrugged again. But I knew then what they wanted me to do.

I sat up straight, explained how both of them were very intelligent, very fair, and knew much more than I did about business. I extolled their respective virtues and how I was loathe to intrude on this honest bargaining among men of good will. Especially under circumstances when each knew the value of the business much better than I. I then explained carefully that I knew that the seller would not reduce his demand one cent, and this was right, *"Ha ragione."* And that the buyer would not offer one penny more, and this, too, was right. And most reluctantly, I said, "Both of you are right, I can't say that either of you are wrong. I could make one suggestion, but because both of you are right, I won't say anything." They then fussed for a while and each implored me to make a suggestion. I lit my own cigar, a Cuban of better vintage that the Italian *toscani* they were smoking, leaned back and said, "Split the difference."

Both smiled and shook hands, and asked me to draw up the papers for the sale of the saloon next door and handle the matter before the Pennsylvania Liquor Control Board. I'm positive that this was the price they were interested in, give or take a few hundred dollars, but it was necessary to go through the formalities in front of "the big lawyer."

A year or so later, Gus, the purchaser of the saloon, burst in my office one night in a very agitated state, interrupting a consultation with a client. "Avvocat. Queek. Queek. Coma my place right now." I ran out with him and he explained, "Some sunnuvabitch I tink died in the backa room." It was pay day at the mill and the guys were three deep at the bar, the jukebox was blasting and we ran to the very dark back room where a bunch of fat old whores were trying to hustle business with some guys who could barely navigate. Gus brought me to a man in one of the booths, apparently passed out. I felt for a pulse in his neck and he was cold to the touch, and looked up at Gus, who said, "I tole you. The sunnuvabitch is dead!" Meanwhile the jukebox is still blasting, the bar talk is still loud and the gals are still trying to make a buck.

"Did you call the police, Gus?"

"No."

"Did you call a doctor?"

"No."

"Who did you call?"

"I called you."

"Why did you call me?"

"You're my lawyer!" he said triumphantly.

I covered the man's head with his jacket, called the police for Gus, suggested that they call the Coroner and went back to the client whose consultation was interrupted. When the morgue ambulance came, I went next door. The guys were still three deep at the bar and juke box still was on. I didn't go into the back room.

So I flew solo and did well that first year. It was a gamble, but it paid off. It was successful for several reasons: My father had a fine reputation in the legal community and was a well known fraternal leader with a host of friends who directed clients my way. I opened a night office in Carnegie and I was the home town boy who made good. I was the kid who enlisted in the Marines as a private, had gone to the Pacific and had come home as a captain; patriotism always ran high in the mill and mining towns that surrounded Pittsburgh. And finally, I was a conscientious lawyer who took no shortcuts no matter how modest the fee and was not timid about walking into a courtroom.

Homer W. King was my best friend. We met in 1940 while undergraduates at Pitt, and returned to law school in February, 1946 after serving in World War II. We were admitted to the bar on the same day, and although at first in offices on different floors in the Jones Law Building, in early 1952 we moved into our own set of offices in the Frick Building on Grant Street directly across from the Courthouse. We were suite mates thereafter until I closed my law practice. We started to have lunch together in December, 1947, and continued to so every business day, if possible, until January, 1962 when I ascended the Common Pleas Court bench. Thereafter, we tried to have lunch several times a month until I moved to California in 1987. For some reason, his mother called him "Bill," and that's what I called him as well. As did my three children who adored "Uncle Bill." He was an extremely able lawyer and a most kind and generous person. He died May 3, 1999. And I still miss him.

HANGING OUT THE SHINGLE

RUGGERO J. ALDISERT

WISHES TO ANNOUNCE THAT HE IS NOW ENGAGED

IN THE GENERAL PRACTICE OF LAW

WITH OFFICES AT

600 JONES LAW BUILDING
PITTSBURGH, PENNSYLVANIA

COURT 0777

On December 8, 1947 I distributed an announcement that I was hanging out a shingle.

Chapter Seventeen
The General Practice

In 1951 I made my final office move as a lawyer, this time to the Frick building on Grant Street directly across from the courthouse and began an office association with Homer W. King. We had been friends since college days, returned from the war at about the same time, finished law school together and had begun our own individual practices on different floors in the Jones law Building. We began an office association that would continue, without one word of disagreement, throughout my remaining years as a lawyer. We maintained independent practices, but formed an operating partnership to share the rent, secretarial salaries, office equipment and supplies. From time to time we jointly hired lawyer assistants, none of whom seemed to work out very well. The great advantage here was that King and I were good friends, respected each other as lawyers, and for the first time in our private practices as sole practitioners each of us was now able to pick the brains of another lawyer on problems presented in our individual practices.

He was also the first suite-mate who actually read law books, and with the installation of my books, he no longer had to do his research in the county law library. We stayed together in the same Frick building office for ten years until I became a Common Pleas Court judge.

I am quick to recognize that there are many great lawyers at the bar today. Superb litigators, civil and criminal, claiming and defending actions in personal injuries to commercial fraud through felonious assaults to white collar crimes. Splendid transaction specialists. Great movers in mergers and acquisitions. Superb tax specialists. Notable constitutional law specialists, with sub specialties like the First Amendment or Civil Rights. Class action managers. Securities experts. Health care and hospital law. Trade regulation. Labor law. Bankruptcy. Energy law. Business organizations. Intellectual property. But these specialists never receive the full service, general practice experience that a sole practitioner enjoyed until about 30 years ago.

Even large law firms with identified departments cannot be classed as full service firms, because the very overhead with in depth staffing makes it impossible for them to represent clients without a substantial five or six figure retainers. The sole practitioner who operates today has to specialize in order to get necessary referrals to make ends meet.

To whom does the working stiff go for legal services when needed today for himself, herself or a member of his family? If you qualify for civil or criminal legal aid, you can trust your luck with a community legal service and hope that you get a full-fledged lawyer and not a series of harried paralegals or lawyer assistants. Otherwise it seems that today you have to go to different lawyers for different problems.

I enjoyed my 14 years in my general practice and learned much. It was a graduate school course in learning much about human nature and the hopes, dreams and aspirations of men and women from all walks of life. What I learned would help me immensely to understand problems that later would come before me, as a state trial judge and a federal appellate judge.

Court opinions and law books and scholarly lectures and bright-eyed law clerks can carry you just so far. Underlying all aspects of court litigation are pressures of society's countervailing tensions, stresses and strains. When judges see consequences of deliberate acts, intentional or knowing, or the repercussions of negligence or carelessness, or the unexpected or unfortunate aftermath of innocent acts, judges must always inquire into what triggered these fallouts or reverberations. They must understand patterns of behavior--configurations of generosity and selfishness, avarice and benevolence, reflective thinking and impulsive decisions, kindness and malevolence. My years at the general practice of law intimately immersed me in social and economic conflicts of society. I enjoyed it then, and many decades later, still look back on this experience with great affection and satisfaction.

I enjoyed tending to office practice matters that send the average working class family to a lawyer--writing wills, deeds, contracts and leases, conducting real estate transactions (although soon I was able to contract out the actual searching of the title), sometimes assisting in preparing tax returns. When it was necessary to go to court, I handled their contracts claims or defenses, personal injuries cases, decedent's estates, divorces, adoptions, guardianships, workmen's compensation, and even an occasional bankruptcy (before it became popular) and admiralty cases. I was at home on the equity side of the court as well, handling everything from property deed reformations to several cases of sensitive church matters where one was buried in a cemetery consecrated under one religious rite which was later changed when the church sponsoring the cemetery changed its affiliation. I was also at home when they ran afoul of the law and I got them out of jail, attended preliminary hearings, and represented them before a judge or jury.

Some of my cases were true human interest dramas, even tracking a modern soap opera, cases you don't get when you represent corporations and merger acquisitions. In 1951 I went before the court in a divorce case with a woman and her 12-year old daughter. We will call her Maria who, as a girl of 21 in her native Italy, married a man named Secondo. They had a child and lived happily for a time; until 1941 when Secondo, then a private in the Italian army, was sent to Greece for the Italo-Greco campaign. There he met a young girl Joannidu Afrodite, yes, that was her name, the mythical Greek goddess of love. Afrodite lured him away from the army and he deserted, and together they took refuge in the mountains while the war raged in the valleys below.

When the fighting was over, Secondo stayed in Greece. Maria reported to the International Red Cross that her dear husband was missing, and Italian authorities found Secondo and brought him back to Italy. But with him came Afrodite and their newborn child. In the spring of 1946, Secondo, Afrodite and the baby all moved in with Maria and her daughter. Secondo lived there with his two separate families all under one roof, professing his undying love to his two "wives."

After three months, Maria, wearied of this arrangement, complained. Secondo dramatically replied:
Then go, the sky is my roof,
The leaves on the trees are my bed,
And I will live on love.

So Maria left. For a time she lived with relatives and in 1949 migrated to America with her daughter to live with an aunt. She met a client of mine who brought her to me with her "problem." First, I arranged proper international service on the Italian consul to serve a divorce complaint in Italy. Secondo did not contest. Next I sent her to the Immigration and Naturalization Service to become a citizen, and in a few years she and her daughters took oaths as American citizens. After the ceremony, mother and daughter came to my office with tiny American flags and thanked me. She then remarried, this time to a solid substantial American citizen. Meanwhile, Secondo had the sky as his roof and the leaves on the tree as his bed.

Handling a case like that--translating Secondo's poetry as a trial exhibit, arranging international service on a defendant with the triple seals and certifications of several layers of government, domestic and foreign--doing all this is much more interesting than checking invoices in a warehouse in an antitrust case.

In the post war years of the Fifties many families came to me with immigration matters. Often my participation was limited to assisting them in the preparation of necessary forms to bring relatives over from Europe. But there were unusual circumstances that put me as a protagonist against the federal bureaucracy. In one case I was forced to file a complaint in the U.S. District Court naming as the defendant, Dean Acheson, Secretary of State.

Mr. and Mrs. Bianco (the name is changed) came in one day with a sad tale. They were naturalized citizens and had a daughter, Angelina, who had been born in America. In the late Thirties the parents had traveled to Italy with their daughter to visit family in the home town. During their visit, war had broken out in Europe and they made plans to return to Pittsburgh. Angelina was the only granddaughter of the husband's parents and they begged him to let her stay for another year. "Let her finish school this year," the grandparents pleaded, "Don't worry about the war. America will never get involved." They acceded to the plea and returned to Pittsburgh without Angelina. A year passed and the grandparents begged that she stay "Just one more year." Again the parents acceded. But then came Pearl Harbor and a few days later Italy declared war on the United States, and Angelina remained with her grandparents for the duration.

At war's end in 1945 the Bianco's attempted to get Angelina steamship passage for the return to America. The port of Naples was in ruins. Piers had been wiped out. Steamship service was virtually non existent. The Italian peninsula was in chaos. Military government was ending. King Victor Emmanuel III abdicated May 9, 1946, and was succeeded by his son, Humbert II. Meanwhile the country was verging on anarchy with a plebiscite in the offing that would determine the future form of government. From the Alps to Sicily thundered a political maelstrom of confusion, disarray, disorder, discord, tumult and turmoil. The country rocked with upheaval, for facing the electorate were two major choices--a Republic or Communism, with a monarchy coming in a distant third in popular support. The plebiscite was scheduled for June 2-3, 1946, a time less than a month after the king's abdication. The unspoken managers of the political conflict were Joseph Stalin and the United States government.

Our State Department took the lead in a vigorous campaign within the Italian-American community, urging our people to write or cable relatives and friends in Italy to vote in the plebiscite favor of the Republic. The State Department knew that the June plebiscite would be the first time in the history of Italy that its people were given the right to vote on the form of government their country would take.. The State Department's campaign in the United States was comprehensive and awesome. It reached every community where Americans of Italian origin were located. Advertisements were taken out in the American press. Circulars and letters were prepared for distribution. Our government sounded one message: "Tell everyone over there to vote. Vote for a Republic."

The June 1946 plebiscite was a smashing success for democracy. Communism was stopped dead in its tracks. The Republic won. Everybody had voted. Including Angelina Bianco.

Shortly after the plebiscite, she appeared at the American Consulate General in Naples, presented her birth certificate and asked for a passport. "Did you vote in the plebiscite?" she was asked. "Yes, I did," came her proud reply. "I voted for the Republic."

"I'm very sorry, miss" came the rejoinder from the State Department bureaucrat. "By voting in a foreign election, you have forfeited your American citizenship. You are no longer an American citizen. You're now an Italian. We're getting a lot of people like you. You can't get back to the States unless as an Italian immigrant and the Italian quota is now filled for many years to come."

That was the sad story, *un sacco di guai,* that Mr. and Mrs. Bianco related to me. I was dumbfounded. As a young leader of the Italian-American community I was intimately familiar with the State Department efforts to get out the vote. Some misunderstanding had taken place, I was convinced. The parents retained me to look into it for them. It just could not be that one branch of the State Department hustled votes all over the world, yet another branch of the same department would construct artificial barriers to penalize the very people who innocently heeded the call from relatives in America at the instigation of the Department. Even Joseph Stalin would laugh at a screwed up bureaucracy like this.

I could not imagine that American citizenship could be forfeited that way, but after making inquiries to Pittsburgh's Immigration and Naturalization Service and to the Bureau of Consular Affairs in Washington, they told me flatly that no relief was available. The law was clear, they told me: Voting in a foreign election was tantamount an overt act of allegiance to that foreign power and a renunciation of American citizenship. I became incensed and decided to go all out for these people without a fee.

My research into the law found no exact precedent, but I decided to build a case on the theory that there had to be a knowing renunciation of citizenship, and unless Angelina had been advised that voting in this popular plebiscite would have these consequences, she did not make a knowing waiver. I got excited about this theory but became even more delighted when I discovered a statute that provided that one who had been in the United States at a prior time and was currently in a foreign country, and now claimed a right or privilege as a national of the United States and was denied such right or privilege by any department or federal agency, could seek a declaratory judgement in a federal district court. Moreover, to plead the case personally, they were entitled to receive a Certificate of Identity from the State Department that would permit them to come to America to appear in court. Angela qualified on all points.

I filed the action seeking a judgment declaring that Angelina was a United States citizen and that she had been improperly denied the rights of an American national and I named Dean Acheson, Secretary of State, as the defendant. I drew up the necessary papers applying for the Certificate of Identity with the American Consul General in Naples. The application was duly processed, and within a matter of months Angelina was in Pittsburgh.

My story should end with how I fought a dramatic courtroom battle and prevailed over the mighty State Department. But it was not to be. A grapevine of immigration law lore exists among people affected by it. In these circles there is knowledge that a foreign national married to an American citizen gets a preference on the Italian immigration quota and could get immediate entry. One day Angelina, her parents and a young man appeared in my office. "This is my husband," said Angelina, introducing me to an attractive Pittsburgh native. I knew without any further explanation what they intended. They processed her admission procedures as the wife of an American citizen without my help and she was duly admitted for permanent residence as an Italian immigrant. The family saw no necessity of paying for the processing of the lawsuit, so I discontinued it.

But there is a footnote. A few years later, Angelina, then married, returned to tell me that she had been advised that, although born here, she now had to apply to become a naturalized American citizen. I responded:

> Angelina, you have your birth certificate. That's your proof of citizenship. It's recognized by all the people in the world except for some bureaucrats. You're back in the States now for good. You're a citizen by birth. You don't need those people any more."

I marked the case closed as a win.

Another case had its start in a split in a Pittsburgh area Ukrainian church with part of the congregation electing to be affiliated with the

Vatican and the other part opting that the church to be an independent congregation. The dispute created a bitter religious war, tearing friends and families apart. The opposing groups would still be Christians, but basic concepts of Christendom were tossed to the four winds and a malignant bitterness descended upon the community, brother against brother, parents against children, friend against friend. Good friends against good friends.

Mike, a waiter in a prominent Pittsburgh restaurant, became a victim of this internecine war. He took an active role in the faction desiring affiliation with the Vatican, and he made his enemies, including his closest friend, a neighbor whom he had first met in a displaced persons camp in Germany soon after the shooting stopped in Europe.

It was almost a miracle that Mike had made his way to the West from the Soviet Union. His home town in the Ukraine had been totally demolished by Nazi armies, his entire family slaughtered in the German holocaust. The Germans put an ultimatum to able-bodied youth in the Ukraine: "You have a choice. Either serve in this military unit and fight the Russians, or we will line you up against the wall and shoot you. We will shoot you just as you have seen us shoot the old men, women and children of your village." It was a Hobson's choice and Mike joined and served in operations against the Soviets.

At war's end, hiding by day and scrambling by night, he evaded the Soviet occupying army, made it to the displaced persons camp, and there met the other young Ukrainian who would become his closest friend. Both were successful in qualifying under our Displaced Persons Act, having proved that they were refugees of concern to the International Refugee Organization (IRO). But IRO guidelines excluded any person who either "assisted the enemy in persecuting civilian populations." or "voluntarily assisted the enemy forces...in their operations against the United Nations." Together they migrated to the Pittsburgh area.

When they applied for refugee status, Mike confided to his friend that he would not reveal in his application that he had been pressed into a German-controlled army unit when the Nazis invaded his village. He withheld this information from the IRO when he filed his application for refugee status.

Years passed in America, the friendship between the two men and their families strengthened. They belonged to the same church, and all was well. All was well, that is, until the split in the congregation occurred. The friend was so incensed at Mike's stand on the church, that he decided to punish him. He went to the Immigration and Naturalization Service in Pittsburgh and reported that Mike, his former best friend, had withheld vital information when he had applied for refugee status.

Mike was subsequently called in, and without benefit of counsel, told his story, in due time machinery was placed in motion to strip him of his American citizenship, and process him for deportation to the Soviet Union; deport him to that country for fighting the Communists during the war. All of this in the Fifties when Stalin's mass execution of enemies was at its zenith.

He was about to be stripped of his American citizenship, when he retained me. "This is pretty late in the game for you to come in," the Immigration people told me. "We have compiled an air-tight case. We have all his statements under oath. There's nothing that can be done. He made a material misrepresentation in his visa application and therefore he will be denaturalized."

It took me a year to reverse the process in the Office of the Director of Immigration and Naturalization in Philadelphia, this being before the days of due process protections, immigration judge hearings, appeals to the Board of Immigration Appeals and further appeals to a U.S. Court of Appeals. In those days, the District Director's power was all-pervasive and an appeal, virtually non-existent.

I saved Mike from denaturalization and deportation. My argument: There was no misrepresentation in the visa application. No necessity to report his military service to the International Refugee Organization. Mike did not "voluntarily assist enemy forces." He was forced to do so. There is a colossal difference between a voluntary act and one that is compelled. The alternative to serving in the local army was death by a Nazi firing squad. By no means could you call this decision a "voluntary" act. There was no material misrepresentation. Moreover, he has been an active anti-Communist all his life and active in a "free Ukrainia" movement in the United States. Deportation to the Soviets would be sending him to his death.

Mike remained in Pittsburgh. He continued as a waiter for a few years, and then served as head waiter at several posh Pittsburgh restaurants. When I would enter his restaurant, he would announce in a loud voice, "Ladies and gentlemen, this is the man who saved my life!"

In time he opened his own restaurant near my home and on occasion my wife and I would bring our children there. He would take them aside and say, "Kids, do you know your father saved my life." The children were impressed on the first rendition, but after many repetitions they would shake their heads and say "not again" when Mike approached our table.

I had another immigration matters involving an anti-Communist, active in anti-Tito activities in this country. The case started one summer Sunday morning in 1952 when I was courting Agatha Maria De Lacio. Our families had been friends for years and since 1949 I had been her father's lawyer, a prominent steel fabricator. Louis R. De Lacio was one of the finest men I ever knew and we were very good friends, but somehow the sparks did not fly in my direction from his daughter. Finally, she agreed to go out with me in the Christmas season of 1950. And I proposed to her on our first date.

On this particular Sunday morning, Agatha and I had gone to church together and was planning to have dinner with her family. An attorney from another county, who often referred cases to me, reached me at Agatha's home and said:

> I have some people in my office who need a good immigration lawyer and need him fast. They have a friend who was picked up by immigration people, is now in custody in the Allegheny County Jail and is slated to be escorted by train from Pittsburgh tomorrow at one o'clock where he will be placed on a Yugoslav freighter and shipped off to Dubrovnik on Tuesday. He's an anti-communist and they will kill him when he gets there.

I said that on Sunday it was too late to do anything. And besides, I told him I was spending the day with my girl friend, and he responded, "Look, I'm sending them down. At least talk to them."

Three men arrived a few hours later and related to me the story of how their friend had been arrested in Croatia for anti-Communist activities in Zagreb, had escaped from jail, and entered the U.S. illegally a stowaway on a vessel. He had been working in the mill when recently some immigration officers had called him in for questioning, that nothing further happened until Friday when agents came to the mill and hauled him away to the Allegheny County jail after advising him that he was to be deported to Yugoslavia on a ship leaving New York on Tuesday.

The case sounded like a real loser, so I gave them a demand that they could not possibly meet. I demanded a retainer of $2000 and an advance of $100 for expenses, and it had to be in cash, because it was Sunday and I did not know them. They shook their heads, and speaking Serbo-Croat among themselves for a few minutes, said that they would return."They won't be back," I told Agatha.

But I was wrong. Within an hour or so, they were back with the money. It was a healthy sum for those days.

I then went to work, trying to reach Charles Garfinkel, the Pittsburgh INS Service officer-in-charge at his home and I was told that he was at Forbes Field, attending the Pitttsburgh Pirates ball game. I had him paged, and explained the dire emergency. He replied:

> I know all about this case, but it's beyond my jurisdiction now. It's entirely in the hands of the District Director in Philadelphia, and only he and nobody else could do anything.

I told him I would fly over to Philadelphia, but would he do me a favor and call the director the first thing in the morning and tell him I will be in his office at nine. I hopped a flight to Philadelphia and checked in to the Bellevue Stratford. I still remember that the charge for a single room that night in the city's largest and most expensive hotel was $7.50.

I was standing at the door when the INS Director's office opened at 9:00 a.m. He was having a staff meeting, but his secretary told me he would see me when the meeting broke.

When I came in to see him, he did not even ask me to sit down. He forcefully told me that nothing could be done, that my client was in the midst of a deportation process, and nothing was to prevent his being on that ship on Tuesday. "In fact, they'll be getting on a train at 1 o'clock," he said, "only a couple of hours from now." I delivered an impassioned plea as eloquently as I could, explaining that my client was an anti-communist, that he had escaped from jail in Yugoslavia, and by sending him back, we would be sending him to his death.

The director was unimpressed. "We can't do anything. I've given you my time. I have other things to do. Goodbye."

I pleaded with him. "Please help this man. Save him."

The director then became outright hostile and told me to leave. I started to do so, and I thought, what the hell, he can't hold me in contempt, so I stopped and exploded:

> Listen, you son of a bitch. Don't give me that bull shit that you can't do anything. You mean, "You won't."
>
> It's you who are sending this guy to his death. I hope you have nightmares about it. I'll sleep well tonight, but you, you won't.
>
> Believe me you won't. You'll have nightmares tonight. You'll have them every night of your life.
>
> And when you go home tonight and your kids ask what did you do today, daddy, be honest with them. Tell them, "Today, I killed a man."

I then turned to leave again and he called to me,

"Now don't get so damned emotional about this. Okay, I'll see what I can do. I'll call Charley and release the guy from custody and we'll schedule another interview. Okay? Calm down."

And he made the call in my presence, and then smiled and said, "Okay? Still mad?"

I smiled, shook hands, profusely apologized for my conduct and walked out of the room, still agitated by my impassioned outburst. I had lost my cool. I had lost my professionalism and had reverted to Marine Corps boot camp language. It had not been a pretense or a deliberate act on my part, but a spontaneous emotional outburst. But it had produced the results, results that I had never expected when I began my tirade.

I telephoned my clients and gave them the good news. I told them they could go to the jail in Pittsburgh and pick up their friend. Additionally, I instructed them to have him in my office at 12 noon the next day so I could prepare for the next step.

"Anything you say, boss," came the reply. "Thanks a million."

On the next day came 12 o'clock noon came and went. My client and his friends did not appear. The day passed and still they did not show. I never saw them again. And I doubt that the Immigration Service did either. The service never called for a hearing. It never asked for an explanation. My client probably moved away, disappeared in the great mass of America, probably changed his name, was working in another mill. But he was alive.

In time I had some very substantial business clients–the developer of one of Western Pennsylvania's first suburban shopping centers, a moderate-sized steel fabricating plant, an enormous wholesale grocery operation, several wholesale produce companies, a retail lumber and building supply company, a manufacturer of felt products and a large trucking company. I organized and became counsel to a general osteopathic hospital and established the first fraternal benefit life insurance society chartered in Pennsylvania in over 30 years.

In time I would also represent about ten building contractors, ranging from small home builders to sizable commercial contractors and land developers, whose problems extended from operations foundering close to bankruptcy to enterprises so successful that they encountered serious tax problems.

I had about 20 retail establishments clients varying from grocery stores and produce markets to a men's haberdashery. I also represented a dozen bars, several beer distributors, a number of funeral directors, an auto parts company, a printing company that printed house organs for most of the Pittsburgh labor unions and was the publisher of a weekly newspaper.

The very diversity of my clientele supplied me with a well-rounded background in commercial, construction and manufacturing practices. A symbiotic relationship in many parts of the construction industry helped immeasurably. In representing many building contractors, I learned that a builder is in the vortex of many conflicting forces--the owner-developer, the architect, the engineer, the sub-contractor, the materials supplier, the municipal building inspector, trucking companies and a number of craft labor unions. It was one thing for me to represent a general contractor and examine the problem from a one-dimensional perspective. But after I started to represent developers as well as architects and subcontractors-- carpenters, excavators and masonry contractors--and a building supply company I learned the flash points of actual and potential conflict. I was able to conceptualize many dimensions of a problem, not the narrow perspective of one client's point-of-view. In giving advice I saw my role not merely to solve problems for them as difficulties arose, but to prevent future problems from arising. More often than not, my major difficulty was to educate my client to changing sloppy and seat-of-the-pants practices.

This portion of my practice developed extensively, and by the time I became a judge, a goodly part of my practice was devoted to representing businesses. These clients--wholesale and retail establishments, land developers, and commercial and institutional builders--were not at all happy about my leaving the practice because I had become an integral part of their operations.

It was while representing an ICC certified contract carrier trucking company when I met Jimmy Hoffa. He was not the International President of the Teamsters International union then; he was president of the Detroit Teamsters local. His conduct in Detroit was a precursor of how he would act when he became the head of the International Brotherhood. My client had ICC rights as a contract carrier to haul finished steel from Pittsburgh mills to automobile plants in the Detroit area. As was the practice then, the trucker owned the ICC transportation rights, ran the business by obtaining hauling contracts and assigned hauling jobs to driver-owners of tractor-trailers who functioned under the trucker's ICC carrier rights. With one or two exceptions, all the big rigs were owned by the drivers, or more properly, by the drivers and their financing banks. These drivers were independent contractors and received a sum certain from the carrier to make the deliveries. They paid for their own gas and oil and any repairs to their rigs. Although they carried modest liability coverage, the major insurance protection was that supplied by the carrier in a fleet policy. Virtually, all of the drivers were their own mechanics, did their own repairs and were very sensitive as to how the rigs were driven. They and they alone drove their rigs. They did not trust outsiders behind their wheels. Every driver was a member of the national over-the-road local of the International Brotherhood of Teamsters..

It was against this background that my client came in to see me on what he described as "a most troubling matter." He reported that the Hoffa's Detroit local was now demanding that as long as the rig operated within the Detroit city limits, it had to be driven by a member of the Teamsters Detroit local. The carrier's drivers rebelled. "We don't want any strangers driving our rigs." they said. The drivers attempted to solve the problem through the International Teamster's office, but were unsuccessful. I arranged for an appointment with Hoffa, and my client and I flew to Detroit.

Hoffa was straight-forward and polite. He was not a "dese and dems" guy, but presented himself in a very low key manner, but was adamant: "No truck moves in this city unless the driver is a member of my local."

"But these drivers are members of the Teamster's over the road local," I said.

"I don't care. This is my jurisdiction."

I suggested that perhaps this was a matter that should be decided by Teamsters International, that this seemed to be a jurisdictional dispute between locals.

"You can take it to International if you want, but in the meantime, my men will drive those trucks while they're in Detroit."

I then suggested that our drivers would join his local, too, and pay the initiation fees and dues. "No can do. I have too many members already looking for work," he said.

After more talk going back and forth, I then agreed that we would pay for a member of his local to ride in the rig while it was being operated in Detroit, but the owner-driver would do the driving.

"We can't do that. If the word got out, it would look like we are featherbedding. Mr. Aldisert, this is a Teamster's local, not a featherbedding railroad union," Hoffa said.

We were at impasse, and I got up to leave, asking him to come up with an amicable solution to the problem. "We will consider anything reasonable you come up with, Mr. Hoffa," I said, "but the we have a bottom line, too, and here it is: These men own these rigs. They are your brothers in the Teamsters International Union, and no one can drive their rigs but them." I told him that we would not appeal to the International and file no unfair labor practice with the National Labor Relations Board. "On our part no NLRB, no publicity, but you have to understand how these men feel," I said. As a parting shot, I said that I'm sure that he had to make deals with other trucking companies, that my client was small potatoes compared to major hauling companies, and that I was confident that he would find a solution.

"Let's see what we can do," he said, smiled and we shook hands.

Hoffa telephoned me within a few days with a proposal: As soon as we crossed the city limits, our drivers would place cardboard signs on the sides of the cabs, displaying the name of a Detroit trucking company. We would pay a hauling fee to that company while on the streets of Detroit. The fee was not too exorbitant and we could live with it. My client was satisfied, and so were his drivers.

We never made inquiries, but there was no question in our minds who was the beneficial owner of the Detroit trucking company.

In the Fifties osteopathic physicians were the orphan children of the medical profession. These men and women were known as D.O.'s, doctors of osteopathy, and not M. D.'s, doctors of medicine. Although some osteopathic schools of medicine were below par, and were little more than chiropractic schools, there were some very fine educational institutions turning out top flight physicians who practiced in excellent osteopathic hospitals. The curriculum in the accredited schools of osteopathic tracked the basic medical school courses with one addition—osteopathy subscribed to a system of healing that some disorders can be alleviated by treatment of the skeleton disorders and musculature using manipulation and massage. But osteopathic physicians also deliver babies, perform surgery, practice internal medicine and treat emergencies.

Although many hospitals now extend staff privileges to D.O.s today, in the Fifties most hospital doors were closed to them. A group of these physicians attempted to organize a hospital in the rural, western section of Allegheny county, but were rebuffed by Pennsylvania Commonwealth authorities on the theory that the state had prepared a master hospital plan and no new hospitals could be established except in accordance with the plan. Rebuffed by the state, these osteopaths from the old coal mining communities of Moon Run, Imperial and Burgettstown came to me to ascertain if I could discover some solution to their problem. I took a retainer to look into the matter, but explained that I was not optimistic.

In researching the law I discovered that Pennsylvania regulated two types of hospital institutions---private hospitals owned by corporations or individuals, and charity institutions, usually operated by some religious order. Stringent state regulations governed each type of institution. To organize a new hospital under either type, applications had to be made to an appropriate state authority that served as a watchdog over existing hospitals and administered regional plans for the creation of new hospitals.

The more I thought about it, the more I decided there was another type of ownership not covered by existing Pennsylvania hospital legislation or regulations. I envisioned a not-for-profit corporation that was neither a private enterprise nor a charitable institution. There was a void in the statute and I was prepared to drive a Mack truck right through it.

Under Pennsylvania laws non-profit corporate charters were issued by the local Common Pleas Court, and not by the Commonwealth's Bureau of Corporations. I presented an application for a non profit corporate charter before Common Pleas Court Judge John Kennedy. In written and oral presentations, I made it clear that the proposed corporation would not be a charity organization. Judge Kennedy peered down from the bench:

> I have been a judge for a long time, Mr. Aldisert, and I have never issued a charter for a hospital. Are you sure this is all right? Do I have authority to do this?

I assured the court that it had the power and explained that the state's authority was limited to private and charity hospitals and that this application was for neither types, emphasizing the limiting strictures of the statute governing hospitals.

"O.K., I'll take your word for it," the judge grumbled and signed the order granting the hospital charter.

We were in business. I drew up a set of by-laws and my clients insisted that I serve on the board of trustees and the executive committee. We purchased an historical landmark, the Old Stone Tavern on Steubenville Pike near the former coal company town of Imperial, which had been the scene of the infamous beating death of John Borkowski by the Pennsylvania Coal and Iron Police in 1928. The tavern, an historical landmark, had been sturdily constructed in the 1850's as a wayside inn and had the size and configuration to be adapted as a small hospital. We had no difficulty with the township government or the rural neighbors. They welcomed the idea of having a hospital in their midst, about 15 miles from Pittsburgh and a like distance from hospitals in the borough of Canonsburg and city of Washington in Washington County. We named it West Allegheny Hospital.

We were proceeding with the purchase of the historic tavern when we were served with a flock of court orders to show cause why the hospital non profit corporation charter should not be immediately revoked because it had not been approved by the Commonwealth of Pennsylvania. I appeared again before Judge Kennedy, but this time opposed by a squad of Commonwealth deputy attorneys general.

> Judge Kennedy zeroed in on me:
> Mr. Aldisert, I took your word that this charter was okay and now you've put me and yourself in a lot of trouble.

He waved the thick blue-backed briefs that had been filed by the Attorney General's office."Did you read all these statutes and regulations that have been violated? Nobody can operate a hospital until they get permission from the state."

I held my ground:
If the court please, the Commonwealth of Pennsylvania has no standing to challenge this charter. This is a non-profit corporation but it is neither private nor charitable. No stockholders own it. Our patients will have to pay. We will take no charity cases. That's in our by-laws. The state has jurisdiction only over private and charity hospitals and we are neither. The statute in clear and limits the authority of the Commonwealth of Pennsylvania to only the types of hospitals set forth in the statute.

"Oh, yes, I remember now. That's what you said. Okay, who will answer for the Commonwealth?" asked the judge

A pompous deputy attorney general drew up to the bar: "The Commonwealth's position is clear and straightforward. There is no such thing as a non-profit but non charity corporation. I challenge my opponent to cite me one."

The judge nodded to me and I replied:

That's easy. His honor probably belongs to Blue Cross and Blue Shield, a non-profit corporation. And his honor pays a premium every month and I'm certain that the subscribers do not consider that to be a charity operation.

The judge smiled. I was on a roll:

And I know that my distinguished friend from the Attorney General's office in Harrisburg received his law degree from the University of Pittsburgh. That's a non profit organization, but you pay tuition. They may have scholarship students, but no charity cases. And there's a difference.

The deputies then huddled for a few minutes and then argued:
The Commonwealth's position is that it's impossible for any hospital not to be a charity organization. A person may be in an automobile accident and carried into the

emergency room, and the hospital will have to take care of him whether he pays or not. That's charity.

The judge asked if that's the best case the Commonwealth could make, he would dismiss all the objections to the charter. When they failed to do so, the judge did exactly that.

As a lawyer I was satisfied because I had accomplished so much for my clients. As a person, I was appalled that a hospital could be set in operation with an operating room and a delivery room and facilities for patients without any prior inspection or approval or supervision by any government agency.

When the hospital opened its doors, the only government requirement that had to be met was one imposed by the Pennsylvania Department of Labor and Industry that the doors and passageways be wide enough for beds to be rolled out in case of fire.

Within a month of its opening, babies were being delivered, broken legs were being set, and the operating room was busy with appendectomies and assorted procedures.

But almost as quickly the Attorney General drew up a proposed statute to plug the loop hole that I had discovered. The General Assembly swiftly amended the law to provide that *all* hospitals come under the laws regulating hospitals. The new statute could not be interpreted retroactively.

And so the West Allegheny Hospital came into existence in the old tavern. The internal administration was rocky, the three doctors being at odds with each other over plans and policies, requiring me to constantly mediate disputes, mainly over funding. They were undercapitalized and I could never pound in their heads that Blue Cross reimbursements were based on patient treatment and not capital investment. A year or so later, upon being elected to the Court of Common Pleas, I resigned all positions with them. Later still West Allegheny somehow qualified for federal money for facility modernization under the Hill-Burton Act, received a healthy grant to finance the erection of a huge new building, made peace with state authorities and functioned well as a regional hospital. I knew nothing about the new management of the facility and lost track of the original incorporators. I closed my files when I closed my practice, but years later when I would occasionally pass the imposing new regional hospital, I felt that its proper name should have been "Loophole Hospital."

The excitement I had in representing businesses however was matched by my personal injuries practice which was an extremely important part of my 14 years at the bar. I was extremely successful in personal injuries work, because I enjoyed appearing before a judge and jury. Because of my extensive experience in my early days in criminal court and being very comfortable in a courtroom, I was never intimated by an insurance adjuster's statement as settlement negotiations seemed to break down, "Well, Aldisert, I guess I'll see you in court." My Smart Alec response would be, "Put that in writing, because I really want to try this case before a jury." I called their bluff several times and when the insurance carriers recognized that they were dealing with an effective trial lawyer, negotiations took on a different tone.

Pennsylvania Rules of Discovery did not become effective until the very end of my time as a lawyer. Therefore, I was not saddled with days of depositions and other bells and whistles of modern day discovery, so much the vogue today. A few interrogatories generally were all that was needed. At trial I was not surprised very often by defense testimony nor they, by mine. Thorough leg work by good investigators--and at first I was my own--produced the results with a minimum of expense. What our own personal investigations did not produce was generally exchanged during settlement negotiations in many "'tis so, 'taint so" sessions.

I loved the give and take of settlement negotiations, but I was equally happy in the courtroom.

Agatha and I in the summer of 1952 after we had become engaged in April. The kindest person I have ever known, she tolerated my cigar smoking, note the cigar in my hand. I quit smoking cold turkey in the spring of 1961, and have not had a puff since. But to this day, I think it's a sign of civilized living to have a good cigar after dinner, and occasionally my fingers involuntarily assume a cigar-holding position after enjoying a gourmet evening repast.

We were married on October 4, 1952 and lived in the Pittsburgh area until July, 1987, when, for reasons of health, I had to move to a more temperate climate, and found it here in Santa Barbara. We have three children. Lisa is president of Pharos Alliance, LLC, a New York City-based business advisory firm specializing in strategic business growth and leadership development. Robert is a partner in the Perkins Coie law firm office in Portland, Oregon. Gregory is a partner in the Greenberg Gusker law firm in Los Angeles. We are a close knit family.

Our wedding day, October 4, 1952

Mother and I are pictured in the yard of my parents' Fort Lauderdale, Florida home. They lived there from 1956 to 1966 when the lure to see their grandchildren more often made them return to Pittsburgh. My mother died in 1996, having attained the age of 100 years and five months.

My Aunt Silvia, my father's sister, pictured in July 1961. This was 55 years after my father came to the United States to rescue her from a foster family who had her, at the age of 13, acting as scullery maid in a boarding house. I was fond of all my aunts, but she always had a special place in my heart.

A kiss from his wife to congratulate the new national president of the Order Italian Sons and Daughters of America (ISDA) in August, 1954 at the William Penn Hotel in Pittsburgh. It had been a contested election, and my opponent had been a long time national officer. Although I had held no previous office in the ISDA, I had been speaking before lodges since high school days. When I returned from the Marines in February 1946, I started to write a weekly column in the ISDA newspaper, *Unione,* entitled "Rambling." I wrote on a variety of subjects until I started to practice law in December 1947.

May 1, 1960, a climax of the Democratic Primaries battle in West Virginia between John F. Kennedy and Hubert Humphrey. The ISDA had a powerful lodge in Weirton, West Virginia and we combined forces to assemble 1200 people at a dinner to honor Kennedy. Earlier in the day I had joined his campaign near Fairmont and had the pleasure of talking with him as we rode to Weirton. I introduced him at the dinner and he told me that by far this was the largest audience he faced in West Virginia.

Chapter Eighteen
Criminal Court

"And Your Honor, we will not permit cross examination in this case." So stated Arthur G. Gatz, assistant district attorney, in addressing the alderman of Pittsburgh's Fourth Ward to whose court office he and two county detectives had taken my client at midnight for a preliminary hearing on charges of robbery and conspiracy. The alderman replied that it was O.K. with him.

"This is totally out of order," I said. "This is a court hearing. I represent the defendant and I have the right to examine any witness called by the Commonwealth."

"Not in my court," came the reply from the political hack-cum-magistrate perched on his elevated bench. In those days you didn't have to be trained in the law to occupy this position, and the alderman's compensation, based on fees, depended on the number of cases brought to you by the district attorney or the local constable. "Now, shut up, or I'll throw you out."

This was in the mid-Fifties in Pittsburgh, Pennsylvania. The 1950's, not the 1850's. And this is how the criminal process worked before "technicalities" like the Fifth and Sixth Amendments and cases like the

Miranda rule were incorporated by the Fourteenth Amendment to apply to state court proceedings.

I ended up in this alderman's office at this hour, after staking out the County Courthouse with two friends, Homer W. King and Arthur J. Diskin, after William S. Rahauser, the District Attorney of Allegheny County, refused to let me know where my client would have his preliminary hearing. His detectives had arrested him five hours before, and had brought him to the District Attorney's Office.

I had been called at my home by the defendant's father and told that county detectives had hauled his son away, and I immediately went to the DA's office on third floor of the Courthouse and was told that I could not talk to District Attorney Rahauser or his first assistant, Robert Van der Voort, because they were personally interrogating my client. I demanded to talk to Bill Rahauser, whom I knew well. Ten minutes later he appeared, shaking his head.

"We're still talking to him," he said.

"The man knows me, please tell him I am here. The family has retained me."

"I'm sorry, Rugi, I can't let you talk to him. We're questioning him now. And, no, I won't tell him that his family has retained you as his lawyer."

"When you are through, you'll be taking him before a magistrate for a hearing. Where are you taking him?"

"Sorry, I can't tell you that but I will say that it will be tonight."

There were three exits from the Courthouse, and I called my friends to help me stakeout the building. It was close to midnight when the D.A.'s people finally hustled him out of the courtyard and we followed. The DA scheduled the hearing at a late hour to prevent my posting a bond before "an impartial judicial tribunal." As it worked out, when I attempted to post bond, his honor, the hack, smiled and said, "The DA says no bond, so it's no bond." At least, however, I got to talk to my client, although not in private.

"Don't say one word. Not a word to anybody. Don't even tell them your name. I'll get you out the first thing in the morning," I said.

I went back to the office, hand-typed (ah, the joys of being a solo practitioner) a petition for a writ of habeas corpus When court opened at 9 o'clock I was first in line to be heard by the presiding judge, John Kennedy. I calmly recited all the events of the previous night--the district attorney's refusal to notify my client that he had a lawyer, his refusal to permit me to advise my client of his right to remain silent, his refusal to tell me where the preliminary hearing would take place, and I climaxed it by relating the district attorney's order that no cross examination would be permitted at the preliminary hearing before the committing magistrate and the order that no bond was permitted.

Responding to my presentation, Sam Strauss, the assistant DA on duty in the courtroom, told the court that I was exaggerating, and that his office, especially the district attorney himself, would not sanction the scenario that I described. I responded:

> Very well, your honor, let's have a hearing right now. I want to put Rahauser, Van der Voort and Gatz under oath and we'll see who's exaggerating. In the meantime, this is a writ of habeas corpus and I want my client brought to this courtroom immediately.

The judge ordered Strauss to produce my client, to look into this matter and report back immediately. My bedraggled client was brought to the courtroom and we conferred. When Strauss returned, he explained to the court that no hearing would be necessary and asked what relief I wanted under the circumstances. Because I was denied the right to cross examination, I wanted transcript of any statement my client made. I also wanted to examine every report prepared by the detectives, every statement from any person who implicated the defendant, and every bit of inculpatory evidence in the possession of the district attorney, including any confidential report in the hands of the detectives.

It was a high profile case that had generated banner headlines in the morning edition of the Pittsburgh Post-Gazette. My client was accused of masterminding the daylight robbery of his mother during which the mother had been pistol-whipped. Two weeks after the actual robbers were apprehended, they made the accusation that the victim's son had planned it.

Strauss shrugged his shoulders and Judge Kennedy ordered the D.A. to accede to my demand. "It's much more than any defendant is entitled to, but that's the price you have to pay for the atrocious conduct last night." Six years later, Bill Rahauser and Bob Van der Voort and I would serve together as fellow trial judges. Still later, Sam Strauss, too, was elected to that court.

Knowledge of today's police procedures is now commonplace. Television shows, movies, and novels have explained the *Miranda* rule, the right of counsel to be present at police questioning, the right to notice of a preliminary hearing and counsel's right to cross examine. We take all these for granted today, even though there are still those who complain that these constitutional protections "coddle" criminals and hamper law enforcement. Midnight preliminary hearings were a disgrace then, and are now generally prohibited.

Would we like to return to the procedures and systems when I practiced law? Would we like to go back to a system where the police and the district attorney played patty cake with the writ of habeas corpus? Here's how they did it.

The Great Writ of habeas corpus traces its ancestry to the year 1215 when King John signed the Magna Carta at Runnymede. Article 39 of that Great Charter provides:

> No Freeman's body shall be taken, nor imprisoned, nor disseised, nor outlawed, nor banished, nor in any way be damaged, nor shall the King send him to prison by force, without the judgment of his Peers and by the Law of the land.

The writ of habeas corpus commands the authority holding the petitioner to present the person before an open court. The words, habeas corpus, means "to have the body," but in 1950, about 700 years after the Magna Carta, the Pittsburgh police and the district attorney's office were able to get around the ringing protections of the Great Writ.

A lawyer representing a person in police custody would file the habeas petition before a judge and then serve the proper authority--the police or the district attorney. In Allegheny County at this time there were 128 separate municipalities and almost as many separate police departments.

Often when an attorney demanded to see his client in police custody and was denied, the Pittsburgh police, anticipating the filing of a writ, would immediately hustle the prisoner out of their jail or holding pen and deposit him or her with a police department of another municipality. It was a cozy arrangement within the old boys police network. Thereafter, when served with the writ, the Pittsburgh police would truthfully respond *nihil habet*, "We don't have the body." And they would continue moving their prisoner from one suburban municipality's jail to another until they had completed questioning, or in many cases, until red marks disappeared from the prisoner's body from snapping at him with wet towels during the grilling. The rubber hose had already fallen into disrepute because it broke too many bones (the prisoner always slipped and fell) or left too many black and blue marks. And besides, until the swelling subsided, the prisoner's injuries failed to square with the police explanation of that the bruises came from "resisting arrest."

This is not to suggest that the police did not accord any rights to a prisoner. For example, in 1949 I had a client in a murder case who had been a night club entertainer. The statement taken by the Pittsburgh police contained these passages:

> Q. Do you realize that you are under arrest charged with the crime of murder?
>
> A. I thought murder was a premeditated killing....
>
> Q. Do you realize that you are under arrest for the murder of L.J. who died as a result of stab wounds on Thursday, September 8, 1949 at about 2:40 AM inflicted by a knife in your hands at...in the City of Pittsburgh, Allegheny County?
>
> A. Yes.
>
> Q C., first of all, I want to warn you that anything you say here in relation to the above killing may be used for or against you in the trial of this case as we see fit to use it. Do you understand this?
>
> A. Yes, that's the stock phrase in all of these things.

> Q. With the knowledge of that you have been warned and appraised of your Constitutional Rights, are you willing to tell us everything you know about those circumstances leading to the killing of the aforementioned L.J. You may answer that question yes or no.
>
> A. Yes, I'll tell you what I know, because there's nothing to hide.

Let us examine those "constitutional rights."
- He was not told that he had a right to remain silent.
- He was not told that he had a right to counsel.
- He was not told that if he could not afford counsel, one would be appointed for him.

These are rights guaranteed by *Miranda* but that case did not come down for another 18 years, not until 1966 after I had been a state trial judge for five years.

> The statement concluded :
> Q. I will ask you to read this statement over carefully and if it is true and correct, are you willing to sign it?
>
> A. Not until I have consulted a lawyer.
>
> Q. You have made this statement of your own free will, without any threats, promises, or coercion on my part or the part of any member of the Pittsburgh Police Department. Is that right?
>
> A. I'll answer that after I've talked to a lawyer.

Defending a murder case was an emotional and rigorous experience, and often called for innovative actions. In 1950 I defended a construction worker who had been in a fist fight with a man in a bar. My client had just arrived in Pittsburgh from the Midwest to begin work on a job. After the bartender and other patrons broke it up, it was the Commonwealth's theory that my client left the bar, went to his pick-up truck and there obtained a large hunting knife, positioned himself outside the bar, and waited for the victim to emerge. When the victim left the bar alone, lit a cigarette and walked a few steps, the D.A. contended that my client jumped him and stabbed him in the back. It qualified as a first degree murder because he was charged with premeditation and "lying in wait." This could merit the death penalty. The old adage is that if the facts are against you, argue the law; if the law is against you, argue the facts. But both the law and the facts seemed against me. I tried another tack.

Really worried about his case, I decided that the best strategy was to take the jury's mind away from the facts of the case. By various delaying motions, I was successful in having the case postponed to Easter week. I had prepared and memorized an opening for closing argument on Holy Thursday to a jury that had been sequestered since Monday:

> This is the April week of 1950, a time, when irrespective of our choice of church, we, and each of us, turn our thoughts to the Almighty in the solemn and reverent contemplation of Holy Week.
>
> It is a time when our thoughts are of home and family. When the desire to be with ones loved is heightened, and when we herald the Pascal reunion our mothers and fathers with children and brothers with brothers, and sisters with sisters.
>
> It is a time when you, ladies and gentlemen, have assumed one of the greatest obligations of citizenship---jury duty on a case that has taken you away from the tradition of this week---from your work, but more important, from your home, from your family circle. You have been patient and attentive in the sacrifice of your valuable time in this most memorable of weeks. And we hope that this demonstration of patience and attentiveness continues as you listen to the summation of this trial.
>
> We of the defense have made a sincere effort to expedite the conduct of this trial as was possible under the circumstances, and at the same time guarantee the full rights and constitution privileges of W.A. who stands before you accused of a crime.

You are soon to retire to a jury room to determine if he is guilty of a crime or whether, he, at the termination of this trial will join his wife, E., and his five children in the consecration of the Easter season.

That decision will not be made by the lawyers in this case.

That decision will not be made by Judge Eagan.

Whether W.A. is guilty or not guilty is a decision that rests on the collective shoulders of you ladies and gentlemen of the jury, and you alone.

I stand before you now simply to suggest what conclusions you can draw from the testimony you have heard and the evidence produced.

I then reviewed the evidence, emphasizing the presumption of innocence. Then I closed with another passage I had written and memorized:

And so rests the case of W.A., the defendant.

Your duty we see is clear: to bring back a verdict that is just, for that which is just can harm no one. That which is unjust can really profit no one.

A great poet once wrote:

> But the sunshine, aye, shall light the sky,
> As round and round we run;
> And the truth shall ever come uppermost
> And justice will be done.

Perhaps it may seem to you that the Commonwealth lawyer and the defense lawyer have gone round and round in this case. For ours has been the duty to present the evidence and the testimony in accordance with the rules of the court and the traditions of American jurisprudence.

But here our duties come to an end; and soon yours begin.

In your deliberations, we ask that the spirit of Holy Week guide you in making a decision based on the facts presented and the law that governs.

We ask that the obligation of citizenship--duty to serve on the jury--has been properly met.

As this Easter Week draws to a close and we celebrate as free citizens the glorious season of Easter, we want our hearts to be open and our conscience to be clear.

And as to your respective churches you go on Sunday, you must greet your neighbors in the knowledge that your mind is free from doubt. And as the spring sunshine streams through the stained glass windows and warms you, as in prayer and meditation you kneel, there must be the inner satisfaction that there is peace and contentment within you.

I will be at peace. I will feel that I have done my best as a lawyer to defend this man. I will be at peace.

But as you retire to the jury room, you must ask yourselves a simple question: Will I be at peace Easter morning? Will I be at peace? And you can only be at peace when you are totally and absolutely, positively, unconditionally and unequivocally convinced. Totally convinced that you have not returned a guilty verdict against a man who is innocent.

Ladies and gentlemen, I will be at peace Easter morning.

The question is: Will you?

Be at peace. And you will be at peace only when you return a verdict of not guilty.

The jury returned a verdict of not guilty. Midway through the trial, the D A abandoned his demand for the electric chair and concentrated on a life sentence. From the very first day I was worried about this one.

After the verdict was returned my client's pregnant wife and I were standing at the Ross Street entrance to the County Jail. She was weeping tears of joy and thanking me over and over "for saving my husband's life." When my client appeared, he said to me:

> I guess I should thank you, but I won't. I paid you to do a job and that's enough. I hate Pittsburgh and all that it stands for. From the first day I arrived here I have been in jail and the only person I've talked to is you. So I hate you. I hate you because you will always remind me of Pittsburgh. You and all of Pittsburgh can go to hell.

Ah, the joy of grateful clients, especially after some sleepless nights when I worried about the lying-in-wait facts and the elements of a death penalty case.

I spent much of my early days in the law--December of 1947, all of 1948 and part of 1949--sopping up experience. As my practice began to develop, I found myself on the third floor of the Courthouse, Criminal Court, only when retained by private clients or appointed by the court in homicide cases. This was no longer a daily trip. Weeks and months would go without appearing in criminal court, and when I did, it was to represent not master criminals or arch enemies of society, but some very unfortunate people referred by friends or clients. These cases ran the full gamut from minor offenses of disorderly conduct, surety of the peace, simple and aggravated assault and battery, drunken driving and indecent assault through the more serious offenses of receiving stolen goods, larceny and burglary, to the very serious charges of robbery, statutory and felonious rape, manslaughter and murder.

Putting aside my early years of pro bono work in criminal court where I gleefully accepted any case to get valuable experience in a courtroom, when I settled into my own private practice, I had greater difficulty in defending cases where the charged crime involved force or violence. This being so, you may appropriately ask why would I deign to represent someone charged with a serious crime?

To understand this you must appreciate the context in which these cases arose. They usually started with a telephone call from a member of the family--a father, mother, wife, brother or sister. "We need a lawyer. Johnny has been arrested and we need help." The person calling would either be a client or a friend of a client or simply a person who had been recommended to me by another lawyer. In the eyes of the family, the person arrested was "a good boy" and "There must be some mistake." Thus, the initial impression I received from the family was not that I was asked to represent a sociopath who had no redeeming moral values.

Moreover, some of the cases that came my way would fit under the current rubric of "date rape," and in these cases, so long as I extended to my client the highest of professional and ethical representation, I was quite content to permit the jury to decide whether the actual or alleged victim did or did not consent. But early on I had some cases that reflect the distinction in community moral standards of the Fifties and those of today. I remember one very clearly.

My client's date was about 19 or 20 years old and arrived home late at night and was walking up darkened stairs to her second floor bedroom when her father turned on the light to remonstrate that she had been out too late and saw that his daughter's hair was mussed up, her make-up askew clothing disheveled and that she was carrying her girdle and stockings in her hands. When he started to shout at her and call her names, she replied, "I've been raped!"

The "victim" was in an untenable situation. She could not admit to her parents that she had been "going all the way," as the then-idiom had it, in the back seat of my client's car parked about two blocks from her home. Nice girls did not do that. Yet it was unfair to charge the boy with unlawful conduct to which she had consented. She quickly made the decision on those stairs that night to protect her reputation at home and persisted in it in a statement to the Pittsburgh police, in testimony before a magistrate and grand jury and before a judge and jury where my client had to answer a charge of felonious rape.

I won that case through cross examination of the "victim." I didn't tear her apart to make her out as a tramp. I made her out as a very fine young lady who did not want her parents to know that she had consented to a sexual act:

> Miss, I have a Bible here, you are under oath and I want you to put your hand on this Bible and look at my client in the eye and I want you to tell us that he committed forcible, felonious rape that night.

"Objection", shouted the assistant D.A.

"Sustained," ruled the court.

But I had made my point.

I put my client on the stand and he described the "victim" as a good friend in extremely positive terms and did not portray her as a tramp. I asked him why she would say the things she did:

"This girl is deathly in fear of her father. Had he not been on the steps when she came home, she would not have said the things she said. I would not have been charged and we would not be in this courtroom. Mr. Aldisert, I'm telling the truth. I cross my heart and hope to die. God can strike me dead if I raped that girl. We both wanted to do it," he said.

The acquittal was returned in 20 minutes.

But there were rape cases at the other extreme. Particularly one from a lawyer who was a regular source of referrals. It was a case of brutal violence and my client was a bus driver who had a very short fuse. I was preparing him for trial and one day, in the presence of his brothers, I acted out the role of a cross examining DA. He was a terrible witness and, telling them so, I advised against him taking the stand. My client became enraged, said I had no business asking him questions like that. "You bastard, you think I'm guilty!" he shouted as he took a swing at me. I ducked in time. He was forcibly retrained by his brothers. I advised them to get another lawyer, but they demurred. Against my advice, he took the stand at trial, the DA chopped him into bits and the jury quickly convicted.

I worried through many cases in criminal court, because by the time the trial approached I had learned to know my client, not as a name on the indictment and a number on the file, but as a human being with mothers and fathers, wives and children, possessed of compassionate, humane and sympathetic attributes, a modicum of heartless and sometimes cruel and vicious tendencies, and, as is the case of most people enmeshed in the criminal justice system—an enormous aggregate of stupidity.

The stupidity factor runs rampant throughout the so-called criminal element, whether measured by my experience as a defense lawyer or as a state trial judge or my tremendous background as a federal appellate judge where I have reviewed convictions of thousands--from the solitary felon robbing a bank simply because he is broke to wealthy members of organized crimes and cartels. The common thread running through most anti-social acts is an overdose of wholesale stupidity, giant economy size. But there is nevertheless an abundance of mean, cruel, debauched people who should never be released to society.

Others get involved in the criminal justice system because they are unjustly accused. This was the case of a prominent Pittsburgh physician named as a defendant in a paternity case. We must look at these cases in the perspective of the Fifties, and not in the current era, where tests are now available to include or exclude with scientific certainty the allegations of paternity. At that time, only one test was available. It had the capability of declaring with certainty that a certain portion of the male population could not be the father of a child. Not to be excluded by this test did not necessarily mean that you were the father. It meant only that you were not a member of the class actually excluded.

In Pennsylvania at that time paternity could be established by a civil action in the family division of the court, or before a jury in criminal court where the accused father was arrested and charged with the common law crime of Fornication and Bastardy. The mother of the child had been my client's receptionist who had taken maternity leave without any accusation against her employer. After the child was born, accompanied by a lawyer, she came to his office and made the accusation for the first time. He denied it immediately and told her it was impossible for him to have fathered the child and offered to take a blood test. This was done and he was not excluded. The woman demanded a substantial financial settlement that was totally rejected. The filing of a criminal information followed.

It was at this juncture that I was consulted by the physician in company of his wife, a very attractive and intelligent woman. He told me the story and related the results of the blood tests. At this point his wife spoke:

> It's impossible for my husband to have been the father of this child. We have one child of our own, now five years old. I had a very difficult pregnancy with a life-threatening delivery. My obstetrician advised me not to have any more children. My husband and I talked about it, and he offered to have a vasectomy performed. This was done almost five years ago. And we told [the woman] and her lawyer about this when they made their accusations.

We went to trial.

At that time in Pennsylvania the district attorney could yield his right to prosecute certain misdemeanors, and permit a victim's lawyer to serve as a private prosecutor. In this case her lawyer, a very successful criminal lawyer, served as the prosecutor. He opened to the jury with a wild accusation that our defense was going to be the vasectomy and that he would prove that there was a conspiracy between the defendant and other physicians and the hospital to alter records; that indeed the vasectomy was performed only after his client made the accusation.

Yet he produced no witnesses to sustain his theory.

When it came to our defense, I produced the urologist who performed the operation long before the gestation period and the hospital records describing surgical procedures. On cross-examination the private prosecutor piled innuendo on innuendo over a constant series of objections on my part. He suggested that the urologist lied as to when the vasectomy was performed, that the hospital records had been changed through a conspiracy of the doctors. He had no evidence of proof to support his insinuations. The trial judge was a visitor from an outlying county, who overruled all my objections: "I believe in letting all the evidence in and letting the jury decide, counselor. Objection overruled," he said.

"But it's not a question of evidence, if the court please, it's improper innuendo without a foundation."

"I've made my ruling, counselor."

I constantly objected and got nowhere with the judge. It was even worse during the closing argument when the prosecutor said:

> Ladies and gentlemen of the jury, I don't need witnesses to prove this point. I ask you to draw upon your wide experience in life. You know the score. You know how things work with doctors. They all stick together. One of them commits a wrong and they close ranks. They won't tell the truth. They lie. They falsify records. They have control of the hospitals. Don't let these rich doctors pull the wool over your eyes.

It no longer had become a paternity case. It was a question of "us against them," the medical profession against what the prosecutor called, "the common people, the working people." The jackass of a judge sat up there drinking it all in. I blew out all stops in my closing speech after reviewing the actual testimony at the trial:

> Go ahead and believe the private prosecutor who is being paid by this woman here. When your child is sick with a raging fever in the middle of the night, don't call the doctor because he's a liar and a cheat. When you have a pain in your belly and you think you have appendicitis, don't call him. He's only a liar and a cheat. Call this special prosecutor here. He'll fix you up. When your mother and grandmother are ill and have to go to the hospital, don't call a doctor, for he will lie to them.

And on and on. The court made a short, straightforward charge and the jury was released to deliberate.

In chambers, the judge ordered us to stand by because the jury would be back in a few minutes with a not guilty verdict. I disagreed. I predicted that it would be out for hours because the court permitted improper questioning and improper argument. I told the judge that the private prosecutor used tactics that no right thinking DA would ever dream of using. "With respect, Your Honor let him get away with it," I said. From jury selection to the close of the charge the trial had taken four hours. The jury deliberated for six hours. Dinner had to be sent in for the jury, and when they returned their verdict, the court had to transport them home.

The verdict was not guilty. We were told that 10 jurors were for an acquittal immediately but two believed that "all doctors stick together." But the 10 jurors hung tough and refused to report an impasse until the two recalcitrants caved in. The jurors were not happy campers when they returned their verdict at 10 o'clock at night.

In the Forties and Fifties, the average lawyer, even an experienced litigator in civil practice, stayed out of criminal court. Certainly there were good reasons then, principally, the abhorrence of associating with those accused of crime. But there were decent fees to be made for the limited hours actually expended in court before the constitutional law revolution of the Sixties and Seventies made every criminal proceeding a laboratory exercise in the Bill of Rights. Today, the average lawyer stays out of criminal court because there are comparatively few defendants who can afford to pay for the necessary representation; the best legal defense work comes from the federal public defenders office and to a lesser extent, because their case load is so onerous, from the state public defenders.

I was constantly asked: "How could you ever represent a client when in your heart you know that he is guilty?" Mine was a stock answer: "Only God and the jury know whether one is guilty, and I am neither. My responsibility as a lawyer is to deliver the best possible professional service that the law and the code of ethics permits."

But there is more to this. Today, most criminals are in organized narcotics crime, urban youth gangs or are individual sociopaths. A special kind of law breaker commits crimes to feed a narcotic habit. The addiction costs money, and to obtain their fixes they resort to robbery, burglary, larceny, car jacking and forgery. Added to this is another category of bad eggs who from early childhood live the life of breaking the law.

Jails are filled with spouse-killers and spouse-beaters who otherwise are so law-abiding that they would never have been charged with jaywalking. Many homicide cases that I defended resulted from barroom brawls. Put aside the whiskey and the six pack, and put aside also the cultural tradition supplied by Hollywood in the Western saloons ("Smile when you say that, stranger"), in most cases both the perpetrator and the victim got caught up in events of a specific moment. A fleeting moment transformed a model, law-abiding citizen into a criminal.

You get to know this as you prepare the defense of a criminal case. You seek to discover the whole person including his family, friends and relatives. You do this so that you can present the best dimension possible before the jury and not the stark facts of the prosecution's version of the criminal act. The more experienced I became, the more I became convinced that persons indicted are not always the mean people of Mean Streets, the arch criminal of the Sherlock Holmes's Professor Moriarty, the ruthless killers who wore black hats in the Westerns. Sometimes they are merely unfortunate slobs who get in trouble because of sheer stupidity. Society still has to decide what should be the proper length of incarceration (plain and simple warehousing behind bars) or supervised release, because the chances of prison rehabilitation are virtually nil.

In my entire experience representing persons accused of crime, I remember a truly base, depraved, wicked person. And this arch criminal was a woman. A sweet ole granny type who owned a home in suburbia, who kept to herself, who didn't bother the neighbors much, but had a lot of female visitors--lots of grandchildren and grandnieces, the neighbors thought. They were wrong. She was operating an abortion mill. She had a lovely appearance with coiffed grey hair and glasses and conservative dresses, but she had the most vile tongue and was the most debauched person, male or female, that I ever met.

A neighbor of hers, a prominent Pittsburgh lawyer, asked me to represent her because she was in some kind of police "trouble." "She's quiet and cannot possibly be guilty of any wrong doing," he said. She was a consummate actress. To her neighbors she was a soft-spoken little old lady who kept to herself, seldom said more than a few words, and seldom ventured out of the house. She used a taxicab when she went to the hairdresser or traveled downtown to shop. Most of her groceries were delivered. When I phoned her, she was most polite and asked me if I would please come to her house.

I found a very different person when I arrived. She talked liked a throwback to the Jimmy Cagney and Edward G. Robinson caricatures from the Thirties. Every other expression she uttered was the f-word and it went down hill from there. Her vocabulary was salted with "pimps" "johns" and "faggots." There were no police, just "bulls" and "dicks," and all of them could be bought for "dough" or a "roll." The police accused her about being an abortionist but she said that this was a bum rap. "A woman came to my door and said she was lost," she said. "The next thing I knew she passed out and I could tell she was bleeding, and the bitch died right there." She told me she would never go to trial.

"I'm payin' you a wad of dough just in case I go to trial, junior, but in the meantime, stay the fuck outta my way," this sweet little old lady said. She peeled off my retainer, a healthy one, in $100 dollar bills and refused to talk more about the case. I went home and took a bath.

In time I received notification of a trial date and telephoned her. She refused to come to my office and insisted that I come out to her house the day before the trial. She adhered to her story. She told me that she offered the woman a glass of lemonade and suddenly she started bleeding. That was the substance of her explanation, except that the words she used were profane and disgusting. The f-word was used as an adjective, noun and, in verb form, as a gerund, a past participle, and especially the imperative mood suggesting that the police and district attorney could do something that was physiologically and anatomically impossible.

The police had told me they had confiscated catheters in her home, that her "patient" bled to death after my client was careless, and kept the dead body in her house for two days until she located some family member to take the corpse off her hands. They were amused at crude attempts to bribe them. They reported that she was a sordid character, had for years consorted with a galaxy of underworld personalities throughout the East and Midwest. She was a well known abortionist who in recent years had moved from city to city and had never been arrested or indicted. The police never could prove anything until this case. She was the most profane and immoral person I have ever met.

At trial she took the stand in her own defense, with the sweet grandmotherly appearance, modest dress, neat grey hair, wire-rimmed glasses, and clutching a large black handbag. I led her through her testimony.

To my surprise she made a fair impression, although I could tell that the jury was not overly impressed by her story, especially her explanation of the catheters:

> Oh my late husband, God rest his soul, had bladder problems and after he passed on I started to use them as knitting needles. I do a lot of knitting and use them all the time."

Sam Strauss, the chief assistant DA, had a field day. In cross-examination he immediately goaded her into a knock-down drag-em-out fight between witness and prosecutor before a packed courtroom. Although she was going to match wits with a master prosecutor, there never was a contest. Strauss was a virtuoso. A taunt here, a wisecrack there, he pushed all the buttons, and the defendant became angry and profane. Still raging when she stepped down from the witness stand and glaring at the DA, she pointed to the catheters on counsel table and in a coarse voice that could be heard by the jury, said: "And don't lose these. I still need 'em."

When the jury returned a verdict of guilty, she turned to me with a sweet smile and said, "You fucked up, junior."

She was sentenced instantly by the court. I never saw or heard from her again.

I started my career as a lawyer on the Criminal Court floor of the Courthouse and devoted most of the first 18 months of practice there, immersed in pro bono defense work for the purpose of developing trial court skills and confidence, skills and confidence that cannot be learned from books so much as from hands on experience. When my practice moved into high gear, I had migrated to the civil side of the court, located next door on the Seventh Floor of the City-County Building and it was here that I spent most of my courtroom time during the 14 years of practice. To be sure, as indicated, I had a number of private clients and referrals from other lawyers that returned me to the third floor Criminal Court of the Courthouse from time to time. Having started out in Criminal Court, I suppose that it was symbolic that the last case I tried as lawyer, before I became a judge, was back in Criminal Court as defense counsel in a high profile murder case.

It started one day in late 1960 at lunch with some lawyers and I offered the comment:

"I'd like to sink my teeth in a good criminal case."

That same evening Agatha and I were watching the 11 o'clock news on television when we saw a man debarking from a plane at the airport in the custody of two county detectives. He was submitting to an interview with a TV reporter. I said to my wife, "My God, that guy is confessing to everything but the sinking of the Titanic."

At 11 o'clock the next morning he was my client.

One of my friends at lunch the previous day had represented this man in domestic relations matters and had been called by him from jail with the entreaty, "I need a good criminal lawyer."

My friend telephoned me and said, "About that good criminal case you'd like to sink your teeth into..."

It was a bad case.

At the time I was retained this was what the police knew: After extensive matrimonial difficulties my client was separated from his wife who lived with their children in a Pittsburgh suburb. He left town and took a job in the South. He admitted to the police that he had arrived in Pittsburgh by train from the South for the avowed purpose of entering the family house surreptitiously to see whether his wife was cheating on him. "I wanted to catch them," he said, *"in flagrante delictu."*

As a disguise he grew a mustache and was armed with a small caliber pistol. At two o'clock in the morning he took a cab from the train station and instructed to driver to take him to a location about a block from the family home and instructed the driver to return to this spot in exactly one hour. Although he had a house key, my client feigned a break in. In the event he was discovered, he planned that in his disguise he would have been taken for a burglar.

He told the police that after he entered the house, "Everything went blank." The next thing he remembered, he said, was meeting the cab, going to the Greyhound bus station and taking the 4 o'clock a.m. bus to Cleveland where he boarded a plane for the South under an assumed name. He was arrested shortly after he landed. When apprehended he had scratches on his face which he explained he received while fly fishing in a nearby stream.

But the police knew more. His children told them that a man had come into the house in the middle of the night and pulled their mother from her bed where she had been sleeping with her eight year old daughter, that the man told them to go back to bed, that the man struck their mother over the head with a club time after time. The club was later identified as a table leg. They told the police that the man then proceeded to smash their mother's head repeatedly against a wall until she was unconscious, and that finally he seized a pair of her stockings, garroted her, and placed her body back in the bed with the eight-year old daughter.

The man, they said, was their father.

My client had an IQ that approached the genius level and he was clearly in control of himself at our first interview. He did most of the talking, telling me exactly what he had told the police and then concluding, "I don't know what happened. Everything went blank." After the interview he decided that he wanted me to represent him. "My mother is from out of town. She is at a local hotel. She will come to your office and pay your retainer." She did, and I took the case. From the very beginning, I worried. It looked like a capital case. It was very high profile, widely discussed by the print and electronic media. District Attorney Edward Boyle announced that he would seek the death penalty. At the Coroner's Inquest I was able to elicit from the homicide detectives the monumental extent of incriminating statements taken from his children. Sitting beside me during the hearing, my client did not display the slightest emotion. I visited him in jail regularly, and he was always composed, tranquil and collected. I was the one who was ruffled and extremely concerned. I told him that he was acting as if he was in jail for a traffic ticket. He laughed and preferred to talk to me about current events and the books he was reading. He was one cool guy in complete command of himself. And he made it clear that he wanted to take his chances before a jury.

When my investigation and legal research was complete we had a very serious discussion. I told him that if we went to trial before a jury, he had virtually no chance at an acquittal. My prediction was that the jury would come back with first degree, with more likely the verdict favoring the death penalty than life imprisonment. His response: "You gotta be kidding."

He was personable, extremely well-informed, a charming conversationalist with a marvelous sense of humor. He loved his children and did not want me to brutalize them with any ferocious cross-examination. I had long proposed to plead him not guilty by reason of insanity. "Hell, I don't want people to think I'm nuts." I insisted that he give me the opportunity to have him examined by a psychiatrist. It took me weeks to convince him to let me do this. A friendly psychiatrist obliged me, but after examining my client in jail, he wrote a devastating report: "He knows what he is doing. He is a very cunning, deliberate person."

After many months, my client agreed to a strategy that I had subsequently proposed. I would seek a plea bargain in which we would plead guilty to murder generally with a panel of judges to hear testimony and then determine the grade of homicide. The panel would decide whether it was first degree or second degree murder or voluntary manslaughter. In return for the plea, the Commonwealth and the judges had to agree that the death penalty would not be returned.

I made a lengthy presentation before the district attorney and his chief assistant. At first they would not even listen to the proposal, saying that it was a cruel and unmerciful crime that deserved the death penalty. In response, I told them that the very heinous nature of the events was going to be my trump card. Such violence, I argued, could only have been committed in passion by provocation, that this was a culmination of years of husband and wife discord and this was classic manslaughter, and not murder. We could not agree, but went back to the negotiating table several times.

They finally agreed to my proposal: I would plead him but the state would not ask for the electric chair. A panel of two visiting judges, Judge David Weiss of Westmoreland County and Judge Alton McDonald of Cambria County, agreed to take the plea under the specified agreement.

We took testimony for two days. All of the children did not have to testify for I agreed that their statements could be read into evidence. I drew a picture of two highly intelligent people--the wife, too, had an extremely high IQ--who got along with everybody, with everybody except themselves. I put my client on the stand and he unfolded a tale of almost constant bickering between him and his wife, that showed that they simply should not have been married to each other. A defense witness testified that he saw the wife once hit the defendant with a golf club and another time threatened him with a butcher knife and screamed at him, "you s.o.b., I'll kill you." During this witness's testimony I introduced into evidence a book belonging to the wife titled, "Spectro Chrome Metry Encyclopedia," written by Dinshah P. Gadiali, and explained that the book was the primary testament of a strange Hindu cult that used projections of colored lights to cure troubles and that membership in the sect by her and her mother cased difficulties between the wife and husband. I produced evidence that her mother was a very active disciple of Dinshah, as the Hindu sect was popularly known, that using colored lights to bring harmony out of controversy. The victim's mother began to shine various colors of lights on her daughter and son-in-law while they were in bed asleep. The newspapers ate it up. A yellow light shining on them for hours would decrease his libido. A red light would make them happy. A blue light would lower voices in their speech to one another. The details of years of marital strife was widely reported by the media. After testimony was closed, I made a three-hour closing argument.

I took the rhetorical model of Cicero's famous repetition of the line, *Cartago delenda est,* Carthage must be destroyed. I would go through one segment of the vicious attack, and then say, "And this is manslaughter, not murder." I would describe another segment and repeat, "And this is manslaughter, not murder." I went on and on in this manner, my strategy being to emphasize the problems in their marriage and the heat of passion of the husband sneaking home to see if his wife was cheating on him. I had to do this to offset the premeditated evidence of planning--the disguise, the taxi arrangement, the bus ride to Cleveland leaving at 4 a.m. the return to the South by plane under an assumed name.

I was a realist. The chance of the judges coming back with manslaughter was remote, but I was hoping for the big compromise--the prosecution wants first degree, the defense, manslaughter; perhaps the judges would compromise and bring back a determination of second degree murder. This carried a sentence of 10 to 20 years.

My dramatic closing argument frightened George Ross, the prosecutor. When I completed, he rushed to the podium and shouted "Manslaughter no! The Commonwealth insists that this court return a finding of death, death by the electric chair.

As he began a serious presentation why the death penalty should be returned, the judges exchanged querulous glances, and then Judge McDonald interrupted: "Mr. Ross, wasn't there an agreement reached that the life imprisonment was to be the highest penalty returned. Wasn't there such an agreement?"

Ross admitted there had been an agreement, but as far as he was concerned, "All bets are off. The Commonwealth is now asking for the chair."

Judge McDonald pounded the gavel and announced that the court wished to see the district attorney himself and counsel in chambers. When told about the "revocation," District Attorney Boyle said that this was nonsense, that the agreement had been entered into by him, that his assistant Ross knew that, and besides, the judges had agreed to accept the plea only with the understanding that the Commonwealth had waived the death penalty. We returned to open court and Ross made an extremely effective speech demanding life imprisonment.

The judges then retired to confer in chambers while we waited in the courtroom. In about 15 minutes they returned:

"We assess the guilt as murder in the first degree."

I had not succeeded in my strategy, but I had saved my client's life. He was immediately sentenced to a life term which in Pennsylvania at that time averaged about 17 years. The defendant was then in his late thirties. He would be in his early or middle fifties before he could be released.

Nine years would pass before I heard more of him. I had already served as a Common Pleas Court judge and was in my first year as a U.S. Circuit judge. In 1969 a lawyer from Miami was then representing my former client and had come to see me about certain aspects of the case, specifically, whether my client knowingly and intelligently had entered a plea of guilty. I was still in possession of the file at that time and supplied him with the appropriate information, including a transcript of the proceeding in which he entered a plea of guilty and waived all protections of rights available in a jury trial He then explained how my former client was spending his time in prison.

About a year after his incarceration, his mother died leaving him as her sole heir with an estate of about $275,000. Using acumen commensurate with his high intellect, he utilized every waking moment studying the stock market. In prison he subscribed to a number of financial services and examined the market daily in the local newspapers and the Wall Street Journal. By prudent investments, he had parlayed his $275,000 in 1962 to over $3 million dollars by 1969. He had become a stock market expert in his prison cell.

Projecting his success, by the time he paid his debt to society in about ten more years—at that time a life sentence amounted to about 17 years incarceration if the prisoner behaved himself--he would have amassed several millions more. And this was before the period of inflation occurred, before the stock market took off for sizzling heights.

The man I defended in the last criminal case I tried as a lawyer was sentenced to life imprisonment for committing first degree murder. But after paying his debt to society he would leave prison a self-made, double-digit, multi-millionaire.

Chapter Nineteen
The Icardi Case: Part One

From 1951 to 1956 I donated a massive amount of time and my best professional services in defense of a friend. Today we call this pro bono work, but I jumped to his aid because the federal government had slaughtered his career with a reckless press release and then proceeded to bend rules of law and standards of integrity, if not common decency, to put him behind bars.

His name was Aldo "Ike" Icardi, a friend whom I had known as a very popular undergraduate at the University of Pittsburgh, head cheerleader and catcher on the baseball team. After the end of World War II, he was a year behind me in law school. Slight in build and prematurely bald, he was always buoyant and exuberant. As an undergraduate, he became a high ranking member of the ROTC, was commissioned a second lieutenant and entered military service immediately upon graduation in June 1942.

He returned from the war a decorated hero, became a fellow law student, and by the summer of 1951 he was married, had two children and was beginning a career in New York City as an in-house counsel for Panagra, the airline jointly owned by Pan-American Airlines and Grace Steamship Lines. The airline operated between the United States and Central and South America.

He was splendidly suited for this position because after receiving his degree from the School of Law of the University of Pittsburgh, he had pursued additional law studies at the Catholic University of Lima, Peru. He was tri-lingual, fluent in Italian and Spanish as well as English.

On the evening of August 15, 1951, his world caved in.

After dinner he had been scanning a newspaper while his wife was clearing the dinner table. The radio had been broadcasting a music program as a prelude to the evening news. The news came on with a lead story:

> Aldo Icardi, New York lawyer, has been accused by the Defense Department of ordering the murder of his commanding officer when they were on an espionage mission for the OSS behind German lines in Northern Italy in December, 1944.

There was no indictment. No initiation of prosecution. Only a press release from the Department of Defense's Office of Public Information making the accusation.

The OSS was the Office of Strategic Services, the World War II forerunner to the CIA. On September 26, 1944, then an Army first lieutenant assigned to the OSS, Icardi parachuted into enemy territory in Northern Italy as a member of a small, special intelligence mission headed by Major William V. Holohan. The mission had been dropped in the midst of Nazi garrisons and Italian fascists on a mountain known as the Mottarone that separated Lake Maggiore and Lake Orta. From the time of the initial drop, its members had been constantly on the move to avoid detection. On the night of December 6, Major Holohan disappeared. Seven years after Icardi had been decorated and honorably discharged, the Defense Department made the accusations in the form of a press release.

Two days after the thunderbolt, Icardi returned with his wife and children to his parents' Pittsburgh home. He had just started his job in New York, had borrowed money from his parents to move his family from South America where he had completed his graduate work, and had paid the initial rent for a house in New Jersey. He was 31 years old and was flat broke.

He telephoned me the day after he arrived and we made arrangements to meet that evening in the privacy of my home. We were to be joined by another law school classmate, Samuel L. Rodgers of nearby Washington County. Ike told us:

> I am not guilty of any crime. I had nothing to do with Holohan's disappearance. The OSS investigated the case while I was still in the service. They even asked me to take a lie detector test. I did so willingly and came through with flying colors. They told me, 'We are absolutely convinced that you are telling the truth.' Now, I'm now being shafted. My career is ruined. I have a wife and two kids and no money. I've returned to Pittsburgh and my parents have given us a roof over our head. I'm turning to you guys as my friends. I want your advice and, God, I need your help.

Sam and I believed him, and the three of us then went to work. The major immediate problem, as we saw it, was to get him back on his feet in his home town. He had passed the bar examination but had not been formally admitted to the Pennsylvania bar. We thought that the first thing was to get his side of a very dramatic story across to the media, to the papers and the radio, television then being in its infancy.

We enlisted friends in the Pittsburgh print and radio media, and in a press conference held in my home, Icardi issued a long detailed account of the disappearance of Major Holohan denying any complicity and asserting that he was innocent of any wrongdoing. His denial made a one day story, with the New York Daily News front page headlines proclaiming:

OSS KILLER'S
OWN STORY

So much for the presumption of innocence.

Our public relations plan was a disaster. Icardi's detailed account was a one day story, a bump in the road. The Defense department release continued to fill newspaper columns and the airways. The official release was based in a story that had appeared in *True Magazine,* a short-lived magazine of that era, that a body purporting to be that of Major Holohan had been recovered from Lake Orta on June 16, 1950, that the major had been murdered at Villa Castelnuovo in December, 1944 on the night he disappeared. And what is more, he was murdered on orders of Lieut. Icardi. The magazine accused Icardi of being a Communist sympathizer. Moreover, *True Magazine* charged the federal government of dragging its heels in investigating the case.

The Defense Department quickly issued the press release without any effort to get to the truth, or to report the official results of the OSS investigation on Holohan's disappearance, but solely to react to the magazine's accusations and those of Holohan's family, our government merely parroted the magazine's story. In major parts, the release used identical passages from the magazine account.

The accusations against Icardi did not go away. His version of what took place failed to get wide media coverage. It was totally ignored.

What then ensued was a public outcry, fed by editorial writers, columnists and politicians climbing over one another to get into the act. It was mass moaning, wailing and lamenting the "fact" that:

- Icardi could not be punished by court martial because he had been honorably discharged from the service.

- Icardi could not be punished by a civil court because the crime, that's right, crime, not alleged crime, was not committed in the territorial limits of the United States.

Not a word about the presumption of innocence until proven guilty. The front page of the *New York Daily News* referred to him as "OSS KILLER." Not a word about a fair trial. Not a word about the accusations in the news release being rebutted word for word by Icardi. The "hue and cry with raucous bangs and crashes" bemoaned only that Icardi could not be punished.

The media barrage continued for weeks, and it was not an opportune moment to move for his admission to the bar, but nevertheless we did it. We were forced to, because, within a matter of weeks, Ike was reduced to driving a cab in order to support his family. We prepared the petitions and requested a hearing.

"No can do," the bar examiners pontificated. "Even though you passed the bar examination, you have to clear yourself of these charges before we'll admit you."

When I protested by reminding them that no formal charge had been lodged against him, that there still was a presumption of innocence until proven guilty, they looked down collective noses with, "This bar admission proceeding is no criminal trial. So long as there's a charge against anyone, that's good enough for us." We emphasized that no charge was extant, only a release from the Army Public Relations Office. But to no avail.

This, of course, was the Fifties. We had not yet entered the era where certain "technicalities" now prevent such autocratic actions. Technicalities like the due process clause of the Fifth Amendment made applicable to the states (including state bar examiners) by the Fourteenth Amendment. The splendid nuances of procedural due process had been hidden in our legal firmament until they finally blazed across our land in the late Sixties and Seventies

But Murphy's law soon went into operation. When things appear to be the gloomiest and it looked like things could not get worse, they do get worse. Stories leaked to the press out of Washington revealed that the Defense Department was asking the State Department to request the newly formed Republic of Italy to extradite Icardi to Italy to stand trial in that country for a crime committed there when, as an American espionage agent, he was spying against fascist Italy.

My role with Icardi then changed--from personal adviser to a lawyer who would actively engage in defending him against baseless charges in three separate courts. For the next five years, hardly a week went by when I was not occupied with some facet of this extraordinary case, one that can be understood only in the context of the political climate in the Fifties, time now known as the McCarthy era. Historians have named this unfortunate time in our Nation's history after Senator Joseph McCarthy of Wisconsin who dominated the front pages with a host of wild, reckless and unproved charges, usually accusing the objects of his wrath as Communists.

I extended the best of my professional services, sometimes working night and day, in Pittsburgh, Buffalo, New York and Washington, D.C.

without even a thought of compensation, and at a substantial personal expense. I did it for three reasons:

- I was convinced that he was innocent.

- I strongly felt that he was a victim of two sinister circumstances totally beyond his control--the anti-Communist McCarthy era in which it was easy to accuse one of being a Communist or siding with them, and a political damage control reaction in which the Defense Department set into motion a series of events originally designed to protect it against accusations made in a sensational magazine story.

- He was my friend. I had to help him. It's trite to say but, "That's what friends are for."

During this period I actively participated in complex, arduous and exhausting court proceedings:

- Defeating an attempt by the Republic of Italy in the U.S. District Court for the Western District of New York to extradite him to stand trial for murder.

- Preparing and filing documents in the Italian court system challenging its right to try him for murder *in absentia.*

- Assisting in the successful defense of charges in the U.S. District Court for the District of Columbia where he was indicted in six counts for perjury for saying six times under oath before a Congressional committee that he was an innocent man.

A comprehensive book has yet to be written on the Aldo Icardi OSS operation behind enemy lines, and I do not propose to do it here. It is sufficient only to share some experiences as his lawyer. First, to describe the unusual nature of the legal briefs filed to defend successfully the attempt to extradite Icardi to Italy; how we utilized Supreme Court decisions, some from the Civil War era, to assert a legal proposition and then applied it to our case by writing a history of the Kingdom of Italy's surrender in World War II. We relied on a legal precept that had been applied to a member of the Union army in Tennessee during the Civil War to an OSS operation in Italy that took place after the overthrow of Mussolini.

But first the factual background of the accusations. On September 26, 1944, First Lieut. Icardi, assigned to the OSS, parachuted into enemy territory as a member of a special intelligence mission headed by Major William V. Holohan. At that time, the Allies had been held up at the "Gothic Line" extending east and west slightly north of Florence and running through Pistoia.

The OSS intelligence mission had two assignments. Their primary one assumed a collapse of the German army along the Pistoia line in the early fall of 1944. In the event of a hasty collapse of the German army, members of the OSS team were to coordinate efforts with the Italian partisans in accepting the surrender until forward elements of the Allied forces pushed through.

Heading the mission was Holohan, who had no previous experience in the field and who did not speak or understand a word of Italian. He was over six feet tall, red-headed and freckled. He was selected because although he was a desk officer he yearned for a job in the field. He was a brave man, a good friend of an OSS commander, and he wanted to do something other than the desk job he had occupied throughout the war. Moreover, as a major he possessed the necessary rank to deal with surrendering German officers. One of his officers was Lieut. Icardi, who was extremely fluent in the Italian language. Other members of the mission included another commissioned officer who was second in command, an army sergeant radio operator, who also spoke Italian, and several Italian nationals.

In event the German lines held strong and no breakthrough took place in the 1944 autumn, the mission was given a secondary assignment: espionage and sabotage, to work with Italian partisans to gather intelligence and supply arms to the partisans engaged in sabotage activities. The mission was to organize and implement air drops of arms and ammunition.

Shortly after the mission landed, OSS headquarters realized that initial intelligence of an early collapse of the Nazis was faulty. An early breakthrough by the Allies was no longer predicted. OSS radioed the mission to proceed immediately into their secondary duty assignment---intelligence gathering, sabotage and arming the partisans.

The mission had originally landed on the Mottarone, a round mountain that sits between two scenic lakes: Lake Maggiore on the East, and the smaller lake Orta on the west. To the south, the Mottarone rolls down gradually to the rich Po valley; on the north it drops off precipitously to the mouth of the Ossola valley. The mountain and the lakes formed a traditional resort area. An incline plane dropped down the east slope to Gignese where a trolley proceeds to the popular resort town of Stresa. At the time the mission parachuted in, the Germans were heavily garrisoned both at Stresa on the east slopes of the Mottarone and at Orta to the west. The Nazis used the Italian lake area for two purposes: for rest and recreation, and for combating the hit and run activities of the partisans.

The OSS mission was designed to operate in the midst of the enemy.

What made the OSS mission operable, however, were two factors. This was wild mountain country with thick forests and narrow roads. This forced the Nazis to limit activity to small patrols. Also, a large part of the northern Italian population was anti-fascist and anti-Nazi. Although divided when it came to political views, most of the population was united in an active opposition to the invading German army.

The partisans were loosely controlled out of Milano by the clandestine *Comitato di Liberazione Nationale*, the Committee of National Liberation, and upon the landing of the OSS mission, representatives of the committee began to work with it. The committee exercised loose control over the diverse partisan bands, groups espousing diverse political views, but united against the common enemy--the Nazis and the Fascists. Partisan groups were organized as Socialists, Christian Democrats, Liberals, Actionists, Republicans and, to be sure, Communists. There was no question that the Communist partisans were a highly trained effective fighting force against the Nazis.

The OSS mission was to be the direct liaison between the Allied 15th Army Group under British Army General Alexander and the National Committee in Milano and its partisan bands in the field. The espionage and sabotage mission began. The other commissioned officer on the mission was assigned to work with a British espionage unit. Icardi then became second in command, furnished with a false name and credentials that identified him as an Italian civilian telephone repairman. He had become an American spy. For months he ranged the area collecting military information to be transmitted back to Allied Headquarters, either by couriers through Allen Dulles' OSS station in Switzerland or by clandestine radio broadcasts.

Major Holohan did not work in the field. He operated only inside various villas that were used as mission headquarters. With no field experience, with absolutely no knowledge of the Italian language, and expecting the mission to be short lived as a coordinating effort to accept the surrenders of Nazi and Fascist troops, he was not professionally trained to participate in an espionage mission. Moreover, as the head of an espionage and sabotage mission behind lines, Holohan took the very unusual position that as an American army officer, he insisted on wearing at all times his U.S. Army uniform replete with oak leaves of his rank. In event of capture he wanted to be treated as a prisoner of war and not shot as a spy. He explained this to members of the mission and through interpreters to the partisans. He also radioed OSS headquarters of his decision. Partisan groups providing security for the mission raised collective eyebrows, but did not discuss the matter with him because of his inability to speak Italian.

The mission constantly had to move its operations center from house to house, because of intense Nazi and fascist patrol activity. By November's end they were at Villa Maria near Lake Orta, but were forced to move to Villa Castelnuovo on the lake shore. On December 5, 1944 they received word that in the village of Orta people in the market place were gossiping that the Americans were located at this villa. This meant that they had to move again. They sought advice for a new location from the partisans providing security for the mission. They waited all day on December 6, 1944 for word to come.

After the war the OSS investigated Holohan's disappearance and recounts that a Nazi-fascist patrol had attacked the villa on that night and OSS team and their partisan security force scattered along the lake. In his book, *American Master Spy*, Icardi described the events of the evening of December 6, 1944:

> The tension mounted steadily higher and our danger seemed to increase by the minute, although nothing was

happening that we knew of. Finally, at ten-thirty, when the fog had blanketed all of Lake Orta, Major Holohan decided that we must move. We would stay out in the open, if necessary, rather than risk being trapped in the villa.

"I don't know where we'll go," he said, "but we're going. I'd rather camp out in the open than risk being trapped in this house. Get your things; and get those porters moving!"

In a few minutes, we were assembled in the kitchen, ready to leave. All that remained was to police the house thoroughly before evacuating.

The furtive little group that now prepared to abandon this villa included five men: three Americans, and two Italians. There were Major Holohan, Sergeant Primo, and me; and Secondo and Terzo who served as guides, boatmen, handymen, messengers, guards, and porters for the Mission. The five of us left Villa Castelnuovo by the side door, at about ten forty-five. It was pitch dark and the air stung with cold. There was no snow on the ground. Fog hung over the lake just a few feet from the shore line. We felt our way down the winding path to the lake.

Sergeant Primo and Secondo had a boat ready. The water lapped about the sides as we loaded all our equipment in the stern. When the loading was completed, we assembled at the bow of the boat and Major Holohan said, "Ike, tell Sgt. Primo to go back and secure the villa." This was standard procedure. It meant that Primo should check to see that all shutters were closed, that the doors were locked, and that nothing had been dropped which would indicate that we had been there.

Primo walked up past the iron gate and disappeared along the winding path, as the rest of us waited quietly and tensely, anxious to be gone. None of us was fearless. We knew our situation all too well: we were 200 miles behind enemy lines, and if we were captured it wouldn't mean much that we were in uniform, carrying side-arms, and displaying our military insignia in a prominent manner--we would be treated like spies. We also knew that the enemy was aware of our presence; and somehow the dark, the cold, the sneaky fog, the water gurgling on the beach stimulated unhealthy images in our minds: the direction-finders of the 17th of November, the betrayal of our former friend Cinquanta, the warning of the two priests the night before. A pebble clattered down the path. We slowly drew our weapons. A twig snapped.

Brrrrt! Brrrrrt! Brrrrrt! Three machine gun bursts! All from the direction of the Villa! I charged to the right firing my .45 amid a chatter of gunfire that reverberated back and forth across the lake. It sounded like a full-scale battle. The details are lost. I only know that I ran to the right along a path skirting the lake. I don't remember seeing another person from the instant the first firing began. I just ran. As I put distance between me and the shore in front of Villa Castelnuovo the firing continued, then stopped as abruptly as it had begun. The world was perfectly quiet. I was alone, running, and my legs wanted to run some more. There was no time for me--just impressions, dark, shadowy, fearful. I remember running into the village of Pella, two miles north of the villa, and unconsciously picking my way through back alleys, and then pounding on a door. It was almost midnight. When the door opened, I was greeted by a friend.[8]

The Defense Department alleged that Icardi ordered Holohan shot and his body dumped in Lake Orta that night and that the official report of a Nazi raid was merely a ruse. It alleged that Icardi ordered the killing for three reasons:

---

[8] Aldo Icardi, American Master Spy 54-55 (1954). I have purposely changed the name of other members of the mission and their partisan security guards. Those still living are now in their eighties and no purpose is served to identify them now.

1. He disliked Holohan and wanted to lead the mission himself.[9]

2. The mission carried $100,000 in gold for its operations. Icardi wanted to steal it.[10]

3. The two men had quarreled over the extent of supporting Communist partisans. Icardi was pro-Communist; Holohan had refused to arm Communist bands.

The 1951 accusations completely conflicted with the citation for the Legion of Merit medal awarded Icardi for his service on this mission:

> On 6 December 1944 upon the capture and disappearance of the mission's chief, First Lieutenant Icardi became the leader of the mission, and in this capacity, directed its activities for five months. The mission operated in the zones of Novara, Torino, Vercelli, Milano, Pavia, Brescia, Verona, Mantova, Ossola valley, and Alto Milanese. Under

---

[9] This was facially incredible. The mission consisted only of three Americans. There was no prestige associated with being the leader of three. This theory was quickly abandoned in subsequent court proceedings.

[10] Official OSS records indicate that the mission was allocated $4,000 in gold coins and not $100,000 as set forth in the Defense Department's news release. At the Italian extradition hearing a U.S., Army major produced certain OSS records in behalf of the Italian government. Asked if he had in his possession. records showing how much money the mission carried with it, he refused to answer. He said that all OSS records were top secret and that only the Secretary of Defense or the Secretary of State could release them. As he stepped down from the witness stand, I handed him subpoenas directed to George C. Marshall and Dean Acheson directing them to produce specified parts of the OSS record in court seven days hence. On the appointed day at least ten army and civilian lawyers appeared before the judge with a motion to quash the subpoenas arguing that the matters were top secret. The court granted their motion, but I had a field day with the media: "Our government releases secret OSS records only to those countries which were enemies during the war and not to Americans," I said.

The murder-for-profit accusation would later be dropped when the OSS disbursing officer was finally interviewed by us and conceded that at best the mission possessed only $4,000 in funds.

the direction of First Lieutenant Icardi, an intelligence network was organized to encompass these zones. The network gathered information on such matters as troop dispositions and identifications, rail and highway traffic, location of ammunition and gasoline dumps, military targets, counter-intelligence activities, and political and economic intelligence. The intelligence thus gathered was transmitted to the base Office of Strategic Services station through four radios. In addition to the independent intelligence work established by First Lieutenant Icardi, he kept in close contact with many of the Partisan Groups in Northern Italy. Through these contacts, First Lieutenant Icardi was able to arrange supply drops to the Partisans, supplying them with approximately one hundred tons of material composed of food, clothing, arms, and ammunition. Due in large part to the successful results of First Lieutenant Icardi's mission, over thirteen thousand enemy troops were captured and the entire zone was entered by Allied troops without bloodshed. He later assisted in the negotiation of the unconditional surrender of the German troops in Northern Italy.

This then was the background in late 1951 when the Defense Department requested the State Department to demand that the new Republic of Italy extradite and then try Icardi for murder in the Italian court systems. The action of the Defense Department was patently illegal. The military knew that no federal court would permit an extradition. The military was thoroughly familiar with a line of decisions from the Supreme Court, emanating from the seminal Civil War case of *Coleman v. Tennessee* in which a member of the Union army occupying Tennessee during the war was charged with the murder of one Mourning Ann Bell while Coleman was a member of the Union Army of occupation. Although Coleman had been tried by general court martial, he was later indicted for the same crime in the District Court of Knoxville, Tennessee. The Court ordered the prisoner to be discharged and ruled that the military had exclusive jurisdiction:

> The fact that war is waged between two countries negatives the possibility of jurisdiction being exercised by

the tribunals of the one country over persons engaged in the military service of the other for offenses committed while in such service. Aside from this want of jurisdiction, there would be something incongruous and absurd in permitting an officer or soldier of an invading army to be tried by his enemy, whose country he had invaded.

The State Department, too, knew the law. Nevertheless, it acceded to the Defense Department request. In early 1952 it was made public that the United States was asking the Republic of Italy to extradite the former OSS officers to stand trial in Italy..

The Italians were extremely hesitant to accede to this request for an extremely important reason: wartime partisans had been very effective, but they were bitterly divided politically in post war aims. Forming and operating the National Committee of Liberation was the *only* time that the various political factions had worked together--from the Communists on the far left, the Socialists on the left, the Liberals, Christian Democrats and Republicans in the middle, the Actionists and Monarchists on the right. In the critical 1946 and 1948 elections and plebiscites the Communists, substantially subsidized by the Soviet Union, had made a serious threat to take over the country. At that time the Italian Communist party was the largest in the world outside of the Soviet Union. Moreover, there was a large number of ex-fascists in the country, especially in the governmental bureaucracy. War and politics had pitted brother against brother, friends against friends, cities against cities, but by 1952, the harsh war wounds were starting to heal. The Italians did not want to open them again, especially to have a trial of an American for the alleged murder of another American against a background of wartime partisans of various political stripes fighting the fascists. It was a no-win situation for the Italians.

Yet they had to accede to the American request. At this time, Italy was entirely dependent on American aid through the Marshall plan to rebuild its war-ravaged country. Economically, the Republic of Italy was a puppet state of the United States, and what the *zio grosso Salvatore* wants, the big Uncle Sam gets. Reluctantly, its foreign ministry started the paper work.

The request for extradition had to be presented to a U.S. District Judge.

THE ICARDI CASE: PART ONE

In Pittsburgh we started to combat it immediately. We assiduously researched every aspect of international extradition law and simultaneously mounted a public relations campaign of our own, especially among political and veteran's groups: "The country Icardi spied against now wants him back to try him for murder." The climate in Pittsburgh was pro-Icardi and Washington soon learned that the political leadership in both parties and local U.S. District judges felt that way too. The State Department then decided to make a test case by deciding that the mission's radio operator then living in Western New York, the alleged perpetrator who allegedly fired the shot, be the first subject of extradition.

This young man was enrolled in school in upstate New York and was petrified when the requisition was made by Italy, a mandate issued by the State Department and an arrest warrant granted by the federal court there. His family retained a lawyer. We immediately contacted him, and to his relief, we agreed to supply all the legal briefs and argument in federal court. We had been working on the case for months. We were ready to take on the Italian government, our State Department, Defense Department and Department of Justice.

By "we" I mean an embattled Icardi and his school friend, Rugi Aldisert, working pro bono, with a great assist from another school friend, Sam Rodgers, when he could find the time to drive in from Washington county. This was the "massive" legal team to combat the platoons of government lawyers from Washington, D.C.

There are great moments in the law when lawyers feel they have reached the summit, when they feel they are standing on Mount Olympus, when they get an inner glow and are confident that they have done something good and rich and fulfilling. With all the drudgery and weary hours that go with the practice, a moment that sometimes appears that enkindles and titillates. Sometimes this happens in a trial when a witness says one sentence that you know will bring the jury your way, or when the trial judge inflects his voice just so in a jury instruction or pauses and looks at the jury straight in the eye in a very special way. When things like this happen, you know that you are going to win. These action moments give you a flush, a flush warmer than when the jury verdict is later read.

I remember well one such moment in the Icardi extradition case. Five decades have passed, over a half century, yet I can still remember that instant in the Allegheny County Law Library late one night when Ike and I were poring over the books to prepare the brief.

"I found it!" I shouted. "Those bastards can never take you back to Italy. We've won this case!"

Previously I had been reading the terms of armistice between the United Sates and Italy on September 23, 1943–symbolically, the day after Icardi had parachuted into the Mottarone. And I was elated. Article 21 of the Additional Conditions of the Armistice had provided:

> Members of the Land, Sea or Air Forces and officials of the United Nations will have the right of passage in and over non occupied Italian territory....

In this context "right of passage" had been defined by Chief Justice Marshall in the landmark case of *The Schooner Exchange*:

> The grant of a free passage, therefore, implies a waiver of all jurisdiction over the troops, during their passage and permits the foreign general to use that discipline, and to inflict those punishments which governments of his army may require.

We had been content with this and were confident that the Armistice terms alone would defeat Italy's extradition effort, but I was determined to learn if anything had been included in the formal Peace Treaty between our countries. Our constitution provides that next to its specific terms and the laws made thereunder, "All treaties made, or which shall be made under the Authority of the United States, shall be the supreme law of the land..."

I wanted to look at the Peace Treaty to ascertain if any "supreme law of the land" would help us. We had asked the county law librarian to locate a copy of the treaty in Washington, D.C., and he had been successful. I was reading the treaty that night when that moment took place. I found a passage in the Peace Treaty between the United States and Italy that became effective September 15, 1947

> The Italian Government agrees that United States forces, military and naval, courts and commissions, shall continue to have exclusive jurisdiction, civil and criminal, over all members of the United States forces in conformity with an arrangement already in force.

At that exhilarating moment, I uttered some extremely statesmanship remark like, "We've got them by the balls!" and Ike and I danced around the library table.

But feeling that warm inner glow of reaching a high point of the law and dancing around the table, fleeting moments in the five year struggle to protect my friend and client, did not offset the revulsion I felt toward certain functionaries in the federal government in the 1950's.

It was bad enough for the Defense Department to make the accusations in a news release to offset widespread criticisms that it had not done enough to close the Holohan case while the alleged participants were still in the military. To be sure, the proper answer should have been: There was a war to be fought and when peacetime came there were universal clamors to demobilize immediately, and besides, the OSS conducted an investigation and there was no proof that Major Holohan was the victim of American foul play. It was even the worse for the State Department. Knowing the law and the tradition that soldiers could be tried only by courts martial for acts committed on the battlefield, the Defense Department's callous request that the State Department demand that Italy extradite and try American soldiers in Italian courts, especially an American spy who spied against Italy.

The conduct of the State Department was reprehensible, disloyal and deceitful. The Department had its lawyers. It had institutional knowledge. In its ranks were active participants who drafted the controlling documents. It was the State Department that drafted the Armistice terms giving our troops "the right of free passage in or over non occupied Italian territory." When the Armistice was signed, the battle was over in the south of Italy. We were occupying it. Rome north was still in the hands of the Germans. This was "non occupied" Italian territory and it was here where the events of December 6, 1944 took place.

Finally, it was the State Department that drafted the Peace Treaty of 1947, only four years prior to the day it demanded in 1951 that Italy extradite Aldo Icardi. It drafted a Peace Treaty in which the Italian government agreed that American military courts would have "exclusive jurisdiction, civil and criminal, over all members of United States forces."

Not only did the State Department demand the extradition, but when the Italian request came through, that same Department issued the formal mandate to the federal courts requesting an arrest warrant for extradition purposes. It issued the mandate with full knowledge that its conduct was illegal.

This was official cynicism of the highest order. It was motivated, I am sure, by the knowledge that Icardi was penniless and that he could not afford to retain a huge law firm to represent him, and that even if he did, the ordinary highly experienced and well paid lawyer did not deal in the stuff of Armistice terms and peace treaties. But the State Department did not contemplate that there are some lawyers who are inspired by the true calling of the law, who would rush to the defense of a friend and who, without expectation of financial compensation, would be resolute in expending hours and weeks of persistent research and analysis, who would do this because this respects the true calling of the legal profession.

The brief that we prepared was exquisite in every detail. "We're writing this for the Second Circuit or Supreme Court," I said. We had the *Coleman v. Tennessee* case ("There would be something incongruous and absurd in permitting an officer or soldier of an invading army to be tried by his enemy, whose country he had invaded.") We had *The Schooner Exchange* case, the Armistice and the Peace Treaty and this was formidable. But we had more.

At lunch one day with the former dean of Duquesne Law School, Morris Zimmerman, who had served as an instructor at the Army Judge Advocate school at Ann Arbor, Michigan, during the war, he advanced an additional theory. In addition to the line of Supreme Court cases in our favor, there was another serious problem with the standing of the Italian Republic to seek extradition. To express this right in 1952, the demanding state, the Republic of Italy, had to prove that it, or its predecessor government, had jurisdiction over the province of Novara in 1944 where the alleged crime took place. We went to work on this theory, and Dean Zimmerman was especially helpful.

Justice Holmes had taught in *Cordova v. Grant* that "Jurisdiction is power and matter of fact," and in *Cunard S.S. Co v. Mellon*, the Court had said: "It is now settled in the United States and recognized elsewhere that the territory subject to its jurisdiction includes the land areas under its dominion and control."

In 1944 when the alleged crime took place, the land area near the city of Novara, was not under the control of the Republic of Italy or its predecessor government, the Kingdom of Italy. Following the Armistice the Kingdom of Italy had declared war against Germany on October 13, 1943. The scene of the alleged crime at the time of Holohan's disappearance was under the absolute control of the German army. The demanding government in this extradition proceeding was not then physically in control of the place of the alleged crime with its armies or otherwise. The demanding country relied on an 1868 extradition treaty between the Kingdom of Italy and the United States. In a 1948 diplomatic note the State Department indicated that the extradition treaty was one of the treaties which it desired to keep in force, but the successor to the Kingdom of Italy had no standing to demand extradition in 1944 because the kingdom lacked control of the area. It had declared war against Germany whose armies were now occupying it.

Related to this extremely formidable theory was another historical fact that we emphasized in our brief. And this dealt with the political events which took place in northern Italy after the overthrow of Mussolini. On July 24, 1943, Il Duce reported to the king that the Grand Fascist Council had voted to restore political power to the monarchy. As he left the king's presence, he was arrested. He was first taken to the island of Ponza where he was placed under house arrest, and was later moved for better security to the island of La Maddalena for a number of weeks. He was then taken by plane and ambulance under Red Cross markings to an isolated ski resort high in the Appenine mountains in the Abruzzi where an entire hotel had been evacuated in order to house the celebrated prisoner.

On September 12, 1943 Hitler rescued his friend. In a brilliant commando operation, a German unit landed from the air on this difficult mountain peak. Its commanding officer, Colonel Otto Skorzeny was expecting armed resistance but not a shot was fired during the five minutes it took to overrun the hotel. Mussolini, himself, helped to clear boulders from the primitive runway from which they took off. His guards, the Carabinieri, still loyal to Il Duce, waved them goodbye.

Mussolini was taken to Hitler's headquarters on the Eastern Front, from which Mussolini announced over the radio to Italy that he was resuming power. He then returned to northern Italy under the protection of the occupying German army, where he established a new fascist republic, called the Republic of Saló, named after the town on Lake Garda where he set up his headquarters.

In December, 1944, therefore, these were the circumstances. Northern Italy was in fact controlled by the German army. Theoretically, its civil government was not the Kingdom of Italy that had already surrendered in the south, but the civil government was Mussolini's brand new fascist Republic of Saló. Our government never recognized Saló, nor did the Kingdom of Italy. We had no extradition treaty with Saló. We had a treaty with the kingdom, and the Republic of Italy was a successor to the kingdom, not the Republic of Saló. The demanding state, the Republic of Italy, was not a successor to Mussolini's new fascist republic. And the United Sates never had an extradition treaty with the fascist republic.

In the U. S. District Court we argued that in addition to the Supreme Court cases vesting exclusive jurisdiction in the military, in addition to the Armistice terms and the Peace Treaty, in addition to the brute reality that the German Army controlled the land and not the Kingdom of Italy, its predecessor state, the Republic of Italy, could not rely on a legitimate predecessor state with power over the province of Novara. We emphasized that in December 1944 that area had come under the civil jurisdiction of the Republic of Saló--which had never been recognized by our country and with whom no extradition treaty existed–and under the military jurisdiction of armies of the Third Reich.

The District Court wasted no time in denying the extradition request, and accepted our major argument:

> It is not disputed that the alleged crimes upon which this proceeding is based were committed on December 6, 1944, at a place in Northern Italy then occupied by the

German armies, the common enemy of the United States and Italy; nor that the demanding government was not then, with its armies, or otherwise, physically in control of the place of the crime.

The main precedent it relied on was the Civil War case of *Coleman v. Tennessee,* and its unambiguous statement that both the Defense Department and State Department winked at:

> Aside from its want of jurisdiction, there would be something incongruous and absurd in permitting an officer or soldier of an invading army to be tried by his enemy, whose country he had invaded.

These were heady days in 1952 and the juices were always running full. The excitement of espionage, true cloak and dagger stuff, writing legal briefs that smacked more of reciting history than citing cases, examining Armistice and treaty documents instead of the latest cases in automobile negligence and manslaughter. Playing David against the Goliaths of Washington and Rome. These were heady days. The good times.

But for Aldo Icardi his troubles had just begun

September, 1951. A planning strategy session in my den at home. From the left, Samuel L. Rodgers, Esq., Aldo Icardi and yours truly. Sam would later serve as a Common Pleas Court judge in Washington County and on the Commonwealth Court, a Pennsylvania appellate court. We often used my family's home in Green Tree, Pennsylvania, as nerve center after the case broke in August 1951. We held radio and press conferences and a national newsreel interview there.

THE ICARDI CASE: PART ONE

U. S. Court Ruling 'Victory' for Icardi

Pgh. Press 8/11/52

Italy Balked In Extradition Of Army Pal

Decision Virtually Frees Pittsburgher

Former OSS Lieut. Aldo Icardi stood virtually free today in the Italian government's attempt to get him back to stand trial for a wartime murder.

ALDO (IKE) ICARDI
Accused in murder plot.

Court Ruling Hailed by Icardi

Attorney Aldisert today called the outcome, "A triumph of American justice."

Plans Legal Action

He said that plans were afoot now to "institute legal action to clear the mud from Icardi's name." He said he couldn't "divulge the nature of the action just at present."

Mr. Icardi couldn't be reached immediately to comment.

He has a degree from the University of Pittsburgh, but took his final work at the University of Lima, Peru, specializing in South American law.

It was in this capacity as a specialist in Pan-American relations that he joined the air line.

Challenge Likely

Attorney Aldisert said that "After Icardi's name is cleared, we presume that he will get back into his legal work."

Judge McKnight's decision today is regarded as "final" in the case, government officials said.

They said unless there is some unusual legal twist in the case, Italy will be unable to challenge the ruling in any higher court.

Neither of the accused former soldiers can be tried in Army or civil courts in the States. The Army has no jurisdiction

Pittsburgh Press, August 11, 1952 "U.S. Court Ruling 'Victory' for Icardi"

Former OSS Agent Declared Victim of Italian Political Plot

Charges Made by LoDolce's And Icardi's Counsel; Former Expected To Be Freed Today in $10,000 Bail

By DICK KOPKE

Federal Judge John Knight last night authorized $10,000 property bail for former OSS agent Carl G. LoDolce as defense attorneys charged he is a victim of an Italian political plot to unmask wartime partisans who spied against Italy.

Rome Tries to Unmask Partisan Spies, He Says

The charges were made by Ruggero J. Aldisert of Pittsburgh, attorney for Aldo Icardi, and LoDolce's counsel, Thomas G. Presutti of Rochester.

Icardi and LoDolce, the latter a 30-year-old Rochester resident, have been charged by the Defense Department with murdering Maj. William V. Holohan eight years ago in the Italian Alps. The three OSS agents parachuted behind German lines in Northern Italy to supply arms to partisan military bands.

Extradition Demanded

The Italian government moved yesterday in Federal Court here to have LoDolce extradited as "a fugitive from the justice of Italy" to face trial on charges of murdering Maj. Holohan. Similar action is expected to be launched later against Icardi, now a law clerk in Pittsburgh.

"The reason for the Italian government's persistence in this case," contended Aldisert, "is not to find a solution to the alleged crime eight years ago.

"Icardi and LoDolce were members of a military mission that developed into a military intelligence operation employing the services of 100 to 150 Italian citizens as spies. The government of Italy figures that if those partisans spied once against Italy they will spy again.

"Italy wants LoDolce and Icardi back to find out who spied against Italy during World War II. They want the names of the partisan spies, not the solution of the death of an American major behind German lines."

RUGGERO J. ALDISERT

Courier Express, Buffalo, N.Y., April 3, 1952

Chapter Twenty
The Icardi Case: Part Two

The federal government's power is awesome. But it is a force that can be unleashed by a single, low level functionary without prior approval of layers of multi-person reviewing authority. I am confident that this is what happened in the Department of Defense and the State Department. I think that's what happened as well in the Department of Justice a few years later.

A single FBI agent can persuade his supervisor to go forward in a case. He in turn can make a phone call to a U.S. Attorney, and in a matter of days or weeks an information can issue or the matter referred to a grand jury. And as the saying goes, a grand jury can indict a ham sandwich.

One person making $50,000 a year can make a value judgment that will mobilize the monumental force of the United States government into action against an individual.

Similarly, one member of Congress, or realistically speaking, one member on a Congressional committee staff, can set into motion the monumental investigative force of a Congressional committee.

After we successfully blocked Italy's effort to extradite Icardi, I still do not know whose idea it was in 1952 to develop the following scenario:

- We can't try Icardi in an American court because the alleged offense did not take place in the United States.

- We can't try him in a court martial because he has been honorable discharged

- We can't have him tried in Italy.

- But here's a way we can get him. We will create a Congressional committee and have a hearing and invite him to testify under oath. When he declares under oath that he is innocent, we will indict him for perjury. What is more, we will indict him for a separate offense for each time he says he is not guilty. It won't be a murder case that we are trying, but it will have the same force and effect.

- And besides, he won't be able to put up much of a defense because he can't bring witnesses in from Italy. He doesn't have the money. He can't use a federal subpoena to bring them in because subpoenas are good only in the United States, but through our resources we will fly in our witnesses at government expense. Those characters will be happy to come because they will be getting a free trip to the States.

Irrespective of who triggered the plan, it was activated and executed shortly after our victory in the U.S. District Court in defeating the extradition attempt. The Armed Services Committee of the House of Representatives appointed a subcommittee "to investigate the circumstances surrounding the disappearance and death of Major William v. Holohan, while a member of the Armed Forces on assignment to the Office of Strategic Services in the Italian Campaign of 1944." This committee conducted private hearings in December, 1951 and January 1952. The subcommittee's work produced legislation enacted into law by the 81st Congress in 1952 which made it possible for the military to recall to active duty a former member of the military after his or her discharge to stand court martial for a crime committed while on previous active duty. Although the legislation had already been enacted--with no retroactive application in accordance with ex post facto strictures of the Constitution--the sub-committee was reconstituted a year later. In March, 1953 it addressed a letter to Icardi:

> The subcommittee desires to hear from you any and all evidence--competent, relevant or material--relating to the subject (the disappearance of Major Holohan) which you may have and may desire to offer. Your evidence...will be received by the subcommittee on Thursday, March 26, 1953 at 2 o'clock in the afternoon in the Armed Services Committee room, No.313, Old House Office Building, Washington, D.C.
>
> If you do not appear, the subcommittee must assume that it is in possession of all evidence required to form its opinion and report, for the information of Congress.

I strongly urged Ike not to accept the invitation."These characters are not out to do you any favors," I said.

But he was adamant: "I think that this will be a good forum for me to clear my name."

"Listen to me. Don't do it. They're out to get you."

"I'm going to clear my name"

The hearing was held in executive session. Members of the media or the public were not admitted. Only the witness and his attorneys. We would later learn that the only other witness called by the 1953 subcommittee was Col. Ralph W. Pierce, former chief, Criminal Branch, Provost Marshals Office, who conducted a polygraph or lie detector test of Icardi in 1947 and testified that as a result of this examination Icardi did not kill Holohan and probably did not know who did.

Two years later after testifying, Aldo Icardi was indicted on six counts of perjury for saying under oath six times that he was not guilty.

I was confident from the very beginning that the prosecution against my client was constitutionally infirm because Icardi did not have the power guaranteed by the Sixth Amendment "to have compulsory process for obtaining witnesses in his favor." This was the Fifties. It was a time before constitutional law and statutes made available public funds for indigent defendants to mount a defense in federal courts. Our favorable witnesses were in Italy, thousands of miles beyond any subpoena power of an American court, and Icardi lacked the funds to transport them here at his expense. The prosecution was under no such constraints. They had Uncle Sam's open check book and the power and prestige to influence and transport witnesses to America and house them in Washington's Mayflower hotel with unlimited room service and a daily cash allowance of $25.

We knew that the grand jury witnesses received this red carpet treatment, because certain of them contacted us and reported:

> We're lucky to earn $25 a month in Italy, yet your government is paying us $25 a day. And they've given us a free trip to the United States!

But that was 1956. In the years preceding this trial, Icardi was desperately trying to put his life in order. He was prohibited from practicing law. He had a wife to support and his family was growing. They had a roof overhead through the generosity of his parents. He began to earn a living, acting as a free lance real estate title examiner for various attorneys and gradually developed a small real estate agency.

Even while engrossed in the extradition proceedings, we continued to hear rumbles out of Washington. We had knowledge that a criminal investigation had been set in motion. We learned this from Icardi's former OSS colleagues who had been called in to testify. Almost unanimously they came to his defense. From time to time, these men would come to Pittsburgh and consult with us in my office and we began to discuss defense strategy in the event an indictment were to be handed down. It was from these defense strategy sessions that a bombshell struck.

The day after we interviewed a former OSS officer, he telephoned me. "Go to a pay phone and call me at this number. It's at an office of a friend." I did as requested. "Give me the pay phone number and I'll call you right back"

I did so, the phone rang and he said "Look, this morning I got a call from the F.B.I. They asked me a shit house full of questions about all the things we talked about yesterday. Wake up Aldisert, they've bugged your office They've tapped your phones and probably have a bug in your car."

The government acquired knowledge of the secret details discussed between attorney and client in the privacy of a lawyer's office. Communications in the law office between lawyer and client are as privileged and confidential as those between priest and penitent.

Under current tenets of constitutional law, the protection of the Sixth Amendment's right to counsel is both absolute and paramount. Neither state nor federal governments may pry into the intimate and protected conversations between a lawyer and his client. This has not always been so. In the Fifties, the Supreme Court had not yet added sinew and muscle to the protections of the Sixth and Fourth Amendments, even in cases involving the federal government. Nor had Congress.

Eavesdropping on intimate conversations between and lawyer and client to learn defense and trial strategy was not illegal in the 1950's. Indeed the very act of bugging or wiretapping without permission or without a court order is now a criminal offense. Things were different in 1953-1956.

Modern precepts of constitutional law prohibit the government in a criminal prosecution from penetrating the sanctity of the defense attorney-client relationship by any listening or recording device. The Constitution prohibits the government from compromising a defense lawyer's investigator to learn the trial strategy of a defendant who is under investigation or has been indicted by a state or the federal government. But this is precisely what agents of the Justice Department did to me in the Fifties when I was representing Ike. They wire tapped. They bugged. They paid off our investigator so that he would report back to them. Today federal agents could be prosecuted for such criminal activity and held responsible in money damages.

After this, we realized my office phone was tapped by federal agents, as well as my line at home and Icardi's home phone. We had a well-founded suspicion that they had placed a bug in my car as well. When we had serious planning to do, I would drive Ike out in the countryside and meet Sam Rodgers and we would then drive to open farm land. We would park my car along side a country road, traipse through open fields to find a defilade which a directional microphone could not cover, and prepare defense strategy.

If you should ask why we did not use electronic devices to sweep the offices or the car, the short answer is that these modern devices were not yet invented. Moreover it was difficult enough to represent a client in an important case without receiving a fee, without incurring additional massive expenses in hiring a professional to conduct periodic electronic sweeps.

One day an important witness, a former ranking OSS officer in the Italian Campaign, came to Pittsburgh for consultation. When he entered the reception area of my Frick Building office, he used a pre-arranged fictitious name. We immediately left the building and crossed the street to the Pittsburgher Hotel where I had previously booked a room under still another assumed name, paying cash in advance. After entering the hotel room, we turned the radio on at full volume and proceeded into the bathroom and turned on the shower. We then conducted our interview in the bathroom, with our visitor sitting on the toilet seat. He was key to our defense on the merits and the government never knew we had him.

After the indictment was returned, we made one of the most important, and fortunately, one of the best decisions in our long representation of Aldo Icardi. Early in 1955, we decided that an indictment was going to be forthcoming in Washington, D.C. and that we should be thinking of a Washington D.C. lawyer to be lead counsel at trial. Sam and I could help immeasurably in legal research and assembling facts, but it bears mention again that this was a pro bono operation, that our client had no funds to pay a lawyer, and that we had our own law practices to tend. We could not move to Washington for months of pre-trial proceedings.

We then embarked on a campaign to recruit a lead lawyer for the trial. We were asking for the moon. We wanted a top flight Washington lawyer, the best trial lawyer possible, but he or she had to work for no fee. There was no Criminal Justice Act in existence, as there is now, where the government pays fees and expenses for indigent defendants in federal court. We had many long sessions at my house--the phone was probably tapped but we were reasonably certain that no bug had been placed in the house because you had to enter the premises to install a listening device. It was easier install a bug in an office building, but was difficult to gain entry into a private house to do it.

We considered names like Abe Fortas, Joseph Welch, Clark Clifford, Tommy Corcoran. And for hours we concocted and designed various approaches to persuade top names in the legal profession not only to take our case, but to be so imbued with the righteousness of the case that he would take it on without a fee.

We made lists of dozens of prominent trial lawyers in the Nation's capital, evaluating their professional careers and analyzing their personalities to seek some clue, some tiny inkling that would suggest that they could be persuaded to be involved in a high profile case of this magnitude. It would be a head-on clash with the force and majesty of the federal government. Three departments--Defense and State and Justice--had actively attempted to put Icardi away. It was not the most popular crusade to mount. The media had not been kind, having rejected his side of the story and constantly pumped up accusations as if they had been proved. Moreover, America was in the midst of the McCarthy era, and insinuations had been tossed about that my client had Communist leanings and that this was a major motive for the slaying.

But the paradigm of anomalies came about. It was Senator Joseph R. McCarthy who drew our attention to one of the greatest American lawyers. It wasn't McCarthy who was our intermediary, but one person, Edward Bennett Williams, a bold young 34-year old lawyer was able to control the wild senator during the critical Watkins Committee censure proceedings in the U.S. Senate. Williams was well known in Washington as a feisty litigator equipped with magnificent courtroom presence and talent. He was adjunct professor of law at Georgetown where he taught evidence and criminal procedure, but was relatively unknown outside of the Nation's capital.

McCarthy had been very much in the news, operating like a loose cannon for years, but by 1954 he had lost his power. He had succeeded in attacking the State department and the Hollywood community and made himself into the most feared man in America until he took on the U.S. Army in a nationally televised hearing. Breaking a promise that his counsel, Roy Cohn, had made that they would not attack Fred Fisher, a young Army Department lawyer, who at one time had been a member of the National Lawyers Guild, McCarthy did just that. Although there was not one iota of proof that Fisher had ever been a Communist sympathizer, McCarthy lashed out against him on national television.

Special Army counsel Joseph Welch then made two statements that caused the total devastation of Joseph McCarthy:

"Until this moment, Senator, I think I never gauged your cruelty or your recklessness. McCarthy thundered on, alienating every member of the Senate committee as well as the viewing audience. Then Welch administered the coup de grace:

"Have you no decency, sir, at long last? Have you no sense of decency left?"

McCarthy was left with very few supporters, in and out of the Senate. A fellow Red hunter, Senator William Jenner, described him as "the kid who came to the party and peed in the lemonade."

By June the Senate was ready to act. A motion was made to censure the Senator from Wisconsin and a series of hearings were conducted under the chairmanship of Senator Watkins of Utah. McCarthy turned to Edward Bennett Williams, who agreed to represent him before the committee with one reservation. A big one at that. Williams was to run the show and McCarthy was to keep his mouth shut. At first McCarthy violated the arrangement and incurred the wrath of the six senators sitting in judgment, but Williams plodded on, slowly and methodically, keeping McCarthy somewhat reasonably restrained. In time the hearing settled down into a boring proceeding.

McCarthy lost his case before the committee and the Senate adopted a resolution of censure. McCarthy never recovered. But his young, 34-year old lawyer became a winner. In *The New Yorker*, Richard Revere wrote, "Edward Bennett Williams is one of the most capable trial lawyers in Washington and an extremely personable young man."

I had followed the proceedings in the media and repeatedly called Ike's attention to the name of Ed Williams, but no approach was made. In time the indictment was handed up, as we feared, charging Icardi with six counts of perjury for saying six times under oath that he was innocent. The government was prepared to try him for the crime of murder during a wartime espionage mission behind enemy lines and it was to do this in the guise of prosecuting him for perjury because he said he was not guilty. It was now the time for decision.

On a Friday in August 1955, Icardi put in a call to Williams' office and was told that Williams was on vacation in New Hampshire. We told his secretary that it was critical that we reach him immediately and she furnished us with the telephone number of his wife's parents, the family with whom he was visiting. Ike placed the call from my house, talked to Williams who said he had read about the case and was familiar with the accusations, and agreed to meet with us at his office the following Monday.

Today's huge law firm of Williams and Connolly was not in existence then. Williams was virtually a sole practitioner, assisted by one associate, Agnes Neill.[11] A third lawyer, Tom Wadden shared office space and assisted Williams in some cases. Williams had not yet achieved the international fame of representing Teamster boss Jimmy Hoffa, Frank Sinatra, industrialist Armand Hammer, Democratic chieftain Robert Strauss, George Steinbrenner, Hugh Hefner, Texas Governor John Connally, financier Robert Vesco, Lee Iacocca, Reverend Sun Yung Moon, Michael Milliken and President Gerald Ford. In 1956 Williams was a sole practitioner with a marvelous researcher, Agnes, and he occupied a rather modest suite of offices.

We sat in his office while Ike slowly told his side of the story, occasionally interrupted by Williams to clarify some points. I explained that Ike, Sam and I had been friends from college and law school and that we were convinced of his innocence. I went into great detail about the legal representation in contesting the extradition proceedings:

> I'm a sole practitioner and this work is not only without fee, it's out of pocket, but there are things that a lawyer has to do because it's the right thing to do. This is a man, a courageous man, a true hero of the war, who is being unmercifully shafted by his government. And some of us simply have to help.

---

[11] Following the death of Williams' first wife, he and Agnes Neill were married. Agnes then retired from the practice of law.

Williams smiled and said:

> Well, I guess you're right. As the man says, there are certain things that a guy's got to do. I'll take the case and we'll all go broke together.

He set down some ground rules. He was lead counsel and in sole control of the case, but we were to supply him with all the legal research we had completed and to continue "burning the midnight oil" as problems arose. And yes, to assist in the investigation. We agreed. A grateful Icardi asked Williams to keep time charts, and that "someday, somehow" some financial compensation would be forthcoming. The arrangements agreed upon were extremely modest.

Thus began my long time friendship with Ed Williams which continued for 35 years until his death in August, 1988. In time he would hold a controlling interest in the Washington Redskins and became the owner of the Baltimore Orioles, but it was in the courtroom where Ed Williams strode like a colossus. It was in the courtroom where he earned the money to purchase professional athletic teams. He was the finest lawyer I ever met, the most effective courtroom presence I ever saw. At the same time he was the source of constant great joy and unflagging good humor. At the darkest hour, he could come up with a quip that would set us all laughing. He laughed at our reports of wiretapping and office-bugging: "Assholes. I don't even bother to sweep my offices anymore and besides, my best strategy sessions always take place in some saloon."

He was especially amused at an incident that took place in Washington when Ike, Sam and I stopped for a drink in the old Men's Bar of the Hotel Statler (now the Capitol Hilton). We had driven down from Pittsburgh and arranged to meet Ed in his office at 8 p.m. It had to be in the evening because Williams was in the midst of a trial. The bar was empty when we entered around seven and we took at booth at the far end of the room away from the bartender. A few minutes later, a man entered. He was clean shaven, white shirt, dark suit, the prototypical FBI agent. He did not sit at the bar, nor at any of the tables or other booths away from us, but parked in the booth right next to us. All three of us knew what was going on. I was quite young at the time, only a few years out of the Marine Corps, and the "pissed off level" was still very low on my psychological thermometer. I got out of the booth and faced him:

THE ICARDI CASE: PART TWO

We know you have a job to do. We know you're with the Bureau. Now, you have two choices, either get out of your booth and come sit with us. We're not going to talk about the case, and you can tell us how you guys tailed us all the way from Pittsburgh. Your other choice is to get the hell outahere. Now!

I glared at him, and he wasn't sure how to react. He fumbled with a cigarette and a match, and then muttered, "I don't know what you are talking about." But he got up and left without ordering a drink.

We saw Ed about a half hour later and recounted the incident. He guffawed: "Junior G-men with tin badges."

They had tapped my phone and bugged my office. They tailed us to Washington and even followed us into a bar. And got caught trying to eavesdrop on a conversation between a defendant and his lawyers in a Washington, D.C. bar. That is how the Justice Department played the game until the federal courts put a stop to it by its rulings on "technicalities" during the Warren Court era.

Knowing that "Big brother was listening," we had our games to play too. Disinformation games. We concocted wild stories about non-existent witnesses: "We'll bring Anasastio in from India and he will corroborate this," and "Guglielmo used to be with Italian CID and although he is now in the foreign ministry in Rome, he's prepared to testify." "Are you sure of our mole in the FBI? Can he still be trusted in getting us the material?" "How about that guy at Justice? What's his name? Frank? Joe? Mike? When did he call and why does he have to call at night?" "And how about Silvia? She's a critical witness. Can we depend on her?" Wild, wild, wild.

And so the "Games People Play" went on all though the case. At first they did not know that we knew about the bugging, but in time they learned that we knew.

Although the law was on our side--the Sixth Amendment and the statutory definition of perjury under federal law--we were determined also to win on the merits. We knew precisely the witnesses the government intended to fly in from Italy, and we knew that much of the government's case was based on hearsay, good copy for the press, but inadmissable in a courtroom, but it was critical that we go to Italy and investigate ourselves.

Ed Williams and I planned to make the trip in January 1956. Ike would scrape up $1,000 for Ed's expenses and I would advance my own. Ike promised, "I'll pay you, Rugi. Sometime. Some year." We had to make plans in utmost secrecy because it was critical that our work not be compromised. At time when Ike and I travelled to Washington we used a series of cutoffs with various automobiles borrowed from friends. And we disguised ourselves, often wearing jeans, western shirts, bandannas and cowboy hats. We met with Williams at various spots in the Washington area, not always trusting the office environment.

The case could not have come at a worse time for me. My wife was pregnant with our second child. We were in the midst of building a new house and were living with her parents. Her teenage brother, Louis, was seriously ill with leukemia and I told him that I hated to leave him but I had to go to Italy.

We were all set. Williams had called upon Robert Maheau, his Holy Cross debate team partner, to make the trip with us and assist in the investigation. A former FBI agent, Maheau had recently formed an international investigative agency staffed with former FBI agents, and had already obtained Howard Hughes and TWA, his airline, as clients. Although we did not know it at the time, Maheau was also on the payroll of the CIA, but this did not compromise his work with us. Maheau was a generous man who agreed to lead the investigation with no advance retainer and only a promise that he would receive payment for expenses when Icardi was able to do so. Maheau would later become the major domo and spokesman for Howard Hughes during the final hermitic existence of Hughes.

Icardi furnished the names of key witnesses we were to interview, including a number of priests who had sheltered the OSS mission, and members of former partisan bands who had first hand knowledge of the activities of Major Holohan. Critical to our assignment was the selection of a person who would act as our guide in Italy. He had to be bi-lingual, trustworthy and intelligent. Maheau found such a person. He enlisted the help of Giuseppe Dosi, the former Italian head of Interpol, the international police organization. Dosi agreed to perform our services for $50 a day for a

THE ICARDI CASE: PART TWO 343

definite number of days, all payable in advance. Icardi borrowed the money from his father and forwarded it through a byzantine arrangement with Canadian and Italian banks.

We let the word go out that the defense team would be in Paris to interview witnesses in a certain hotel and made arrangements for the three of us to stay in one room. We announced this in advance so that military intelligence could arrange with that hotel to assign us a certain room so that they could properly bug it. I was about to complete passport arrangements, when Louis De Lacio, Jr.'s condition worsened considerably. His physician warned me that he didn't think that Louis would last the month. I decided that I could not leave the family at such a time. I withdrew from the expedition.

But the plans went forward. Williams and Maheau purchased airline tickets to Paris, but did not go from the airport into the city. Instead, they boarded a plane bound for Calcutta with an intermediate stop in Geneva. They left the plane in Geneva and took a train to Milano where they met Dosi. All was well.

Dosi was magnificent. He brought Ed and Bob to each witness in northern Italy. Williams was superbly equipped to record every statement through then state-of-the art recording equipment furnished by Maheau. This was the fall of 1955 and miniaturized tape recorders were not yet on the scene, but Maheau had produced a compact wire recording device that could be carried in a brief case and operate silently. It was fed by two microphones on Williams: one in a tie clip, the other in a wrist watch. By adjusting his tie clip Ed was able to turn the machine on and off.

Williams would ask the question in English, Dosi translated it into Italian and also translated the answer into English. All of this was recorded. In the authorized biography of Edward Bennett Williams, *The Man to See*, Evan Thomas, the author (also assistant Managing editor of *Newsweek*) relates:

> The first step was to sneak into the country so that they would not be followed by U.S. intelligence and Italian authorities....It took two and a half days for the authorities to catch up, and by then Williams had found what they had been looking for. At first the partisans who

had fought with Icardi had not been friendly. One flicked his switchblade throughout the interview before finally throwing them out with a burst of obscenities. But the two Americans picked up their first hint of what really happened to Major Holohan when they obtained photos of his corpse. The photographs showed that Holohan's hand had been chopped off---the gruesome signature of the Communist underground in Northern Italy. Then they found the man who had ordered the murder: Vincenzo Moscatelli, a leader of the Communist partisans in the Po Valley where Holohan had been killed.

[They interviewed Moscatelli.] The two Americans plied Moscatelli with wine over lunch at a little cafe' in Rome, the Ristorante Pancrazia, while trying to stay sober themselves. As the recorder silently spun in the briefcase, Moscatelli freely told them that he decided to remove Major Holohan--a Wall Street lawyer who spoke no Italian and insisted on wearing his uniform so he would not be shot as a spy if captured by the Germans---because he was a liability to the partisans. Icardi, he said, had nothing to do with the murder....

The investigating trip was a smashing success. Williams was absolutely convinced that his client was innocent. We were ready for the trial.

In preparing for the trial I did the heavy lifting on the government's burden under the federal perjury statute. I concluded that the subcommittee before whom Icardi testified had to have a valid legislative purpose and had to be really looking for information that was for a valid legislative purpose. This went to the issue whether the statements Icardi made under oath to the subcommittee had been made to a "competent tribunal" and related to a "material matter." Further, the government had to show that the six questions on which the indictment was based, the six times that he said he was innocent, were pertinent to this purpose. The sub-committee chairman, Congressman Sterling Cole, was to be called as the government's first witness to do just that on the first day of the trial.

At breakfast that morning I teased Ed Williams. "You've got to prove that they can't meet that burden here, and the only way you can do it, is to pull it out of the Congressmen's mouths without them knowing what you're doing."

He laughed. "We're rolling the dice on this one, and to do it I have to violate the cardinal rule of cross examination. I have to ask questions to which I do not know the answer."

Cole took the stand and the government had him discuss why the subcommittee was formed and what it was doing. Ed was very calm and very respectful when he started his cross examination. He then proceeded into the make-or-break series of questions:

> Q. Did you talk to anyone, I say, anyone at all, sir, before Mr. Icardi was invited to testify with respect-did you talk to anyone with respect to setting up a perjury case against Mr. Icardi?
>
> A. I cannot quite subscribe to setting up a perjury case. I can, in response, say that the question of perjury was a subject of discussion.

* * *

> Q. Tell me the substance of what was said about perjury in relation to Icardi before he was called.
>
> A. The substance of perjury is perjury itself.
>
> Q. Tell me the substance of your conversation, sir.
>
> A. It would only be repetition. The subject of swearing Mr. Icardi was discussed. It was determined to swear him. He offered no resistance to being sworn as a witness. It is my recollection that the question of prosecution for perjury was entered into in the discussion of the question of swearing him under oath. Now I cannot particularize beyond that.
>
> Q. But this was all before he was invited to testify?
>
> A. Well, it wasn't limited to that time.

Q. But you did have this discussion before he was invited to testify?

A. I can't swear positively that we did. I say it is my best recollection that we must have.

Q. Didn't you have a conversation with your counsel and with Mr. Kilday (the other member of the sub-committee) during which you discussed inviting Icardi to testify, during which you discussed that you would swear him if he accepted the invitation, and during which you discussed that a perjury case could be spelled out against him if he testified in accordance with the reports that you then had in your committee files obtained from the Army?

A. I cannot deny that that happened. On the other hand, I cannot swear that it did happen. I could very readily say that in all probability it did happen.

Q. And your best recollection here today is that it did happen?

A. It could very well have happened.

Q. And that is your best recollection here today?

A. I would not swear that it did, but it is my recollection.

Q. It is your recollection that it did, is that your answer, sir?

A. Yes, sir.

MR. WILLIAMS: I have no further questions.

Bingo! Congressman Cole said the magic words without realizing it. He explained that setting Ike Icardi up for a perjury charge was in their minds. This testimony effectively killed the government's case.

You do not violate the federal perjury statute if the oath was not administered by a "competent tribunal." And a committee of the legislature that sets up a hearing for the purpose of setting up a witness for a perjury rap is not a "competent tribunal." Moreover, because the legislation relating to the Holohan disappearance had already been enacted into law, no information Icardi could offer could relate to any "material matter" before the U.S. House of Representatives.

After the government rested its case of proving the "competent tribunal" Williams moved for a directed verdict of acquittal. Argument was held and it was no contest. The district judge did not miss a trick. Judge Richmond Keech directed a verdict of not guilty. And in the opinion supporting his ruling, the judge discussed Congressman Cole's testimony at length:

> Chairman Cole testified that the subcommittee already had in its possession sufficient information on which to base its report to the Congress, including Icardi's prior statements on many occasions, and that the purpose of asking Icardi's appearance before the subcommittee was to give him an opportunity to tell his side of the story. Chairman Cole further testified that, to the best of his recollection, before asking Icardi to testify, he discussed with his colleague and counsel for the subcommittee the calling of Icardi, putting him under oath, and the possibility of a perjury indictment as the result of Icardi's testimony. It is unnecessary for the court to determine for which purpose Icardi's testimony was sought or obtained, since neither affording an individual a forum in which to protest his innocence nor extracting testimony with a view to a perjury prosecution is a valid legislative purpose.

* * *

> While a committee or subcommittee of the congress has the right to inquire whether there is a likelihood that a crime has been committed touching upon a field within its general jurisdiction and also to ascertain whether an executive department charged with the prosecution of such crime has acted properly, this authority cannot be extended to sanction a legislative trial and conviction of the individual toward whom the evidence points the finger of suspicion.

On the basis of all the evidence before it, the court therefore finds, as a matter of law, that at the time the subcommittee questioned the defendant Icardi it was not functioning as a competent tribunal.

Judge Keech concluded his opinion:

The facts sought to be elicited by the questions which are the subject of this indictment all dealt with the issue of Icardi's guilt of the crimes with which he had been charged. The court has not overlooked the government's argument that the matters sought to be elicited by these six questions were material because, Icardi had impressed the subcommittee with his credibility and had produced substantial corroborative evidence, the subcommittee might have concluded that he was innocent. In the face of the evidence that, as of the time he was questioned, Icardi's answers could have no effect upon the subcommittee's conclusions in the field of legitimate congressional investigation, this slim conjecture cannot support a finding by this court, as a matter of law, that Icardi's answers related to a material matter. Whether Icardi denied or confessed guilt by his answers, his testimony could not have influenced the subcommittee's conclusion on subjects which might be legitimately under investigation, namely, whether existing law adequately covered the prosecution of crimes committed under the circumstances of the specific charge under investigation, and whether the Defense Department had functioned adequately in its investigation of the Holohan disappearance.

Therefore... the court holds as a matter of law that the alleged false answers by Icardi were not material to the subcommittee's authorized investigation.

There were tears in Ike's eyes as he embraced all of us.

The ordeal that began on August 14, 1951 ended on June 17, 1956.

All the trauma of fighting extradition, avoiding a murder trial in Italy in the very area where he had functioned as an American spy, preparing to battle the charge of perjury, thwarting the government's efforts to tap our phones and bug my law office--all this was over. All, including the secret trip that Ed Williams and Bob Meheau made to Italy. All, including the necessity of total secrecy to prepare our defense.

But we later learned that all the secrecy was for naught. The fake hotel reservations in Paris, boarding a flight from Calcutta, deplaning in Geneva, taking a train to Milano to meet our agent Dosi surreptitiously. The clandestine arrangements were to no avail, but we did not know this until about a year after the trial.

Icardi learned it one day while walking on Grant Street in Pittsburgh when an acquaintance stopped him:

> Now I can talk to you. I am no longer in Army Intelligence and the Icardi case is over, but do you remember Dosi, that Interpol guy who was your agent in Italy? You guys paid him $50 a day. He was a double agent. We contacted him and he agreed to work for us at $50 a day, too. He did a good job for you, but every night he would telephone us at the Embassy in Rome and give us an oral report of the day's activities. He would follow it up with a written report.

Icardi slapped his forehead and staggered away.

The Icardi case was an accelerated post-graduate course in the machinations of the federal government. I will not forget the Defense and State Departments' abortive attempts to have Icardi extradited to Italy, when they knew that Supreme Court case law prohibited this, and the terms of the Italian Armistice and Peace Treaty absolutely forbade it. I will not forget that officials would release to a foreign government top secret OSS materials from the United States military operations in World War II to process the extradition, but, on the ground of national security, absolutely deny any access to an American citizen fighting for his life.

They could not get away with this today. What they did then is now prohibited by law or discouraged by today's causes of action for civil damages and criminal sanctions against federal officials. Today a citizen can sue agents of the federal government for violating his or her constitutional rights. And Uncle Sam has to pick up the tab, even the plaintiff's attorneys fees.

I will not forget my experience with a Congressional Committee, or the conduct of the Justice Department and Army Intelligence while I represented a defendant indicted for perjury. The Congressional committee had before it the results of a polygraph test that completely exculpated Icardi, but nevertheless they went through with what a district judge would later describe as an "illegal legislative trial." The Justice Department had in its possession the confession of Vincenzo Moscatelli, Italian Senator for life, that he, as the leader of Communist partisans, ordered the death of Holohan for stated reasons. The Justice Department had in its possession this information from their own double agent, Dosi, the former Interpol officer whom we had hired as our investigator.

I will not forget the Gestapo tactics of the Justice Department's bugging my law office and my office phone and my home phone. I will never forget being tailed when I was with my client, requiring us at times to disguise ourselves to achieve some semblance of privacy. I will not forget how my client's defense was compromised, when the United Sates government bribed our investigator on an ongoing basis at $50.00 a day to disclose the secrets of the attorney-client relationship.

If it is true that we judges come to our robes with the stigmata of past experience, those were five years of an acute learning experience. What then did I learn from August 15, 1951 to June 17, 1956, the years of pro bono professional representation of a friend in need of help? Only my wife bears witness to the time I contributed to this case, exhaustive time that took me, a sole practitioner away from serving clients who paid for services. Abraham Lincoln is known for the aphorism, "A lawyer's time is his stock in trade." And from a dollar and cents standpoint, it was an significant drain of what I could have earned for my family during this time. But once I committed myself because I believed in the innocence of a friend, I never looked back. And I never have had any regrets.

Voices of great professors in our law school throughout our Nation, who today rush in defense of those oppressed by government, were totally silent in the Fifties; silent at a time in our history when their talents were desperately needed; silent when we were steeped in the McCarthy era.

Not one professor of law stepped up when four separate powerhouses of the federal government--the Defense Department, the State Department, the U.S. House of Representatives and the Department of Justice--formed a mighty juggernaught to crush a brave young man, a decorated war hero, who had risked his life behind enemy lines as an OSS espionage agent gathering important military information. No professor of law, that is, except one--Professor Morris Zimmerman, former dean of the Duquesne University Law School. One solitary academic voice out of the hundreds in the law schools. As reported before, Professor Zimmerman volunteered valuable assistance when we resisted the attempt to extradite Icardi to stand trial in Italy.

Over a half century has now passed from those events. I have had the time to reflect quietly and it still boggles my mind that our government would do what it did in the Fifties. But the total experience in defending my client was a source of magnificent psychic and professional satisfaction. We never felt that we were Don Quixote tilting against windmills, but rather we were David against the Goliath of big government. At bottom, I guess that's what lawyers are supposed to do.

Oliver Wendell Holmes once said that a citizen must turn square corners in actions against his government. I have turned this around, first as a state judge and almost four decades as a federal appellate judge, and say that when it comes to personal liberties, the government must turn square corners with the people. I suppose that this is the big lesson that I have learned. The government represents organized society. Once it suggests that a person had broken the rules of society, the government as the instrument of society, must never, absolutely never, break society's own rules.

But there is a footnote to the perjury case.

In May, 1956, Frank Costello, the prime minister of the New York underworld, boss of bosses, *capo dei tutti capi*, had been sentenced to five years in a federal penitentiary for income tax evasion and the U.S. government was seeking to deport him to Italy.

Costello needed a good lawyer.

He needed the best in the country, the best that money could buy.

It was only ten days after the U.S. District Court for the District of Columbia directed a verdict of not guilty in our case when I received a call from Ed Williams:

> Rugi, forget about my fee in the Icardi case. Forget about reimbursing me or Bob Maheau for our trip to Italy. Tell Ike that we're all square.
>
> As the result of the Icardi case, I got Frank Costello as a client. Let Frankie baby pay for it.

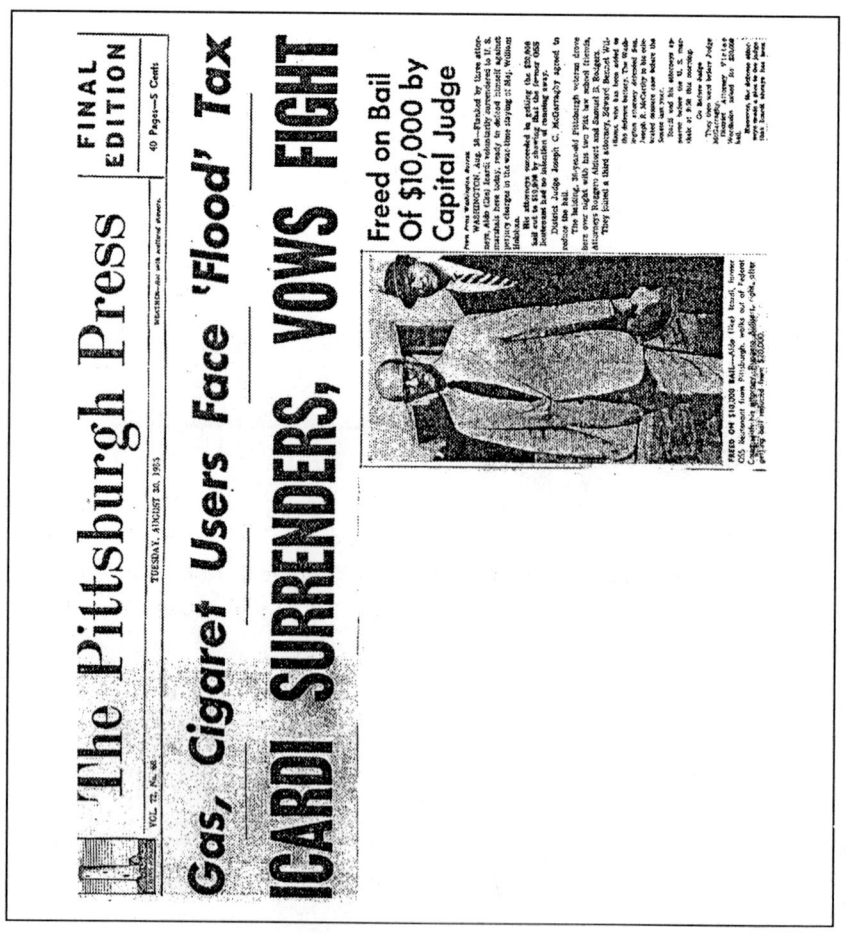

Aldo Icardi and I leave the U.S. Courthouse in Washington, D.C. on August 30, 1955 after posting bail as reported by The Pittsburgh Press.

The jury was empaneled chosen On Monday, April 16, 1956, but the trial came to a sudden end only three days later when the U.S. District Court ordered the jury to declare Aldo Icardi not guilty because the congressional committee had acted improperly. The front page of The Pittsburgh Press on April 19, 1956 reports the acquittal.

Aldo Icardi is jubilant as the U.S. District judge in Washington, D. C. rules that he was not guilty. Pittsburgh Post Gazette front page, April 19, 1956.

Edward Bennett Williams and I remained good friends in the years following the Icardi case. He is pictured here in 1965 in Pittsburgh where he spoke at the Allegheny County Bar Association annual dinner. From a sole practitioner in 1956 (only nominally he had a partner), Williams had expanded his office to become one of America's most prestigious law firms. He billed out at $1000.00 an hour for his services, and was fond of saying, "I bill even when I am in the shower thinking about the case." The firm still carries his name, Williams & Connolly, and has 200 lawyers. A partner, Brendan Sullivan, represented President Clinton in the Whitewater case, the impeachment proceedings and the Paula Jones case.

Chapter Twenty-One
The Road to the Common Pleas Court

On Monday, January 15, 1962, I mounted the bench in Courtroom Number Three, Court of Common Pleas of Allegheny County on the seventh floor of Pittsburgh's City-County Building. I was to preside over my first jury trial. The case was *Gorshenhausen v. Griffin*, No. 591 Oct. Term 1958, with Sanford Chilcote and Arthur Stein representing the plaintiffs and William Acker and Rhody Brenlove, the defendants. My minute book, one that I still have after these many years, indicates that I adjourned court at 3:30 p.m. and reconvened at 9:30 a.m. on Tuesday, proceeded until the lunch break, adjourned for lunch, reconvened at 1:30 p.m. Thirty minutes later the case settled for the princely sum of $1200. It had cost the taxpayers much more to process this private quarrel.

I immediately called for another case which began late that afternoon, proceeded throughout Wednesday and finally settled for $4000. My third case began on Thursday and extended through Friday, Monday and Tuesday when the jury returned a verdict for the defendant. Thus, during my first week on the bench, three cases, with three separate juries and three sets of lawyers had come into my court room. I was off and running as a brand new judge.

But it took two elections in 1961 to get there. First, in the May primaries to get nominated, then in the November general elections to get elected. Then, as now, in Pennsylvania, judges run for their first ten-year term in a partisan election.

My run for the robes had begun in February when I received a call from David L. Lawrence, governor of Pennsylvania, a good friend who had been the long-time mayor of Pittsburgh. He told me that one of the Common Pleas Court judges was retiring, that I could be a strong candidate for his position and that he would be pleased to recommend me to the Allegheny County Democratic Party Executive Committee. He asked me to give it serious consideration and to "take a few days if necessary." After my talk with the governor, I went immediately home to consult with Agatha.

This was a major decision, and my wife and I talked for hours. We dispassionately set forth the pros and cons of making a major career change. On the positive side was my genuine love for the courtroom. I was comfortable there. I enjoyed trial work. I was thoroughly familiar with the type of cases that would come before me because I had been a trial lawyer in that court for 14 years. It would be a comfortable life, an enjoyable one. Every trial lawyer, down deep, would like to sit on the bench.

But there was the downside. My practice had burgeoned after 14 years and I was hitting my stride. I had developed a good number of business clients, and a large number of families leaned on me as their family counselor. I enjoyed what I did, drinking fully deep draughts of total independence as a sole practitioner. Moreover, I had established a satisfactory personal injuries practice and was earning an income that bordered on the affluent. My earnings had increased every year, and I had a reasonable expectation that they would continue to grow. If I took the judgeship I would be taking a substantial cut in income. The position paid only $23,500 a year and I would be denied the income and perks I enjoyed as a lawyer.

We had a young family with three children - Lisa, Rob and Greg - ranging in age from seven to two. We had to plan for future college expenses. We knew our life style would be curtailed. I had recently purchased a Cadillac, the third in less than 10 years; then and now, you don't buy Cadillacs on a judge's salary. We were living the good life, belonged to a country club and frequently entertained. Even in 1961 I felt naked if I didn't walk around with $300 cash in my pockets. That's equivalent to $1800 today, but credit cards were still a few years off.

We were living in a beautiful home in one of the finest residential sections of the county, Virginia Manor of Mt. Lebanon Township--five bedrooms, two dens, a family room, four full baths and two powder rooms. From time to time we had live-in help. We had bought a large wooded lot shortly after our marriage and had taken our time to design and build a home to fulfill our expected family needs. Our only debt was the mortgage; monthly payments were not too oppressive. I enjoyed the life we were living and the profession I was practicing. To make the move was a very important family decision.

We had to consider also my wife's personality. A very private person, she was not anxious to begin life in a goldfish bowl. She had concerns about our children, how being children of a judge would affect them, because, like children of clergymen, their behavior would be minutely scrutinized. We gave the question of finances serious consideration, and finally decided that we could live a good life and still educate the children on a judge's salary. Clearly, we had not anticipated the brutal advent of inflation that descended upon us within the next ten years.

When it came to the final decision, my wife said, "It's your call. Whatever you decide will be okay with me." It was typical Agatha. She was the wife and mother, and her husband and children always came first. I called the governor in the morning and immediately took his advice to make the rounds of key Democratic leaders. I solicited their support, and within a few days, received the county committee's endorsement. And the primaries campaign began.

Sixteen judges sat on the Court of Common Pleas, but by a quirk of retirements and deaths, seven positions, almost half of the court, would be filled at one election. Endorsed by the Democratic Party County Executive Committee were the President Judge, a Republican, running for his fourth 10-year term; serving by gubernatorial appointment were two other incumbent judges seeking their first full terms; two County Court (court of limited jurisdiction) judges vied for a promotion to a higher court; a prominent Pittsburgh councilman made his run for the robes. I was the seventh.

I had never held political office, and aside from my time in the Marine Corps had never held a full time government position. Because all my running mates held public office and had extensive name recognition, I entered the primaries with full knowledge that I had the hardest race to run.

The political environment today differs drastically from that of 50 years ago. If you have a satchel full of money, you can hire a political consultant who will arrange slick television spots, create photo opportunities for the media, design fancy direct mailings, and as did a former Santa Barbara Congressman, Michael Huffington, (Adriana's former husband), prepare and mail a video tape to every registered voter in his party. Spend five million dollars, as did my former Congressman, and voilá, you have the best Congressman money can buy. Spend five million dollars for 120,356 votes, all of which comes to $41.66 per vote.

This is an extreme, and it was a Congressional race, but we see the same thing happening today in judicial, as well as in other local and state elections. If you decide today that you want an elective office, all it takes is a pile of money to make it today. Dig into your own family coffers, take out a second mortgage on your house, put the arm on some PAC's by making outlandish promises, or prostitute yourself to organizations of lawyers who will be appearing before you and get yourself elected without making one campaign speech.

Today the strong political organizations do not exist as they did when I ran for office in 1961. In Pittsburgh and Allegheny County a rock-solid Democratic machine held sway under the direction of Governor Lawrence. Some 827,000 voters were registered in the county, with 523,000 registered Democrats. The party's base was Pittsburgh with 225,000 registered Democrats and 80,000 Republicans. The Democrats had but a slight edge in the 128 other municipalities in the county---the boroughs, 168,000 to 101,000, and townships, 99,000 to 90,000---and the conventional wisdom was that a candidate had "to leave" Pittsburgh with a substantial lead in order to capture the county.

In Presidential elections, and to a lesser extent in Congressional and Senatorial races, political philosophy traditionally plays an important role, but when it came to county-wide races for the judiciary, the key to success was the county Democratic organization. Most city and county employees were political appointees--only police and firemen below the rank of captain or lieutenant were protected by civil service. This coterie of government workers was known as "the payroll." They had to be in the good graces of the elected county committee persons and ward chairman or his counterpart in the borough or township. The payroll was expected to make a financial contribution in each campaign, (the newspapers called it "macing") and had the duty to bring in the vote to support the slate endorsed by the county committee.

As Pittsburgh's mayor, Lawrence had developed an efficient machine in the city and had established an effective working arrangement with elected county officials. Under normal conditions, endorsement by the executive committee was tantamount to nomination, but the situation was not normal in the 1961 primaries for the Common Pleas Court. Seven positions—almost half of the court—were up for grabs. In judicial elections you may cross file in both the Democratic and Republican primaries, so in 1961 many lawyers filed for the nomination, hoping that lightning would strike. In the end 26 candidates jumped into Democratic primaries for the seven seats. However strong the Democratic party was, it was no sure bet that the organization could carry all seven endorsed candidates to victory.

Your place on the ballot was determined by picking numbers out of a hat. I was hoping to draw number one or a place high on the list. Ballot position is critical in multi-candidate races. I closed my eyes and drew, and ended up the absolute worst position--25 out of 26 names. I would gladly have settled for last place, but next to the last was deadly. My campaign got off to a disastrous start. Before serious campaigning began, I knew that I could win only if two circumstances fell into place: first, the organization had to bring in a sufficient number of voters to support the seven endorsed candidates; and second, I had to create my own personal organization to offset my political novice status.

I turned to the membership of the Order Italian Sons and Daughters of America. In 1954 at the age of 34, I had been elected national president of this fraternal organization, had been re-elected three times, and by 1961 was generally recognized as the leader of the Italian-American community of Western Pennsylvania.

Following the lead of John F. Kennedy who had organized the famous Kennedy "teas and coffees" in Massachusetts when he first ran for the

Senate, I organized an elaborate series of daytime meetings at private homes to sponsor what Kennedy had called a "coffee klatch." Each hostess would invite ten of her friends for coffee and cookies, and the plan called for me to be present for an hour; make some informal remarks, discussing generally the law and the court system and my own experience as a lawyer and convince them to support me. The coffees worked extremely well, and after my original remarks, I would chat informally with them, and closed with a double exhortation: "Please vote for me and help me by contacting ten of your friends to ask them to do the same. I can only succeed, if we have a massive chain reaction like a chain letter."

We ran the coffees six days a week from mid-March to early May, scheduling four or five a day. Volunteers at my headquarters did the recruiting and scheduling. They grouped the coffees regionally so that I would not have to cross the county to get to one from another. A good number of invited guests at one coffee offered to sponsor another for me in their homes. Many volunteered to work on telephone banks at my headquarters, to distribute literature and to work at the polls on election day.

In January before I had become a candidate, I had bought a new Cadillac. You do not campaign in a Cadillac in Greater Pittsburgh, so I could not use it. An automobile dealer client who also served as my campaign manager donated the use of a small, white Pontiac as a campaign car. My name was boldly displayed in red letters on the sides and the roof so that the car could serve as a mobile billboard. We rented a public address system which we often used to make rolling announcements. A friend took a furlough from work and I retained him as my driver--night and day--for the duration of the primary and general election campaigns

My own committee headquarters had a bank of telephone volunteers constantly calling numbers at random asking people to vote for me. Well known in the Italian community, I was the guest speaker at almost every lodge function. In addition to being head of the Italian Sons and Daughters of America, I was also president of the Fraternal Society of Greater Pittsburgh, an umbrella organization that coordinated activities of ethnic Irish, Hungarian, Polish, Russian, Carpatho-Russian, Slovak, Croatian, Serbian, Ukrainian, Lithuanian and Slovenian organizations. I became the featured speaker at their meetings and banquets and was invariably introduced as "One of us. One of our people." I was invited to meetings of volunteer fire departments, veteran posts, local unions as well as service club luncheons.

Most of the evenings were devoted to meetings sponsored by the Democratic organization, organized by "the payroll." I attended political rallies in every one of the outlying cities, boroughs and townships as well as in each of Pittsburgh's 32 wards. Only the seven endorsed men of the 26 candidates were invited to speak at these political rallies.

Unfortunately, it was one thing to enforce party discipline at the general election by instructing all to vote the straight Democratic ticket: Pull the one lever representing the Democratic Party on the voting machines or mark one X on the paper ballot and this automatically counted as a vote for every Democrat running for office, local, county, state or national. But when it came to primaries, the voters had to examine a long list of candidates and cast an individual vote for each candidate.

In the city wards and outlying communities controlled by the Democratic party, political rallies were widely enthusiastic. The candidates would tour individually and appear at various times. In addition to the county-wide judicial elections, it was a year for municipal elections-- mayors, burgesses and members of council, township supervisors, the minor judiciary and local constables. The rallies attracted enthusiastic audiences.

Generally, three or four meetings took place every weekday evening; to plan your traveling was a matter of logistics. As soon as judicial candidates would appear, the local chairman would accommodate us, give a rousing introduction, we would respond with a few remarks encouraging that all present vote for the endorsed ticket in the community as well as the county-wide judicial slate. It was speak and run except for the final stop of the evening; it was expected that any judicial candidate who appeared would remain and "press the flesh" and partake of the refreshments and always hot dogs and sauerkraut, sausage and kolbassi.

Then up at five in the morning to be at the mill gates at six to shake hands when the third trick left the mill and the daylight shift came on. Mill gate appearances were mandatory not only because of the large number of candidates in the field but also because of the activities of two particular unendorsed candidates. Anticipating election campaigns of the 80s and 90s, one lawyer retained an advertising agency to plaster his name in giant billboards and large newspaper ads, and radio commercials. Moreover, he was the first political candidate to purchase television time, a medium then in its infancy. He spent close to $50,000 and garnered only 61,000 votes.

The other major unendorsed candidate posed a more dangerous threat to me. He was the beneficiary of a power play by district directors of the United Steel Workers International Union. These labor leaders had sought a major role in the slate-picking by the Democratic party executive committee. When rebuffed, they decided to teach the party leaders a lesson. They decided to pick one judicial candidate, support him to the hilt, have him "bust the slate" and therefore flex their political muscle in party circles. The man they chose was an unknown lawyer who had drawn the last place on the ballot, number 26, right next to mine. They could only succeed if they endorsed six of the seven judicial candidates and cut one of the seven. I was deemed the weakest and was chosen by the Steelworkers Union to take the fall. The "Steelworkers Ballot" was widely distributed in the same color and layout as the official Democratic Party sample ballot. With one difference. It had X's printed next to all six of my running mates and their candidate. I was shut out.

But I had my friends in the labor movement, some of whom had assumed leadership roles in my campaign and were active in Italian Sons and Daughters of America. For the most part, they were members of various Teamster Locals and the American Federation of Labor (AFL) craft unions–carpenters, electricians, plasterers, painters, barbers and all the trade unions involved in newspaper production. Our plan was to make this a union battle between the Teamsters and the AFL on one side and the Steelworkers (CIO) on the other.

The strategy worked. I was successful, came in seventh with a little over 100,000 votes, but only 600 behind one of my sitting judge running mates, 20,000 ahead of the Steelworkers candidate and twice as many as the $50,000 candidate.

After the primaries, we began the campaign for the general election immediately, because the picnic season was upon us. Democratic headquarters supplied a list of picnics and throughout June, July and August. The campaign began in earnest on Labor Day where we repeated the rounds of the political rallies throughout the county. My "war diary" for Sunday September 3, 1961 was typical:

> 8 a.m. Mass at St. Patrick's and then speak at communion breakfast.
>
> 10 a.m. Brunch at Poli's restaurant. Speech
>
> 2 p.m. Glassport Democratic Committee picnic. Broadway Roller Rink. Broadway and Ohio Ave. Chairman Joseph Witkowski
>
> 5 p.m. Liberty Borough Democratic Committee. Gliva's Farm, Liberty Way. Chairmen: Dan Ivkovich and Adolph Dominick.
>
> 4 to 10 p.m. Candidates picnic. Lodge, North Park. Women's Division, Democratic Headquarters. Chairlady Marie C Aurentz.

Finally, November 7 came and it was over. We all made it, all seven of us. I came in sixth with 298,000 votes.

Running for office is a great leveler. Although it is humbling, it is also a splendid educational experience; it exposes a judicial candidate first hand to the feelings, endeavors and dreams, the longings and yearnings, and yes, the superstitions, of a broad spectrum of the public.

My election campaign family picture. Rob was 5, Greg 2 and Lisa 7. They are still my pride and joy.

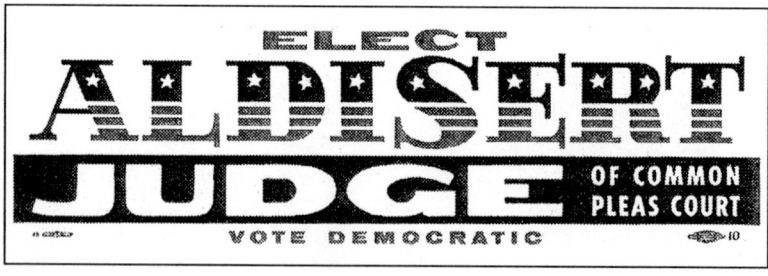

Bumper stickers came in handy.

My Common Pleas Court running mates, the winning team, pictured on the day we were sworn in on January 3, 1962. From the left, first row, David Olbum, William H. McNaugher and James G. Legnard. Second row, Frederick G. Weir and John G. Brosky; to my right, Ralph H. Smith, Jr.

My political sponsor, David L. Lawrence, Governor of Pennsylvania, long time Mayor of Pittsburgh, Democratic National Committeeman from Pennsylvania, confidante of Presidents Roosevelt, Truman, Kennedy and Johnson The largest auditorium on the campus of the University of Pittsburgh and the Pittsburgh Convention Center bear his name today.

THE ROAD TO THE COMMON PLEAS COURT 369

My campaign card in the General Elections, November, 1961.

R. J. ALDISERT

- Trial lawyer with extensive experience in Common Pleas Court.
- Community leader in fraternal and civic activities... health and welfare charities.
- World War II Veteran... Major, U. S. Marine Corps, South Pacific service.

"The University of Pittsburgh recognizes R. J. Aldisert as the Senior Man of the Class of 1941 who best combines character, scholarship, leadership, activities, and social bearing."
—JOHN G. BOWMAN
Chancellor

No. 25 on Democratic Ballot
No. 11 on Republican Ballot
PRIMARIES: TUESDAY, MAY 16, 1961

Reverse side of campaign card in the May Primaries, 1961.

Chapter Twenty-Two
The Trial Judge Years

One always remembers the beginnings of a new experience. I remember my first days in high school. My first days at college. My first job. My traumatic introduction to the Marine Corps boot camp. My return to law school after the war. My first court trials as a lawyer. I remember also my early days on the trial bench.

I remember those days as a very pleasant time, devoid of tension. Because I had been an experienced trial lawyer, the move from counsel table to the bench presented no trepidation. I merely changed seats in the courtroom. From the first day I seemed to relax on the bench because I was free of the apprehension–heavy or minimal, but always there--that any good trial lawyer feels when being "on stage" every moment when appearing before a judge and jury.

I was assigned to civil jury trials in 1962, and my minute book indicates that from January through September I presided over 54 jury trials with these results

Verdict for plaintiff	17
Verdict for defendant	7
Settled at or during trial	24
Compulsory nonsuit	3
Directed verdict for defendant	1

Hung Jury	1
Mistrial	1
Total	54

This would prove to be a fair cross section of the flow of civil cases which would come into Courtroom Three during the times I was assigned to jury trials in a busy metropolitan court. With population changes in Cleveland and Pittsburgh making it a give or take proposition, at that time we were either the eighth or ninth largest trial court in America.[12]

Most trials involve personal injuries where questions of law centered on the admissibility of evidence, but a fair number presented more interesting issues. My rulings and published opinions as a trial judge over 40 years ago were a precursor of an evolving judicial philosophy that would characterize me in later years as a federal appellate judge.

As early as 1962, while we were still balancing the law of defamation with the First Amendment, I made a ruling in a libel suit in favor of a daily newspaper published in the mill town of Homestead that in retrospect was a harbinger of what the celebrated teachings of *New York Times v. Sullivan* would pronounce as the law of the land:

> There have been times when our American newspapers, parading under the banner of fair comment, have abandoned the authorized routes of propriety and recklessly burst forth into fields of defamation.
>
> In other cases the line of demarcation between fair comment and defamation is thin and occasionally imperceptible.

---

[12] Counties by population (1960 Census):

Los Angeles	6,038,771
Cook (Chicago)	5,129,725
Wayne (Detroit)	2,666,297
Kings (Brooklyn)	2,627,319
Philadelphia	2,002,512
Queens (N.Y.)	1,809,578
New York (Manhattan)	1,698,281
Cuyahoga (Cleveland)	1,647,895
Allegheny (Pittsburgh)	1,628,587

> But in the case before us, it is our belief that the statements of the defendant were well within the area of propriety.
>
> For our press to remain free, and more importantly, for our citizens to receive the maximum benefits of an unfettered and unshackled press, it should be the province of the court, operating within the principles of the law of defamation, to expand rather than circumscribe the area of free speech, and the reporting of it.[13]

Balancing conflicting precepts, federalism and national labor policy, I declined to exercise jurisdiction in deference to the NLRB where certain employees had charged the company with conspiracy. What I said then was influenced by my early days in the mill and mining town of Carnegie:

> Traditionally a common law state, and proud of our judicial tradition, we are loathe to abdicate jurisdiction; and very reluctantly, and only upon good cause being shown, do we close our doors to those who would seek remedies for invasions of their rights.
>
> Pennsylvania is the industrial heartland. It has been the setting for the development of American labor relations history. In the twentieth century growth of the mighty Pennsylvania industrial complex, the sturdy stock of native sons and daughters were joined by hundreds of thousands of immigrants who left the old world, landed on these shores, crossed our mountains, and settled in the mining camps, mill towns, and urban factory centers of the Commonwealth. To protect these miners and mill workers and factory hands were only those jurisprudential principles we had inherited from the common law of England.
>
> As we increased industrial posture as a state and nation, it became apparent that our common law tradition had to be modified. It had to be augmented by legislation affording some standards of stability and protection to the employee.

---

[13] <u>Volomino v. Messenger Publishing Company</u>, 110 Pgh. Legal J. 435, 442 (1962)

> The absolute monarchies of company towns and some mill cities controlled not only the hours the employees labored, but the shelters wherein they lived, and the stores from which they bought their food and necessaries.
>
> We first witnessed the Norris-La Guardia Act outlawing injunctions in certain industrial disputes, and saw the enactment of Pennsylvania's Anti-Injunctions Act of 1937. The Wagner Act gave legitimacy to the NLRB, following the demise of NIRA with it section 7a.
>
> Collective bargaining and protection of union membership became an integral part of our society, and the rights, privileges and immunities flowing therefrom found more and more protection under state and national legislation.[14]

Later that same year I was faced with a labor-management issue that would rise time and again in the U. S. Court of Appeals--compulsory arbitration of a labor dispute. In ruling that a union had the right to compel arbitration of a contracting-out dispute, I described the essence of a collective bargaining agreement:

> To give [the agreement] proper meaning we must apply the standard principles of commercial contracts, but at the same time our appraisal must not be *in vacuo*. It is important that such a writing be recognized as a code of behavior, a charter of labor-management government, and subject to what has been variously referred as the "law of the shop" or "industrial jurisprudence."
>
> Its terms were forged in the crucible of hard negotiations at the hands of skillful practitioners. Some of its provisions are deliberately clear, others are purposely vague....
>
> The terms of all collective bargaining agreements transfer certain management prerogatives from the employer either directly to the employee or to an area of joint employer-

---

[14] *Smith v. Pittsburgh Gage and Supply Co.*, 111 Pgh. Legal J. 188, 190-191 (1962).

employee responsibility. Without such a contract the transfer of these functions does not normally take place; and under no-contract circumstances labor-management government becomes in effect an absolute monarchy with the employer reigning supreme over subjects who choose to be so governed.[15]

We are all familiar today with the alumnium can for beer and sodas with its convenient lid with a tab riveted to its center which can be lifted or pulled in opening the can. Today it is the world-wide mainstay of the brewing and soft drink industry. In 1963 it was new on the world scene. Its manufacturer was Pittsburgh's own Alcoa who was testing the new product in various markets. The testing resulted in a lawsuit between Pittsburgh's two largest breweries which landed in my courtroom. The dispute was not over the use of the can because Alcoa had supplied both the Pittsburgh Brewing Company (Iron City beer) and Duquesne Brewing Co. (Duquesne Pilsener) with the can for original test marketing. Rather, they were fighting over the name used to describe the new can. Iron City accused its rival Duquesne of purloining its common law mark, "Snap Top," in describing the can, and charged it with unfair competition. I ruled in favor of Iron City and held that the company's use of "Snap Top" in an aggressive and very expensive advertising campaign gave the term a secondary meaning. Presented to me was evidence showing that Iron City had tripled its sales in a four month period in the test area featuring the expression "Snap Top can." In determining that a common law mark had been established I noted:

> We are dealing with an ancient, if not gnarled, branch of the law. It is at home in equity. Some courts intimate that there is a special tort called unfair competition, the ingredients of which have not been minutely spelled out. Other courts indicate that what is involved here is simply the hand of equity restraining and prohibiting trespass upon property, inducement to breach of contract and interference with relations, breach of trust, libel and slander.

---

[15] *United Steelworkers of America v. Westinghouse*, 111 Pgh. Legal J. 142,147 (1962)

> What is definite, however, is that equity traditionally has been permitted to stride in the arena of the marketplace where commercial gladiators are constantly slugging it out, and occasionally, by decree, will haul away certain of the combatants and tell them that their tactics have transcended current standards of fair play....[The law of unfair competition], if sired by uncertain fathers, is constantly being given new perspective by the courts charged with the interpretation of myriad fact situations, no two of which are precisely the same....The ultimate offense always is that the defendant has passed off or is attempting to pass off his goods as and for those of the complainant. It is based on the simple premise that man has no right to sell his goods as the goods of another.[16]

As early as 1963, I emphasized that custody of minor children should not always be awarded to the mother, and in so doing, reflected standards of contemporary community moral standards of a period that is now at least two generations past. The mother had been given custody following the divorce but was now charged with having an affair with a married man "where it can be inferred that some of the intimate incidents occurred in the presence of eight and six year old children." At that time adultery was a criminal offense in Pennsylvania. I wrote:

> The mother's right, however, is not absolute and must yield to the best interest and welfare of the child which is still the paramount consideration. Therefore, while it is normally true that the needs of a child are best served by the mother, she may forfeit her right to custody by neglect or by conduct which is unchaste or improper.
>
> The question is whether such misconduct affects the welfare of the child. Certainly so long as present conduct is not objected to, a temporary lapse from moral standards is not controlling. This is true even if the lapse involves adultery or other infidelity, but if the parent's immoral

---

[16] *Pittsburgh Brewing Com. v. Duquesne Brewing Co.*, 111 Pgh Legal J. 351, 357, 359 (1963).

> conduct is persistent and flagrant, it is impossible to disregard what is best for the child.
>
> We objected only to the respondent's conduct with this particular married man under the same roof as these children. Once her behavior conforms with proper standards prescribed by society and by law of this Commonwealth, her right to these children should be re-examined, and we set a period of six months for this purpose.
>
> On the other hand, if she continues to flaunt acceptable codes, then even the question of her partial custody two days a week should be subject to further appraisal.[17]

Re-reading this case from the perspective of current acceptability of cohabitation with "a significant other," it is doubtful that the result would be the same today, given the changes of what I previously described as "standards prescribed by society" and "acceptable codes."

But it was in a dissenting opinion in 1963 that I first demonstrated a keen interest in the allocation of competence between trial court and a reviewing court. I began to define the proper standards of review, a subject that often would command my interest as an appellate judge. I was a member of a three-judge court in banc (at that time Pennsylvania utilized a court in banc in equity matters to decide demurrers, post trial motions and exceptions to decrees nisi) and a challenge had been leveled to the facts found by the chancellor. The majority discarded the facts, and reviewing the evidence, found facts of their own. Dissenting, I expressed a philosophy that I would later strongly endorse and amplify when I became an appellate judge:

> Our inquiry is sorely limited. The proper scope of inquiry of any court en banc with respect to findings of fact is solely limited to a determination of whether competent evidence supports the findings of the chancellor, and only

---

[17] No citation. I see no necessity of hanging out dirty linen in public at this time.

in clear cases where there is not such evidence may such a court overthrow his findings.[18]

In that same opinion I quoted sources outside the law books, a practice that I have continued over the years:

> [It is the confidential relationship which has to establish the presumption of undue influence. And you cannot have an undue influence with one person. Daisy Smith cannot enter into a confidential relationship with herself, and Daisy Smith cannot exercise undue influence over herself.

As J.D. Salinger wrote: "You cannot clap with one hand."[19]

But there was a lighter side to my life as a trial judge. For the previous 14 years I had been a sole practitioner, and this meant that there was not too much time for extended vacations. To be sure, we took long week ends and a week here and there, but it was not until I because a judge–especially in a court that operated on a reduced summer schedule because courtrooms lacked air conditioning–that my family and I had extended vacations. For three summers we traveled the West extensively and learned to know intimately much of our country at a time before the Interstate was opened; it was a time when national highways ran though the main streets of Midwest, West and Far West towns and cities. We all fell in love with the West.

At the same time Agatha and I made our first trip to Europe in 1965 as a participant in a Medical-Legal Seminar in Italy, sponsored by Cyril H. Wecht, a Pittsburgh forensic specialist, a doctor-lawyer from Pittsburgh. Thereafter, until recent years, Agatha and I went to Europe almost every year; and also thereafter, we had became extremely close friends with Dr. Wecht and his wife Sigrid, a wonderful friendship between our families that continues to this day.

After a year and a half of civil jury trials, I received a new assignment that, in part, was responsible for a major change in my professional career. I

---

[18] *Smith v. Berg*, 111 Pgh. Legal J. 311, 322 (Aldisert, J. dissenting).
[19] *Id.* at 323.

was named to the newly created post of Calendar Control Judge and given the responsibility of implementing a plan to eliminate the four year backlog on the civil side of the court. I became so successful in this program that our court became widely known for what the Judicature Society described as *A Metropolitan Court Conquers its Backlog*.[20] As the chief architect of the plan, I became a national figure in court administration as the creator of innovations for use by metropolitan courts.

The "Pittsburgh Plan" was the offshoot of the election of six new judges in 1961 and the subsequent addition of three more in 1963 in an expansion that brought our court to a strength of 19. New blood produced new ideas. On our bench was one judge who was 80, one 70, two in their 60's and 15 in their 50's or younger. The new judges decided that we had to do something about the dreadful situation on the civil side where a litigant had to wait four years to get a case to trial after pleadings were closed.

We new judges, numbering 9 of the 19, were serious about doing something about it, and considered several solutions. Because I was fresh from the trial bar, I submitted a plan to the Board of Judges, and my plan was adopted. My colleagues chose me as the first Calendar Control Judge. This position was the heart of the new plan, and the Board of Judges gave me the authority to implement it in an experimental program that began in September 1963.

Our court had 4200 civil jury trial filings a year. Starting with that annual case load figure, I set out to devise a plan that would first eliminate the backlog, and then strive to dispose a number of cases each year that equaled the annual filings, and thus prevent future backlogs. I called for three prerequisites:

- An adequate supply of available jury trial rooms. I insisted on having 10 or 11 courtrooms available during the civil jury trial terms, and that these rooms operate simultaneously and be staffed by vigorous judges.

- A strict, even at times, harsh, policy of refusing to postpone cases once they appeared on the trial list. To

---

[20] 51 *Judicature* January, February, March 1968

execute this policy, trial judges abandoned all power to postpone cases after I assigned the case to them.

- Two tiers of compulsory settlement conferences presided over by judges.

The key to the successful implementation of calendar control was a refusal on my part to continue a case at trial once it was placed on the trial list 90 days prior thereto. Motions for continuances had to be timely made after the list was published. I explained to the bar:

1. A request for a continuance on the day of trial is presumed not to be bona fide.

2. The cases which are subject to most requests for continuances usually settle, once the parties realize the case will be tried immediately.

3. When the case does settle under these conditions, it usually settles for what the case is worth, without injustice on either side.

We established an elaborate calendar procedure. Counsel were given 60 days advance notice of the day of trial. If they had a problem or a conflict, that was the time to make a motion for adjustment. Two weeks before a six-week jury trial period, a week of compulsory mass conciliation conferences took place, the conferences scheduled at half-hour intervals before twelve judges. This meant ten conferences a day per judge or a total of 120 conferences each day, or 600 for the week.

These were no-nonsense sessions. Cases not settled at mass conciliation remained on the trial list. But before the parties could pick a jury, they had to appear before me, the Calendar Control Judge for a final mediation session.

The calendar control judge was vested with more power than any other judge:

- The daily trial list was called before me every day at 9:30 a. m. in open court. Only the Calendar Control Judge had the authority to postpone a case. I announced and adhered to a stringent no-continuance policy.

- In accordance with tradition, juries were chosen in the Assignment Room with facilities for the selection of four juries simultaneously. No judge presided over jury selection, but the Calendar Control Judge ruled on any voir dire question.

- The Calendar Control Judge ruled on all discovery matters. Routine contested discovery motions could be heard on Friday afternoon only. I dubbed this session "The Happy Hour." Emergency discovery motions could be presented to me any morning at 9 o'clock.

- Cases listed for the first Monday of a six-week jury term were called on the previous Friday and juries selected on that day. On opening day, each of 12 judges was assigned a jury, was able to start the trial at 9:30 a.m. Meanwhile other juries were chosen so that as soon as a trial judge sent out one jury for deliberation, another jury could be sent to him or her so that there would be no delay in the process.

After the daily case list was called, the parties were required to participate in a final settlement conference with me in my chambers. It was a last ditch, do-or-die settlement conference conducted under optimum circumstances: the sole alternative to settlement that hour was an order to choose a jury immediately. Neither party could rely on further delays. It was fish-or-cut-bait time. No other judge had the authority to postpone a case.

First a plenary session with all sides present took place. The plaintiff had to be present in my antechamber so that his or her lawyer could consult with the plaintiff immediately. Because most cases involved insurance casualty company coverage, I insisted that a company representative who had the power to settle accompany defense counsel. I explained to the bar: "I want the man with the sugar." Because I had been an experienced personal injuries lawyer, and for two years I had presided over jury trials, I was thoroughly familiar with the value of personal injuries cases.

In the plenary session I wasted no time. I demanded that the parties cease all posturing and maneuvering and that this session was the last opportunity to settle before trial. They knew that the alternative to settling was to pick a jury immediately. I insisted that the plaintiff state a reasonable demand and that the defendant disclose the best offer available. This was followed by off-the-record, private sessions with each side, which I called "the confessional." I publicly promised that I would not divulge what was told me in confidence. These private ex parte sessions were the most valuable aspect of mediation efforts because the disagreement between the parties was not so much over the facts or the law, but over the value of the law suit. After hearing both sides privately, I had optimum tools to work out a deal. I then reconvened the plenary session resumed, and was then usually asked for a suggestion as to value. Because I would not be the trial judge, I was given great freedom in these relationships and had no hesitation in expressing a value.

The program was a magnificent success, essentially because I soon earned the respect of the trial lawyers. What lawyers want from a judge is equal treatment to all. I operated in a fish bowl, all motions dealing with any case had to be presented in open court with from 20 to 40 lawyers present at the call of the list every morning. When lawyers realized that I played no favorites and absolutely refused to postpone any case, and took an active role in the settlement process based on my 14 years experience as a trial lawyer and two years as a trial judge, they were willing to cooperate. Soon experienced personal injuries lawyers and insurance company representatives began to understand that I knew the value of cases based on my knowledge of the verdicts our juries were returning. My settlement conferences produced a very high success rate, sometimes described as a hot knife cutting through butter, and within a two year period I conducted approximately 5,000 conferences.

Our program received national attention and was the subject of a lead article by Murray Teigh Bloom in the *National Civic Review*, which, in condensed form, later appeared in the *Reader's Digest*. The articles emphasized:

> [In charge was] Judge Ruggero Aldisert-one of the 19 judges who then made up Allegheny County's Court of Common Pleas-as calendar-control Judge Aldisert's job:

to get as many cases settled as rapidly as possible before trial. Aldisert, then 43, had been a successful negligence lawyer before going on the bench. "The first thing we discovered," Aldisert told me, "was that the lawyers would cooperate only if they knew that we would get tough." One of the first get-tough areas was continuances. A trial would often be delayed because one of the lawyers did not want it tried and asked for a continuance. Pittsburgh's courts began a policy of giving no continuances which were asked for on the day of trial. Lawyers then came in with pleas of heart attacks. "When I wouldn't budge," Aldisert recalls, "the attorneys started claiming that they had a trial that day in federal court, which traditionally gets precedence over local court trials. Most of these excuses weren't valid, so we began a regular conference between our clerks and the federal-court clerks on pending cases to get an honest picture of which lawyers would be needed where and when. That ended the phony federal-court excuse."

Mr. Bloom also noted:
But soon a new obstacle emerged. Most cases were being handled by a comparatively small group of lawyers. About 20 law firms represented some 81 percent of all the plaintiffs in the area, and about 14 law firms did nearly all the trial work for the insurance companies. Inevitably, these busy lawyers would get so jammed up that the court calendar would call for their trying two or more cases at the same time. Aldisert quickly made it clear that delays would not be allowed on this ground. The solution: the court arbitrarily assigned ready cases to other lawyers in the overburdened attorney's office...

After two years, we reduced the lag time from 48 months between close of pleadings trial to 11.1 months. Other metropolitan courts had dismal records:

Court	Lag (Months)
Cook County (Chicago)	64.3
King County (Brooklyn)	52.0
Suffolk County (Boston)	45.0
Philadelphia	54.1
Essex County (Newark)	30.4

The Pittsburgh Plan succeeded. I was much in demand to present the Pittsburgh Plan to other metropolitan courts, traveling to the 12 largest state trial courts to explain our plan to boards of judges. Bloom concluded his article by emphasizing the hands-on efforts with lawyers that made it a success:

> By their efficient and imaginative methods Pittsburgh's courts have been able to get 83 percent of their cases settled before trial, and only about seven percent of all cases actually get as far as the jury verdict.

Aldisert believed that even this percentage left too many cases on the docket. He began analyzing the work patterns of lawyers who seemed to have a disproportionate number of trials. Every year at a bench-bar conference, the Calendar Control Judges (there are now two) meet with representatives of the leading law firms. Says Aldisert, "We tell these lawyers exactly how many of their cases are being settled, and at what stage, and how many went to trial. One firm, for example, had three times as many cases going to trial as the average. I told them that by insisting on trial they were not only costing the public money but were losing money themselves.

"What Pittsburgh did is now being copied by other cities," Judge Aldisert told me recently. "And maybe it is time for all of us to think seriously about related problems that don't get as much attention as crowded court calendars, yet have a strong bearing on them. For example, should the taxpayer have to bear the entire burden of civil-court cases over auto accidents? If the litigants knew that they had to pay a good part of court costs, you'd see less haggling over small amounts."

The calendar control program that I instituted in 1963 still operates in the Common Pleas Court in Pittsburgh. I look back on it as one of my greatest accomplishments as a judge, being convinced that active participation in pre-trial settlement negotiations is as important a judicial role as sitting on a bench and ruling on evidence questions and instructing juries.

By September, 1965 I was ready for a breather and was assigned to Criminal Court. But my criminal court assignment was truncated because I was needed back on the civil side to insure that "the Pittsburgh Plan" would not run into glitches. During six months I presided over 306 criminal cases which represented a fair cross section then coming into the court system. Notably, the largest number of cases dealt with violations of the Motor Vehicle Code. Although I had 50 of these cases, they are now handled exclusively by the minor Pennsylvania judiciary. Prior to the Pennsylvania Constitutional Revision in 1968, most crimes were based on Common Law precepts. Although staffed by Common Pleas Court judges, criminal courts had truly ancient Common Law names. Indictments of misdemeanors were handed down to the Court of Quarters Session of the Peace; felonies, to the Court of Oyer and Terminer and General Jail Delivery. In actual practice the same judges and courtrooms were used to handle these cases.

My records show that I presided over the following jury and non-jury cases:

OFFENSE	NUMBER	PERCENTAGE
Violations, Motor Code	50	16.3
Burglary	40	13.1
Driving Under the Influence	26	8.5
Larceny	24	7.8
Simple Assault	21	6.9
Surety of the peace	21	6.9
Prostitution	9	2.9
Robbery	7	2.3
Aggravated Assault	6	2.0
Assault with Intent to Kill	5	1.6
Rape	5	1.6
Failure to Support	5	1.6

Murder	5	1.6
Narcotics	4	1.3
Other	63	20.9
Total	306	100.0 %

I would return to criminal court only for summer sessions taking guilty pleas and non-jury cases.

In the Sixties regular sessions of the Allegheny County Common Pleas Court were not held in July and August. There were two reasons for this: first, Pittsburgh summers are hot and muggy and there was no air conditioning in the courtrooms; second, members of the bar typically took their vacations in July and August.

For my remaining tenure in the court from January 1966 until I resigned in August 1968, I was assigned to civil jury trials and took my turn as law and motion judge. Records show that I presided over 358 trials, (with some procedural dispositions not necessary for inclusion here):

Equity trials	21
Non-jury trials	30
<u>Jury trials:</u>	
Verdict for plaintiff	152
Verdict for defendant	31
Settled during trial	115

Many U.S. Circuit judges previously served as U.S. District Court judges, but I went straight to the U.S. Court of Appeals from the Pennsylvania Court of Common Pleas. When I practiced law, the U. S. District Courts were sleepy little courts handling admiralty, bankruptcy, railroad worker injuries and vessel worker injuries. The rush to federal courts created by landmark decisions revitalizing the Civil Rights Act of 1874 (42 U.S.C. §§ 1983 and 1981) through *Monroe v. Pape* and opening wide the concept of federal habeas corpus of state criminal convictions through *Fay v. Noia* had yet to come. Nor did we have the Title VII cases of the Civil Rights Act of 1964 and state habeas corpus cases under 28 U.S.C. § 2254, and the other anti-discrimination statutes that followed. Bankruptcy was a dark mysterious practice. It would take the Bankruptcy Reform Act of 1978 to let the sunshine in, or more particularly, the sparkling new set of bankruptcy procedures. Later, as a U.S. Circuit Judge, I would be intimately involved in this project, chairing the Bankruptcy Rules Committee that deep-sixed all previous esoteric practices and a created a new set of rules that tracked the Federal Rules of Civil Procedure as much as possible.

During my years as a lawyer I practiced essentially in the Common Pleas Court. When you add eight years as a judge there, that makes 22 years as a state court lawyer and judge This explains, in part, why I respect concepts of federalism today, insisting that federal courts must always be mindful that there are 51 state jurisdictions and judicial systems out there (including the District of Columbia) and that they function as sovereigns independent on all state law matters.

It also explains what I often say, "You can take the judge out of the Common Pleas Court, but you can't take the Common Pleas Court out of the judge."

On the bench in Courtroom 3, Court of Common Pleas of Allegheny County, Pennsylvania, Seventh Floor, City-County Building. This photograph was taken by my tipstaff (court officer) John J. Bodnar, who administered oaths to witnesses, handled the juries, maintained order in the courtroom and made all entries in my official miunute book. John was my First Sergeant when I was a Private First Class in the Marine Corps Officer Candidates Class at Quantico, Virginia in 1942. When John retired from the Marines in 1962 after 30 years service, I hired him for the position. We became close friends. I deeply regretted that I could not take him with me when I went to the U.S. Court of Appeals.

1965 Agatha and I had an extremely active social life as Common Pleas Court judge and national president of the Italian Sons and Daughters of America (ISDA).

A favorite ISDA project was supporting Boys Towns of Italy; an important project for teaching democracy to war-torn Italian orphans. Joe Di Maggio was featured in a program that raised $30,000 in one evening. He is pictured with Boys Town director Msgr. John Patrick Carroll-Abbing. This photo hangs in my chambers. A former law clerk once observed, "Judge, I have seen you pictured with two Presidents and two Popes, but when I see you with Joe Di Maggio, I know you have arrived!"

Growing up while their father is on the trial bench in 1963 are Lisa, Rob and Greg.

Rob is a now a partner in a Portland, Oregon law firm, but he still plays his music, now a stand-up bass. He was a professional jazz and rock musician in New York City for eight years before going to law school. He and a few friends in Portland rehearse every week. In 1966 he was already a serious guitar player, accompanied by sister, Lisa at the keyboard.

Easter was always an important holiday. In 1964 Greg tells Rob what the Easter Bunny had brought him.

Another Easter photo of Greg in the Mid Sixties. He did not know then that when he would become a lawyer he would represent a wide range of entertainment clients, including Mike Tyson, Quentin Tarantino, Jennifer Lopez, Wayne Gretsky, Brian Wilson...and others.

And the kids grew older....

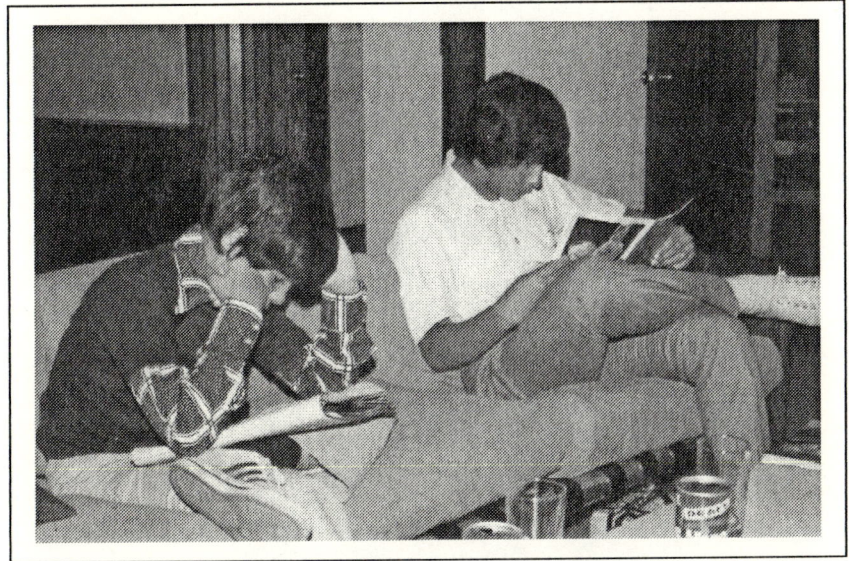

Greg and Rob at Aspen Colorado

Lisa at Aspen

In March 1965, a private audience with Pope Paul VI. What do you say when Agatha and I have a private audience with the Pontiff? You talk about your kids, of course. When I brought out their picture, Pope Paul, dressed in ceremonial robes with the full retinue behind him, said, "For this I have to put on my glasses." He reached in to robes, put on his glasses to examine it with a smile, and we talked about family life in Pittsburgh. When we returned home, we told the kids that now they *really* had to behave because the Pope was always watching them.

March 1965, at the Vatican with two of the Pope's personal attendants. From the left, Severino Sorressi and Franco D'Agostini. We met them while waiting for our audience. Afterwards, I asked if the Vatican photographer could take a picture with them in their uniforms designed by Michelangelo. The four us became good friends, always having lunch together when we visited Rome. One year we had dinner in Franco's home with his wife Teresa and son, Stefano. Severino and Franco were *Pietrosani*, citizens of the Vatican state, and often escorted us through private rooms in St Peter's Basilica and the Vatican, including the Papal Apartments. They regaled us with stories of previous Pontiff. In 1975, Severino spotted us in the public audience of Pope John Paul II, the present pontiff. "You should have let me know you were in Rome," he scolded us. "I must arrange for you to sit in the first row, and have a *bacciamani* (kiss the hand audience)." We protested, but Severino would not be denied. "There is one condition," he told Agatha. "The *bacciamani* is for couples celebrating their 25th wedding anniversary. You must be sure to tell him that." Agatha responded, "I cannot tell a lie to His Holiness! We've been married only 23 years." He responded, "No problem, someday you'll be married 25 years, so its no falsehood." Fortunately, the Pope John Paul II did not ask any questions, and Agatha's conscience is still free from hellfire and damnation.

Chapter Twenty-Three
The Long and Rocky Road to the Court of Appeals

In November, 1967 Austin L. Staley, of Pittsburgh, long time U.S. Circuit judge of the U.S. Court of Appeals for the Third Circuit, announced his retirement as an active judge and his intention to take senior status. The media gave the announcement scant coverage. His retirement was not even the subject of discussion by the lawyers and judges on Grant Street.

Shortly after I read the announcement, I received a call from the Washington office of the Democratic U.S. Senator from Pennsylvania, Joseph S. Clark, and was asked if I was interested in the vacancy, and if so, the senator would be pleased to discuss it with me. Two days later I was in his office on Capitol Hill. He explained that he received a call from Warren Christopher, the Deputy Attorney General, and that my name came up in the conversation.

Senator Clark and I were friends, and previously we had talked at length about problems in the judiciary. A Philadelphian who had been a prominent senior partner in a leading law firm before becoming the successful mayor of his city, Clark was interested in court reform. He was not the prototypical machine politician; well-to-do (his mother was an Avery, as in Avery Island, Louisiana where McIlhenny Co. makes Tabasco, the pepper sauce), extremely independent, he was not beholden to the old Lawrence machine in Western Pennsylvania, then headed by Pittsburgh Mayor Joseph P. Barr, or the Green-Tate machine in Philadelphia. He was not popular with old line politicians. He marched to the beat of his own drummer, but our paths had crossed on the banquet circuit, and I found him highly intelligent, extremely knowledgeable and very interesting. When my travels had brought me to Washington, I often looked in on him on the Hill. In time we had become fairly close. He followed my Common Pleas Court reform activities, heard me speak at bar meetings and read some of my writings.

By 1967 I was well known in judicial circles, especially in Pennsylvania. Clark was very much interested in installing my calendar control techniques in the Common Pleas Court of Philadelphia. That court was in a shambles with a six year back-log in civil cases. We had talked or corresponded at length about this on several occasions.

> When I met with him that day in Washington he said: Judge, it will be my honor to support your appointment to the Third Circuit. You are the type of judge I truly admire. But we must walk carefully.
>
> Unlike a district judge, a circuit judge is a White House appointment, and LBJ and I are not bosom buddies. But I know Ramsey Clark and Warren Christopher well at Justice. They respect me and I have good friends on the White House staff who I think could go to bat for us.

On the same day, at Clark's suggestion, I met with the Republican Senator from Pennsylvania, Hugh Scott, then the Minority Leader in the Senate. Senator Scott had been a frequent guest at activities of my fraternal organization; we had been friends for many years. Scott was very effusive at our interview, and telephoned Clark in my presence explaining his total support of my nomination.

That was November, 1967. I was not nominated until eight months later, on July 17, 1968, was confirmed by the Senate on July 29 and took my oath of office on August 9. It required a nine month gestation period to become a U.S. circuit judge, and during most of this time I was never free from morning, afternoon or evening sickness.

THE LONG AND ROCKY ROAD TO THE COURT OF APPEALS

At first everything went well. By December Senator Scott had talked to President Johnson personally in my behalf and informed the President that Senator Clark was solidly in my corner. Although I was supported by both senators, it was Scott, the Republican Minority Leader in the Senate, who had more influence with the President than Clark, the independent Democrat. Up for re-election in 1968, Clark decided to take a long trip to the Far East, explaining to me that he wanted to be rested and totally free for the grueling election year.

Then the first shoe dropped. Pittsburgh Mayor Barr, who was the Pennsylvania Democratic National Committeeman, announced that he would not seek re-election as Pittsburgh mayor, and desired to take care of his City Solicitor David Stahl, who coveted the Third Circuit vacancy. As the National Committeeman from a large state, Barr was extremely close to President Johnson. Although my nomination had progressed from the Justice Department to the White House, Barr was able to stop the nomination dead in its tracks. With Clark out of the country, Senator Scott heard about Barr's action, and immediately went public in support of my nomination.

Under a headline "SCOTT BACKS ALDISERT FOR COURT OF APPEALS", the Pittsburgh Post-Gazette on January 10, 1968, reported that Senator Scott praised my war record and added:

> In a letter to President Johnson, made public by the senator's office, Scott recited Aldisert's educational, civic and professional record, and concluded:
>
>> "It has been my privilege to know Judge Aldisert for many years and I have the highest regard for his personal integrity and professional competence and achievements. I respectfully request that you consider Judge Aldisert for nomination to the vacancy on the Court of Appeals."

On the next day the Post-Gazette ran another story:
Scott, Schweiker Back Him

**ALDISERT GETS BOOST
ON FEDERAL JUDGESHIP**

> A bandwagon acclaiming Common Pleas Judge Ruggero J. Aldisert for appointment to the U.S. Court of Appeals for the Third Circuit is rolling.
>
> Democrats, especially followers of U.S. Senator Joseph S. Clark, don't know whether to cheer or scream "foul," because the Republicans are providing fuel for the wagon.
>
> The first GOP endorsement of Judge Aldisert, a Democrat, came Tuesday from U.S. Senator Hugh Scott, Philadelphia.
>
> The second was yesterday from U.S. Rep. Richard S. Schweiker, Montgomery County, who is seeking the Republican nomination for the U.S. Senate.
>
> Strategy behind the endorsement was what they meant to the Democratic Johnson Administration but could swing Italo-American votes over to Republicans.

But these were Republicans. The opposition of Mayor Barr continued. I had been a protege of Governor David L. Lawrence, but he had died. I had grown up in the same wing of the Democratic party as Joe Barr. We had been active in the Young Democrats as far back as 1940 when I served as Pennsylvania vice chairman, charged with organizing Roosevelt College Clubs from Harrisburg to the Ohio border in the Roosevelt-Willkie Presidential campaign. Friends for a long time, Joe and I had been running mates in 1961 when I ran for Common Pleas Court and he was up for re-election as Mayor.

But now he told me flatly that he wanted to take care of his long-time City Solicitor and that Stahl had insisted on the Third Circuit position:

> I'm stepping down as Mayor next year and this is an excellent chance for Dave. All he has done is to work in the city Solicitor's office and this will help him out after I retire.

THE LONG AND ROCKY ROAD TO THE COURT OF APPEALS

After we parted, still on friendly terms. I went to work to see if I could solve the Stahl problem. A colleague on the court of Common Pleas, the veteran Sammy Weiss, former Congressman, football referee and longtime judge, not only agreed to take retirement but arranged a commitment from the Republican governor Raymond P. Shafer to name David Stahl in his place. Judge Sammy Weiss and I went to Barr with this proposal. Barr turned us down cold.

Undaunted, I explored the circumstances in U.S. District Court for the Western District of Pennsylvania. Judge Joseph P. Willson told me that he was planning to take senior status and this would create a vacancy on the district court in Pittsburgh. I hurried to Barr with this solution. Again, he turned it down:

> Rugi, you've got a lot of friends. Even Chief Judge Wally Gourley is willing to take senior status to create a vacancy. He called me and told me, but Stahl does not want to be a trial judge. He wants the circuit.

I blew up. A prominent state judge, the Republican governor of Pennsylvania and two federal judges were willing to create the opportunity for Stahl to become a state or federal trial judge, but Barr was adamant. Dave Stahl and I were friends and I had great respect for him. I had never been beholden to Barr, and had an extremely strong political base of my own as the acknowledged leader of the Western Pennsylvania Italian community. I had gained a national reputation in metropolitan court reform and had been active with U.S. Supreme Court Justice Tom Clark in the court reform movement in big-city court systems throughout the Nation.

I reminded Mayor Barr of all this in a loud outburst to no avail. I reached a crescendo with a few choice four letter words. As I stormed out of his office I called him an ingrate.

Barr then tried to placate me by having the state Democratic committee slate me as its nominee for the Pennsylvania Superior Court, the state's intermediate appellate court, and in doing so, did not ask permission to present my name. I learned about it in a telephone call from Philadelphia Mayor James H. J. Tate, who was one of my staunch supporters for the federal judgeship. He explained that when Mayor Barr told him he was presenting my name to the state committee, Tate asked him if I had agreed to it. Barr responded, "He'll take it." I thanked Tate for informing me and told him that I was not interested in the Superior Court and gave a General Sherman statement: "If nominated, I will not run, if elected I will not serve." I thanked Mayor Tate for his steadfast support of me for the Third Circuit position and gave him a concise, albeit crude, message to convey to Mayor Barr at the state committee meeting to take place the next day.

Tony Zecca, Mayor Tate's executive secretary, later told me what happened at the Democratic State Committee meeting in Harrisburg. Barr placed my name in nomination to be the endorsed Democratic candidate for the state-wide office of Superior Court judge. The nomination was received with general approval, but Tate asked Barr some questions:

"Do you have Aldisert's permission?"

"He'll take it."

"That's not what I asked. Do you have his permission, because my information is that he is interested only in the Third Circuit?"

"I told you that he will take it."

"That's strange, Joe, because he's in Philadelphia this week, and I talked to him at 10 o'clock last night. He told me to give you a message, 'You can shove it!'"

But Barr would not be deterred. He had the meeting adjourned for a week, and returned with a recommendation that the committee slate Judge William F. Cercone, the nephew of Pennsylvania Supreme Court Justice Michael A. Musmanno. Bill was then endorsed for the Superior Court post. Barr then telephoned Senator Clark and told him that the state committee had endorsed Cercone, also an American of Italian descent, for the Superior Court. Under these circumstances, Senator Clark should no longer support me. "We can't have two Italians vying for two judicial posts. You should drop your support of Aldisert."

Clark refused to budge in his support. He told Barr that there should not be a quota system for Americans of Italian origin. Putting in a dig, Clark told Barr that he never heard of a quota system for Irishmen vying for judgeships. Barr was not amused.

Later, Justice Musmanno got into the act, sending an incredible message through Barr to Clark that the senator should support his nephew, Bill Cercone, for the Third Circuit position, and if he didn't do so, he would instruct his nephew to withdraw from the Superior Court race. The senator's response to Barr was vintage Clark:

> Tell Musmanno that I'm sticking with Aldisert, and if his nephew wants to withdraw from the Superior Court race, that's okay with me. No one asked me, but I would have preferred to support Judge John G. Brosky for that post anyway.

Bill stayed in the Superior Court race and would be elected in the November, 1968 election and served in that post with distinction for many years. I'm confident that he had nothing to do with his uncle's Machiavellian machinations.

That then, is how I entered that memorable year of 1968. The Vietnam war protests escalated; the country was torn apart. On March 16, Robert F. Kennedy formally announced that he was running for President, thus joining Eugene McCarthy as an active candidate against Lyndon Johnson. On March 23 the Gallup poll showed Democrats preferring Kennedy to Johnson by 44 per cent to 41 and Johnson to McCarthy by 59 per cent to 29. On March 31 in an address ostensibly to address the nation on the Vietnam war, President Johnson announced that he would not seek re-election. I watched his presentation at home and turned to my family: "Well, there goes my chance."

Four days later Dr. Martin Luther King, Jr. was assassinated and our cities rocked with demonstrations. The nation was ripped apart by an unpopular war, the Democratic party was totally splintered and the death of Dr. King had brought riots to our city streets. This was not the best of times to try to push political buttons for a circuit judgeship. Filling the Staley vacancy became frozen in time. Barr still had the clout in the White House to put a stop to my nomination, but Senators Clark and Scott flexed their Senate muscles. They sent word to Barr and to the White House that no nomination except Aldisert would get through the Senate. It was the quintessential Mexican standoff. We waited.

In the meantime, I was on the Common Pleas bench every day, presiding over civil jury trials from January through the end of the spring term in June. The last case I had as a Common Pleas Court judge was *White v. Zelenak* on June 17, a non-jury case that started at 1:30 p.m. and concluded 45 minutes later when I announced an award of $1500 for the plaintiff. Representing the plaintiff was Attorney James Hornick. A former law clerk, Sandy Reiter, was the defendant's lawyer. These were the last attorneys to appear before me as a state judge, because a serious family emergency arose.

My father was suddenly stricken while visiting my sister in Washington, D.C. I flew out of Pittsburgh to attend my father, my loving father, whom I adored. The family posted a vigil in the hospital, but we knew that there was no hope. He would die a few days later and I would accompany him in the hearse in the long sad return from Washington to Pittsburgh. I would not let my father be alone, in death as in life. We buried him on June 24.

It was not the best of times. It was a springtime of riots and confrontations on civil rights and the Vietnam War, a springtime of national discord, of campus uprisings and the disaster of the Ohio National Guard opening lethal fire on student protesters. Teaching a course at the University of Pittsburgh's School of Law, I had become very close to university students. I knew at first hand their almost universal protest to the war.

During this period of personal distress over my nomination and the Martin Luther King riots and Vietnam war protests and the bitter confrontations in the national Democratic Party that started with Senator Eugene McCarthy's attacks on the President, during this period of travail, tumult and turmoil, a very gratifying and congenial relationship developed between two men---Joseph S. Clark, the wealthy patrician U.S. Senator from the mainline of Philadelphia--educated Chestnut Hill Academy, Middlesex School, Harvard College and Pennsylvania Law School--and Ruggero J. Aldisert, son of an Italian immigrant.

This was a relationship that had begun in the previous summer with his interest in my views on court reform. It strengthened when he supported my Third Circuit nomination. In the weeks that followed, as we discussed the prospects of my nomination, our conversations began to expand to other issues. Using me as a sounding board, he asked my advice on many matters. Finding himself in a bitter primary battle in May against a very popular Western Pennsylvania Congressman John Dent and although endorsed by the state committee, Clark was not convinced that the Western Pennsylvania machine was giving him total support. He was especially suspicious of Mayor Barr. He knew that Barr and Congressman Dent were close friends.

Agreeing with the senator's assessment, I advised him to open a Western Pennsylvania office. "Senator, there's a heckuva lot of Pennsylvania west of Philadelphia," I said. He opened the office, and on my recommendation, installed Ron Bua as his administrative assistant in charge, a young Pittsburgh attorney who recently had served as my law clerk.

Joe Clark was not the prototypical politician. He had been elected Philadelphia Mayor and later U.S. Senator as a reform candidate. He was not a glad-hander, not a hail fellow well met, nor one who could roll up his sleeves and make a rousing speech at a United Mine Workers hall or before the Croatian Fraternal Union or an American Legion Post. He was not comfortable pressing the flesh at mill gates. But he spent most of his waking hours in Senate Committees and on the Senate floor introducing and supporting legislation most sympathetic to these constituencies.

In time I would learn that this highly regarded, national figure, who attracted almost universal approval from the Washington press corps and editorial page support, was indeed a very private and lonely man. He had thousands of acquaintances, but very few intimate friends. And as time went on during that memorable spring of 1968, we talked by telephone several times a week, often late at night, and for long periods we did not talk about my nomination, discussing only his re-election campaign.

We constantly talked about community tensions. We always discussed the Vietnam war and the civil rights movement. He later thanked me for introducing him to feelings of neglect so widespread felt by immigrant families from central, southern and eastern Europe, the so-called "ethnic" groups in Pennsylvania. I told him that large groups in Pennsylvania felt neglected by the national political apparatus--the Poles, Russians, Carpatho-Russians, Ukrainians, Hungarians, Lithuanians, Croats, Serbs, Slovenians and Italians. They were not part of the "establishment" and were subject to discrimination socially, politically, economically. I told him that a widespread segment of the liberal community even on University faculties--who would never think of telling a joke disparaging an African-American or a Jew--had no qualms about publicly telling derisive jokes about Poles and Italians.

He emphasized that he was a leader in the legislation to protect all of these groups in the Civil Rights Act of 1964, that outlawed discrimination because of national origin. I told him that this was not enough. "You have to get out among these people. That they belong to the unions that endorse you is not enough. You must go to their fraternal conventions, attend their banquets, kiss their babies, eat their 'strange' foods and insure that your messages somehow appear in their many publications." He survived the bruising Democratic primaries.

With all the political pushes and tugs and shoves in many camps over my nomination in that fateful spring of 1968---maneuvering by my supporters and Mayor Barr's office and the staffs of two United States Senators--no one had noticed that a federal Omnibus Judges bill had passed the Senate and was now before the House Judiciary Committee. The bill called for an increase of U.S. circuit judges in several courts, including an addition for the Third Circuit that would increase the court from eight to nine judges. I learned about this from Joseph F. Weis, Jr., a prominent lawyer, who came to my chambers and told me that he had discovered this information in some legal news source. He said that he knew of my difficulty and that perhaps this would be the solution to my problem. I thanked Joe profusely. Joe Weis and I had been friends as lawyers and I was proud to keep our friendship as he became a Common Pleas Court judge, a U.S. District judge and a close colleague of mine for over 30 years on the Court of Appeals for the Third Circuit.

If the bill was enacted and an additional judge allocated to the Third Circuit we could break the deadlock--both Stahl and I could be appointed to the court.

I explained my plan to Senator Clark's staff. A few days later the senator called and we made an appointment to see him in Washington. When I arrived, he filled me in:

THE LONG AND ROCKY ROAD TO THE COURT OF APPEALS

> We're having trouble. Manny Cellers is sitting on this bill. It won't go anywhere without his O.K., and he won't release it because he's afraid that President Johnson will appoint some red-neck good ole boys down south to the Fifth Circuit.

Emmanuel Cellers was chairman of the House Judiciary Committee.

Clark knew that I had a personal relationship with the Kennedy family because I had told him that I had worked hard in the West Virginia primaries in May 1960 when Jack Kennedy was locked in a bitter primary struggle with Hubert Humphrey. I helped arrange for the largest audience Kennedy would face in the West Virginia campaign: On May 1, 1960 I introduced him at a dinner in Weirton, West Virginia that attracted over 1200 people. Four years later, when the Academy of Trial Lawyers of Allegheny County presented me with its Outstanding Merit Award for accomplishments as a judge, then Attorney General Robert F. Kennedy flew to Pittsburgh to make the presentation. Clark told me that one person could get Cellers to release the bill and that person was Bobby Kennedy. Clark suggested that we talk to Senator Kennedy personally. Bobby had announced his candidacy for the Presidency and Joe Clark was an early supporter.

Bobby Kennedy graciously welcomed us in his office. As Senator Clark introduced me, Kennedy said he knew me well and recalled coming to Pittsburgh in 1964 to present the lawyer's award to me. After Clark explained the problem, Bobby quickly agreed to help. In our presence, he telephoned Congressman Cellers:

> Manny, I need your help. I'm sitting here with your good friend, Joe Clark and his friend, Judge Aldisert, from Pittsburgh. It will mean a lot to me for my candidacy if I can do something for Judge Aldisert right now.

Senator Kennedy proceeded to explain our standoff with Mayor Barr and how important it was to get an additional opening on the Third Circuit. Kennedy added a twist of his own. He assured Cellers that Clark would get Hugh Scott to help him on the Judiciary committee to make sure that the wrong people were not placed on the Fifth Circuit.

"Manny, I need your help and I need it today," he said.

Cellers agreed. Without much fanfare, the judges bill was reported out of the House Judiciary committee. I learned about it indirectly in a story that appeared in the Pittsburgh Post Gazette on May 16, 1968:

> FBI Conducting Routine Check
> JUDGE ALDISERT SEEN
> NEARING SELECTION
> TO FEDERAL COURT
> Washington, May 15--Rumors are buzzing here that the FBI is looking over Allegheny County Common Pleas Court Judge Ruggero J. Aldisert.
>
> Since this is a necessary preliminary to presidential appointment, and since it does not usually occur until the President has pretty well made up his mind, the speculation here is that Judge Aldisert will soon be nominated to the Third Circuit Court of Appeals.

There were now two vacancies to be filled on the Third Circuit. I later called Mayor Barr, who, although the Pennsylvania Democratic national committeeman of the Democratic party, knew nothing about the creation of the additional judgeship or that the President had signed the bill. I told him that both Stahl and I could now be appointed to the court because there were now two vacancies on the Third Circuit. Barr was effusive, "This is wonderful. It will solve all our problems."

Two weeks later, after winning the California primaries, the one person who ultimately made my nomination possible, Senator Robert F. Kennedy of New York, was assassinated on June 4.

My nomination actually came through on July 17 and I learned about it during a round of golf at the Westmoreland Country Club where I was playing with Judges Dave Olbum and Harry Montgomery and Attorney Abe Cohen. Having called my chambers after the ninth hole, I was told

THE LONG AND ROCKY ROAD TO THE COURT OF APPEALS

that Senator Scott had asked me to call him as soon as possible. Using a public phone near the tenth hole, I called his office and was connected directly to the Minority Leader on the Senate floor. He said: "Judge, I saw the President an hour ago just before he got in his chopper. He told me that he was sending your name up to the Hill today. I wanted you to know this as soon as possible."

I did not tell members of my foursome about the call. There had been so many slip ups in the tortuous months since the past November and I still was not certain. When we approached the eighteenth green, however, I encountered some friends. They shouted congratulations, having heard on the radio that the President had nominated me. I immediately called Agatha who told me that she had heard about it from news reporters and the radio was broadcasting the story. She said that she had been besieged with telephone calls.

It was a time of exultation and celebration, to be sure, but the enthusiasm was dampened because this had come to pass only a few weeks after the death of my father. Very close all my life, we had talked every day for months about the pending nomination. He was in his eightieth year when he was stricken in Washington, D.C. His last words to me before lapsing into a final coma were: "When is that White House going to announce your nomination? What's holding up those fellows?"

As the family sadly maintained the hospital watch those mournful days and nights, I passed the hours reviewing the life of this noble man who had taught me so much and was such a vital part of my life. This immigrant boy with the bright blue-green eyes who in 1905 started a life in the strange new world with his 14 year old sister. This steadfast man had who accomplished so much in life, who revered his adopted land, who savored its vigor and its purpose, who became sensitive to its variegated sociological and political ideals; this magnificent man would, by the accident of a casual visit to his daughter, spend his final hours in the capital city of the country he first saw from the steerage deck of the S.S. Prinz Adelbert 64 years before. He died in the capital of the United States, the country he would choose to call his home and rear a family and have a son who would become the first American of Italian origin to be named to a U.S. Court of Appeals in the history of the great Eastern Seaboard.

Receiving the nomination was tantamount to actual appointment, but this was the summer of 1968, the summer of a year that went from one national crisis to another. One of these national crises now would affect me directly--the retirement of Earl Warren as Chief Justice of the United States.

Warren made his announcement at the close of the Court's Term in June and the President had an immediate successor chosen for the post--his close friend Abe Fortas, then serving as an Associate Justice on the Supreme court. He nominated Fortas to be Chief Justice of the United States, and Fifth Circuit Judge Homer Thornberry of Texas, also an intimate Johnson friend, to fill the Fortas vacancy. But by July of 1968, the lame duck President no longer could control the Senate, even the Democrats, especially the Southern Democrats who were not enamored with liberal decisions of the Warren Court and Fortas's participation in them.

On the very day my nomination was sent to the Hill, a bruising hearing on the Fortas nomination was taking place in the Judiciary committee. Committee Democrats McClellan, Ervin, Byrd and Long opposed the nomination for a variety of reasons--antipathy to liberal decisions of the Supreme Court either written by Fortas or joined in by him declaring as constitutionally protected certain materials which these Senators deemed to be obscene. *New York Times* reporter Fred Graham had written a scathing piece, *The Many-Sided Justice Fortas* which raised a separation of powers issue. The article detailed many instances where Fortas, while a Supreme Court justice, had served as an intimate political adviser to President Johnson. On their part, Republicans raised serious questions over the propriety of a Supreme Court justice serving as a confidential adviser and speech writer for the President.

The Fortas hearing before the judiciary committee opened on July 11. Republican Senator Robert Griffin of Detroit was the point man for the opposition. He said that the Fortas-Thornberry nominations were "cronyism at its worst, and everybody knows it." He was to follow Attorney General Ramsey Clark as a witness, but decided instead to deliver a scathing speech on the Senate floor sounding variations on the cronyism theme. In his speech Senator Griffin raised the question whether a lame duck president had the right to make lifetime judicial appointments in the final hours of his office. Fortas began his testimony on July 16, was on the stand for four days and underwent a blistering attack. When Fortas concluded his testimony, McClellan moved that the committee delay reporting out its recommendation for a week. Congress would stand in recess on August 31.

This then was the political climate when Warren Christopher, Deputy Attorney General, called to inform me that my hearing before the Senate Judiciary Committee would take place Monday, July 29. It was one week after the Fortas bloodletting, the first meeting of the Judiciary Committee after one of the most acrimonious sessions in its history. Christopher told me not to worry. But I did. I had reason to. The media kept fanning the flame of the propriety of a lame duck President making life-time appointments of federal judges. The issue was made more dramatic when the polls kept showing that Richard Nixon would smother Hubert Humphrey in the November elections.

The papers continued to run front page stories highly critical of Johnson, their accounts quoting Senators of both parties that it would be difficult for any Johnson judicial appointees to be confirmed. But some silver linings appeared. The Pittsburgh Post Gazette ran a story:

> Approval Seen Tied to Fortas
> ALDISERT'S POST
> IN POWER PLAY
> Washington, July 18--Confirmation by the Senate of the nomination of Common Pleas Court Judge Ruggero J. Aldisert to the U.S. Third Circuit Court of Appeals appears certain before Congress adjourns.
>
> Aldisert's and other judicial appointments to lower courts are being made part of the power play over the nominations of Justice Abe Fortas to be chief justice and Fifth Circuit Judge Homer Thornberry to be a justice of the Supreme court.
>
> Judge Aldisert was one of eight persons whose names were sent up to the Senate. Reportedly the President plans to send up about 20 other nominations to federal courts before many days pass....

President Johnson could have filled most of the places before. Some Senators believe he has held back on the other nominations in order to be able to use them to persuade balky senators to vote for the confirmation of the nominations of Fortas and Thornberry.

Five days later the Pittsburgh Press reported:

Despite Fortas Controversy

ALDISERT OKAY EXPECTED SOON

Washington--Judge Ruggero J. Aldisert of Pittsburgh may be confirmed soon for the federal judgeship despite the controversy over Supreme Court Justice Abe Fortas' nomination.

Warren Christopher telephoned again to give assurance that they felt that I would be confirmed, but he advised that I not talk to any representatives of the media. "Go into hibernation and avoid them," he counseled. Senator Clark said, "I think you will be confirmed." But I was most anxious to talk with Senator Scott who was as a member of the Judiciary Committee and finally reached him on the Friday before my Monday committee appearance. He, too, advised against talking with the media and concluded:

> Judge, you must remember that when you go before that committee on Monday morning, I will be there. I will be there to make sure that all will be well.

I thanked him, but the Sunday editions still carried stories of a lame duck President making lifetime judicial appointments. Under ordinary circumstances, a circuit judge nominee appears before the Senate Judiciary Committee with his wife and children in tow. This is to show members of the committee that he or she is family-oriented, and is also an opportunity for family members to hear the praise heaped upon the nominee by witnesses.

I did not bring my family when I took the plane to Washington. Having gone through nine months of problems with the nomination, neither Agatha nor I expected that there would be smooth sailing at the

THE LONG AND ROCKY ROAD TO THE COURT OF APPEALS 413

hearing. The Fortas specter loomed large. After a fitful night at the Capitol Hilton on Monday morning and breakfast in my room, I turned on the NBC "Today" programs for the news. What I saw and heard almost made me cry. After the announcer described preparations for the Republican National Convention slated to begin in a few days he said:

> We now take you to Miami for a meeting of the convention credentials committee. Some fireworks are expected there because certain delegations are being challenged. We now take you live to the opening session of the committee. Hugh Scott of Pennsylvania, Minority leader of the Senate, is presiding.

I then saw Senator Scott wielding a gavel in Miami, calling the credential committee meeting to order.

Senator Scott in Miami. On Friday he told me not to worry because he would be sitting with the committee at my hearing in Washington. I died then and there. I simply died.

But Senator Clark was smiling and quite jaunty when I hooked up with him a half hour later and we walked to Room 2228 of the New Senate Office building where the hearing was scheduled. I soon learned that my fears were not well taken. The hearing turned out to be a love fest. Only one member of the committee was present, Quentin N. Burdick of North Dakota, in place of Chairman James O. Eastland of Mississippi. Senator Clark introduced me saying that I had been active in civic and philanthropic affairs and "has the qualifications to become an excellent Federal Appeals judge. I heartily support the nomination. He is the kind of man we badly need in the federal judiciary."

Clark was followed by my own Congressman James G. Fulton, Republican, and Ernest Freisen, Director of the Administrative Office of the U.S. Courts, who attested to my work with Justice Tom Clark in the National Conference of the Metropolitan Courts in which Freisen had served as executive director. Extremely favorable reports from the Pennsylvania and American Bar Association were read into the record. Senator Burdick concluded the hearing:

> The full committee having previously approved the nomination of Judge Aldisert subject to the report of

this sub committee, the approval of this sub committee is hereby given.

He rapped the gavel and the hearing was adjourned. I then realized how bipartisan support could bring daylight out of my long darkness of night.

Freisen and I then went over to the Supreme Court building to pay my respects to Justice Tom Clark. We had lunch in his chambers and had a fine visit. It was then time to return to Pittsburgh, but first I made a courtesy telephone call to Senator Joe Clark's office. His secretary greeted me:

> Judge Aldisert, we've been looking all over for you and have already called your home. The full Senate has already voted on your nomination and you have been confirmed as of this day.

I telephoned Agatha with the news but she had already heard it on the radio. I had finally come the end of the long and rocky road. I had become a U.S. Circuit Judge.

> The Pittsburgh Post Gazette editorialized:
> The U.S. Senate has recognized professional competency in confirming President Johnson's nomination of Common Pleas Court Judge Ruggero J. Aldisert to be a judge of the United States Court of Appeals for the Third Circuit.
>
> Judge Aldisert has demonstrated both administrative ability and legal learning during his service on the state trial bench here since 1961. His energetic performance on the Common Pleas Court will be missed. But he deserved the elevation to the federal appellate court, for which the Senate has now given its approval.

I ascended the bench on August 9 in that frightening August of 1968 that saw Nixon nominated as the GOP standard bearer in Miami and Hubert Humphrey named at the Democratic convention debacle in Chicago amid bloody street riots, where war protesters were clubbed by the police and gave rise to the saga of the Chicago Seven. George Wallace became a third party candidate for President and made the election of Nixon all but assured.

I took my seat on the U.S. Court of Appeals for the Third Circuit that August when America was being ripped apart by protest and reaction, charge and counter charge, with an unpopular war in an obscure Far East country that daily generated obscene body counts on our television screens, with our highest court lacerated by the Fortas allegations, with Congress in recess and totally impotent, with a lame duck President witnessing a mangled Democratic party at war with itself. To top it off regiments of Russian tanks rumbled into Czechoslovakia. August of 1968 was not the best of times.

We caught our breath in September. Joe Clark kicked off his re-election campaign on Labor day, but took one day off to celebrate the first anniversary of his remarriage and invited Agatha and me to join Iris and him in a quiet dinner in Philadelphia. A few days later I mounted the bench in the Ninth Street federal courthouse for my first Third Circuit sitting with Gerry McLaughlin, appointed by President Franklin D. Roosevelt, and Harry Kalodner, a Truman appointee.

That year I would return to Philadelphia for two more sittings and an in banc session of the court, and Agatha and I flew to Philadelphia on the afternoon of election day.

We were not optimistic that Senator Clark would be re-elected. Humphrey was trailing in the polls nationally and in Pennsylvania, but even more serious was the frantic activity of the National Rifle Association against Senator Clark. He was one generation ahead of his time, having come out strongly for hand gun control, the elimination of the Saturday night specials, but the NRA translated this into an opposition to hunting rifles and proceeded to circularize the entire state of Pennsylvania with a well organized effort to defeat him. They succeeded.

I had not appreciated the loneliness of politics until the election night of November 5, 1968. We had dinner with Joe and Iris Clark alone in a suite in the Hotel Bellevue Stratford. Several floors away the Clark headquarters was in full force with a bountiful buffet, drinks and a jazz band. Aides posted scattered returns coming in from all over the state. But the Senator was content to watch only the television reports in his private suite in company only with his wife--and the Aldiserts.

That night he received no calls from the White House or Senate colleagues. No calls from the newspapers that had endorsed him throughout the state. No calls from Philadelphia political co-workers, or associates from his life in public service for almost 20 years---Philadelphia City Controller, 1949-51, Mayor, 1952-1956, and U.S. Senator since 1957.

Shakespeare could pen a verse to describe the lonely moment. But Joe Clark was not bitter in defeat. He wrote out a gracious concession statement, and read it at his public headquarters for the television and radio audience, in which he thanked his workers and bade them goodnight. He retired to his suite and the four of us reminisced for a while and then Agatha and I got up to go. He embraced me, then shook my hand and said: "At least I gave them a good federal judge." Senator Joseph S. Clark had made possible my elevation to the federal appellate bench. He had opened the road to a new set of robes which I have worn proudly since 1968.

What we do in the black robes sitting high in the courtroom is constantly subject to profound analysis. Lawyers and professors study and examine our opinions rendered in the past to predict how we will rule in the future. Predictions are important in the law, indeed that is precisely how Oliver Wendell Holmes defined law: "The prophecies of what the courts will do in fact, and nothing more pretentious, are what I mean by the law." To ruminate on the law, to recollect a lifetime on the bench – I have been a judge for over half my life – is to plow through written opinions, now numbered in the thousands that go back over 40 years. Since taking senior status I have sat also with the Fifth, Seventh, Ninth, Tenth and Eleventh Circuits. I have published four books on the law and over 30 articles in professional journals; these reveal a jurisprudential profile and reflect if not a philosophy of law, at least a point of view I was willing to express and defend at that time.

Newly found insights always produce a willingness to re-examine views on the law, even those once strongly held and loudly voiced. Concepts of community morals change. Notions of proper social conduct change. Rules of society change. And with all this, the law, too, should change. Roscoe Pound , long time dean of the Harvard Law School, was fond of saying, "The law must be stable, but it must not stand still." The passage of years and the opportunity of reflection should effectuate an increase in wisdom. But as Thomas Wolfe once reminded us: "Some things will never change. Some things will always be the same."

Some things remain constant. And when it comes to judges, the substance of decisions may change, but methods of reaching those decisions remain the same. The ways, the manner, the techniques used to make decisions remain the same. The personal approach to the law does not change even though end results may differ over time.

How a judge decides, as distinguished from *what* a judge decides, remains constant. The judge's procedures, working concepts, rules and postulates have been influenced by more than classes in law schools, treatises read, briefs studied, or arguments followed or rejected. Processes, techniques or approaches employed in the solution of a problem are the end product of many intangible factors. How the judge reached the age of reason as a child, family influence in formative years, social attitudes formed in the elementary and secondary schools, success or failure on the college campus, membership on a sports team or other school activity, military experience, the nature of a law practice, especially the extent of interpersonal relationships; the extent of participation in church or community groups or political organizations, marital or parenting successes or failures – all these are as important, as Holmes would say, in predicting what the judge will do in fact as are past judicial opinions and articles and treatises. These are but milestones, whether clearly defined or faintly observed, on any judge's road to the robes.

In these pages I have attempted to share some of mine with you.

Senator Joseph S. Clark of Pennsylvania pictured with me and Agatha at a dinner in Atlantic City, New Jersey, in August, 1968 shortly after I took the oath as U.S. Circuit Judge. He was one of most dedicated public servants I ever knew.

Senator Hugh Scott of Pennsylvania, a long-time personal friend, was a great supporter of the ISDA campaign for federal action or legislation to combat the Mafia. Here we are showing him a full page newspaper advertisement under the banner, "The Mafia: Its 12 million Real Victims." From the left, Senator Scott,

THE LONG AND ROCKY ROAD TO THE COURT OF APPEALS

Victor Frediani, former ISDA Pennsylvania state president, publisher of the ISDA weekly newspaper, *Unione*; and Tullio G. Leomporra, then ISDA national vice-president. Leomporra is still active as a retired United States Magistrate Judge for the Eastern District of Pennsylvania. From the point of service he is one of the oldest and most respected magistrate judges, grandfathered into the program while serving as a U.S. Commissioner, and re-appointed for a series of terms until he took retired status.

On May 25, 1964, Robert F. Kennedy, as Attorney General, came to Pittsburgh on behalf of the Academy of Trial Lawyers of Allegheny County, to present an award to me. On the left is Abe R. Cohen, president of the academy. Four years later I was playing golf with Abe and Judges David Olbum and Harry Montgomery when I received the news that President Johnson had nominated me as a U.S. Circuit Judge.

420 ROAD TO THE ROBES

In May, 1968 Senator Robert F. Kennedy of New York was instrumental in breaking the log jam in Congress that created an additional judgeship for the U.S. Court of Appeals for the Third Circuit. Without his help I could not have been appointed a U.S. Circuit Judge. A few weeks later he was assassinated.

THE LONG AND ROCKY ROAD TO THE COURT OF APPEALS

President Lyndon B. Johnson invited me to the White House to extend congratulations on the Senate's confirmation of my appointment to the U.S. Court of Appeals for the Third Circuit. I was one of his last Court of Appeals appointments in the troubled year of 1968.

About the Author

Ruggero J. Aldisert is a well-known federal appellate judge and author, and has served as an adjunct professor at several law schools. He is a Senior U.S. Circuit Judge of the U.S. Court of Appeals for the Third Circuit in Philadelphia, but has had the unique experience of also serving by designation since 1987 in other Courts of Appeals from Atlanta to Seattle. He was appointed by President Lyndon B. Johnson in 1968. Previously he served as a trial judge on the Court of Common Pleas of Allegheny County, (Pittsburgh) Pennsylvania, 1961-1968; before that he was in the private practice of law. He served as the Third Circuit's chief judge, 1984-1987 before attaining senior status

He was Adjunct Professor of Law, University of Pittsburgh School of Law 1963 -1986, and a visiting professor at schools of law at New York University, University of Virginia, Augsburg University in Germany, University of Texas and Arizona State University.

A graduate of the University of Pittsburgh, he has been awarded the LLD honorary degree from four colleges and universities, including the Dr. iur.h.c. from Augsburg University

He served on active duty in United States Marine Corps for four years during World War II, attaining the rank of captain. While serving the USMC reserves for five years thereafter, he was promoted to the rank of major.

His other books include: *Winning on Appeal: Better Briefs and Oral Argument* (2d Ed NITA 2003); *Opinion Writing* (West 1990); *Logic for Lawyers: A Guide to Clear Legal Thinking*, (3d. Ed) (NITA 1997) ; *The Judicial Process: Text, Materials and Cases* (2d.ed.) (West 1996). In addition he had written over 30 articles in professional publications.

He has lectured before lawyers, judges and students throughout the United States and Canada, as well as in England, France, Italy, Germany, Poland, Croatia and Serbia.

An example of the professional respect accorded the author is the comment of Harry A. Blackmun, Justice, United States Supreme Court, 1970-1997) in the Foreword to Judge Aldisert's book, *The Judicial Process: Text, Materials and Cases*:

> Judge Aldisert loves the law. He yearns to know its history and its character or, to use the word he has employed effectively used in this volume, its anatomy. He wants to know what it is, why it is what it is, and how all of us who labor in its vineyard use of misuse it.